# German Mysticism
## from Hildegard of Bingen
## to Ludwig Wittgenstein

SUNY Series in Western Esoteric Traditions

David Appelbaum, Editor

# German Mysticism
## from Hildegard of Bingen
## to Ludwig Wittgenstein

A Literary and Intellectual History

Andrew Weeks

State University of New York Press

Published by
State University of New York Press, Albany

For information, address State University of New York
Press, State University Plaza, Albany, NY 12246

Production by M. R. Mulholland
Marketing by Fran Keneston

**Library of Congress Cataloging-in-Publication Data**

Weeks, Andrew.
    German mysticism from Hildegard of Bingen to Ludwig Wittgenstein :
a literary and intellectual history / Andrew Weeks.
        p.   cm. — (SUNY series in western esoteric traditions)
    Includes bibliographical references and index.
    ISBN 0-7914-1419-1 (cloth : alk. paper).   — ISBN 0-7914-1420-5
(pbk. : alk. paper)
    1. Mysticism—Germany. 2. Mysticism in literature  3. German
literature—History and criticism.  I. Title. II. Series.
BV5077.G3W36   1993
248.2'2'0943—dc20
                                                                92–8641
                                                                    CIP

10 9 8 7 6 5 4 3 2

To my friend Willis Barnstone
whose universal interest in literature and ideas
encouraged me to undertake this study

# Contents

# Preface

This book will chart a circumscribed course through the virtually boundless literature by and about the German mystics. My primary objective is not a survey of Christian spirituality or mystical experience, but rather a profane essay in comparative literature and the history of ideas. The student of spirituality reacts to the mystical text from the vantage of faith, attending to the spiritual "drink" (rather than to the cup, the hand that bears it, or the extraneous circumstances of its ministration). The consistent student of spirituality presumably recognizes in every significant mystical work the same spiritual drink.

This spiritual focus of attention can find its complement in a study of comparative literature and intellectual history. The skeptical comparatist begins with the simple question: If all the mystical texts of a particular tradition are thought to voice the same overriding authority, why do the texts appear so distinct in character? What, inquires the comparatist, can possibly validate these disparate texts, if not their store of common biblical and traditional themes, their abiding nucleus of traditional literary materials? And what can account for the differences, if not the diverging personal and historical circumstances of the mystics—the temporal "darkness" surrounding the eternal "light" of their invariant spiritual authority? The comparatist pursues a middle course between an affirmative attitude that takes the authority of the mystic for granted and a defensive reaction which shrinks from the very word *mysticism*. The intellectual historian places the issue of authority at the center of investigation, examining it with reference to tradition and with regard for the formative influence of each unique historical context.

The present study of German mysticism grew out of my last book, an intellectual biography of the seventeenth-century mystic and philosopher, Jacob Boehme. In my previous study, I examined the "illuminism" of the Baroque theosophist with respect to the question whether Boehme should be read critically like other writers, or set apart as an "illuminate" who can only be accepted or rejected wholesale. In answering this question, it seemed to me that the affirmative alternative—the approach which begins by confirming that what Boehme wrote stemmed from an immediate intuition of an ultimate

truth—would lead to contradictory results. The theory that a momen-
tary flash could generate an oeuvre of many volumes seemed unlikely
on the face of it; and it was contradicted by the evolving contents of
Boehme's writings. Sources could be found for almost all components
of his work.

This posed further questions. Why did Boehme and his followers
insist on their orthodoxy—despite a mysticism that appears to encompass so many extrascriptural and nontraditional elements? How does it
happen that his writings are so distinct from those of Hildegard, Eckhart, or Silesius (so disparate in fact that some scholars of the history of
spirituality pass him by in silence)? I addressed the disparities by examining his period of sweeping change and confessional conflict with its
peculiar historical challenge to doctrines rooted in the Bible. After initially viewing him as an enemy of doctrine, I came to the realization that
the Baroque mystic was preoccupied with Lutheran teachings. More
generally, I recognized that canonical texts, doctrines, and their historical contexts are constants and variables of the mystical tradition. The
present study expands my work on Boehme in order to argue that German mysticism as a whole developed from a specific core of materials
and evolved by responding to recurrent challenges to authority.

Since the objective of this study was not that of a survey, the
essay form seemed the most appropriate one. Where a survey covers
the full ground, an essay breaks down barriers and offers new perspectives. If a survey calls for an exhaustive compendium of the facts,
an essay is avowedly tentative and incomplete, and hence more conducive to questions that point beyond its admitted limitations. An
essay is freer to concentrate on salient figures and representative
works in arguing its thesis.

The more general objective of this essay is to shed light on German literary and intellectual history in its entirety. After Paracelsus
and Boehme, mysticism began to lose its prominence in the intellectual life of the Germans. Instead of considering all the subsequent representatives of religious mysticism from the eighteenth through the
twentieth century, I have chosen to take into account the dispersal of
mystical themes in literature and philosophy as a whole—a procedure
which veers from the narrower focus of my title in order to serve the
interests of my subtitle.

For helpful suggestions, editorial assistance, and friendly
encouragement, I am endebted to Ann Barker, William Dickey, Peter
Erb, Matthew Lage, David Lee, Kelly Mickey, Megeen Mulholland,
Erwin Streitfeld, Elke Segelcke, Avery and Carl Springer, Heinz
Strotzka, Veronika Strotzka, James Van Der Laan, and Mary Weeks.

# Introduction

*De toutes les nations, celle qui a le plus de penchant au mysticisme, c'est la nation allemande.*

—Madame de Staël[1]

By present standards, de Staël's magisterial pronouncement sounds brash, sweeping, and perhaps a bit rude. No longer do we equate cultural history with national character, or suggest that mystical penchants can be weighed and measured between nations.

Yet at any level of knowledge, arguments can be mustered in favor of her pronouncement. Those familiar with the outline of German literary history will recollect that several periods knew important figures and movements of a mystical cast: Hildegard of Bingen, Meister Eckhart, Heinrich Seuse (Henry Suso), and Johannes Tauler in the Middle Ages; Paracelsus and the "nature mysticism" of the Renaissance; Jacob Boehme, Angelus Silesius, and the Pietists in the aftermath of the German Reformation; and Novalis among others in the Romantic period. What is remarkable, however, is not the number or prominence of the German mystics, but rather the degree to which their influence channels into the German tradition as a whole, shaping even those achievements not commonly associated with mysticism. This applies to the Reformation, to German Idealism and Romanticism, and to the secular voluntarism that begins with Schopenhauer and Nietzsche and exerts a strong influence on modernism. The very concept of *deutsche Mystik*, "German mysticism," was coined by the disciple of Hegel, Karl Rosenkranz. The term was originally intended to suggest that the great achievements of German philosophy stood in a line going back to medieval religious mysticism.[2] De Staël intimated a general affinity of German Idealism with German religiosity: *D'ailleurs, l'idéalisme en philosophie a beaucoup d'analogie avec le mysticisme en religion: l'un place toute la réalité des choses de ce monde dans le pensée, et l'autre toute réalité des choses du ciel dans le sentiment.* Is it an error to suggest that German imagination and thought on the whole exhibit the introvertedness and cosmic-visionary expansiveness associated with mysticism?

Two of the most resolute German opponents of mysticism were Luther and Kant. What are we to make of the well-documented fact that their respective developments and impact had much to do with mysticism? Early in his career, Luther was impressed by mystical authors and concepts. He greatly admired a mystical tract that he edited, and which soon became known as the *Theologia Deutsch*. Although Luther later turned against most forms of mysticism, his early impulses were reawakened in Protestant dissenters, Spiritualists, and Pietists.

Moreover, even the influence of the consummate anti-mystic, Immanuel Kant, was soon to converge with a revived interest in mysticism. There is some irony in the fact that Kant had been stimulated to transform metaphysics into the science of the limitations of human reason and knowledge by his early satirical assault upon the influence of Swedenborg's *Arcana Coelestia*. Yet two decades after the inaugural shot fired against the Swedish "Nordic Seer," Kant's friends in Königsberg and Riga, including Hamann, were as preoccupied with Swedenborg as ever.[3] More significant still, by Kant's death in 1801, the philosophical movement initiated by him encompassed a broad spectrum of tendencies, including, not least of all, a revived preoccupation with mysticism.

We will need a workable understanding of mysticism and its evolving forms to interpret its presence in German intellectual history. Is it one phenomenon or many? What are its sources and why does it flourish in some periods more than others? But what is altogether untenable is the common tendency to place whatever can be called *mystical* outside the mainstream of intellectual history. The influence of medieval mysticism and the *Theologia Deutsch*, the impact of Paracelsus on the Northern Renaissance, Protestant mysticism and Pietism in the aftermath of the Lutheran Reformation, the revival of mystical themes during the Romantic period, and, generally speaking, the significance of German words such as *Innerlichkeit, Geist,* or *das Absolute*—these and similar considerations confer an oracular solemnity on de Staël's brash pronouncement.

Whoever undertakes to examine the holdings on mysticism in any major library is likely to find a fascinating and forbidding array of titles by scholars, scientists, poets, and luminaries. They promise hidden doors to secret worlds: *Cosmic Consciousness, The Mystic Path to Cosmic Power, The Silent Path, A Road to the Spirit, At One with the Invisible, L'Experience interieure, Die große Glut, Der siebenfarbige Bogen.* In some cases, these works deserve more serious attention than they receive; they should be regarded with the open-minded but critical attitude of William James's classic study *The Varieties of Religious Experience*. However, precisely to the degree that the diverse presentations in these books succeed in shedding light on this or that aspect of mysticism, they inadvertantly undermine the very assumption on which much of the relevant literature rests: that there exists a universal mystical experience. Recent scholarship has rejected this postulate.

In interpreting mystical literature, one is confronted by the choice between two "models." One can assume that the mystic is moved by a psychological affectation beyond true description. If so, then what the mystic says or writes is a mere stammering and grasping, which almost by chance avails itself of a language acquired from a store of knowledge derived from sacred books and confessional doctrines. Presumably, this ineffable experience would stand in an *incidental* relationship to the sacred books and doctrines, since they are embodiments of a particular religious tradition, while the experience is univerally the same.

Alternatively, one can approach mysticism from the perspective of religious literature, confessional doctrine, and tradition. Prior to any mystical experience, the mystic's mind is immersed in the literature and imbued with the religious doctrines of a tradition. From this vantage point, one recognizes that the written or spoken word comes first and last in the mystical experience. The word does not stand in an incidental relation to an ineffable experience, but rather is decisive. This word-based model corresponds to the general characteristics of confessional mysticism. Recent scholarship has favored this model. Moreover, it is implicit in much of the best scholarship of the past. In this study, I will adapt arguments advanced by Gershom Scholem and Steven T. Katz: What is known about mystical experience in general is known mainly through mystical literature; and mystical literature is *conservative* in that it reflects the literature and tradition of particular confessions, rather than an identifiable universal experience.[4]

Where other concepts fail because of a lack of precision in their fringe applications, the concept of (German) mysticism is controversial and ambiguous in its core. There is no agreement among scholars on the question of who ought to be classified as a mystic. Important scholars currently adhere to the opinion that even the two most widely studied "German mystics" ought to be removed from the canon: Hildegard of Bingen (as a visionary) and Meister Eckhart (as a theologian or philosopher of Christianity). Hildegard is excluded because in her visions she experienced no union with God. As it happens, however, Eckhart—the classical mystic of unification—reports no such experience, and his works do not encourage the expectation of raptures or ecstasies. Kurt Flasch, a leading proponent of the philosophical interpretation of Eckhart, points to the fact that philosophers from Parmenides to Wittgenstein have articulated themes that can be considered mystical.[5] With considerable effect, Flasch cites a passage from Kant's *Religion Within the Boundaries of Simple Reason*, in which the rationalist approvingly writes of what is the *locus classicus* of all Logos mysticism—the identification of Christ as the Word with the divine word of creation in Genesis. Flasch argues that we can find mysticism in philosophers from Plato to Wittgenstein, but that if we do so, we must be prepared to accept certain dire consequences. The fronts in the mysticism debate cut across the lines of religious and ideological persuasion. On other grounds, the Jesuit scholar Heribert Fischer has rejected the classification of Eckhart as a mystic.[6]

Alois M. Haas is their most frontal opponent. Haas insists on a mysticism of *Erfahrung* (but adds that Christian "experience is always accompanied by language"). Haas maintains that there is a fundamental "incommensurability of the mystical experience" with the "resonance" of human possibilities and abilities.[7] It would seem from this that anything we might say about mysticism is subject to the rejoinder that we are talking about something that is absolutely beyond us. Whatever can be said in favor of this view, it discourages any discussion that doesn't begin with a declaration of faith or skepticism. In scholarly debates over mysticism, the postulate of the mystical experience curtails the discussion in the same way that confessionalism and the doctrine of verbal inspiration once impeded biblical scholarship. It is perhaps ironic that scholars of all persuasions can now carry on productive discussions of the Bible as literature, while mystical literature still occasions blanket declarations of faith and doubt.

The German character of German mysticism and its internal periodizations are also subject to controversy. (Certainly, many German mystics were quite comparable to counterparts in England or Italy.) To the problem of distinguishing philosophy from mysticism, one can add the Protestant theological objection to the idea of a "Christian mysticism." This objection was articulated most definitively in Emil Brunner's *Die Mystik und das Wort*—but it remains perceptible both in Catholic and Protestant scholarship. Brunner argued categorically that, as a revealed religion, Christianity is incompatible with mysticism. His argument, however, was largely a polemic against the theology of Schleiermacher. A fairer and more comprehensive Protestant view of German mysticism has recently been provided by Gerhard Wehr's *Die deutsche Mystik*.[8]

At least until the wave of new studies appearing during the last decade, the standard survey of German mysticism has been the work of the Germanist Friedrich-Wilhelm Wentzlaff-Eggebert, *Deutsche Mystik zwischen Mittelalter und Neuzeit* (1943, 1946, 1968).[9] The strength of his survey lies in its philological perspective and renunciation of confessional blinders. *Deutsche Mystik* follows a thematic approach, defining mysticism in terms of the mystical union with God; but it also recognizes that the German mystics were more speculative than affective. The criterion of the unification experience is oddly inappropriate for the German mystics. It applies more in some cases than in others, and often enough—as in the case of Renaissance "nature mysticism"—scarcely at all. It is also evident that the mystic may teach of mystical union or illumination without claiming it as a personal experience. This extension of mysticism to *mystagogy*, the teaching of mysticism, is explicitly accepted by Ruh and Haas as well.

The Germanists Wentzlaff-Eggebert and Josef Quint tacitly accept a thematic analysis. We will fare better if we do so explicitly. Wentzlaff-Eggebert and Quint both in effect expand the *unio mystica*, the union of human and divine subjects, to a union of metaphysical objects, a union of time and eternity, or of the divine world with the created world.[10] This extension of the *unio mystica* from a union of persons to a union of "worlds" needs to be highlighted at the outset of any discussion of German mysticism. We can avoid much confusion by discarding the *criterion* of experience altogether, by approaching mystical experience and thought as the content of a literature by authors whom we accept quite simply as writers.

As in any other literature, we are confronted with themes rather than with unmediated authorial experiences; and themes can only be defined as ideal types. The Faustian theme exists as a coherent cluster of motifs that have more or less ascertainable sources. Since the theme has a constructed objectivity, we are not consternated if the features of the Faustian material happen to be clearer and more pronounced in one literary treatment than in another. We know perfectly well that the same theme can be treated in various forms of literature, with variations of style or purpose. We expect themes to cut across genre and ideology, to be taken up by writers with divergent outlooks and intentions. The discussion of mysticism should therefore possess at least the same detachment as a discussion of love literature. The theme of romantic love is virtually universal and rooted in psychological experience, but it is also determined by the changing conditions of culture and history. In selecting a canon of love poetry, we would not be decisively swayed by the question whether this or that poet had actually

experienced romantic love (though this question would be of profound biographical interest). The nature and authenticity of the poet's
experience would not be of the essence. Nor would it be essential that
the researcher of the theme be a romantic lover, or even a believer in
romantic love. The scholar who personally experiences romantic love
might well have special insights into the nature of the love theme. The
scholar who lacks such experience might enjoy the advantages of
detachment.

Our point of departure, then, is not a universal, ineffable experience beyond literature, but rather the literature of German mysticism.
Our initial question is whether a common denominator, a constructed
ideal theme, can be formulated that can guide the analysis of diverse
writings. What do the visions of Hildegard (which are already very
different from those of other nuns) have in common with the reflective
exhortations in Eckhart's sermons? What do either of these have in
common with the philosophizing theories of nature in Renaissance
mysticism, with the personalism of Pietistic confession literature, or
with the finely crafted epigrams and impassioned poems of Angelus
Silesius or of Novalis?

All these forms of German mystical literature thematize *a God-
given knowledge of God*, or to put the matter more generally, a divinely
inspired knowledge of things divine. If the divine is understood to
mean not only God, but also the world of the angels or that of the eternal spirits in God, then our definition is broad enough to include the
visionary mysticism of Hildegard, the reflective mysticism of Meister
Eckhart's sermons, and the nature mysticism of Boehme. "Illumination" as well as "union" is covered by our definition. The concept of
mysticism as a knowledge *from* the divine source and *of* the divine
object is appropriately applied to the Protestant Spiritualists in the
wake of the Reformation. Although German Pietism appears to return
to a nonmystical devotion, it is still perceptibly nourished by mystical
currents. In knowing of God through God, the knowing being communes with, or indeed may be united with, the divine object of knowledge. Knowledge of God through God may coincide with a higher
form of self-knowledge.

No path of deduction leads from the putative experience to the
diverse manifestations of mystical writings. But conversely, the specific manifestations of mysticism in our literature can be accounted for
by our definition. The distinctive characteristics of Eckhart's theme of
knowledge as union can be derived from the more general definition
of the mystical theme; but any attempt to explain what Eckhart says

about his theme of divine knowledge by reference to an *unio mystica* experienced by Eckhart has to rely on assertions with no foundation of evidence in his work.

As a divine knowledge of divine truths, mysticism entails a devaluation of human knowledge as the precondition for divine knowledge. In accordance with the classical stations of the mystic's path, there is a kind of noetic *purgatio*, preceding *illuminatio* and *unio mystica*. Eckhart urges his listeners to take leave of everything "creatural." Cusanus demonstrates the inadequacy of all finite knowledge. The proper devaluation of all human or creatural knowledge may actually coincide with the divine knowledge. For Eckhart, becoming "empty" of all "images" results in the "birth of the Son in the soul." For Cusanus, Christ—adumbrated by the union of opposites—is the corrective for the inadequacy of the finite mind.

By this same definition of a divine knowledge of the divine, it is possible to speak of nature mysticism—provided that nature appears to the illuminated mind as a manifestation of the invisible powers of God. Paracelsus distinguished between the light of nature and the light of the spirit; however, these two kinds of knowledge converge in the invisible forces or "virtues" that stem directly from God and inform the creation as it is known to the senses and mind. The Paracelsus who based his authority even as a physician on an unmediated intuition of the all-informing unity of the Creator and the creation stood within the German mystical tradition. The human microcosm and the natural macrocosm can only correspond to one another because both reveal the divine nature. Paracelsus as a physician focused upon created nature, but his speculations are implicitly or explicitly centered in the nature of the Creator. The German mystics who came after him recognized and highlighted this latent core of his thought.

If our definition of mysticism as a divine knowledge of the divine is broad enough to accomodate both the classical theme of the "union with God" and the less intense mystical knowledge by "illumination" (in which the distinction between human subject and divine object is retained), the double criterion of the divine should also demarcate our theme from certain related phenomena. The vision of a medieval nun, to whom Christ reveals himself in bodily form, is indeed mystical. However, the auditions of Joan of Ark (which came from God, but were concerned rather with the salvation of France) are not. Nor is systematic theology mystical; for, though its object is a knowledge of God, it advances by Scripture, tradition, and logic, not by mystical intuition. The conservative, mature Luther who insisted on the "scriptural principle" as the limit of knowledge of God was no mystic. But the Protestant Spiritualists who were influenced by the earlier Luther and who wrote that the scriptural "letter" is "dead" without the inner revelation of the divine spirit within the believer are justifiably classified as mystics. Ecstatic experience, understood as a psychological state involving no knowledge or experience of anything sacred or transcendent, is excluded by our definition. An encounter with ghosts or demonic supernatural phenomena stands outside our purview (though it may be the case that a terrifying knowledge of the devil predisposes the mystic to seek God). Johannes Kepler regarded his initial intuition concerning the structure of the solar system to be a divine revelation of the divine plan of creation.[11] Hence, his intuition can justifiably be called *mystical*. But in pursuing this intuition, he proceeded as a scientist and mathematician, not as a mystic.

The mystic receives a knowledge of God from God. Both the transcendent reference and the transcendent source are essential to the association addressed by our definition. Yet this can still be a matter of degree. Newton, who employed mathematical techniques to derive the date of the Judgment from allusions in the Book of Revelation,[12] ought to strike us as further removed from mysticism than Melchior Hoffmann, who learned of the date through prophetic dreams; and Hoffmann is in turn less a mystic on the issue of the Apocalypse than Jacob Boehme who conceived of the final age, not in worldly dates and times, but rather as the dawning of eternity, signaled by the emergence of a knowledge of the divine eternal nature. In Boehme's case, the knowledge imparted by the Holy Spirit was its own object and fulfillment.

It might be objected that our definition leaves it unclear whether the Old Testament patriarchs and prophets were mystics, or whether common practices of prayer are mystical. But these difficulties could be obviated if instead of treating the term as a shibboleth, we were to analyze it as a concept, by asking why it seems either applicable or objectionable. To do so would reveal that the debate revolves around the claim or attribution of divine authority.[13]

Is the psychological "experience" of the religious mystic anything but the intrinsic certainty accompanying a God-given knowledge of divine things? The divine truths revealed to the mystic are said to be secret things, but when we search for the specific esoteric contents, what we discover can invariably be found as well in the Bible or in the interpretive writings of the tradition. Whatever is not found in the Bible is at least justified by means of biblical references. What appears to go beyond is the motif of an "unknowing"—the sense of an outer limit, attained or surpassed, of human, communicable knowledge. However, even if we were to grant that this motif reproduces a distinct experience, it is by no means alien to the mainstream of tradition. Pseudo-Dionysius is the most important source for this motif. Though relegated to the realm of the apocryphal now, Dionysius the Areopagite occupied an almost apostolic status throughout the Middle Ages.

As mysticism, the divinely inspired knowledge of a divine truth may range from the ecstatic "unknowing" of an inexpressible union with God to the inspired scientific hypothesis of a Kepler. The divine knowledge may elude every positive formulation, or it may be knowledge of the quotidian things of our world—which are recognized in their essential being in God. In all events, what typifies German mysticism is not a personal union of the human *I* with the divine *Thou*. In its most characteristic representatives—in Hildegard, Eckhart, Paracelsus, Boehme, or Novalis—German mysticism is speculative: concerned not, or not mainly, with a union of persons, but of "worlds." The *I* and *Thou* of a personal mysticism are globalized by the categories of transcendence and immanence. These lend the mystical knowledge a metaphysical cast. To be sure, German mysticism also shares many motifs with the mysticism of the Romance cultures: it shares the ecstatic union of bride and bridegroom and the physical emulation of the Passion of Christ. However, the most productive theme of the German mystics is the unity of time and eternity, of the finite and the infinite, of the visible and the invisible, or of the divine one and the created many, centered in a plurality of self-knowing individuals. The terms *microcosm* and *macrocosm*, which are commonly associated with Renaissance theory, are in fact characteristic for German speculative mysticism from Hildegard on. German mysticism is preoccupied with large and small "worlds," ranging from the absolute world of divinity to the microworlds encompassed by the smallest organism, space, or discrete thing. Jacob Boehme stood squarely within the tradition when he wrote that he could discern the entire world in a single stone or clump of earth, or the transcendent principles of divine being in the life of the soul.[14]

The objection might be raised that, in choosing between our two "models," we are merely deciding whether to apply to one and the same object of investigation a psychological-experiential or a literary-thematic coat of paint. Nothing could be further from the truth. In removing the psychological characterization from German mysticism, we discover something altogether different in what the mystical writers actually recorded. Remarkably enough, when we disregard the postulate of the universal experience and instead consider the literary-thematic aspects of mysticism, we may arrive at a better understanding of the mystic's experience. The contrast can be outlined point for point with regard to the traits commonly associated with the mystical experience. In outlining the contrast, I am guided more by the common stereotype of mysticism than by the more differentiating, though still problematical, presentation of Evelyn Underhill.[15]

1. As postulated experience, the *unio mystica* is ineffable. Yet instead of ineffability, we discover that a recurrent motif of much German mystical literature is the "expressiveness" of all things. The "signature of things" is a motif anticipated already in the writings of Hildegard and Eckhart. It acquires prominence through Renaissance naturalism, and it is influential even beyond the sphere of mystical literature.

2. As experience, the mystical union is a seamless merging, a coalescing of subject with object. The experienced oneness is personal, though selfless. By contrast, the *theme* of oneness is concerned with reconciling the one with the many, the individual conscience with the common standard of faith, freedom with order. The literary structure corresponding to the experienced union is that of *synthesis*. The origins of the mystical synthesis can be traced to various views of God and the world, voiced in distinct passages of the Bible or in conflicts of doctrine or philosophy. Mystical literature is a synthesis of sources: its main sources, Philo Judaeus, John the Evangelist, the Apostle Paul, Plotinus, Pseudo-Dionysius, Origen, and Augustine can in turn be analyzed as syntheses of diverse currents.

3. Guided by the notion of an unutterable union with God, we might expect mystical literature to be carried by a solitary rapt voice. But, in fact, the literature of the German mystics often reveals itself to be remarkably "polyvocal" (to borrow the term coined by Bakhtin for Dostoyevsky's novels). Mystical literature counterpoints the voices of God and woman in Hildegard's work, or the voices of all the "masters" in Eckhart's sermons, or those of contending doctrinal opinions in Boehme's writings.

4. A mysticism grounded in the universal experience of union is frequently thought to transcend doctrine, confession, and the particularities of culture and historical period. But, quite to the contrary, the German mystics express the conditions of their cultures, periods, and confessions. In spite of its metaphysical breadth, German mysticism remains Christocentric, at least until the Romantic period. The personal union of the divine and the human equates with the all-informing and world-generating Word. The Word is rendered visible by

Hildegard or Boehme in symbols drawn from nature. Christ is spiritualized by Eckhart or Tauler as the "birth of the Son in the soul," conceptualized by Cusanus as the intellectual construct of an *absolutum
maximum contractum*. The Christocentrism of German mysticism is
conveyed in paradoxes that shatter literal representation, rather than
in consoling images that encourage emotional identification. Paradox,
as the crux of the mystical encounter of transcendence with immanence, is carried over into secular German literature and thought. The
influence of mysticism extends by way of Schopenhauer—a pivotal
secularizer—through Nietzsche to German modernism.

      5. Christian German mysticism is not only Christocentric, it is
doctrinal. The notion of the undogmatic nature of mysticism has roots
in Pietism. But, in fact, doctrines, including highly contested ones,
have played a role. The classical case is that of the Eucharist, a cause of
contention that elicited visionary revelations in the prescholastic Middle Ages and gave rise to elaborate theories in subsequent times.[16]
Eucharistic doctrines have been influential in shaping the content of
German mysticism, including Boehme's Protestant mysticism.

      6. Mysticism purports to be atemporal in its universality. How-
ever, German mysticism has been clearly molded by its contexts in
intellectual history. The themes and symbols of the German mystics
overlap with the metaphysical, scientific, or literary themes of appearance and reality, nature and spirit, subject and object, or sign and signification. The German mystics were not otherworldly researchers
into occult secrets. To a surprising extent, they were women and men
of affairs, engaged in practical activities and preoccupied with wide-
ranging ordinary interests. The historical periods in which they lived
were characterized by confrontations and conflicts. These often pitted
ecclesiastical and secular powers (the institutional embodiments of
eternity and time in the social-historical context) against one another.
In significant instances, these conflicts helped shape the German mystical theme.

      7. An aspect of the theory of mystical experience criticized by
Steven T. Katz is the association of mysticism with heresy or radicalism.[17] This association accords with the oversimplified notion of a universal, nonconfessional, nondoctrinal religious experience. Noting the
conservative, confession-bound nature of mysticism, Katz has argued
that the mystics were more traditional than radical and that their association with heresy is therefore incorrect. Although much can be said
in favor of Katz's view, a finer distinction has to be drawn. Heresies
can originate in "conservative" campaigns to reform the Church for its
own good. It is more difficult to ascertain which doctrines or move-

ments were intentionally heretical than to find out who has been burned by whom.[18] Mysticism can be conservative regarding tradition and at the same time heretical. Although it is not nonconfessional, German mysticism does count universalism and tolerance among its themes. The mystic asserts a divine knowledge of divine truth. Depending on the mystic, this claim may validate the demand for conformity or justify the individualism of the dissenter. There is a tension between the confessionality and the toleration of the mystic, but then this same tension exists in the confessions as a whole and cannot be reduced to a simple and consistent formulation.

8. The German mystics were men and women of conviction, with beliefs and ideas. Beliefs and ideas possess their own inherent defects and strengths. Yet the actual performance of beliefs and ideas in history surely depends ultimately on the roles created for them—on the "setting" and "cast of characters." At worst, German mysticism—caricatured virtually beyond recognition—provided Nazi ideologues with the mystique of the perennial aristocrat of the Aryan race. At the opposite end of the spectrum, mysticism helped create a culture of pluralistic tolerance premised on a mystical interpretation of the Pauline dictum that "the letter kills, while the spirit gives life" (2 Corinthians 3:6).

9. This quickening "spirit" merged with the other motif that occurred throughout the tradition from Hildegard to Novalis (and with distant echoes in the literature of this century): the motif of the expressionistic relationship of the transcendent and immanent worlds. Hildegard interpreted the cosmos as a whole and in detail as the materialized expression of the divine will and intention. Mechthild of Magdeburg compared the triune God to the inner and outer form and the spirit of the book that was her life's work. Meister Eckhart preached that every "creature" and created thing is a "book," which, if it were properly understood, would render any sermon superfluous. (*Der niht dan die crêatûren bekante, der endörfte niemer gedenken ûf keine predige, wan ein ieglîchiu crêatûre ist vol gotes und ist ein buoch.*)[19] Paracelsus wrote that "all created things are letters and books which describe the human being's [divine] origin" (*dan alle creata seind buchstaben und bücher, des menschen herkomen zu beschreiben*).[20] The German Renaissance and Baroque mystics elaborated theories of the divinely configured "signatures of things." The motif of the signature pertains to the "book symbolism" cited by Curtius, but it goes beyond the rhetorical flourish or topos. The signature of things outlasts the Enlightenment and is revived with original insights by Novalis and others during the Romantic period, and reinterpreted by Schopenhauer in a secular sense.

Though modern German literature and philosophy flourishes in a world of belief distinct from that of the mystics, its visions and concepts have also courted the boundaries of transcendent and immanent realms, recapitulating the symbolism of the meaning of things. Whether or not modern German literature and philosophy contain an authentic mysticism, they are assuredly replete with mystical elements and allusions.

10. The above characteristics of German mysticism will be shown to be closely related to the central problem of authority. The word of traditional-biblical authority, which is challenged in the sphere of common experience and reconfirmed by the special knowledge of the mystic, is decisive for our interpretation of German mystical literature. Undoubtedly, *the mystical*—like all other conscious affectations—*is experience*; assuredly, too, any profound experience has unutterable recesses of meaning that elude translation into words. But by shifting attention from the elusive "experience" to the accessible patterns of tradition, of challenged authority, and thematic knowledge, we will be better able to integrate mystical literature into intellectual history.

Historical context is what distinguishes the characteristic German mystics, whether they wrote in German or Latin, from the Scholastic authors of mystical treatises. German intellectual history is less complete when its mystics are abstracted from it, and they are less intelligible when they are considered outside their historical setting. The objective of this study is to place these figures in their own world in order to render them more comprehensible for students of literature and intellectual history.

# 1

# The Union of Worlds

## Biblical and Augustinian Sources of German Mysticism

A student unfamiliar with mystical writings, who approached them expecting to encounter reports of arcane experiences, might be dismayed to discover so many open secrets. Much of what is found in the writings of Hildegard, Eckhart, or Boehme could have been said or written in a nonmystical context—indeed was written elsewhere without pressing any claim to an immediate knowledge of divine things. Eckhart also expressed the themes of his mystical sermons in his discursive treatises. The many-faceted theosophy of Boehme can be traced in large measure to sources that are not *per se* mystical.

What makes the traditional theme into a mystical theme? In instance after instance, the German mystics were confronted with crises of authority. Either their own or their contemporaries' certainty of the received word of scriptural, ecclesiastical, or philosophical authority came under challenge. Under challenge, the received word was reborn as mysticism, taking on new life in the vision or audition, through prayer or contemplation, in the illuministic theory, or as the Pietistic awakening. If German mysticism possesses a secret, it should be sought in the world rather than in the word.

From our vantage, mysticism is not something that occurs or exists in and of itself. To debate whether there is mysticism in the Bible or Augustine is pointless. Even granting that the Fourth Gospel has given rise to a Johannine mysticism, and that Augustine's vision at Ostia was clearly a mystical experience, it is not the case that a self-perpetuating mysticality is rekindled by an isolated Johannine or Ostian spark which leapfrogs the remaining biblical and Patristic-Augustinian tradition. A study focusing only on the *unio mystica*, on Dionysian elements, on the mystic as heretic, or, in whatever mysterious way, as *Other*, would be like a mountain range charted to show only the peaks that extend above the cloud cover. We can gain a sounder view of the lay of things by reversing this perspective. It is misleading to characterize the mystic as an outsider devoted to the

path of Pseudo-Dionysius. Thomas Aquinas was hardly less devoted
to him than was Eckhart; and Johann Wenck, who accused Cusanus of
error, was probably at least as taken with the "Father of Western Mysticism" as the man whom he accused.[1] The mysticism of Eckhart,
Cusanus, or Boehme originated in a more complex interaction with
authority than the indictments of orthodox accusers or the idolizations
of some modern admirers would lead us to suspect.

The theme of German mysticism to be delineated and studied
here is derived from canonical passages of the Bible. As sources of
mysticism, they do not require interpretation by means of the allegorical or anagogic modes of exegesis. Not Dionysius, but Augustine is
the Patristic source whose interpretation of the seminal scriptural passages introduced them into the mainstream of Western thought in the
form that is decisive for our theme.

The preeminent speculative theme of German mysticism is what
might be called the "union of worlds." Its scriptural subtexts are two
passages of the Bible that begin with the words, "In the beginning...":
the first verse of Genesis and the Prolog to the Gospel of John. Behind
the conflation of these "beginnings" lies a convergence of philosophical and religious traditions—Jewish, Hellenistic, Gnostic, and Christian—a convergence first represented by Philo Judaeus of Alexandria
and then carried on by Origen, Clement of Alexandria, and many centuries of Platonizing Fathers of the Church. To the German mystics, the
authors of the two seminal passages are Moses and John the Evangelist, as interpreted by Saint Augustine.

In addition to the two "beginnings," with their distinct para-
digms for the relations of creation, creature, and Creator, other biblical
motifs enter into the pattern. A constellation of texts establishes the
structure of the divine knowledge recorded by the German mystics in
their writings. Genesis 1:27 indicates that the human creature was created in the image of the divine Creator. This is also a source for the
motif of creation as a form of imaging and of self-knowledge as mystical knowledge. The intertestamental Wisdom literature, as well as a
number of Pauline dicta (especially Romans 1:20 and Acts 17:28),
extend the concept of a creation in which the visible things in nature
are symbols for the invisible qualities of God, or for his immanent
presence in the creation. The Pauline term for God as *omnes in omnibus*,
all in all,[2] not only sustains the view that God is in all things: it eventually yields the implication that all things are contained in all other
things. Immanence and transcendence, creation and Creator, visible
and invisible, part and whole—these are the parameters of distinct,

yet symbolically related spheres. The visible, external, finite, temporal, and natural world consists of an array of symbols and systems of symbols, expressing in time the eternal being of a transcendent deity.

Hildegard of Bingen, Meister Eckhart, and Jacob Boehme are the three outstanding representatives of the varieties of German mysticism: the visionary, the reflective, and the nature mystic. Though their works are characterized by considerable differences, they nonetheless approach the common theme of the relationship of transcendence and immanence by way of the same canonical texts; and they arrive at a similar solution: *the created world is to its Creator as an utterance to its speaker*. The world means God, and has been meant by God into being. Created through the Word, the world is wordlike for all who are open to discern its significance. This wordlike character of all things lends an authority to the German mystic, who characteristically appears in a period of crisis for traditional, institutional, and personal standards of authority.

Before we turn to the nonscriptural, philosophical sources of our theme, we should first consider the degree to which the biblical passages offered the requisite material of imagery and idea for the themes and authority of the mystic. Since we will repeatedly encounter the juxtaposition of the two "beginnings," we should consider what the pertinent passages are capable of contributing aside from their traditional reception. Both begin with the words, "In the beginning," but then proceed to recount the coming into being of the world in rather different terms. According to Genesis in the New International Version (NIV):

> In the beginning God created the heavens and the earth. Now the earth was formless and empty, darkness was over the surface of the deep, and the Spirit of God was hovering over the waters. And God said, "Let there be light," and there was light. God saw that the light was good, and he separated the light from the darkness. God called the light "day," and the darkness he called "night." And there was evening and there was morning—the first day. (Genesis 1:1–5)

On the second day, God created the expanse or firmament and separated the waters above it from the waters below it. On the third day, God gathered the waters below the firmament into one place; the dry ground became the land, and the waters the seas. God let the land produce vegetation, sprouting seeds and bearing fruit, and pronounced it

good. On the fourth day, God created the lights in the heavens, separating day from night and marking the seasons, days, and years with
stars, sun, and moon. On the fifth day, God filled the seas with living
creatures, and the sky with birds. And on the sixth day, God created
animals, seeing to it that they would reproduce according to their kind.

Then last, but apparently most important of all, God created the
human being as a twofold creature:

> So God created man in his own image,
> in the image of God he created him;
> male and female he created them. (Genesis 1:28)

Upon them, God conferred *dominion* over all living things. Genesis goes on to survey the parameters of dominion by revealing the
consequences of disobedience. The disobedience of the human creature plunges humankind into the state of nature in which laws and
punishments become necessary. If the entire Bible commands obedience to God, the command in Genesis not to eat the forbidden fruit
exalts obedience over understanding. The point is not to understand
why; the point is to obey God. Genesis is in this sense patriarchal and
hierarchical.

Until surprisingly recent times, the six days of creation in Genesis provided the cornerstone for philosophical and scientific theories
of the natural world. These included free speculations, expanded
beyond the literalism of a world brought into being in six calendar
days. Precisely for those whose expectations were honed by absolute
faith in the scriptural word, Genesis left many questions unanswered.
How could there be "evening" and "morning" on the first day—
before the heavenly bodies and the sun had been created on the fourth
day? What sort of light shone prior to the creation of the sun? When
were the angels created? (For created they must have been, since otherwise the absolute priority of God would have been challenged.) Out
of what material was the world created? Was the stuff of the world
coeternal with God, or was the material of the world made out of
nothingness by God prior to the six days? And if God created everything, what was the source of evil in the world—prior to the fall of
Adam? And above all, how were all the questions that had been left
unresolved by the creation account in Genesis related to the paramount one of why a God who presumably didn't need it should have
chosen to bring the world into being at all?

What were the dark waters that were parted by the firmament on
the second day? Could they be identical with the crystalline seas that

appear in the course of the world's destruction in the last book of the Bible? And, if so, might this be a secret hint that the end returns to its beginning, that creation is not only circular in space (as we see from the heavens) but also circular in time—circular in salvational history? And, if so, what does this circularity reveal to us about the still-hidden significance of the world? How does it relate to the Savior who is called the "light of the world," who is the Alpha and the Omega, who exalts the lowly and humbles the proud?

And why is "separation" so decisive—the separation of the waters, the separation of light from darkness? The faithful but polyvocal reading of the Bible discerns the voice of an "author" Moses, who wrote of things he could not have witnessed—but who also may have known far more than he was able to write. Peering behind the veil of Moses became a term for the mystic's quest.

Notwithstanding all the unanswered questions, one thing is certain: Genesis accounts for the origin of the world in terms of the coordinates of the *created world*, in accordance with *space* and *time*, of *above* and *below*, as *a sequence of events*, within an implicit *hierarchy*, in which what is above is higher, and what is below lower, and in which what comes last in order of creation is first in order of importance. If God is transcendent in Genesis, the perspective of his act of creation is nevertheless immanent.

The origin of the world appears in a different perspective of immanence and transcendence, when we attend to the voice of the fourth Evangelist recounting the "beginning":

> In the beginning was the Word, and the Word was with God, and the Word was God. He was with God in the beginning. Through him all things were made; without him nothing was made that has been made. In him was life, and that life was the light of men. The light shines in the darkness, but the darkness has not understood it. (John 1:1–5)

Here the perspective of space, time, and nature has shifted to one of timeless immediacy and presence. No longer is there a sequence of distinct events. Here, event has aspect rather than sequence. The beginning is not a first followed by a second and a third. The "beginning" is an eternal present and ground of all that comes into being and lives. The Word or "Logos," according to Kittel's dictionary of the Greek New Testament, is unique in this usage. Clearly, the Word is Christ. But why this peculiar terminology? The reader may recall the translation challenge that Goethe's Faust labored over at the beginning of his journey of discovery through the created world. As in Faust's interpretation of John 1:1, "the Word" can be interpreted as "sense" (*Sinn*), "force," (*Kraft*), and even as "action," (*Tat*), since the unfolding of the world is the same as the "action" of divine creation in Genesis. Cross-referenced with other passages, especially from the Wisdom books, "the Word" could also signify the divine "order" or divine "mind," and there are surely even more possibilities.

But beyond these valid interpretations, "the Word" can mean quite simply "word," that is, any spoken, written, or conceived utterance, sign, or command. It can be taken as the "Let there be" of Genesis, or taken as the hidden intention, the word within the word that Genesis does not reveal. If "the Word" is taken in its literal sense, as *a* word, then the world itself becomes figural—it is transfigured into a "Book of Nature": the world is an external revelation of the divine will, before it was recorded by Moses, or revealed in Christ. Books are after all collections of visible letters revealing the invisible meanings of an author. In its philosophical sense, "cosmos" signifies order. Pondering the natural, human, and scriptural orders, the mystic attempts to look from creation, from "macrocosm" and "microcosm," to a hidden divine intention, concealed in the Bible. To be sure, the Bible itself offers the precedents for this. The Apostle Paul, echoing motifs of the intertestamental sapiential literature, exhorts the idolatrous Romans that they should recognize the invisible things of the Creator from the visible things of creation (Romans 1:20): "For since the creation of the world God's invisible qualities—his eternal power and divine nature—have been clearly seen, being clearly understood from what has been made..." With the same reasoning of natural theology, Paul tells the Athenians who have erected an altar "to the unknown god" that, as for the true deity: "in him we live and move and have our being. As some of your own poets have said, 'We are his offspring'" (Acts 17:28). The transcendent-immanent deity is invisible, yet omnipresent in the world. God is wholly above human beings, yet—so it appears here—as innate to them as their own human genesis and lifeblood.

In the Prolog of John, the Word is paradoxically immanent and transcendent. The Word acts in creation, yet remains unto itself, remains *with* God, and *is* God. The self-identity of the eternal Word is therefore dynamic: an identity that gives rise changelessly, which resides in eternity while entering into time. This duality is matched by the light that shines in the darkness, but cannot be comprehended by the darkness. Where the creation account in Genesis represented God through his actions, and his actions in terms of our world of time, space, matter, and number, John instead places transcendence and immanence abruptly vis-à-vis one another. The becoming of the world is refracted through the eye of eternity. If we regard the created world as a riddle, implicit in Genesis, this riddle now moves into the forefront in John. To the darkness, the light is an incomprehensible and elusive mystery. Where Genesis left us with unanswered questions regarding the world, the language of the Fourth Gospel encourages us to see the world and life as an ever-present mystery. For the devout mystic the answer is, to be sure, never lacking. What is lacking is a full appreciation of the mystery itself.

The most original German mystics place this mystery at the creative center of their work. In *The Book of Divine Works*, Hildegard perfects her synthesis of Genesis and John by treating the creation in time as a symbolic formulation of the eternal Word. Eckhart emphasizes the Prolog in his Latin treatises and highlights its symbolic dualities in his sermons. One sermon subliminally inserts the mysterious imagery of the Prolog into the seventh day of Genesis, thereby equating the sabbath of divine creation with the Dionysian darkness of absolute divine transcendence:

> "In principio"—this means in German as much as a beginning of all being, as I said in the school; I said this in addition: it is an end of all being, for the first beginning is only there for the sake of the final end. Indeed, God himself does not rest there where the first beginning is; he rests at the final end and resting place of all being.... What is the final end? It is the concealed darkness of the eternal deity, and is not known, and was never known, and will never be known. God remains there unknown in himself, and the light of the eternal Father has eternally shone into it, and the darkness does not comprehend the light.

> *"In principio" daz sprichet als vil ze tiutsche als ein angenge alles wesens, als ich sprach in der schuole; ich sprach noch mê: ez ist ein ende alles wesens, wan der êrste begin ist durch des lesten endes willen. Jâ, got der ruowet selbe niht dâ, dâ er ist der êrste begin; er ruowet dâ, dâ er ist ein ende und ein raste alles wesens... Waz ist das leste ende? Ez ist diu verborgen vinsternisse der êwigen gotheit und ist unbekant und wart nie bekant und enwirt niemer bekant. Got blîbet dâ in im selber unbekant, und daz lieht des êwigen vaters hât dâ êwiclîche îngeschinen, und diu vinsternisse enbegrîfet des liehtes niht.*[3]

Here, Eckhart the preacher superimposes onto the imagery of John the Dionysian motif of the superessentiality of God as a "darkness" beyond all knowing, and then returns to the context of the Prolog, in which the light is eternally shining into the darkness. But notably the overriding message of this sermon to Dominican nuns in Cologne is that the believer should love rather than fear God (*Der mensche ensol got niht vürhten, wan der, der in vürhtet, der vliuhet in*[4]) and should therefore desist from striving for a knowledge of God in images and instead recognize that all created things are nothing in themselves, yet are God in God. In view of this purpose, it seems unlikely that Eckhart intended to confound his listeners by drawing them ill-prepared into an unwonted adventure in negative theology. The Dionysian mystery is assimilated to the authority of Scripture. The Johannine-Dionysian light and darkness reinforce the preacher's chiaroscuro symbolization of interpenetrating yet distinct aspects of being—as well as his consoling message that time is entirely overshadowed by eternity. Gnosis and agnosis are both absorbed in divinity.

Equally mysterious, but again incorporating the same scriptural materials, is the cosmogony in Boehme's *The Three Principles of Divine Being*: Before the world was born, writes Boehme, there was a dark matrix in the void, like a nothingness; then into it shone the eternal light, arousing a desire for the light within the darkness. But since the craving within this reified darkness (or "dryness") could find no object for its desire, and could not hold the eternal light, the desire contracted upon itself. This contraction gave birth to and became the material of the world—in which the forces of life are rejuvenated through the power of the divine light.[5] After recounting this strange cosmogony, the author deciphers it for the reader as an allegorical transcription of the Johannine Prolog—which he then praises above every book of the Bible.[6]

In Eckhart's sermon, we risked missing the message to love rather than fear God, risked overlooking the familiar references to John, interpreting the sermon as pure Dionysian negative theology aimed above the heads of the simple nuns of his flock. In Boehme's cosmogony, we could easily fail to notice the similar message that fear can be vanquished because the power of light pervades everything—a message that merges the two "beginnings" in the single moral: "Thus one truly understands how the light of God is a cause of all things" (*Also verstehet man gar eigentlich, wie das Licht Gottes aller Dinge eine Ursache ist*).[7]

One might want to interpret Boehme's visionary cosmogony as a contamination with Gnostic influences of the kind represented by Basilides. Yet the birth of the world is an elaboration of the motifs of the Johannine Prolog. The light shines into the darkness: its inability to comprehend the light is what constitutes nature as forever in need of

redemption from its own congenital blindness. Eckhart's cryptic conclusions and Boehme's mysterious cosmogony aim at stimulating a
sense of the wondrous depth of experience, an awareness of a profound
riddle awaiting its solution. But we notice that the answer is encoded
into the puzzle. Instead of referring back to some obscure psychological
experience—and far from involving Gnosticism or pantheism—the
solution lies in Scripture and in established articles of faith. The astute
reader or listener can be expected to hear a familiar voice of authority.

The key is the eternal Word, embodied in time and spoken by the
God become human in the Gospel of John: "no one can see the kingdom of God unless he is born again" (3:3); "Flesh gives birth to flesh,
but the Spirit gives birth to spirit" (3:6); "God is spirit, and his wor-
shipers must worship in spirit and in truth" (4:24); "the Spirit gives
life; the flesh counts for nothing. The words I have spoken to you are
spirit and they are life" (6:63); "I am the light of the world. Whoever
follows me will never walk in darkness, but will have the light of life"
(8:12); "...become sons of light" (12:36); "A new command I give you:
Love one another" (13:34); "Remain in me, and I will remain in you"
(15:4); "Though I have been speaking figuratively, a time is coming
when I will no longer use this kind of language but will tell you
plainly about my Father" (16:25). Christ embodies the union of immanence and transcendence. As the Word, he is both in the Father and in
the world, both historical and present, outer as well as inner. The
believers are in him, and he in them. True to its mysterious Prolog, the
Fourth Gospel elaborates the dichotomy of transcendence and immanence in its teachings. John generalizes in contrasting life, light, spirit,
love, and truth with darkness and flesh, and hints that the figurative
language of these teachings is to be supplanted in time by a more
direct mode of expression. The meditative path that Eckhart's auditors
or Boehme's readers could be expected to follow need never have lost
sight of biblical authority in the play of association and interpretation.

Their mystagogical pronouncements invited misunderstandings
and rendered them vulnerable to charges of heresy. However, no serious evidence has ever indicated that these mystics harbored the covert
intention of subverting the canonical status of the Bible or overturning
fundamental articles of faith—much as we might prefer to see them as
radical outsiders. In some cases, the mystics indeed seem to have
clashed with the authorities as in Dostoyevsky's parable of the Grand
Inquisitor who threatened to have a returned Christ burned at the
stake. But there is just as little reason to sanctify the mystic as such, as if
every claimant to divine knowledge were a saint or martyr. Ultimately,
it is pointless to argue over the charge of heterodoxy against Eckhart or

Boehme. Heresy is defined by the institution which holds the power of judgment and enforcement. Our claim is simply that the message of the German mystics—whether orthodox or heterodox, whether doctrinally admissible or deviant—found its point of departure in the scriptural word—in a word mediated, as Katz says, by tradition.

The German mystical tradition is not only scriptural but also Augustinian. It is Augustinian, not in reference to an Augustinianism of doctrine, but rather in reference to a writer and his dynamic and sometimes contradictory synthesis of themes. The difference cannot be emphasized enough. The *doctrine* of the creation *ex nihilo* may distinguish the orthodox thinker from the heterodox one. Yet the thought of *the continuity of the eternal being of the Creator with the temporal being of his creation*—the idea that in some sense *nature was in God before creation, and that God remains in nature after creation*—these are *themes* that are elaborated by the heterodox and the orthodox alike, even in similar terms.

Augustine viewed immanence and transcendence in light of the eternal Word and the created world, and at the same time in terms of Scripture and philosophy. His universal influence introduced our theme into the tradition in an enduring form. He embodies the theme of the union of worlds as if in person. His conversion was a bringing into focus of a Neoplatonic *Logos* in the revealed Word as Christ, a union that persists in the tradition founded upon his work. Here, we need to regard him not as the Father of the Church, nor even as the great philosopher, but as the author whose works were known directly or indirectly to nearly everyone. Not a doctrine, nor even a philosophy of Augustinianism, but rather the breadth of the man, replete with his many unresolved contradictions, makes him seminal for German mysticism.

The perennial importance of Augustine puts into a different perspective the theory of mysticism as an irrational subcurrent welling up periodically and inexplicably into the mainstream. Luther read him extensively in the decade before the *Ninety-Five Theses*. Descartes's *cogito ergo sum* looks back to Augustinian reflections even as it anticipates Kant. In addition to the weight of tradition, his work is of relevance to the *historical* environment of the seminal German mystics. Their representations of eternity and time were, like his, paralleled by institutional counterparts, by conflicting ecclesiastical and secular voices of authority.

Book eleven of *The City of God* lays a groundwork without which the tradition of German mysticism could scarcely have developed its characteristic forms. In the previous ten books, the author has made various replies to the enemies of the City of God. Now he proposes to treat "the origin, and progress, and deserved destinies of the two cities (the earthly and the heavenly, to wit), which, as we have said, are in this present world commingled, and as it were entangled together." The author proposes to begin by showing "how the foundations of these two cities were originally laid, in the difference that arose among the angels" (CD 11.1).[8] The historical context evoked by Augustine is as if designed to resonate with the characteristic historical dilemma of the Germans who, from Hildegard to Boehme, likewise found themselves in a crisis-ridden world, a world in which two realms were vexingly entangled or at war: the Holy Roman Empire. At the beginning of the second chapter of book eleven, he writes in an exultant and visionary formulation that,

> It is a great and rare thing for a man, after he has contemplated the whole creation, corporeal and incorporeal, and has discerned its mutability, to pass beyond it, and, by the continued soaring of his mind, to attain to the unchangeable substance of God, and, in that height of contemplation, to learn from God Himself that none but He has made all that is not of the divine essence. (CD 11.2)

This soaring trajectory of the contemplative mind that passes beyond the world of created mutability to merge in thought with the eternal being of God is akin to the salient project of several German mystics. Like him, they ascended above "cities" that were "commingled" and "entangled" in their own times—the secular city of the Empire and the spiritual city of the Church. Like him, they also endeavored to view the earthly world from the vantage of heaven. Again, as in book eleven, the German mystics were guided in their reflections by the two beginnings of Genesis and John, fixed poles between which their reflections developed with a surprising constancy and an equally surprising latitude of originality. Their Christology, like Augustine's, is set within a cosmic and philosophical perspective.

Of central importance for us are Augustine's many and varied reflections on eternity and time. Often in the background can be glimpsed the challenged principle of authority—personal, social, or doctrinal, whether in his conversion, in the controversies with the Donatists, Manicheans, and Pelagians, or in the dispute over the rival claims of pagan virtue and Christian faith. Pondering the union of eternity and time, he characterizes possible approaches to philosophical problems that he cannot claim to solve. He visualizes the created world as contained in an infinite sea of divine being. The world is like a sponge: surrounded by, but also saturated with, the infinite being of God (Conf. 7.7). He considers the question posed by the philosophical critics of Christianity: Why should God have created the world at one particular moment in time and not at another? He reasons that time and the world were created together, so that although the world does have an origin, there was no time before it (CD 11.6). He notes that the presence of God within the world cannot be construed in the manner of part and whole. Like the divine presence, the incorruptibility of life in any living body is entirely present in every part of the body (CD 11.10). In his many reflections, Augustine repeatedly juxtaposes the first verses of Genesis with the Prolog of John, and cites Paul's injunction to the Romans to recognize the invisible things of God from the visible things of creation. He interprets this as an instruction to proceed from the sensible things to the supersensible ones, from the realm of nature to the intellectual sphere of God and the angels. He notes that God does not reveal himself in visions or voices to the outer human eye or ear, but rather speaks by means of truth itself to those who are prepared to perceive it (CD 11.2). He writes of a twilight knowledge of things when they are regarded in themselves, and of a noonday knowledge when they are regarded in God (CD 11.29). Rational, empirical, scriptural, and visionary-mystical arguments are all combined in his reflections. These were in turn formed by the historical context of conflict and dissolution, by the conflicting interests of the earthly and heavenly "cities." In the historical environments of the German mystics, these motifs will be adapted to new assertions of authority.

The Augustinian synthesis therefore presents a thread of continuity. This is not to deny all the earlier and later—all the Christian and non-Christian—sources that contribute to the tradition. But no other source, including Pseudo-Dionysius, is capable of reemerging in such distinct forms. Centered in the relations of Genesis and Word, there is an alternation between temporal and eternal poles: these are variously embodied in the visible and the invisible, the outer and the inner, the finite and the infinite, letter and spirit, part and whole.

1. For Hildegard, it is the visible world of nature that refers us to the invisible things of God. Involvements in time are counterposed with the contemplation of eternity. There are echoes of Augustine's struggles with the Donatist and Manichean heresies, of his City of God and its satanic enemy, and of the endtime battles that conclude with the triumph of the faithful, followed by a final restoration of the new heaven and new earth. Hildegard may have drawn on sources unknown to us. Certainly she reflects the intellectual climate of the

twelfth century with its revived Augustinianism and its symbolic interpretation of the visible world in the Scholastic mysticism of Hugo of St. Victor. (Though Hugh was by some accounts a German from Saxony, he is customarily assigned to the history of Scholasticism rather than to the annals of German mysticism.)[9]

2. For Meister Eckhart, the relationship of the visible to the invisible directs us no longer to Hildegard's close study of nature, but rather beyond all visible or imaginable "images," to the supersensible that lies within, in the "ground of the soul," contiguous with the ground of God. Eternity with its serene calm overshadows time with its harsh struggles. The balance therefore swings back to the Neoplatonism of Augustine—and beyond him to a speculation on unity represented by Dionysius, or later by Moses Maimonides.[10] Yet even as it swings, the pendulum is anchored in tradition: much of what seems radically mystical and heretical in Eckhart is an interpretation of Augustinian motifs.

Eckhart might seem to characterize himself for us as an introverted fugitive from the world by his assertion that the truth lies within; as a pantheist by his teaching that God did not create all things and then turn aside, but rather remained in things; and as a Free Spirit by his word that none other than the Son of God is born in the soul of the believer. Yet Eckhart cited the first two assertions from Augustine; the third is an attenuated variant of a Patristic motif with Pauline scriptural precedents.[11] Conceptual prerequisites for the motif of the birth of God in the soul can also be found in considerations concerning the mind in Augustine's *On the Trinity*. Eckhart's Dionysian mysticism of unity is a magnification of his biblical and Augustinian motifs, which recognize in God the true being of creation and associate knowledge of God with knowledge of the soul, drawing the final consequence from the common tenet that only like can know like.

3. For Nicholas of Cusa, Augustine is present in the paradigm of a finite world encompassed by the infinite being of God and in the philosophical essaying from the conceivable toward the inconceivable.

The reaction against Aristotle and Scholasticism in Renaissance mysticism revived the speculative fertility of Augustinian creation theory. Again, this was not a matter of an Augustinian doctrine, but of an inquiry that speculated between the options of creation *ex nihilo* and a creation from an eternal ground of nature in God (the Word before and within creation), or, put differently, between dichotomizing God and nature and recognizing the divine presence in nature.

4. Protestant Spiritualism interwove the relationships of time and eternity with the relations of letter and spirit. Again Augustine

provided precedents by interpreting letter and spirit as law and grace
and by accepting (as a stepping-stone to his own conversion)
Ambrose's teaching that what appears meaningless in the Bible taken
literally can have an allegorical or spiritual sense (Conf. 6.6).

5. Boehme's synthesis of the mystical tradition takes its point of
departure from the doctrine of a nonpantheistic divine omnipresence.
According to views of ubiquity articulated by Augustine or Luther
and recapituled by Boehme, God is wholly present in every part of the
world. The divine wisdom that enlightens the human spirit also
guides the movement of every leaf. In this, Boehme not only confirms
Lutheran doctrine but also recapitulates Augustinian motifs. Boehme
broke with certain earlier mystical traditions by characterizing the
eternal grounds of creation in animistic and alchemistic terms, by
acknowledging the substantive existence of evil, and by seeking the
root of evil in the divine being. Nevertheless, the context framing his
theories is in numerous respects an Augustinian one. Though not doctrinally Augustinian, Boehme's writing carries on the thematic tradition rooted in a biblical approach to nature. Nearly all his seminal
notions are enhanced variants of Augustinian themes: the instantaneous and continuous creation in which the seven days correspond to
an ever-present pattern, Creation and Word, all the motifs of the Fall
from grace, the idealization of a prelapsarian Adam, and the recovery
of his angelic knowledge. Moreover, close textual scrutiny offers evidence of a minor but unmistakable paraphrasing of Augustine.[12] The
recapitulation of Augustinian themes distances Boehme from his precursor Paracelsus, in whom the same influence is less distinguishable.

6. In the Pietistic turn inward toward a personal fervor and
devotion, the voice of Augustine could still carry—as intimately as if
he were not an African bishop of the Roman Church, dead for twelve
hundred years, but seated, prayer book in hand, within the Protestant
conventicle. A popular book of prayers was compiled by Martin
Moller, the Lutheran pastor of Boehme's home city of Görlitz. A precursor of Pietism, Moller was placed by Johann Valentin Andreae in
his Preface to *Christianopolis* (1619) on a par with Johann Arndt. Pastor
Moller's German-language prayer book, *Meditationes Sanctorum
Patrum* (1592), drew some fifty of its sixty-eight prayers from the writings of Augustine (with four each from Tauler and Saint Bernard and
one from Dionysius).[13] The Augustinian *Meditations and Soliloquies*
were among the most common translations printed in the late sixteenth century.

The distant Augustinian background looms as large behind the
*Innerlichkeit* of Eckhart and German Pietism, as behind the divine

powers of creation envisaged by the Renaissance nature mystics, or even behind the cosmic attraction of love which the German Romantics recognized in nature. Augustine is considered to have inspired the medieval metaphysics of light, as well as the historical-eschatological schemes in the mysticism of South German Anabaptists. His mind could countenance a seemingly enlightened critique of ancient astrology, along with a superstitious acknowledgment of demons. Both sides of Augustine were echoed in the Renaissance. Always with references to an existential center and perpetually referring back to the two beginnings of Genesis and John, his inspirational fecundity ranged across most fields of science, philosophy, and theology.

The conjunction of Creation with the Word is at the root of the theme designated here as the union of worlds. Under thematic analysis, the union of worlds breaks down into several disparate, but conceptually interrelated motifs. Most of these motifs have a basis in Augustine, though in certain instances their classical articulation may lie elsewhere.

The mystical mind travelling like Augustine from this world toward the eternal one may pursue a variety of courses traced or intimated in his writings. Under closer scrutiny, the paths prove to be variants of a single conceptual theme. The pragmatic consequence of this is that—despite the absence of an experienced mystical union— the varieties of German mysticism can be appropriately studied as variants of a common theme of divine knowledge.

1. There is an *upward* path of ascent, which the mind pursues *gradatim*, "by degrees." This path is spectacularly projected in book eleven of the *Confessions*. The path of hierarchical ascent is a frequent mystical motif, associated with the "affirmative" and "negative" theologies of Pseudo-Dionysius.

2. There is an *inward* path of the mind that goes into itself to seek God. This is the avenue described in *On True Religion* (39.72), cited by Eckhart: "Do not go out. Return into yourself. Truth dwells in the inner man." Prior to his conversion, Augustine had been fascinated with a Plotinian philosophy familiar to him from the work of Marius Victorinus. This had encouraged the reflective tendencies of his thought. In remarkably abstract yet compelling reflections, Plotinus guided the philosophical enterprise from the outer world of the senses, inward to the soul and transcendent spirit, and to the unity of the superessential deity from which all being emanates: "to find ourselves is to know our source" (Ennead 6:9, 7). The soul that knows itself becomes like, indeed one with, the divine Spirit which has its

being in the thinking of its own being. In Augustine's understanding of his conversion to Christianity, the Platonic concept of truth as a supersensible reality rediscovers itself in Christ, as the Logos become flesh. Guided by revealed truth, the soul's self-knowledge therefore leads toward, indeed is, a knowledge of God.

3. There is also a speculative path of retrospective inquiry that looks back to the beginning of the world, as in Augustine's Genesis commentaries. Later, combining Augustine with Dionysius, Gregor of Nyssa and other sources, Erigena's *De Divisione Naturae* recognized a cosmic progression or return (*reditus*) of all things to God. According to Augustine, God could not have created the world without a plan or idea in the form of the eternal grounds or reasons: the *rationes aeternae* present in the divine Word and Wisdom. The creation in Genesis was instantaneous. Its continuation is perpetually implemented by the invisible "seeds" of the *rationes seminales;* these effect the orderly origination and growth of all things. Hence, order, permanence, and growth in nature are a profound mystery with sublime implications. The Augustinian concept of the eternal seeds of the creation in time is of Neoplatonic and perhaps Stoic origin (*logoi spermatikoi*).

After Augustine, Erigena's naturalistic mysticism posited *causae primordiales* at work in an ongoing creation. Among the German mystics, the same function (with or without the reference to Augustine or Erigena) is fulfilled by Hildegard's notion of a "greening" of things, as the work of the Word, or by the divine virtues or forces. In Eckhart's doctrine of ideas (*rationes*), these mediate between eternity and creation. So also do the "forces" (*krefte*) "poured into" all created things by God in the nature theories of Paracelsus. Boehme's seven "source-spirits" (*Quellgeister*) dwell in an eternal nature and are active in the ongoing creation and revitalization of the world.

Despite their many differences, all these concepts—from the Augustinian *rationes seminales* to Boehme's *Quellgeister in Gott*—serve to bridge the chasm between the eternal world in God and the created world in time. To some degree, all are construed in the sense of an objective agency or medium, intermediate between the absolute transcendence of the deity and the visible world of nature. German mysticism went far beyond Augustine by breaking with his teaching of the creation *ex nihilo*, but did so in order to implicate the life of the world and the life of God in one envisioned development.

For the ninth-century Irish theorist Erigena, as well as for Boehme, the Word, understood as a divine cause, helps to resolve the question whether God created nature from nothing or from some pre-existent material. As Gershom Scholem has observed, a *creatio ex nihilo*

was required by the idea of God's absolute omnipotence—yet philosophy dictates that nothing can arise from nothing.[14] Between these two
options, Erigena recognized the dialectical synthesis of a creation of
the world out of *nothing other than* God's own eternal being: comprised
of divine primordial causes in the Word. A systematic thinker *par excel-
lence*, Erigena surpassed Augustine's interpretation of creation with a
theory of theophany in which knowledge plays a more dynamic role.

Through speculations of this kind, the Augustinian trajectory of a
knowledge that soars up toward the City of God eventually merged
with a vision of the completion of being, the perfection of the world in
which God is understood as all in all. Knowledge is a divine self-creat-
ing process in nature, in which we with our imperfect knowing take
part. All things are in all other things: to know this suggests that the
beatific vision, or the completion of the world-process, is near at hand.
As the Romantic poet Novalis still believed: mystical knowledge not
only spans and unites worlds, it brings them into being and completes
them.

4. The motifs of the ascending, ingoing, and returning paths to
God are reinforced by further motifs concerning the nature of knowledge and its objects. The hierarchical path upward is also a path
inward: the highest created thing is the soul. Thus for Eckhart, the
motif of hierarchical ascent does not contradict the motif of an immediate "breakthrough" (*Durchbruch*): a spiritual event which occurs
without degrees. Moreover, the immediacy of divine knowledge is
emphasized as much by the nature mystics, Boehme or Paracelsus, as
by the reflective mystic Eckhart. All characterize the knowledge of
divine things as "immediate" (*ohne Mittel*). In seeing, the mind can
pursue the outer path of the senses; the inner one of imagination or
spirit; or the one that is both innermost and uppermost in the mystical
scheme of routes—that of the illuminated intellect.

In his *De Genesi ad Litteram, Libri Duodecim*, Augustine divided
the temporal and eternal perspectives on Creation into: (1) nature as
we now experience it; (2) nature as it came into being during the six
"days" of creation (which is interpreted as an instantaneous creation);
and (3) nature as it existed prior to the creation, in the eternal Wisdom
or eternal Word (Gen. ad litt. 5:28 ff.). These three aspects of creation
match up with three modes of knowledge: the sensory, the imaginative, and the intellectual. The third is the supersensible divine knowledge—Augustine's interpretation of the "third heaven" into which the
Apostle Paul was transported in the indescribable rapture recounted
in 1 Corinthians 12:3-4. The ground of created nature—as laid out in
the eternal Wisdom and Word of God—is known only through an

ecstatic transport of the kind experienced by the Apostle Paul. An entire concluding book of *De Genesi ad Litteram* is devoted to this mysterious ecstasy. To bolster the authority of their own interpretations of the created world, the German mystics defined Paul's rapture to conform to their own modes of knowledge. For Hildegard, Paul's incomprehensible words were an influx of wonders that conveyed the order of natural virtues and imparted prophetic knowledge[15]: that is, the kind of knowledge Hildegard claimed for herself.

In the sixth chapter of book twelve of *De Genesi ad Litteram*, the three kinds of knowledge are illustrated by means of Christ's commandment from Matthew 22:39, "Love thy neighbor as thyself." The eyes recognize the letters. The imagination recognizes the neighbor who is not present. Only the third, intellectual, mode of knowledge can discern those things which have no image at all: the love for one's neighbor. The third kind of knowledge is free of images, even as it recognizes the highest things of God (Gen. ad litt. 12:16 ff.).

The innermost and highest vision in Augustine's interpretive scheme coincides with love, making the divine love tantamount to the invisible spirit beneath the letter of the divine injunction. This is echoed in the mysticism of the Protestant Spiritualists, in Sebastian Franck's understanding of the "inner word." Boehme's mysticism dropped the three heavens of the Pauline-Augustinian tradition in favor of three "births" and "principles" of divine being, yet he still saw knowledge as a penetration and rebirth that strives for what is innermost and coincides with divine love. Whether or not Boehme and Franck were consciously alluding to Augustine in this motif, they were guided by the structures he had propagated.

5. Augustine declared that he wanted to know but two things: God and the soul. Knowledge of grace comes only from revelation; however, the measure of the certainty of truth is self-knowledge. Scriptural revelation is therefore balanced with the inner truth of a reflective self-certainty. While I can doubt all else, he concludes, I cannot doubt that I am. All truth is one, anchored in an inner certainty that is independent of sensory experience: "For we have another and far superior sense, belonging to the inner man, by which we perceive what things are just, and what unjust—just by means of an intelligible idea, unjust by the want of it.... By it I am assured both that I am and that I know this; and these two I love and in the same manner I am assured that I love them" (CD 11.27). The improbable German transition from Kantian rationalism to a new Romantic mysticism was in some sense anticipated by the Augustinian counterpoising of his own keen philosophical introspection with his passionate will to believe.

The inner trinity of being, self-certainty, and love enables the human mind to intuit an unconscious power pervading nature: "is it not obvious enough how nature shrinks from annihilation?" Love, the life of the soul, also acts without as a power causing all things in nature to rise, fall, or grow (CD 11.28). Though Augustine cannot, like Schelling, call this power the world-soul, only a small step would be needed to do so. A further step, and one might interpret the world-soul as a world-generating Will, as did Boehme and, long after him, the Romantic philosopher Schopenhauer (who still cited our pertinent themes from Augustine and the mystics).

6. If in German mysticism, there are more paths to God than the classical *purgatio, illuminatio,* and *unio,* there are indeed far more way-marks. The Book of the World is inscribed without and within. Everywhere there are analogies, signs, and symbols. Book thirteen of the *Confessions* provided a model for interpreting the Creation as a type of the Church. Augustine's theory of signs as words, or as things meaning other things, was expanded by those who came after him. Beyond the sign, the symbol can betoken that which is transcendent and infinitely distinct.[16] Taking issue with Augustine and at the same time citing Dionysius and Hugh of St. Victor, Saint Thomas Aquinas systematized the notion of created things as signs. God means not only in words, but also with things. When a word of Scripture refers to a thing which is also a divine sign, we are faced with the "spiritual" sense that is founded upon the literal sense of Holy Writ. The thing as sign is thereby integrated into the doctrine of the fourfold meaning of Scripture.[17]

A long tradition interprets the "unlike likeness" of Creator and creation by way of "analogy," as participation in the essence of the Creator. This encouraged a symbolism based on allegorical interpretations of nature and Scripture; this has been summarized by Armand Maurer:

Influenced by Philo, Clement of Alexandria makes frequent use of symbolism. For him, symbolism expresses the basic unity of all things, despite their multiplicity and diversity. Invisible harmonies, likenesses, and proportions bind the universe together, and these can be interpreted by symbols and allegories.... Augustine prefers the term 'sign' to 'analogy.' A sign is any word or thing that leads to a knowledge of something else. If it points to the divine, it is a *sacramentum.* The universe itself is holy (a sacrament, for it contains signs leading the mind above itself to God).[18]

Eckhart formulated a more radical variant of the medieval theory of analogy; in conformity with it, he made some of his most extreme sounding statements about the nothingness of all creatures *per se*.[19] Yet no less a medievalist than Josef Koch was unequivocal in concluding that the roots of Eckhart's theory of analogy lay in Augustine.[20]

Applied to the Book of Nature, the concept of analogy can reveal that forms correspond to things revealed in Scripture by the author of both these encoded works. Everywhere in nature, wrote Augustine, there are traces of the divine Trinity. The first vision in the second book of Hildegard's *Scivias* submits (in a divine pronouncement) that there are three forces in a stone, three in a flame, and three in a word; in each case, the three allude to the Trinity. The equivalent symbols for the three forms in one are inexhaustible in mystical literature. The nature mysticism of the Renaissance employed the trichotomies made famous by Paracelsus, thereby instituting a wider latitude for new hypotheses in chemistry and medical theory. But the Baroque mystic and poet Johannes Scheffler (Angelus Silesius) gives away the open secret of the Paracelsian *Tria Prima* in the *Cherubinischer Wandersmann* (book 1, no. 257):

> That God is Triune any plant will show you,
> Since Sulphur, Salt, and Mercury are seen in it as one.
> *Daß GOtt Dreyeinig ist / zeigt dir ein jedes Kraut /*
> *Da Schwefel / Saltz / Mercur / in einem wird geschaut.*

The triad of principles, Sulphur, Salt, Mercury, can be construed respectively as root, stem, and flower. But what made them seem so clearly visible to Silesius was his belief that the invisible things of God are revealed in the creation. In the mysticism of the Renaissance and Baroque periods, the mystical-philosophical trichotomy of body, soul, and spirit was revived. Accordingly, nature, anthropology, and divinity were all structured alike.

The principle of likeness can also be expressed in complex numerological symbols, as in Augustine's construal of the six days of creation as "the first perfect number" (an alternative to assuming that God was so slow that he required six calendar days to perform his work): "For the number six is the first which is made up of its own parts, i.e., of its sixth, third, and half, which are respectively one, two, and three and which make a total of six" (CD 11.30). To Augustine, this confirmed the biblical-apocryphal Book of Wisdom (2:20), that the divine Wisdom "ordered all things in number, and measure, and weight." The divine Wisdom is synonymous with the Creator Logos.

Order and number in nature therefore attest, as do the visible properties of things, to the transcendent being of God.

If it is permissible to think of this universal order and coherence
of things as a grammar of the Book of the World, then its semantics
also owes much to the obscure author of *The Divine Names*, Dionysius,
called the Areopagite. (According to a legend universally accepted
during the Middle Ages, the author Dionysius was the Athenian man
converted when Paul preached in the Areopag at Athens.) Dionysius
came to be considered the founder of Christian mysticism, the propa-
gator of the *via negativa* and *via affirmativa*, and the *via triplex* (the
above-mentioned stages of purgation, illumination, and union); as
well as the sovereign mystic who recognized the divine superessential
darkness. For this rhapsodist of absolute transcendence, the eternal
outshines everything historical in Christianity. If Paul authorized the
whole tradition of reading the visible things of nature in order to discover the invisible things of God, his legendary Athenian convert
Dionysius enhanced the sign with an aura of the symbolic.

The human horizon is altogether too narrow and too low for conceiving God. In praising God beyond every conceivable thing and quality, *The Mystical Theology* of Dionysius in effect places God beyond the
horizon of human thought and contemplation. What results from this is
a kind of refraction of the supreme mystery back into certain things and
qualities: "the divinest and highest of the things perceived by the eyes
of the body or the mind are but the symbolic language of things subordinate to Him who Himself transcendeth them all."[21] Eventually, in
Eckhart and in subsequent mystics it seems that the disappearance of
God leaves behind a kind of afterglow of the divine insurpassability in
the fullness of all things. Since, in *The Mystical Theology*, the two paths
to God, positive and negative, are complementary, we can find prerequisites for the species of reverse pantheism, known, too blandly, as
pan*en*theism: all things are in God. In *The Divine Names*, the enormity of
divine transcendence appears as if reflected back onto the created
things, thereby highlighting in all names the unnamable One.[22]

The unutterable Creator contains all things prior to creation. This
was a stimulus to ideas of creation as an unfolding of what is latent in
the Creator, of the theophany of a developing God, and of the symbolic divine meaning that is revealed in all things as the end comes full
circle to its beginning. The rhapsodic divine nomenclatures of Dionysius supplanted the scriptural and traditional symbolism of order and
number with a distinctive geometrical symbolism of line, center, circle, and spiral, a symbolism adapted by Mechthild of Magdeburg,
Nicholas of Cusa, and Angelus Silesius.[23]

The correspondences of macrocosm and microcosm and the many symbolic codes of the Book of Nature would engage Hildegard and her contemporaries.[24] Unscriptural as this kind of thinking may appear now, nothing suggests that Hildegard saw it as alien to the Bible or the Fathers of the Church. Since the authorities had had relatively little to say about natural science, Hildegard or Bernard Silvester probably thought of themselves as reconfirming the canon by applying it correctly. Even when the specifics of Hildegard's readings of things stand on no particular biblical foundation, the divine textuality of nature is always legitimized by the primacy of its Authorship, its creation through the Word.

In the course of this tradition, it came to appear evident that every symbol was rife with hidden meanings. Augustine, as well as Dionysius and Erigena, contributed to the interpretation of the Pauline motif of *omnes in omnibus*.[25] For Gertrud of Helfta or Tauler, God as "all in all" enhanced the authority of the individual. Moreover, since all things are in God and God is in all, all things are in all other things. For Cusanus, this would signify the presence of all numbers and figures in all other numbers and figures. In Renaissance mysticism, *omnes in omnibus* would prove compatible with the adept or symbolic project of alchemistic transformation. Like the castaway stone on which the Temple was founded, even the most extraneous object of contemplation could relate back to the omnipresent center of all meanings. Boehme thus stood squarely within this tradition in proclaiming that he could recognize the entire world in a stone or clump of earth.

All the motifs and correspondences merge in the coherences of Word and world—a common denominator of mystics who otherwise appear very dissimilar. German Logos speculation unites such distinct figures as Hildegard, Eckhart, Tauler, Seuse, Cusanus, Boehme, and Silesius. Alois Winklhofer has drawn attention to the extraordinarily wide dispersal of *Logosmystik* in Germany in the high Middle Ages[26]; it can be traced on down through Baroque mysticism and beyond the confines of Germany.

Our normative analogy for the German mystics and their tradition is the mountain range, not the archipelago. The Logos theme was by no means exclusive to the German mystics. Nor did they draw solely on the Word as Christ. Renaissance Kabbalah and naturalistic speculations converge in the tradition.[27] Nor were the German mystics inspired solely by Christ as the Word. It should suffice to consider the medieval bridal mysticism, or the Lutheran contemplation of the Passion. However, no mystical theme has proven more fertile in German literature or in intellectual history as a whole. The world-creating Word ties the writings of the German mystics into the broadest conceivable context. From Hildegard to Novalis, and ultimately beyond the religious tradition (through Schopenhauer to Wittgenstein), the meditation on the unity and meaning of the world has inspired a remarkable variety of formulations.

# 2

# The Visible and the Invisible

## Hildegard of Bingen and Female Visionary Mysticism

The great female mystics of medieval Germany were visionary nuns or Beguines. The greatest male mystics were the Dominican masters and preachers whose gift was a mysticism of reflective inwardness—purest in Eckhart or Tauler, creatively mixed with other elements in Seuse. The mysticism of the women was often oriented toward perceptible operations of faith, toward works, sacraments, and the liturgy. The mysticism of the Dominican men turned from works and ceremonies to seek the divine birth within.

In the form of expression, there is also a contrast between the medieval female and male mystics to be studied here. As if to round out the contours of a female mysticism richer in sensory sounds and images and also given more to the outer enactments and realizations of faith, the women created literary and artistic works to document or propagate their unique experiences. This applies to the well-executed masterpieces of Hildegard, Mechthild of Magdeburg, and Gertrud of Helfta, as well as to the less artful documentations of the nuns' *vitae*. By contrast, the great mystical productions of Eckhart and Tauler are transcripts of sermons held in routine fulfillment of their office in the Order of Preachers. Eckhart's *Liber Benedictus* and the books of Seuse are exceptions among the Dominicans, and the Franciscan mystics, David of Augsburg, the mentor of Berthold of Regensburg, and Rudolf of Biberach, author of *The Seven Ways to God*, a mystical tract in the tradition of Bonaventura, should not be forgotten.[1] Nevertheless, the generalization is an informative one; for if the exceptions suggest that this was not a gender difference, the rule directs our attention toward an institutional typology of mysticism.

The Dominican preachers enjoyed authority by virtue of their office, while the women mystics acquired it by their exceptional achievements and experiences. Hildegard of Bingen and Elisabeth of Schönau gained wide renown as prophetic visionaries. To the women visionaries who lived and wrote at the Cistercian convent of Helfta—

Mechthild of Magdeburg, Mechthild of Hackeborn, and Gertrud of Helfta, called "the Great"—fame and high example were accorded (at least within their monastic environment) for their distinction as seers. The convent chronicle literature of the early fourteenth century augmented the prestige and tradition of the individual convent. Ernst Benz has drawn attention to the fact that the content of female visionary mysticism compensated for the absence of institutional authorization by providing a "visionary sense of mission."[2]

Peter Dinzelbacher has assembled and interpreted what is known of the lives and experiences of medieval male and female visionaries. Prior to the twelfth century, a broader perceived distance cut off the temporal world from what lay beyond it. The "Renaissance of the Twelfth Century" discovered romantic love. Dinzelbacher, as well as Johanna Lanczkowski, see Saint Bernard of Clairvaux as a watershed in the mentality governing the rising spiritual expectations.[3] Bernard taught the human nearness of a deity no longer conceived solely as the *rex tremendae maiestatis*. Gradually, a humanization of the image of God engendered rising expectations of spiritual experience among women and men. This narrowing of the perceived distance between the divine and human gave sustenance to the desire for a mystical knowledge of God.

The legitimation of feeling was accompanied by what appears to us as a shadowy and irrational side. Visionary mysticism was frequently, though not always, combined with illness or physical suffering, often cruelly self-inflicted. Frequently, symptoms of hysteria were present.[4] The manifestations varied from visionary dreams to reported stigmatizations. If these phenomena were pronounced in the nuns' mysticism—sometimes involving markedly sexual visions and delusions—similar ascetic practices could also characterize the mysticism of men, including Seuse.

Not only the world of God, Paradise, and the angels was seen. Hell, Purgatory, Satan, and the Apocalypse appeared to medieval visionaries. Nevertheless, it is not advisable to allocate all visions to a category distinct from nonvisionary mysticism. A nun or monk who knew God sometimes visibly and sometimes inwardly did not alternate between being a visionary and being a mystic. Various gradations and modes of seeing are found in medieval visionary mysticism: there were night dreams, waking visions, and visions associated with illness. Much of the visionary mysticism of the medieval nuns was of the sensory kind.

The visionary mysticism of Hildegard of Bingen incorporates sensory, allegorical, and philosophical elements. At the outset of

*Scivias*, she announces that the things she has seen and heard have been perceived, "not in dreams or in frenzy, nor with the bodily eyes or the ears of the external human being"—but rather with those of "the inner human being" (*non...in somnis, nec in phrenesi, nec corporeis oculis aut auribus exterioris hominis, nec abditis locis percepi, sed eas vigilans, circumspiciens in pura mente oculis et auribis interioris hominis, in apertis locis secundum voluntatem Dei accepi*).[5] The invisible has become visible to the inner spirit. The world she sees is symbolic. It does not appear before her like a Paradise or Hell to be entered into or fled from, but in order to instruct and teach. What is seen and heard by Hildegard is to be made visible and audible to all.[6] To put her in a category of visionaries distinct from that of the mystics, Eckhart and Tauler, ignores the fact that she, no less than they, labored to instruct her fellows. To focus on her visions as psychological or supernatural experience would divert attention from the purpose and historical context of her work.

The predominantly inner or imaginative nature of Hildegard's visions is no less essential to their proper assessment than the sensory stimulus expounded in the intriguing and plausible theory of Sabina Flanagan, concerning the pathological generation of the forms of light that appeared to Hildegard from early childhood—as a rare form of migraine.[7] Though Flanagan does not suggest that the full articulation of the visions might be understood as migraine symptoms, a misperception nevertheless arises from any rationalization of the miraculous aspects of medieval mysticism. The temptation to reconcile the medieval miracle with the modern scientific understanding of the world (no less than the impulse to disprove the miracle in the name of our science) ignores the fact that, to Hildegard, experienced nature could be miraculous in the very occurrences we now regard as prosaically natural. Moreover, there is a modern prejudice in reverently pretending that visions like Hildegard's were objective manifestations in the fullest sense. The error arises in the assumption that she recognized our implicit distinction between the natural and the miraculous. We distinguish between our own normal experience of nature or imagination and an extraordinary "experience *X*" and we attribute to the visionary the claim of a miraculous experience, contrasting with what *we* gauge as normal and natural. In fact, however, Hildegard's natural world presented itself as wondrous in the very processes we now perceive as prosaic. If she perceived her visions only by the organ of her imagination, this need hardly have detracted from the honest miracle for her. In assuming that the authority of the visionary report depended on the preternatural authenticity of experience, one easily forgets that a supernatural event could have been the work of the devil.

There can be no doubt that the supernatural was of immense importance in the religious life of the Middle Ages. However, authority just as certainly depended on conformity with the Scriptures and doctrines of the Church. For Hildegard, the imprimatur of the highest churchmen was added as well. Even after receiving her direct command from God to record and proclaim what he had revealed to her (indeed, even after he had visited an affliction upon her for not obeying at once), she solicited the sanction of her superiors before publishing her visions. Not psychological circumstances, interesting though they may be, but rather the references of authority should be decisive for the interpretation of mystical literature.

Like so many medieval mystics, Hildegard of Bingen spent her life—a remarkably active and many-faceted life—wholly absorbed in the service of her order. Born in Bermersheim in the Rhine region near Mainz in 1098 of a free or noble family, she was the youngest of ten children, four of whom devoted their lives to the Church. By her own account, she experienced visionary phenomena, manifestations of light, from early childhood on.[8]

At the age of eight, her parents sent her to be brought up by the anchoress, Jutta von Spanheim. Jutta, a woman of noble birth, lived as a recluse in a cell attached to the Benedictine monastery of Disibodenberg. If the actual degree of Hildegard's seclusion as a ward of the recluse Jutta is not ascertainable, it was assuredly a greater isolation than that of other children. The life of an anchoress was understood as a dying to the world and being buried alive. However, Hildegard did not lead the life of a Kaspar Hauser. Through Jutta or others at the monastery, she acquired not only some knowledge of Latin (the language in which her books were composed with the help of the monk Volmar), but also a schooled curiosity regarding all aspects of nature. The cloister with its strict devotional discipline remained the center of her life and aspirations. At age fifteen, she took the vows of a Benedictine.

The example of Jutta attracted a number of women who became the core of an independent convent. When Jutta died in 1136, Hildegard was chosen as its prioress. In this role, she took upon herself the tasks of a founder, leading her nuns to a new site at Rupertsberg and eventually establishing another convent at Eibingen. In the sundry tensions and altercations which were attendant upon initiating and directing these institutions, she demonstrated considerable skill, courage, and imagination. Her many activities as a prioress were diverse enough to include the waging of ongoing legal feuds and the composition of liturgical music, some of which is still performed today. In addition to her administrative role, Hildegard always took a keen and active interest in matters both theoretical and practical, from medicine and cosmology to the current struggles between the ecclesiastical and secular authorities. She interacted and corresponded with the great men of her time, with emperors, kings, and popes. The diversity of her interests and her involvement in the life of her times are reflected in her mystical writings.

Hildegard the visionary acquired fame as the "prophetess of the Rhine." As in her other roles, the prophetess directed her energies toward practical objectives, that of strengthening the moral conduct of her sisters, of combatting heresies and errors in her region, and of mobilizing the active will of Christians. Soon after her death in 1179, she was revered as a saint.

Though we know more about Hildegard's biography than about that of other medieval mystics, we should also consider her life through the prism of her visionary writings, since these convey her own conception of her existence. Even if this conception is generalized and allegorically stylized, it is an image with which Hildegard clearly identified. Our objective is to understand the revelatory dialectic guiding the evolution of her visionary work. The distinction between the visible and the invisible is also a threshold of admission or exclusion, of exposure or security.

In Hildegard's first work, *Scivias* (*Know the Ways*), we see the visionary *I* as a forlorn figure, at the mercy of a natural sphere shaken by instabilities and infiltrated by the poison of Satan. Within this world, there is a personified sanctuary of salvation: the all-embracing, embattled female personification of the Church. In the fourth part of Hildegard's first vision, the path of the soul through its earthly life passes from a prenatal introduction in the womb of an earthly mother, through the world of demonic torments and persecutions, and then into the holy tent and tabernacle of faith that is impervious to attack. Faith and its ecclesiastical embodiment are the womb into which the soul is reborn in preparation for eternal life; however, faith requires a perpetual struggle to build and defend the fortified City of God (which is rendered in intricate symbolic detail in the third part of *Scivias*). The human soul requires a firm sense of the whence and whither of its existence in order to engage in this struggle.

Even before the inception of the soul (which, notably, takes place only after the bodily embryo has acquired its human form), divine providence knows in advance of the soul's path through the world. Even before its earthly life can begin, its human parents through their seed endow it with its qualities of mortal strength or weakness. Since all is known to God in advance, the awareness of divine providence can cause the soul to lose courage. To the soul, frightened by God's preordained certainty, the divine voice offers the council that human presumptuousness in reacting to the divine foreknowledge is the devil's way; and that, by struggling and persevering, the human soul, if it is not fatally flawed, is to overcome its handicaps and serve God's purposes in this world. Of these purposes none receives greater emphasis than the defense of Mother Church, the embattled bulwark of faith, against a host of besieging enemies. All hope and security lie in the enclosing institutional sanctuaries.

Hildegard's writings evince a keen interest in the nature and history of the world: she regards it always with an eye for its meaning in the drama of salvation, and with a mind open to the practical ends of healing and living. Her work is enriched by the coincidence of two perspectives: the first is set in time and focused on a struggle of the elect against evil; the second encompasses the inherent structures and latent goodness of the natural world and of life itself. The first perspective of the soul's exile in a fallen world is complemented by the second, which recognizes the prelapsarian goodness of the divine work of creation. In accordance with the first perspective, Hildegard knows that the world is dominated by evil; in accordance with the second, she eagerly explores the intricacies of nature. One way of approaching her work is to ask how these two perspectives are coordinated. A related question is why the message of her work should have taken a visionary form at all. Moral instruction and natural curiosity are not inherently mystical. Even in her time, a woman might have pursued these interests by writing a work such as the devout and instructional *Hortus Deliciarum* of Herrad of Landsberg. Hildegard, however, wrote with the authority of a visionary to whom God has revealed himself by voice and by means of images. In principle, she directed her message to the entire world. We must therefore review her times and situation in order to consider what sort of needs might have been addressed by the authority of the visionary mystic.

The historical moment that saw the emergence of Hildegard's great visions fell within a period of transition and crisis. The misogyny of the Middle Ages was apparently never more restrictive than in the centuries preceding her ground-breaking public role. Dinzelbacher's book on medieval visionary writings notes that the rise of the literature authored by monastic women begins in the second half of the twelfth century. Dinzelbacher suggests that this came about in reaction to the "accentuated misogyny of the eleventh and twelfth centuries"—an interval of two hundred years during which no more than four women gained papal recognition as saints (whereas, significantly, the absence of female visionaries during the prior centuries had coincided with a greater number of saintly women and an above-average number of abbesses).[9] This seems to warrant the conclusion that the rise of female visionary literature was a compensation for the avenues of external activity barred to women.

But what of Hildegard? In her mature years, she suffered no dearth of practical tasks and no want of human contacts. Why was she compelled to pursue her course as a visionary author, and why was she not only allowed, but even encouraged, to assume a public role? The answer lies in the urgent crisis of her time. Hildegard began writing in a period when the unity of Christendom appeared to be threatened with impending disaster. Toward the middle of the twelfth century when she emerged as a visionary, an array of new forces was challenging the old order. These forces included not only the steady rise of cities and commerce, and the perennial conflicts between *imperium* and *sacerdotium*, but also an intellectual challenge to authority posed by the critical spirit of Peter Abelard (1079-1142), and a doctrinal one posed by the rampant spread of heresies. Externally, Christendom was about to overextend itself in the Second Crusade of 1146. After the Muslims recaptured an important base from the Crusaders in 1144, Bernard and Pope Eugene III preached the cause of crusade, hoping, to no avail, to unite Christendom in securing its most sacred shrines. In Germany, this was a period of irreconcilable tensions. After the election in 1138 of the first Hohenstaufen, Conrad III, as German king, rival houses were fighting over the royal succession.

By midcentury, the threat of heresies and rebellions had begun to acquire dangerous proportions. Herbert Grundmann has reconstructed the role of these heresies. Stimulated by the official movement for monastic and clerical reform, itinerant preachers who were often monks or priests called for apostolic poverty and denounced a venal, sinful clergy. When the preachers made a nuisance of themselves by exceeding the allowable limits in their invective, they were excommunicated and persecuted as heretics.[10] To the dismay of the conservative churchman Bernard, the heretics were known to find their staunchest adherents among women. Thus, the heretic named Henry who first preached in Le Mans in 1116 had been accused of marrying off his supporters to prostitutes in order to save the women from their life of sin. The status of women was implicated in these heresies in two ways: because of the violations of chastity committed by the corrupt priests, and because of the eagerness of lay women to participate more fully in spiritual life.[11]

Soon after 1140, the Cathar heresy, with its dualistic or Manichean features, penetrated Western Europe from the Eastern Mediterranean.[12] It flourished in Southern France and spread up the Rhine during Hildegard's lifetime. In her old age, Hildegard took the unusual step of travelling on extensive tours to preach against Cathar heretics. According to the conclusions drawn by Grundmann, the new heresies cannot be regarded as a foreign body without influence upon the life of the Church. Their apostolic spirit was directed against the performance of the sacraments by corrupt priests. The Church's own doctrine of the sacraments as an *opus operatum* (the subsequent target of Luther's fury against "works righteousness") was, according to Grundmann, formulated in part against these heretics.[13]

Even within the Church itself, the leadership was threatened by a new dissension and rebellion due to the intellectualism of Abelard. Bernard succeeded in having Abelard and his teachings condemned at the Council of Sens in 1140; but the new spirit continued to flaunt itself in Arnold of Brescia. Disciplined with Abelard, Arnold refused to be silenced. When Pope Eugene III sent him to Rome to do penance, Arnold instead joined and led a burgeoning uprising of the Roman Commune. In upstart Rome, Arnold's religious intentions again found strong support among women. Declaring themselves a republic, the Romans actually drove the pope into exile from the Eternal City. It was not until the year 1155 that Eugene's successor, Hadrian IV, was able to have Arnold burned at the stake as a rebel.

In the world of Hildegard, it therefore appeared as if in every quarter infidelity and rebellion were running rampant. It may indeed have seemed as if the perniciousness of Abelard's new critical dialectics—associated at every turn with the vicious waywardness of women, heretics, and disobedient priests and monks—was poisoning the entire body of Christendom, striking even at its heart in Rome— and this at the very moment when the armed determination of Christendom was flagging in the Holy Land. Like the Saracen foe, the Cathar heresy was of the East. The new heretics even allowed women to become priests (*perfectae*). As the Cathar heretics made their presence felt—soon in Hildegard's Rhineland—this assuredly aggravated the sense of an impending catastrophe. Between 1140, when the conditions eliciting Hildegard's response to crisis began to unfold in a fateful succession of events, and 1151, when she finished *Scivias*, conditions were thus far from normal. The Church indeed must have seemed to its adherents like the beleaguered maternal figure and besieged fortress of Hildegard's vision. The acute challenge to faith, received doctrine, and the institutional church allowed and called for the response of a woman.

There could not have been much doubt about her allegiance when Hildegard arose to denounce the weakness and infidelity of the *tempus muliebre*, the "womanish age." *Scivias* could scarcely have been more insistent in condemning error and disobedience, in damning torporous inaction, or in chastening insolent inquiries of the human mind into divine secrets. Berta Widmer has argued that the title *Scivias* ("Know the Ways of the Lord") was a reply to the work of Abelard, *Sci te ipsum*, condemned at the Council of Sens in 1140 just before she began work on *Scivias*.[14] It is, in any event, certain that her repeated admonitions against probing into divine matters and asking too many questions in theology placed her in opposition to the dialectician Abelard and firmly on the side of his opponent and her powerful supporter, Bernard of Clairvaux. In Hildegard, the patriarchal power structure therefore found a champion who was able and determined, precisely because she had a mind of her own and a conviction that women had a special role in conserving the challenged order and hierarchy of the Church.

Many passages in *Scivias* must be understood as admonitions against critical thought, rebellion, and even against the Cathar heresy, which in her lifetime became rampant in Cologne and the Upper Rhine valley. In specifics, we cannot be certain, since Hildegard always formulated her views without topical references, and since we do not know how soon the Cathar heresy acquired the reputation of a non-Christian, Manichean creed. But *Scivias* in any case warns that there cannot be (as the Manichean dualism may have been understood to proclaim) "two gods" (which is to say not two creators), but rather only the true God and the false devil. The good Creator made all things good. The disobedience of the willful creature ruined creation by attempting to divide (as do the heretics, Manichean or Christian) the wholeness of divinity: "When [this] proud angel lifted himself up as a snake, the devil received the confinement of the lower world, because the devil was not able to be stronger than God" (*Cum superbus angelus ut coluber se sursum erexit, carcerem inferni accepit, quia esse non potuit ut ullos Deo prævaleret*). As if to warn both against dividing the inner faculties through disobedient thoughts and the domain of God by usurpation, the voice asks: "And how can two hearts be in one breast? Similarly, two Gods should not be in one heaven" (*Et quomodo conveniens esset, ut in uno pectore duo corda essent: sic nec in coelo duo dii esse debuerunt*).[15] The sin of inquiring too much originates in Lucifer's first schism. (*Sed præsumptio hujusmodi sciscitationis orta est in primo schismate...*).[16] One should not "investigate the secrets of God too much" (*secreta Dei non debes plus scrutari...*).[17] Mother Church is wearied by "diverse blows," sorely oppressed by the attacking "heretics and schismatics" whose errors burgeon into all manner of vicious crimes.[18]

The warning against disobedience and rebellion is loud and clear in *Scivias*. Supreme authority resides in the fact that the God who has created all things out of nothing appropriately proscribes the knowledge of human beings who cannot know whence they come or how they subsist:

> Now tell, me, o people: What do you think you were when you were not yet in body and soul? You truly do not know how you were created. But now, o people, you wish to examine heaven and earth and to decide the justice of those in the order of God and to distinguish the highest of things.... God who created you in the first man foresaw all of these things.[19]

> *Nunc dic mihi, o homo, quid putas te fuisse cum nondum eras in anima et corpore? Tu vero nescis quomodo creatus sis. Sed nunc, o homo, coelum et terram vis perscrutari, et justitiam eorum in constitutionem Dei dijudicare, et summa dignoscere.... Qui te in primo homine creavit, ille haec omnia prævidit.*[20]

Human knowledge is restricted to a world in which creation is the visible likeness of the invisible divine will. Appropriately in view of her attack on unbelief, Hildegard here paraphrases Paul's argument to the Romans:

> God—who formed all things in the divine will—created those things for the understanding and honor of the divine name, not only showing by these things those things which are visible and temporal, but also manifesting by these things, those things which are invisbible and eternal.[21]

> *Deus qui omnia sua voluntate condidit, ea ad cognitionem et honorem nominis creavit, non solum autem ea quæ visibilia et temporalia sunt in ipso ostendens, sed etiam illa quæ invisibilia et æterna sunt in manifestans.*[22]

The fact that all things have been created demonstrates the supremacy of the good Creator whose word is the Son. The Son of God is made manifest by the origin of the creation, since Christ is the Word through which all things are made. The Bible, the Church, and created nature therefore all concur in commanding the human being to obedience and to dutiful travail for the honor and glory of God. The sacraments are highlighted as the holy institution of the Church. The injunction to perform works of faith has a sacramental character. Hildegard's actual Christian world may have been challenged in its tenets and divided in its will, but the Christendom of her visions is embracingly whole: symbolized not only by Mother Church rising above the besieging rebels and heretics, but also by the stalwart cluster of the faithful who are destined to triumph over the enchained beast of the Apocalypse. The path of faith points us from the visible to the invisible. The path of works renders the invisible visible. Active faith transforms the invisible power of God into the City of God in order to complete the work of creation.

Because of its roots in conflict, *Scivias* possesses a high drama and vivid clarity rare in mystical literature. The work is composed of three books, the first comprising six visions, the second seven, and the third thirteen. Each vision is told in the first person. The characteristic opening is a variant of "I saw..." The vision is then elucidated by the voice of God, which sounds forth from within the visionary manifestation seen and heard by the inner spirit.

The first book opens with an image that still fascinated Tauler and his congregation of nuns two hundred years later: the great vision of the majesty of God, symbolized as a mountain the color of iron, with windows through which myriad human faces can be seen. Atop the mountain, a figure of glorious light is enthroned, pouring down beams onto the head of the childlike figure representing the visionary. A second figure at the foot of the mountain is covered over and over with eyes. This figure stands for the fear of God, as the beginning of all Wisdom. The enframed faces signify that the omniscience of God recognizes and judges all human actions—those that are upright, and those lazy and remiss in their pursuit of God's ends. The divine voice that rings out is wholly purposive, commanding Hildegard to proclaim how one enters upon the final restoration of all things. People are to be instructed about an inner sense of the Scriptures which, though it is known, is not being propagated sufficiently. The magisterial insistence of the divine voice, with its call to awaken and to speak out and its sweeping evocation of the final state of the world and of the inner meaning of the Bible, invests the opening of *Scivias* with a magnificent forcefulness.

The unity of *Scivias* is a unity of purpose. Roughly put, the first book of *Scivias* lays out the nature and fall of the creation and creature; the second concentrates on the redeeming institution of the Church; and the third on the Heavenly City that is being built. Rather like a Crusader's fort, the City is a bulwark against the enemy, as well as a glorification of God's will and commandment. If the inner sequencing of visions at times seems inconsistent and random, each vision is directed toward the overriding aims of instruction and encouragement. The fact that the message is conveyed by means of intelligible images orients the viewer toward situations and tasks in time.

The foreground perspective embodying the call to action is overlaid by a second perspective invoking the beginning and the end of all things. If the temporal foreground perspective is more urgent, it is reinforced by reminders of cosmic completion before an eternal background. The second book of *Scivias* reintroduces the figure of the Savior and focuses on the path of Christ, as well as on the role of the Church and the sacraments. In the second to the last vision of the second book, the Satanic beast is presented in chains. But the last vision portrays the constant temptations to which the flesh is subject—as if to remind us that there is no escape from temptation here below. The temptations are depicted as merchants who hawk their wares of self-indulgence—an image appropriately chosen to contrast with the spiritual discipline expected of Hildegard's sisters. The architecture of the Heavenly City is elucidated in intricate symbolic detail in the third book.

Set against this foreground perspective of temptation and action, there is the eschatological background, superimposed by means of a circle symbolism and with references that cut across the sequence of visions and cause distinct phases of the cosmic and salvational history to appear as aspects of a larger pattern. For example, the cosmos is said to be surrounded by a skin of dark fire separating the fallen world from the spheres of the angels. Similarly, the human souls that are swept up into the net of Mother Church—to be reborn through her by water and spirit—also have a dark outer skin to be shed in rebirth. Even the elements of nature, which only became agitated and inimical as Adam and Eve disobeyed the will of God, are to cast off their dark aspect, just as in the final restoration of all things the world is to be returned to the erstwhile calm permanence of its Paradise lost. This circular progression of creation and return becomes even more prominent in later mysticism.

Within the conceptual structure of Hildegard's visionary symbolism, the linearity of time is subtly resolved into the circularity of permanence. Eternity provides the model for surmounting the depredations in time. Schipperges has shown that Hildegard's world of the angels is exemplary for the human world.[23] This utopian vision of the angels is not an isolated motif among the German mystics. Influenced by Augustine's twelve-book Genesis commentary and by the Dionysian celestial hierarchy, Eckhart presented the hierarchical sub-ordination within the angelic principalities as exemplary for the proper order within the soul and within human society.[24] Similarly, Boehme's *Aurora* revealed the harmony of the angelic world as a utopian model for the strife-torn human world. What the imitation of Christ is for the individual, the imitation of the angelic orders is for human society.

Hildegard's superb vision of "the Savior" at the beginning of the second book of *Scivias* is suitable for demonstrating her method of visual symbolization. This vision is dominated by the transformations effected by a flame which she sees as omniscient and inextinguishable. The flame is complex. There is an inner brasslike flame within an outer fire. Tongues of fire or sparks leap forth to fashion a sphere of darkness that is subsequently illuminated by the works and creatures which light up within it. The tongue of flame then warms into life the piece of clay that becomes a human being. The flame extends a blossom to a created man, but the man only smells it without grasping or tasting it. He thereupon plunges into the darkness, which spreads throughout the created sphere. Next, three bright stars are ignited within the darkness. Many others, both large and small, follow, ending with the great star that shines toward the flame. On the earth, an aurora then appears, and the flame pours into it, eliciting a luminous being. This radiant figure thrusts his light toward the darkness, but the darkess rebuffs it. The luminous figure then strikes out at the resistant darkness, thereby arousing the human creature trapped inside it, and transvesting him with garments of light. The luminous "son of the aurora" rises up to shine forth with an immeasurable glory, a glory that is to continue glowing in the fragrance of all natural fruitfulness.

After this vision has been enunciated in the voice of the mystic, the celestial voice rings out in order to explicate it. In effect, the sequence of mystical vision and divine commentary serve, respectively, as riddle and key. Assumedly, the attentive monks and nuns who hearkened to the words of *Scivias* would have known most of the answers to the allegorical riddles from Scripture and tradition. The chief nonscriptural detail of the flower of obedience to God demarks—one might say: with an "x"—the central message of the book: what the nuns and monks were to ponder most intensely. The vision's implication that Christ is manifested in everything that flowers or is fruitful within the world carries the point beyond action and obedience to the contemplation of the surrounding world. In Hildegard's final work, this contemplation of nature takes precedence over the call to action of *Scivias*.

Without a doubt, *Scivias* is one of the most singular and compelling works of medieval literature, a monument to Hildegard's strength and convictions. It is a striking sign of the marginalization of mysticism and of women in intellectual history that Charles Homer Haskins's classic *The Renaissance of the Twelfth Century* neglected Hildegard, though her work would have sustained his arguments. Recent studies more sensitive to the role of women in medieval history have revived interest in, and cast a fresh perspective on her work. Hildegard had a keen awareness of the special abilities and higher calling of women. Having been made from Adam's rib, not from coarse earth, women are graced with the skills that require sensitivity; women are summoned to the eschatological task of restoring what has been lost through the faithlessness of Eve. In addition to her stern warning against divorce, Hildegard also voiced a recognition that marriage should be based on love.[25]

However, these points aside, *Scivias* has an authoritarian undertone that is reactionary in a basic sense: again and again, the voice of God commands against asking questions of God or the Church. *Scivias* brooks no challenge to authority and displays no tolerance for error. The world is divided into two camps: those who err or disobey do so because their will is corrupt and evil. All the problems and confusions of the world can be traced to the devil's vanity and rebellion and to a correlative human disobedience.

Hildegard may have been opposed to using violence in the suppression of errors or heresies; however, her oversimplified view of the world led her to overlook violence committed in the name of faith. This is true even in instances that should have been familiar to her. The terrible massacres of Jews during the First Crusade (1095-1099) in her native Rhineland were within the memory of her elders by one generation. It is possible that she led such an insulated life that she knew nothing of these events, and that her views of such things were in universal currency. But as an adult, Hildegard was generally open to information from the surrounding world. The Rhenish pogroms were not minor incidents, and subsequent mystics who lived in times of widespread prejudice did rise above the views voiced by Hildegard. Yet in *Scivias*, it is the allegorical figure of the Synagogue that is stained with the blood of a murdered Christ. The contrasting figure of the Church is beyond reproach. What makes this view reactionary is not our retrospectively "sensitized" outlook, which has the Holocaust in mind; it is the fact that her lack of information necessarily resulted from her injunctions against asking questions where the sanctity of the Church was at risk.

Hildegard's attitude can neither be presented as a given of her faith, nor divorced from it. Later German mystics were more critical than she of persecutions committed in the name of faith. What she shares with them is the premise of unity. Hildegard affirmed a unity of suppressed contradictions within the manifest order of her ideal world. The German Spiritualists later postulated the unity of an invisible church, understood to be in conflict with the sanctimoniousness of all existing ecclesiastic institutions. This entailed a shift in perspective: from the temporal perspective of salvation history toward the perspective of permanence or eternity, a shift coinciding with an emphasis on the eternal Word in nature and in the inner human being. This shift, if not the corollary tendency toward toleration, becomes evident in Hildegard's later visionary works, written at a time when ecclesiastical and secular figures of authority were beset by continuing heresies and struggles that aroused longings for a perspective of permanence and stability.

We would do Hildegard an injustice if we were to regard her as the toady of a reactionary establishment. For better or worse, she was passionately committed to her beliefs. She was too independent in her relationship with kings and popes, too rounded in her interests, and too inclined to interpret her articles of faith in a broad context to qualify as a shallow propagandist.[26] As her work gradually developed, her focus evolved toward a perspective anticipating the more reflective and independent mysticism of a later period.

In the works that follow *Scivias*, there is a gradual shift in thematic focus, accompanied by a restructuring of her claim to authority. The *Liber Vitae Meritorum* was composed in the years 1158 to 1162. This work in six parts begins with less visionary fanfare. Like *Scivias*, it juxtaposes vision and voice. However, the new book projects its visionary framework by superimposing the colossal figure of God upon the world. The figure of God rotates his gaze to the objects to be described and explicated. The visionary framework is a bracket which, instead of directly quoting God as in *Scivias*, attributes the contents of the work cumulatively to divine authority. If, artistically, the effect is weaker, the change can be fairly interpreted as a sign of increasing confidence. This second visionary work is less precise in distinguishing the voice of God from the voice of Hildegard, and the contents are also more mixed and varied.

We have seen that, in effect, *Scivias* was a book of riddles in which the visionary images constituted picture puzzles, and in which the divine voice also gave the key to their solution. In the *Liber Vitae Meritorum*, the cosmic image and the voiced word are attended to *per se*. The balanced harmony of the created world is interpreted as a warning to humans to follow the ways of divine wisdom.[27] The voiced utterance *per se* is broken down into sound and word: "sound" is equivalent to the Old Testament law and "the word" to Christ as the true meaning of the Law.[28] By extension, the word is equivalent to the inner meaning of the external utterance which constitutes the world. Visible nature is increasingly shown to be the real puzzle. The second book of visions also redirects the call to action that *Scivias* had exclaimed to the whole world, toward the daily moral challenges within the convent. Where *Scivias* knew faceless human types, the moral struggles of unique individuals now become apparent, if only in the great variety of virtues and vices.

After the second book of visions has exhaustively considered the myriad powers of virtue and vice in the world, the third book shifts to nature as a whole. The third book is called either *Liber de Operatione Dei* or *Liber Divinorum Operum*, depending on the manuscript version. This *Book of Divine Works* was composed in the years 1163 to 1173.

A lengthy explication of John's Prolog, *In principio erat Verbum*, is included in chapter 105 of Vision Four. Conceptually, this passage ties together all the analogues of authority within her work: Bible, nature, the cosmos, mental activity, humanity and divinity—all are subsumed in the eternal Word through which all things have been created. In creating the world, God made countless mirrors in which to regard his own countenance. The analogy of visible to invisible in chapter sixty-two of Vision Four reinforces the view of a kind of guiding world-soul. The world-soul is like the soul within the body, but conceived realistically as a guiding stratum of air above the earth. The ever-present greening effect of this force is the work of the Word. In effect, this unveils contemplation of the fruitfulness and harmony of the world as the positive "flower" of obedience that Adam passed up in Paradise when the struggle against evil began and human failure cried out for obedience to the law.

In *The Book of Divine Works*, Hildegard refers back to the vision of the world as an egg in *Scivias*: the transformation of the world-image in the last book recognizes that the cosmos is harmoniously proportioned by concentric circles (as was the angelic world in *Scivias*). Hildegard's term *medietas* indicates the central place of the human being in the creation, which is like the place of the Son in the heart of the Father.[29] The two biblical mainstays of mysticism, the themes of the human image of God and of creation through the Word, are merged in Hildegard's symbolic interpretation of the created world. *The Book of Divine Works* shifts to symbols of universal harmony. God is identified with reason, with a life reassuringly constant.[30] Not only does the universe appear more tranquil and regular in structure than in *Scivias*, the soul is said to be a reasonable spirit, and the rhythm of the brain to be like the rhythm of the natural world.[31] This anticipates the naturalism of Renaissance mysticism in which the human being is like nature since both are like God.

At the core of this ordered and stable vision is Hildegard's explication of the eternal Word—a notion of the musicality of all creation and mind much accentuated by her Latin:

> As the word of God resounded, this word appeared in each creature, and this sound was the life in every creature. Hence also from the same word, the human reason effects its works, from this same ringing, calling, or singing sound bringing forth its works, as in the creature, it lets cithara and timpani sound, resounding through the acumen of artistic gifts.

> *Quando enim verbum Dei sonnuit, idem verbum in omni creatura apparuit, et idem sonus in omni creatura vita fuit. Unde etiam de eodem verbo rationalitas hominis opera sua operatur, et de eodem sono opera sua sonando, clamando et cantando profert, quia per acumen artis suæ in creaturis citharas, et tympana sonando sonare facit...*[32]

Hildegard's role as a visionary cannot be divorced from the problem of her self-assertion. In her correspondence with the powerful men of her time, she claimed validity for her judgments by attributing them to the voice of God. Flanagan has analyzed these assertions. Hildegard was flexible in pursuing her goals, but she assumed her prophetic role in disputes even when strong legal arguments could also be cited. Flanagan reaches the surprising conclusion that, "Hildegard's use of the prophetic persona in adversarial situations was never in itself sufficient to prevail over the opposition." Often, Hildegard's decisions followed upon intense deliberation and bouts of physical illness, after which her resolve presented itself as divine:

> The way Hildegard used the prophetic role in her life paralleled her use of it in her writings. Her conviction that she was privy to God's will gave her the courage to assert herself where she might

otherwise have hesitated, and to stand up to her superiors when she thought they were in the wrong. In cases where there was a clear legal remedy she was prepared to appeal to it, but not without also insisting on her superior knowledge of God's intentions.[33]

This conclusion is of particular interest because it allows us to regard the visionary work of Hildegard within the overall context of her other writings and activities. Not only did the acute challenge of personal and institutional self-assertion in a time of crisis give her opinions their visionary cast, Hildegard went on to invoke prophetic authority in a quarrel over whether her beloved young helper Ricardis should leave Rupertsberg to become an abbess elsewhere.[34] It says much about her contemporaries' understanding of her propheticism that, when her revelation went against the interests of power, she was summarily ignored.

Many details in Hildegard's visions correspond to the naturalistic objects of interest discussed in her nonvisionary writings on science and medicine. Though the truths of Scripture and doctrine are beyond dispute, the manner in which they were reconfirmed by creation stimulated imaginative inquiry. Reflecting on nature, Hildegard could be remarkably open-minded. Thus, sexuality does not appear to be vile in itself, nor because it pertains to the flesh. However, characteristically, lust is unspeakably vile when its indulgence entails disobedience, as when the vow of chastity is broken. For then it leads from bad to horrid, to the sodomy and bestiality which the *Liber Vitae Meritorum* condemned in a vision of souls being boiled in foul excrements.[35] Yet her naturalism and understanding of the coherence of all things also allowed her to formulate a view of women, more positive than that of the traditional account of Eve's role in the fall from grace.

Hildegard's visions gradually increased in naturalism. In *Scivias,* the visions subordinated real elements to envisioned ensembles in conveying allegories confirming church doctrines or biblical injunctions. Continuing and magnifying the third vision of *Scivias,* Hildegard's *Book of Divine Works* draws most of its envisioned ensembles directly from reality: from the order of the cosmos and the human body, the months and seasons of the year, or the universal processes of growth and life. This shift from the miraculous riddle to the confirmation that the world is wondrous in itself anticipates later German mysticism. In Hildegard's final visionary book, the materials are no longer special gifts to her graced person as in *Scivias.* The materials reflect life and nature. What Father Chenu has written regarding the outlook of Hildegard's contemporaries applies equally to her:

It was no longer the extravagant occurrences that interested them, those marvels which entranced their forebears and rapt [sic] them into a world all the more real in their eyes for its very capriciousness. On the contrary, they were interested in regular and determinate sequences, especially in the area of vital activity.[36]

Everything stands on a common footing as the expression or configuration of the Word become flesh, the Word through which all things are and reveal their meaning. If the Logos as Creator Mundi was a common motif in the art of her age,[37] Hildegard was to excel in liberating the motif from pictorial personification. Her work evolves toward the centrality of the Word and toward the corollary integration of the spheres of knowledge—an evolution associated with a more assertive role of the author. Beginning in the last part of *Scivias* and culminating in *The Book of Divine Works*, the transitions from the magisterial utterances of God, to the reflecting and explicating voice of the "ignorant woman" (*mulier ignota*) are increasingly fluid. Authorial autonomy grows apace with the significance of nature, keyed to the conflation of Genesis and John. Their joint exegesis in the Fourth Vision of *The Book of Divine Works* establishes that the Word has formed the human and natural spheres to be in harmony with one another—the former in discerning truth, the latter in comprising the great system in which all parts and orders are coordinated with one another in a manner that combines cause, symbol, and natural law. The cosmos, the body, and the inner life of the soul can thus be interpreted by Hildegard as if they were correlative columns of ciphers.

Hildegard's work is both unique and grounded in tradition. According to Schipperges, her theories of nature cannot be traced to contemporary sources.[38] Nevertheless, her originality was congruent with contemporaneous ideas. Certain aspects of her thought place it squarely in the "Twelfth-Century Renaissance."[39] She was in step with its new fascination with nature, a nature now viewed in its entirety *qua* universe, personified as the all-animating life force and interpreted by paralleling microcosm with macrocosm. Like Hugh of St. Victor, she sees in nature a tableau of sacramental symbols. Expression and causation are seen as inseparable in natural processes. In interpreting every part of nature with respect to the whole and in her confident compiling of a knowledge drawn from observation, independent thought, and folk sources, she anticipated the mystical nature philosophy of Paracelsus. Hildegard may in fact have influenced Paracelsus by way of the Benedictine monks of the monastery of St. Paul's in Carinthia (founded by monks from Hildegard's region), through Trithemius of Würzburg, or the 1513 edition of Hildegard, Elisabeth of Schönau, and Mechthild of Hackeborn, published in Paris by Jacque Lefèvre d'Etaples.[40]

What is referred to by scholars, somewhat uncomfortably, as *Frauenmystik*, "female mysticism," takes wing in Hildegard's age. The varieties of female visionary mysticism in Germany are represented by several major figures or currents: 1. Closest to Hildegard is her younger contemporary, the Benedictine Elisabeth of Schönau. A correspondent of the prioress of Rupertsberg, Elisabeth responded to Hildegard's direct influence. 2. In the thirteenth century, a new type of mysticism emerged in Northern Europe in the lay piety of the Beguines, represented in Germany by Mechthild of Magdeburg, a Beguine whose individualistic and poetic writing embodies a new "mysticism of love" (*Minnemystik*). Mechthild's *Flowing Light of the Godhead* (*Das fliessende Licht der Gottheit*) is akin in conjugal motifs to the *St. Trudperter Song of Songs* of the mid-twelfth century, though her work is more passionately personal in tone and content. 3. Mechthild's influence endured in the convent of Helfta, where she spent her last years as a close friend of two Cistercian nuns, Mechthild of Hackeborn and Gertrud the Great. These women were transitional between her individualism and the convent mysticism soon to follow. 4. In the first half of the fourteenth century, in Switzerland and South or Southwest Germany, Dominican nuns, some of whom had formerly been Beguines, produced the "convent chronicle literature" of the *Nonnen-viten* or *Schwesternbücher*. Though in part authored by monks, these were mainly collections of the spiritual experiences of nuns, living or remembered. The mysticism of the *vitae sororum* is varied. Sometimes it involves extreme asceticism. Often the mystical experiences coincide with occurrences of the liturgical calendar. In a few instances, this literature already documents the influence of Eckhart.

1. Elisabeth of Schönau (approximately 1129–1164) had been sent at an early age to live in the convent of Schönau in Nassau. Like Hildegard, she was frequently ill. After an early period of demonic visitations, Elisabeth began experiencing divine visions. Many of these were of a symbolic and prophetic nature. Her *Liber Visionum* follows the liturgical calendar. Her *Liber Viarum Dei* (1156–1163) is close to Hildegard's *Scivias* in title and in its criticisms and instructions to the estates. These and the other works of Elisabeth were composed with the help of her brother, the monk Ekbert. They were widely distributed in the Middle Ages in Latin or in German translation.

Elisabeth of Schönau's prophetic visions possess a fearful solemnity and power. She is confronted with great symbols of time and eternity—symbols of order and authority in this world and in God's. She sees a white bird perched precariously atop a great turning wheel; witnesses an assembly of all the apostles, martyrs, and saints; views a great staircase and rainbow, and a man with hair like pure white wool. She sees that from head to foot his body appears to be made first of gold, then of silver, of bronze, of steel, of iron, and finally of earth. Within this stark vision, St. Gregory advises her that only the men who are trained in reading Holy Scripture would understand the meaning of such things. The expert men to whom such deference is accorded would undoubtedly have solved the riddle of her visionary images by referring to the biblical passages underlying them, to Daniel 7:9, with its prophetic vision of divine majesty. ("As I looked, thrones were set in place, and the Ancient of Days took his seat. His clothing was as white as snow; the hair of his head was white like wool," etc.)[41] For all their uncanny particularity, the details of Elisabeth's vision rest on firm biblical authority.

2. Mechthild of Magdeburg (who lived from about 1210 until about 1290) follows Hildegard by a full century and represents a new and distinct type of mysticism. This was the period in which religious life was expanding beyond the cloistered monasticism of Hildegard's time. In Northern Europe, this trend led to the establishment of Beguine houses—lay communes of pious women who were not attached to any convent. The male equivalents were the Beghards. The derivation of their name (probably a corruption of *Albigensian*) betokens the air of heresy that clung to these pious Christian souls because of their independence. An earlier theory that they were economically motivated plebeian self-help communes is no longer generally accepted. As a lay affiliation dedicated to a life of single-minded devotion, they anticipated Protestant Pietistic and dissenting circles of later centuries.

The character of the Beguine mystic Mechthild of Magdeburg is distinguished by great tenderness and humility, combined with bristling defiance and individualism. She became a mystic early in life (though not as early as Hildegard's childhood experiences of light). At age twelve, Mechthild received the "greeting" of the Holy Spirit that became the luminous "flowing" of her work.[42] The divine conflux is a classical mystical symbol which, with its many variants, offers a barometer for the relations of the divine and human spheres. The divine and human worlds are joined in a mediating fluidity that enfolds the soul with God, nature, and humankind. In Hildegard's visions, the immanent and transcendent objects remained circumscribed; the flow was more on the order of a conduited transfer of power and light: the flow *bound* the human to the divine. In the visions of Mechthild, the flow of light is characterized less as a bond than as a form of play, *spîl*, a term conveying both a kinetic and a visual imagery (as in the play of light on water). As a play stirred and driven on by love, this is a flow in which discrete beings are wholly carried away. The mystical *spîl* can therefore appropriately allude to a new ideal of attachment that came to prominence in this period: the ideal of the service—free yet wholly subservient—of the courtly knight, a *Minnedienst* or labor of love that dedicates itself body and soul to its beloved. Mechthild's birth coincided with the flowering of courtly poetry in the Hohenstaufen-governed empire. She was born around the time that Wolfram von Eschenbach wrote *Parzival* and Gottfried von Strassburg *Tristan and Isolde*—works in which scholars have discerned mystical aspects.[43] Gottfried's *Tristan* with its anarchic apotheosis of love provides a parallel to the passionate intensity of Mechthild's devotion.

Far more than Hildegard's visions, those of Mechthild embody the personal and inexpressible manifestation of mysticism. It is true that Mechthild's work, like Hildegard's, has instructional and public purposes, but the highly personal and allegorical nature of her writing certainly seems to reserve it for the like-minded few. A marked individualist, Mechthild left home and resided in Magdeburg where, she writes, she knew only one person. Most of her life was spent as a social outsider in the city. Her work articulates scathing criticisms of priests and holds up her own spiritual intensity as exemplary for true piety—in contrast to the immoral conduct of the representatives of the Church.

Mechthild's single work, *The Flowing Light of the Godhead*, was written in German. Her book is theological and allegorical, infused with a militantly personal sense of validation, unlike the sense of submission toward superiors informing the work of many nuns. It is difficult to imagine Mechthild going to her superiors to ask for permission to write. Nonetheless, her confessor, the Dominican Heinrich of Halle, was instrumental in persuading her to write; and a Dominican influence is perceptible in her insistence that one should not only love, but understand what it is one loves. According to her confessor, she began to write in 1250; assumedly, this was after her thirty-one years of increasingly intense visitations, perhaps in order to revivify and recollect them. Her visionary visitations appear less visual than those of Hildegard or Elisabeth—more a play of allegorizing thoughts than an array of images. Hildegard's image held center stage, an inexhaustible store of meaningful details. Mechthild's allegorical thought barely clothes itself in imagery.

Her few written remarks about her life suggest a continuity of her mystical devotion with the piety of her childhood prayers. The early intrusion of evil and hypocrisy in the form of clerical falseness (a lascivious priest?) catalyzed an idiosyncratic path of development. She sought independence in order to attend to the flowing inspiration of the Holy Spirit. This was visited upon her, she claims, daily and with increasing intensity for no less than thirty-one years. During these years, God made her aware of "holy knowledge" and "incomprehensible wonders" (*helige bekantheit...unbegriflich wunder*—110).

Mechthild is keenly aware of her defiance of a male world. Even when her soul is in dialog with her five senses, these are men—her chamberlains—determined to bend her to a hierarchy of consolation in the Virgin, the martyrs, the apostles, the angels, and so on. Imperiously, she silences these gentlemen who do not know what she means, and reserves herself for him whom she knows best (68). She shuns all things in favor of God—her father by nature, her brother by humanity, her bridegroom by love. The soul takes leave of its chamberlains and is united in nakedness with its object. But the union cannot last: "Where two lovers meet in hiding, they must often go off from one another without parting" (*Wa zwöi geliebe verholen zesament koment, sie müssent dike ungescheiden von einander gan*—32).

The desert into which Mechthild had fled in order to receive these gifts was a desert within the city and within her own soul. In her twelve-point delineation of existence in "the true desert" (25), the Beguine social ethos shows in an injunction to tend to the sick. But the introverted, fiercely independent stance is dominant. Mechthild created a symbolism of the individualist in quest of the absolute comparable in intensity to Nietzsche's images of solitude and self-consuming fire.

Warned that her book would be either buried or burned, she prays, as in her childhood, to her "Dear One." The answer she receives from God is that he himself has commanded her to write it, and truth can be burned by no one. The book is threefold. The parchment ringing it, she learns, is an image of God's pure white humanity that suffered death for her. The words are his miraculous divinity, flowing hour by hour from his mouth into her soul. And the sound of these words explains God's living Spirit, disclosing in Spirit the truth (68). Her book is the incarnate light. The metaphor of confluence holds together an assortment of poems, dialogs, literary visions, and rhymed or rythmic prose, in seven books. The *I* and *Thou* of bridal mysticism are its main voices. All things began with a creation for the sake of love. The creation of the soul was decided in heaven for the sake of a courtly game of love. This creation is not a central theme, but her delicate conception of it fulfills the customary function of an empowering myth.

As in *Tristan*, the sadness of parting informs the work. In a dialog with the soul incorporating paraphrases from the Song of Songs, God explains where he is when he departs from her: "I am in myself in all places and in all things, as I was ever without beginning" (*Ich bin in mir selben an allen stetten und in allen dingen/ als ich ie was sunder beginne*—66). This noteworthy passage should be kept in mind as a standard of comparison when we turn to the reflective mysticism that later arose under the influence of the Dominicans. As the sense of the visible and external God waned and the intimacy of the divine communion grew, the light—still literally present for Hildegard—receded into a Dionysian darkness and concealment, leaving an afterglow of the divine presence lingering in all things.

3. Mechthild zealously guarded her independence against any threat of intrusion—a stance like that of the Beguine women who went to the stake without recanting their alleged heresies. Yet despite the intensely private tone of her book, she intended it to be an example of true piety for all. Despite her fierce independence, she concluded her life in the Cistercian convent at Helfta, where she was revered by two nuns, her juniors, Mechthild of Hackeborn (1241/42-1299) and Gertrud the Great (1256-1301/02). These two kindred spirits had spent their entire lives from early childhood on following the rule of St. Benedict. As a result, they were guided more by the liturgical rhythm of the convent and devoted more to veneration of the Virgin Mary than their Beguine sister. But like her, they yearned for an immediate and vivid experience of the objects of faith. The Cistercian visionaries combined the heightened personalism of Beguine devotion with a strong attachment to the objective context of the liturgical calendar.

From her fiftieth year, Mechthild of Hackeborn was ill and bedridden. It was in this condition that she experienced the visions and auditions that she communicated to her intimates. Her experiences were recorded by her erstwhile pupil and friend Gertrud as *The Book of Special Grace* (*Liber Specialis Gratiae*).[44] Mechthild of Hackeborn's visions excel in symbols reminiscent of the images of flowing light, but often combined with liturgical and sacramental events in the convent. The regal majesty of Christ as the King of Glory places God at a distance. Yet out of the enthroned figure two pure brooklets flow forth: the grace of the forgiveness of sins and of spiritual consolation.[45]

Gertrud (who was born in 1256 and posthumously called "the Great") arrived as a child in the Cistercian convent at Helfta. The abbess (also a Gertrud) was the older sister of Mechthild of Hackeborn. Within this family-like monastic setting, the young Gertrud excelled in her studies of Latin, the liberal arts, and theology. After 1270, the Magdeburger Mechthild contributed to Gertrud's development. She felt authorized to undertake her theological studies by a vision of the year 1281. Between 1289 and her death in 1301 or 1302, she composed most of her *Legatus Divinae Pietatis* (*The Messenger of Divine Love*),[46] the remainder being brought to completion by her sisters. Liturgical events, the Mother of God, Christ as the Celestial Bridegroom, veneration of the Heart of Jesus,[47] and trinitarian contemplations are her salient themes. Nearly all of Gertrud's experiences are woven around scriptural passages and injunctions.

The visible presence of a personalized Christ appears with the celebration of the Communion. Holding the Christ child in her arms, Gertrud feels transformed; she comprehends the meaning of 1 Corinthians 15:28, "God will be all in all": at the end of time, divine truth and love prevail everywhere (25). Elsewhere, she meditates on Paul's wish to forego salvation for the sake of his brethren (Rom. 9:3), a verse similarly inspiring to Eckhart. She recognizes in it an imperative to renounce mystical nearness to Christ in order to benefit one's fellows (35). Caroline Walker Bynum has analyzed the "authorizing" role of Christ for the Helfta nuns, who faced a common dilemma of choosing between "service or withdrawal, action or contemplation."[48]

Gertrud's work contains harbingers of a new sensibility. Pausing in the courtyard to partake of a quiet mood of nature and observe the bright transparent stream of water, the green trees, and doves, she senses a flow of grace paralleling the bounties of the cloistered font (16). Observing the tranquil life in nature, she attends to the quiet life in her soul. After the two Mechthilds with their elaborate allegorical arrangements, Gertrud begins to court an intrinsic significance in nature and life, anticipating a new kind of vision that sees itself already within the realm of divine serenity.

Within the close network of convent society, Gertrud's fame, evinced by her resounding epithet, should have spread rapidly to the Dominican convents of the South and Southwest, where the broadest wave of mystical literature was just getting underway about the time of her death.

4. The growth of the mendicant orders from the thirteenth century on allowed the impulses that had blossomed in Helfta to become something like a movement, expressed in the nuns' *vitae* of the con-

vent chronicle literature. Scholars have debated the role of the monastic institution. According to Wentzlaff-Eggebert, "imitation" diminished the force and originality of the previous century. Others have suggested that the corporate prestige and group spirit of the convents required the "hagiographic legend"—a genre in which literary originality mattered little.[49] Since imitation can also be a form of veneration, the two approaches are not mutually exclusive.

The Dominicans were established as a preaching order for the conversion of Albigensian heretics—a purpose already addressed by Hildegard in her old age. The Blackfriars (or "white monks," as they were known in Germany after the inner garment of their habit) were disciplined, politically astute, and intellectually trained. They were the order of the inquisition, as well as of the great minds of the High Middle Ages: Albertus Magnus, Thomas Aquinas, and Eckhart. They differed from the Franciscans with whom they shared the vow of poverty by their special resolve to employ reason and knowledge in the defense of faith. Dominican nuns recorded the mystical *vitae.*

As preachers, the Dominicans made a powerful impression on women, as had the heretical preachers of the previous centuries. If convents and Beguine houses were eager to become affiliated with the Dominican order, this was not only for the protection that it afforded against heresy charges but also for the sake of instruction and ministry. Somewhat reluctantly, the preaching order undertook to oversee, instruct, and minister to the ever increasing numbers of women religious. The nuns thus instructed and guided by the Dominican friars were probably more receptive to sophisticated theological arguments but less fluent in Latin. The coincidence of these two factors, eagerness for instruction coupled with a necessary reliance on the vernacular, created the preconditions for Eckhart's sophisticated sermons in German.

The mysticism of the *Nonnenviten* or *Schwesternbücher* varies. Clearly, we would do the female mystics an injustice by treating their spirituality as a simple neurosis, or by attributing their mystical inclinations to their restricted sphere of experience. Facile psychological interpretations based on our own assumptions about the psychology of women or nuns are to be avoided.[50] The forms of female mysticism are far too diverse to be considered a common product of bored and frustrated women. Nevertheless, we would also be misled if, out of respect for the spirituality of the nuns, we were to ignore certain extravagant features of life in a fourteenth-century convent.

Walter Blank's study of the literature of the nuns in the fourteenth century summarizes aspects of the *vitae* that are sometimes passed over politely or disapprovingly in scholarly discussions of the convent chronicle literature. Miraculous events came to pass in the convents. The coffers of the church were wondrously filled. There were stigmatizations, torments, and miraculous cures bringing relief. The dead were sometimes called back to life. It could even happen that around Christmas a nun might recognize symptoms of pregnancy in her womb. The nuns might feel the body of Christ stirring in the Eucharistic oblate. The infant Jesus might be heard at night, crying out for maternal solicitations. Religious relics and images could take on a magical life, like the wooden doll of the Christ child in a cradle that Margaretha Ebner reported having suckled at her breast.[51] Appearances of the supernatural light were frequent in the convents, and levitations became ever more widespread toward the end of the Middle Ages. As these visionary events became increasingly common, individuals as well as entire convents were encouraged to consider them the measure of merit and "special grace," to pray for their conferral and take it as a sign of disfavor if nothing of the sort came to pass.

Remarkable sounds also insinuated themselves into the muted contrabass of cloistered routines. The unbelievably sweet tones of an angelic music and the resounding harmonies of the spheres could be heard. Communications could be carried out in silence, telepathically across great distances, or in a secret language understood by two sisters who enjoyed spiritual harmony. Even the practical-minded Hildegard had constructed a secret tongue which she called the *Lingua ignota*: in it, "God" was *aigonz* and "mother" *maiz*.[52] Latin—ever-present but imperfectly understood by many sisters—must have reinforced the notion that the divine world conferred grace in an alien language, like the Pentecostal miracle of "speaking in tongues" that was practiced in ecstatic glossolalia in some convents. According to Muschg, when Bernard of Clairvaux preached for the Second Crusade, his Latin sermons had a spellbinding effect on the common people—an effect that was lost when his words were translated into the vernacular for the crowds.

Muschg considers that an older strain of convent mysticism was ascetic, dominated by blood and suffering. A few later cases reveal the influence of Eckhart. However, visionary mysticism prevails on the whole. The transition from the grimly ascetic type to a mysticism influenced by Eckhart is illustrated by the chronicle of Elsbeth of Oye (Eiken). Her story is known from her own memoir, which circulated in German and Latin during and even after the Middle Ages. In its edited version, it is of interest because of its transitional aspects from an ascetic and physical to a more reflective mysticism; and also because Elsbeth shows how the thematic coalescence of creation and divine generation could form the core of an ecstatic union with God.[53]

A child of the convent since the age of six, Elsbeth knew a burning desire to achieve through suffering the signs of divine love. She scourged herself with a whip reinforced with needles that became embedded in her flesh. She bore wooden crosses day and night with protruding nails that drew blood. Racked by pain and terrified by the worms that she saw or imagined in the folds of her decaying clothing, she received comfort and encouragement from God in these efforts to be "crucified with Christ." After nine years, God indicated to her that she had succeeded in this purpose. Even after laying aside her outer cross, Elsbeth was plagued by inner torments, by invisible knives that stabbed at her or flying pikes which plunged at her.

All the while, Elsbeth carried on thoughtful inner dialogs with God. Gradually—possibly as the influence of Eckhart made itself felt—the tone became more reflective. God wanted to be with her in an essential presence in the innermost ground of her soul. "What does your essential presence do?" she inquired childishly. God explained to her in further questions and answers that from all eternity he had generated his natural Son in a hidden treasure chamber of his divinity. Even before the creation of the world, Elsbeth had been present as a joy of God's heart, predisposed to become oblivious to all images of created things or creatures.

Now, God was fulfilling her desire to become like Christ. Closing her mind to her external senses, Elsbeth knew herself to return to the origin from which she flowed. God was drawing her thither with such a burning desire that being forced to go back out to the external things became as bitter as receiving a wound. The divine voice echoes the terminology of Eckhart, who may have counselled Elsbeth. Muschg sees it as a mere embellishment of the chronicle when Elsbeth asks God, "Lord, what is the loveliest joy of your heart?"—and receives in reply: "The flowing out and flowing back in of my eternal Word."[54]

Divergent text versions permit disagreement on the extent of Elsbeth's adoption of reflective motifs; however, for her, as for Seuse, the ascetic imitation of the Passion clearly combined with the generation of the Son in the believer. In the version cited by Muschg, the creation of all creatures combines with Johannine immediacy in an ecstatic equivalent of the speculative union of worlds. Her Eckhartian terminology of a return to God along with all creatures is utilized not only by Seuse in his letters to Stagel, but also in the abidingly popular sermons of Tauler. Elsbeth's symbolism of the flowing of all things out of God even as they remain in God was sufficiently widespread to have had an almost conventionalized semiotic status. Eventually, this same sort of imagery appears in the language of the *Theologia Deutsch*, and in that of its editor, the young Martin Luther.

An incident from the chronicles discussed by Otto Langer may offer a hint concerning the link between the semiotics of the new non-visionary mysticism and the psychological implications of the switch from Latin to the vernacular. In this incident discussed by Langer, Sister Hailrat—an "inhumanly beautiful" (*unmenschlich schone*) and musically talented sister in the Dominican convent of Engelthal—was instructing and leading her choir in singing the liturgy for the fourth sunday of Advent, when she came to the response, *Virgo Israel*. Slipping into her vernacular dialect, she sang: *Ich han dich gemint in der ewigen minne, da von han ich dich zu mir gezogen mit miner barmhertzikeit* ("I loved you with eternal love, and therefore I drew you to me with my mercy"). As soon as Hailrat had unthinkingly rendered this verse into German and sung it with her angelic voice, the other nuns spontaneously comprehended the meaning of her slip. Collectively overwhelmed, they fell as if "slain," before coming to their senses to finish singing their matins "with great devotion."

Hailrat's slip into translation and her sisters' reactions presuppose that she and they had worked through and internalized the meaning of the Latin verse. Langer's interpretation appears convincing: Hailrat recognized that the verse had revealed its truth in her person, as the *Virgo Israel*.[55] This recognition was communicated to her sisters by an unspoken sympathy, issuing in a collective joy of recognition through her. The event suggests how a new dialectic of *beyond* and *within* was taking root in the life of the group, replacing the invisible with the inner.

Illustrating the impact of the vernacular, the incident can serve as a contrast to the power of speech exercised by Bernard of Clairvaux in the twelfth century, when his preaching in Latin to an awed but uncomprehending multitude impressed them as if his were a voice from an inaccessible beyond. In Hailrat's case, the divine voice instead comes from within and announces to those who hear it that the sacred is unexpectedly present in their midst. No longer does the divine voice ring out from an invisible world. What is experienced and sung now appears as a living echo of the unifying Word of creation.

# 3

# The Outer and the Inner

## The Reflective Mysticism of Eckhart, Seuse, and Tauler

The aging Hildegard corresponded with the first great Hohen-staufen emperor, who died in 1190 during the Third Crusade after bitter quarrels with the pope. The young Eckhart would have heard the shocking news of the last Hohenstaufen, executed in 1268 at the age of sixteen. Between the death of Hildegard in 1179 and the birth of Eckhart around 1260, the ideal of a Holy Empire, *Sacrum Imperium*, gave rise to dreams and nightmares. Ideals were crushed and Germany threatened with dissolution in struggles between *sacerdotium* and *imperium* and within either.

Around the year 1300, the Church was locked in a contest for political hegemony—the pope against the ascendant power of the French monarchy. Philip IV ruled France during Eckhart's stays in Paris as a student and professor. Philip counteracted the papal attempt to attain supremacy by instigating an assault on the person of Pope Boniface VIII, forcing the relocation of the papal seat to Avignon. Philip expelled the Jews and acted in collusion with the office of the inquisition to eliminate the crusading order of Knights Templars. Symbolizing the ideal of selfless service, the Order of Templars had inspired Parzival's Knights of the Holy Grail, but they had grown enviably rich and powerful, if not perverted, as the inquisition charged. The public rhetoric of denunciation became violent enough to dismay and confuse a common people over whose heads the fierce volleys were exchanged.

In the thirteenth and fourteenth centuries, dissatisfaction began to assume more radical and dogmatic forms. The most spectacular of these was the Joachite movement that aroused expectations of a world soon to be prophetically transformed. The brightest of these hopes had been dashed by the mid-thirteenth century, but the persecution of the Joachite Franciscan Spirituals continued. Toward the close of the century, the forward-looking expectations were replaced by or subsumed within the Flagellant movement. Its adherents inflicted fearful public floggings upon themselves for the disobedience of the world. Moving from city to city in Italy and Germany, the Flagellants became the lay champions of penitential practices exercised by the cloistered religious from around the year 1000.

The violent and repressive aspects of public life, coupled with the natural catastrophe of an especially harsh winter at the beginning of the fourteenth century, make it appear plausible to interpret the mysticism of Eckhart as a turn inward in the face of outer hardships and despair. The interpretation is attractive for a number of reasons. Since we know almost nothing about his reaction to the conditions of his historical environment, it is seductive to suppose that he turned his back on the world. The great themes of his sermons are concerned with the inner being: "the birth of God in the soul," and the "small spark" (*Fünklein*) in the soul. Eckhart advised against praying for the fulfillment of human needs and desires, against external works or religious exercises as intended to bring about such responses from God.

Like Hildegard's visions, Eckhart's "inwardness" cannot be interpreted without allowing for the difference between his world and our own. Upon hearing his invocations against "time, place, number, and body," our inclination may be to interpret him in a post-Kantian manner, or in the sense of a purely philosophical Neoplatonism. The Scholastic theorist and the spiritual adviser who counselled against entertaining *Bilder*, "images," in prayer and the contemplation of God, did have a peculiar perspective on the world of appearances, but this relationship should not be interpreted outside its institutional context. The world from which Eckhart exhorted his monastic flock to turn inward was a worldliness that penetrated the cloistered cells, prayers, and thoughts of the religious. The dark and superessential Oneness of God was found not only in the desert of the soul, but also in an evanescent union of freedom and order, of *vita contemplativa* and *vita activa*, in the ideal society of the cloister. We shall see that Eckhart's invocations to rid the soul of "place, time, body, and number" sanction an interpretation of *place* as the authority of the high position of the pope or emperor, and hence of *time* as the times. *Body* could have meant physical well-being in an age in which good health was rare, or perhaps flagellation in a period in which asceticism was on the rise. *Number* recalls a rising mercantile class whose ethos challenged the mendicant orders, which were dependent on largesse and troubled with a growing penchant for personal possessions.

Far from counselling quietism or withdrawal, Eckhart cited Origen in urging his listeners to find God in every creature and activity: "I tell you—and it is true—: In each good thought or good meaning or good work, we are perpetually born anew in God" (*Ich spriche—und ez ist wâr—: in einem ieglîchen guoten gedanke oder guoter meinunge oder guoten werke werden wir all zît niuwe geboren in gote*).[1] Just as the image of the quietistic mystic does not fit with Eckhart's dual emphasis on the *vita activa* and *vita contemplativa*,[2] the dismal panorama of four-teenth-century calamities likewise has no room for the outgoing thir-teenth century, a golden age for Scholasticism and monasticism—the formative period and field of the young man Eckhart. Moreover, while nature and society were apparently of no interest to him, they are by no means excluded from his mentioning.

Eckhart the preacher was not an anchorite, estranged from the world. The environment of his activity was a powerful order in which he rose meteorically: as a student and *magister*, as a priest, prior, vicar, provincial head, spiritual instructor, and counsellor. At the height of his administrative career, the scope of his responsibilities might have matched *mutatis mutandis* those of a regional boss in a modern interna-tional corporation. His mystical sermons were not private meditations, but part of his guiding role. Much of what strikes us as otherworldli-ness in Eckhart has to do with a real world distinct from our own.

However, this does not solve the problem of Eckhart's relation-ship to a surrounding society. The order he served was not only that of the great minds of High Scholasticism; his was also the order of the inquisitors who were condemning heretics and their books through-out much of his career, sometimes even in his vicinity.[3] Was Eckhart an intellectual somnambulist who knew all the masters of the present and past, who could urbanely quote from "Rabbi Moyses" (Moses Maimonides), who saluted Plato as "the great priest"—yet saw and heard nothing of the inquisition's offices? Was Eckhart concerned with the ordeals of the Dominican nuns, but indifferent to the martyr-dom of innocent Beguines and Beghards? It would be senseless to con-sider these questions from an anachronistic vantage, to confront Eck-hart with options that were nonexistent in his time, or to reconstruct his life minus the vow of obedience at its core. However, it is an equal failure of perspective to write about Eckhart's understanding of faith, as if these persecutions committed by the Church were an irrelevant backdrop, like perennial bad weather.

In interpreting Eckhart, we can benefit from a number of recent scholarly studies written from opposing points of view. In addition to the philosophically oriented overviews by Fischer or Waldschütz, the Bochum school represented by Kurt Flasch and Burkhard Mojsisch offers a challenging view of the "philosopher of Christianity" whose declared purpose in all his treatises and sermons was to explicate the truth of faith and Scripture by means of "natural," that is, philosophical, arguments.[4] This school has much to commend it, but it leaves us with an Eckhart who seems out of place in his nonintellectual activities. The opposing school represented by Alois M. Haas reclaims Eckhart for the history of Christian spirituality.[5] This school has the advantage that it can address the whole Eckhart, who was not an alienated intellectual or an open rebel against society. The more recent books by Kurt Ruh and Otto Langer are crucial efforts at fleshing out the wider historical world of Eckhart.[6] Ruh has undertaken the difficult task of interpreting an evolution within Eckhart's oeuvre in view of the events of his times. Langer's study evaluates results of some previous researches and provides valuable new insights into the forms of female monastic piety that confronted Eckhart. By expanding on arguments dating back to the nineteenth-century debate between Preger and Denifle, these new books highlight the range of possible approaches.[7] Any integrated study of Eckhart's work, life, and times can be expected to take them into account. An interpretation should address the contrastive aspects of his life and work, doing so without playing one aspect off against another, without neglecting the scholastic *Lesmeister*, a thinker of great subtlety, or the *Lebmeister*, a man of practical counsels; neither ignoring the independent mind and voice whose utterances were at least redolent of heresy, nor the humble servant of his order, consistent to the end in his vow of obedience.

A guiding idea of this study is that mysticism arises when the authority of doctrines or articles of faith is challenged. In Eckhart's time, the highest achievements and aspirations of the schools and orders coincided with the mortification of the Church by its secular opponents and by its own representatives. It would be difficult to imagine a more extreme clash of spiritual aspirations and historical realities. I will argue that Eckhart in effect elevated obedience to a transcendental plane. Not only the willful self, but all the powers and correlatives of immanence, of space, time, body, and number, were shunned in this absolute stage of obedience. Paradoxically, renunciation led to autonomy by rendering humility so immediate before God that all external authorities commanding the obedience of the outer man or woman became irrelevant to the inner human being, assimilated to God by mystical knowledge.

Eckhart's earliest work is the *Talks of Instruction*. These were informal lectures for the spiritual orientation and training of his younger Dominican confrères. The instructions were given in Erfurt sometime between 1294 and 1298 by the young prior who had recently completed his studies in Paris. Compared with the difficult later sermons, these talks are readily comprehensible and practical in their spiritual advice. The talks can therefore offer a point of reference, giving us something like a base tone for the normal monastic life, from which the more subtle mystical pitch of the later sermons rises.

True and complete obedience is the virtue of all virtues. God assuredly enters into those who surrender to him in absolute obedience. In prayer, one should seek to become united with God in body and soul; above all, one should abandon one's own selfish will completely.

The mystical virtues of *Abgeschiedenheit*, distance from all things, and *Gelassenheit*, serene abandonment to God, are thus a part of the monastic life Eckhart urges upon his fellows. The virtues of "distance" and "serenity" require a self-knowledge that overcomes self. Eckhart's most compelling advice to his fellow monks is that they should not worry so much about what they ought to *do*, but rather more about what they *are*: our actions are justified by our being, not our being by our actions (*Die rede der underscheidunge*, 4). Being and knowledge, spiritual distance and serenity—these are chords that will be sounded again in a new and metaphysical key in the later sermons.

Returning to Paris to teach in 1302, Eckhart was obliged to participate in academic disputes and to elucidate the Bible. His so-called *Questiones Parisienses* were prepared for such disputes. The first of these questions was whether being and knowing are identical in God.[8] Eckhart embraced the position that in God knowing *precedes* being. Though, obviously, the divine knowing did not come before the divine being in time, *intelligere* is the foundation of *esse* in God. Eckhart's position can therefore be interpreted as a metaphysical heightening of the Dominican and Thomistic emphasis on knowledge. There are ambiguities in the theology of Eckhart.[9] The later *Opus Tripartitum* states: *Esse est deus*.[10] Since both positions are expressed in Eckhart's German sermons, with intellect more often and more prominently taking priority, it is not possible to offer a contradiction-free Eckhartian theology. Here, the main questions to be considered are the scriptural and philosophical authority on which his doctrines of being and intellect stood, and how these doctrines related to the lives of the nuns.

Eckhart's speculations on the Word played a key role in his philosophical work. The paradoxes of the preacher are grounded in the Platonism of the theologian who identified the "beginnings" in Genesis and John with the *logos* or *ratio*, as the Idea in which all other "ideas" (prototypes) of creation have their ground: *De primo sciendum quod principium, in quo 'creavit deus caelum et terram' est ratio idealis. Et hoc est quod Ioh. 1 dicitur: "in principio erat verbum'—Graecus habet logos, id est ratio....*[11] Repeatedly in his sermons and treatises, Eckhart cites John 1:1, interpreting the divine Word "in the beginning" as *intellectus*. As the cause of all that is, God's essence is higher than his being, and God's "purity of being"—*puritas essendi*—amounts to the divine knowing. Mojsisch has shown that Eckhart was in line with the Scholastic avant-garde in a thinking influenced by the theory of the active intellect of his fellow Dominican, Dietrich of Freiberg.[12] In an age of speculative systems rivalling the Gothic cathedrals in their ingeniousness, a thesis such as the Eckhartian *deus est intelligere* undoubtedly seemed less abstruse than it may now.

Eckhart's theory of analogy is pivotal to the understanding of the riddles and paradoxes of his sermons. This famous theory maintained that the transcendental predicates of oneness, being, living, knowing, goodness, or justice were imparted by the higher term, God, to the subordinate term of the analogy as an image is imparted to a mirror, or as light to luminous air. Without the source, the image or luminosity is nothing. The image is the creature, the source or exemplar the Creator. The theory of analogy grounds many puzzling usages of the sermons, including the apodictic statements that creatures are purely "nothing," or that the Son, born in the soul of the believer, is none other than the selfsame Son of God.[13]

In his Scholastic treatises, Eckhart refers back to certain signally important passages in Augustine. In chapter seven of the *Confessions*, Augustine recalled having found in the books of the Platonists the Word, but not the humble human incarnation of God. Attempting to go beyond Augustine, Eckhart is resolved to reconfirm the truths of Scripture by means of natural arguments, thereby proving that Moses, Aristotle, and Christ all reveal the same thing. According to Eckhart, faith (Moses) and knowledge (Christ) are related to one another as an opinion is related to its proven certainty.[14] The program is philosophical without departing from revelation.

The *tertium comparationis* of the treatises and sermons is the interpretation of the Word. Mojsisch documents that Eckhart's paradox of the divine universals (as both entirely *within* and entirely *outside* the things) has a long tradition.[15] The sermons vest the Word with the plastic contours of an utterance, doing so reflexively: the Word as Creator is likened to the word spoken by the preacher to his congregation. The inconceivable paradox of *totus intus, totus foris* is rendered understandable by the complementation of inner intention and external expression: If it were possible to divorce the expression from what remains within (the thought or intention), the world of created place, time, body, and number would be as insubstantial as the images caught in mirrors. If it were possible to divorce what remains within from what goes out in the act of creation, the Word would not stand in the eternal self-knowledge that is the *puritas essendi*.

The distinctions between inner and outer and between the immediacy of grace and the nothingness of the creature were of relevance to the heresies of the day. Ruh sees Eckhart's final teaching stay in Paris as decisive for his mysticism.[16] A year before Eckhart's return to Paris in 1311, a celebrated heresy trial and execution took place in the city. The prosecutor was a Dominican inquisitor who lodged in the same monastery as Eckhart.

The victim was the Beguine Marguerite Porete. Marguerite was the author of a mystical treatise called *The Mirror of Simple Souls* (*Miroir des simples âmes*). This small book was a work of deep spirituality that would endure as few others in the Middle Ages. *The Mirror* had given offense by appearing to contradict accepted doctrines. Marguerite had written that the soul which was "annihilated" by God took leave of the virtues. The virtues stood at the disposal of the soul.[17] This smacked of the heresy of the Free Spirit. We have to ask to what extent the ideas of Marguerite and of her kindred spirits threatened the prevailing order. An older interpretation holds that many of the Beguines and Free Spirits were genuine rebels and heretics,[18] but other scholars have written that the victims were for the most part devout independents, senselessly persecuted by the Church.

There is a third possibility between the conscious heresy and the random victimization. As an author, Marguerite was a proselytizing independent. Her "noble soul," having "abandoned" itself to God, can say nothing more of God. Since the soul lives only in its love of the deity, it is beyond virtue or vice. The "great church" is set off against a "small church" of the humble souls. If this was taken literally, the Church was explicitly divested of its foundation of authority as the exclusive arbiter of truth about salvation. Even if Marguerite intended no heresy, this was at least obnoxious during a period in which the standing of popes and churchmen had already taken quite a thrashing. The office of the inquisition may have had grounds for regarding the spiritual independence of Marguerite as an affront, as a potential rallying point for popular anticlerical scorn, if not an outright threat to their battered and tarnished authority.

Eckhart was confronted with this case. Ruh submits that he may have acquired her book from one of three Parisian theologians who dissented from a first judgment against her. The essential point is that Eckhart, like the author of *The Mirror of Simple Souls*, increasingly came to reject the external aspects of faith. Although the elements Eckhart shared with Marguerite were already present *in nuce* in his earlier work, it may indeed be true that an encounter with Beguine mysticism accentuated these elements. Citing the findings of Edmund Colledge and J. C. Marler, Ruh contends that it was only *after* 1311 that Eckhart's Scholastic theories became infused into his mystical teachings: Eckhart may have taken this step in order to provide a defensible theological foundation for the allegorical formulations of the Beguines.

Like Mechthild of Magdeburg, Marguerite employed allegory and personification. Eckhart the dialectician now adapted his Scholastic theories in order to rationalize the spirituality of the Beguine *unio mystica*. The "analogy of the mirror image" made it possible to assert the identity or union of the believer with Christ. Accordingly, the ideas of Marguerite's *Mirror of Simple Souls* were deepened and transformed by the Neoplatonizing philosophical thought of Eckhart. Thus the hypothesis that Eckhart knew Marguerite's *Mirror* and took over decisive statements from it, giving them a more precise and defensible form by means of his own Scholastic theories, can integrate Eckhart's work with his life and times. Even without an encounter with Marguerite's mysticism, Eckhart's academic and pastoral duties confronted him with a potential conflict of pursuits and involvements. His resolve to reconcile them, to speak with the same voice to his students in Paris and to his spiritual charges in the convents, can account for many features of his mystical sermons.

After his last stay in Paris, Eckhart was entrusted with the duties of providing spiritual counsel in the Dominican convents of the Upper Rhine region. Other developments were simultaneous with this renewed activity. The Council of Vienne (1311-12) was admonishing against the Beguines and Beghards who had numerous adherents in Strasbourg and Cologne. These two main cities of Eckhart's later career were considered suspect: the mendicant orders were coming under the suspicion of aiding the Beguines in their path of error.[19] The nuns were also making themselves heard in the convent chronicle literature. Since the recorded *Lives* extended back into the previous century, the chronicles provide a background for the ascetic and visionary impulses in the Dominican convents of the Upper Rhine prior to and during Eckhart's activity there.

Eckhart's reflective sermons raised the love mysticism of the free Beguines to a plane of high intellectuality and at the same time disengaged the visionary mysticism of the Dominican nuns by denying that phenomenal experience can be the realm in which the believer communicates with God. Interpreted in this manner, Eckhart's "negative theology" falls into place with his real concerns and environment. Other churchmen also discouraged "corporeal" visions. Langer has shown that the visions included self-oriented experiences. Self-flagellation and the extremes of self-doubt were symptomatic of an evolving convent spirituality in which self-oriented supplications prevailed over prayers of praise or thanksgiving.[20]

Against a disturbingly achievement-oriented and self-centered piety, Marguerite's precept that "the noble soul desires nothing" must have appeared to Eckhart as a beneficent antidote. This can be recognized in a programmatic tract written at the beginning of his period of pastoral activities on the Upper Rhine: the *Liber Benedictus*, with its attached treatise on the noble being (*The Aristocrat*).[21] The *Liber Benedictus* begins with a philosophical precept alluding both to the metaphysics of analogy and to the mystical trope of the birth of the Son in the soul: "Goodness is neither created nor made nor born; yet it is birth-giving and gives birth to the good being (*den guoten*); and the good being, insofar as he is good, is unmade and uncreated, and yet the born child and son of goodness" (*...diu güete enist noch geschaffen noch gemachet noch geboren; mêr si ist gebernde und gebirt den guoten, und der guote, als verre sô er guot ist, ist ungemachet und ungeschaffen und doch geborn kint und sun der güete[22]*). The theory of analogy is adapted here to rationalize what soon becomes Eckhart's *leitmotiv* of "the birth of the Son in the soul."

The small tract called *The Aristocrat* (*Von dem edeln menschen*) begins by presenting, without context, Christ's words in Luke 19:12: "A man of a noble birth went to a distant country to have himself appointed king and then to return." Whereas in Luke this sentence merely sets the stage for the parable of the master and his servants, Eckhart focuses on the sentence and states that much of Holy Scripture is already touched upon in it. The "nobility" is found in the human soul.

As *The Aristocrat* interprets this nobility, Eckhart's focus winds inward, from the whole of Scripture implicit in the words, to the words by themselves, and then to self-knowledge—the key which unlocks the path back to the broader scope promised at the beginning of the tract. Eckhart moves from his decontextualized and open-ended sentence to a single word, then by way of it—as if he were passing through the focal point of all truth—back out to the broad plane of the universal. This is the characteristic movement of many of his sermons.

In the sermons, the project of the noble soul absorbs all his themes. In the Word as the ideal ground of being, God knows himself. This transparent knowing of God is the divine image in accordance with which the human soul is created. According to the preacher: "(God's) image is that he knows himself through and through and is nothing but light. When the soul touches him with proper knowledge, it is like him in this image" (*Sîn bilde ist, daz er sich durchkennet und all ein lieht ist. Swenne in diu sêle rüeret mit rehter bekantnîsse, sô ist si im glîch an dem bilde*).[23] Not only are Genesis and John two accounts of the same origination; the principle of creation lies within the soul: "in the innermost and in the highest [part] of the soul, God creates the entire world" (*in dem innigsten und in dem hoehsten der sêle schepfet got alle dise werlt*).[24] God's speaking is his creating. Speaking as creating and creating as knowing encompass the crux of Eckhart's homiletic mysticism. What could this have meant to the Dominican nuns who were not trained in the subtleties of a *magister* from Paris?

The nuns who heard his sermons were absorbed in an act of speaking that dominated their lives. Prayer, both liturgical and private, was the rhythm and focus of their existence. In prayer alone, their lives could be miraculously and perilously creative. Prayer and contemplation could result in exultation, illness, terror, and deliverance. It could confront the nuns with visions of Christ and transport them into heaven or hell. The extremes of heaven and hell were known by two of the Swiss nuns within Eckhart's pastoral circle: Jützi Schulthasin and Anna of Ramschwag.[25] In the piety of many nuns, a mixture of traits surfaced: a concern with personal salvation and a resultant unstable alternation between ecstasy and fear, giving rise to visions; a preponderance of prayers of supplication; and the expectation that the conferral of grace should take the form of perceptible signs. If Eckhart could hope to have an effect on the lives and the thinking of the nuns, this influence could only be exerted through their absorption in prayer.

In his instructions to his Erfurt confrères, the *Lebmeister* had recognized both the necessity and the pitfalls of the path pursued by these nuns. He had urged his brethren to pray so as to unite themselves in prayer with God: "So powerfully should one pray that one would wish that all human parts and powers, eyes and ears, mouth, heart, and all the senses should be directed to it; and one should not stop before one feels that one is intent upon uniting oneself with the one whom one has present and to whom one prays, that is God" (*Also kreftlichlîche sol man beten, daz man wölte, daz alliu diu gelider des menschen und krefte, beidiu ougen, ôren, munt, herze und alle sinne dar zuo*

*gekêret wæren; und niht ensol man ûfhoeren, man envinde denne, daz man
sich welle einen mit dem, den man gegenwertic hât und bitet, daz ist got).*[26]
Eckhart had recognized the dangers of a self-directed or misguidedly
ambitious spirituality. He had instructed his novitiate brethren that
even if they were experiencing the ecstasy of Paul, it would be better
for them to come out of it in order to give a sick man soup.[27] In Strasbourg and Cologne, Eckhart's thinking developed a dynamic unity of
antitheses: the movement inward, toward union with God and away
from the world of common experience, is joined by the movement outward, back to the world of shared life and activity.

The paradoxes of immanence and transcendence, of communality
and single-minded devotion, resound in homiletic reformulations of
the philosophical *totus intus, totus foris* motif: "It is a miraculous thing
that something flows out and yet remains within. That the Word flows
out and yet remains within" (*Ez ist ein wunderlich dinc, daz ein dinc ûzvliuzet und doch înneblîbet. Daz daz wort ûzvliuzet und doch inneblîbent...*).
"God is *in* all creatures, insofar as they have being, and yet is *above them*.
With the very thing that he is *in* all creatures, with that he is above
them" (*Got ist* in *allen crêatûren, als sie wesen hânt, und ist doch* dar über.
*Daz selbe, daz er ist* in *allen crêatûren, daz ist er doch dar über*).[28] Eckhart's
central paradox confronts us with the material of John, creation
through the Word—here in the figure of an existential continuity with
the act of speaking or praying. The inexpressibility of the Godhead is
superseded by the expressiveness of all things and words:

> When the Father gave birth to all creatures, he gave birth to me,
> and I flowed out with all creatures, and yet remain within in the
> Father. Just like the word that I now utter: It arises within me;
> second, I abide upon its image; third, I utter it forth, and all of
> you discern it; yet it actually remains in me. Just so have I
> remained in the Father.

> *Dô der vater gebor alle crêatûren, dô gebor er mich, und ich vlôz ûz mit
> allen crêatûren und bleip doch inne in dem vater. Ze glîcher wîs, als
> daz wort, daz ich nû spriche, daz entspringet in mir, ze dem andern
> mâle sô ruowe ich ûf dem bilde, ze dem dritten mâle sô spriche ich ez ûz,
> und ir enpfâhet ez alle; nochdenne blîbet ez eigenlîche in mir. Alsô bin
> ich in dem vater bliben.*[29]

We can extend this from the sermon to the prayer, and from the voiced
word and concrete image, to the prayer of silence which asks for nothing from God. The total absorption without images encouraged by

Eckhart passes over into a contemplation and love of all things and creatures as expressions of God. All things have a wordlike character: they are expressions of a substantial intention that remains within, even while uttering itself as the generative power which communicates being and life in creation: "Whoever were to know nothing more than the creatures would not need to think about any sermon, for each creature is full of God and is a book" (*Der niht dan die crêatûren bekante, der endörfte niemer gedenken ûf keine predige, wan ein ieglîchiu crêatûre ist vol gotes und ist ein buoch*).[30]

The material of ideas in Eckhart's sermons and treatises is received doctrine from Scripture, tradition, and contemporaneous Scholasticism. Quoting perpetually from these sources, he could scarcely have intended a wholesale rejection of such common and traditional opinions. However, the German sermons are far from being academic lectures. They stand on the principle that all knowledge presupposes a universal faculty for recognizing truth. This universality is dramatically evidenced by the very fact that the erudite sermons are addressed to the nonscholarly nuns. The noetic faculty is the human image of the transcendent One, whose knowing is the same as his being and creating. In persuading the nuns that God created the entire world within them, he was not espousing an esoteric form of idealism; he was confirming their divine right as knowing beings, capable of giving birth to truth within themselves. From Hildegard to Luther, the opposing view deprecating human knowledge was linked to an adjunct doctrine of creation (created out of nothing with no comprehension of its whence and whither, the mind is subject to external authority).

Eckhart's sermons have a stock of recurrent themes: there is the knowledge of God (or self-knowledge in God); the distance or detachment (*Abgeschiedenheit*) from things; the self-abandonment or "releasement" (*Gelassenheit*) to God; the removal of "images" (*Bilder*) from the soul; the "ground" or "small spark (*Fünklein*) of the soul, which seeks God and desires the good; the birth of the Son in the soul; the divine darkness of the Godhead; the silent desert in the soul; the generation of all creatures through the Word; the paradoxical interiority and exteriority of God; and others. However imperfect the resultant composite image, all these terms and themes should be thought of as aspects of one single theme.

The term *gelassen* survived through Tauler and the *Theologia Deutsch* to provide a slogan and ideal for dissenting Protestants of the Reformation era. Even now, this word retains a certain suggestiveness, implying serene calm and ease. With Eckhart, it came into use between the terrors of hell and the beckonings of paradise. The reflective knowledge associated with the calm of *Gelassenheit* is the eye that is both the seeing and the seen, the ear that is both the hearing and the heard—the mystical knowing of a monk or nun whose life is absorbed in prayer.

The calm of *Gelassenheit* is the silence in which, as Eckhart repeatedly preaches, God utters the eternal Word: this utterance is the same as the birth of the Son in the soul of the believer. The soul is emptied of "images" (*Bilder*)—of all representations of God in terms of time, place, body, and number—to be filled virtually by its emptying with divine essence. Through the power of a deity beyond representation in images, the soul conceives in itself the birth of the Son. The birth of Christ in the heart or transformation of the believer into Christ is, as we have seen, a Pauline motif with a long tradition.[31] But Eckhart's statement that the believer is *none other than* the eternal Son of God substantiated the heresy charges against him. The believer is transformed by truth and knowledge into the divine object of knowledge. The annihilation of time, place, and number as qualifiers in the divine knowledge has as its corollary this identity of human subject and divine object.

In place of the special grace sought by some visionaries, Eckhart's mysticism recognizes in each soul the divine force or spark created in the image of the transcendent Godhead: "Within the soul, there is a power for which all things are equally pleasing; indeed, the very worst and very best are entirely equal for this power..." (*Ein kraft ist in der sêle, der sint alliu dinc glîche süeze; jâ, daz allerboeseste und daz allerbeste daz ist allez glîch an dirre kraft*).[32] In regarding all things with equanimity, this power leaves place and time and self behind to become empty and free of self. The soul's emptiness is filled by the Father with the Son in the power of the Spirit, through which the Son is reborn again and again. This birth and rebirth in an eternal Now is identical with the utterance of the eternal Word in John 1:1.

Various metaphors designate the innate faculty within the soul: it is a force, a spark, a ground; and it is the highest and the innermost part of the soul. In replying to his inquisitors, Eckhart presented the ground as created, but in the image of God. Approached theoretically, it undoubtedly relates to that knowing which precedes being in God. Understood practically, the spark of the soul implies that those to whom he preached were capable of a divine knowledge, effected not by seeking, but by ceasing to seek. When all images have been expelled from the soul and all supplications of the self have been suspended, the ground is made ready for this birth. *Seeing*, Eckhart preached, goes out through the senses, while *hearing* remains inside and receptive. Several Middle High German terms are equivalents of the Latin *cognitio* and *intelligere*.[33] Quint renders almost all of them with the German *Erkennen*, a verb that is specific neither to hearing nor to seeing, but which instead generally implies a recognizing *as true*. Infinitive as well as substantive, *Erkennen* thus denotes both the noetic capacity and its fulfillment.

Though not without inconsistencies, the theme of knowing occupies the high ground in the sermons. The mystical knowing of the soul is a divine self-knowledge: "The same knowing in which God knows himself is none other than the knowing of each detached spirit. The soul receives its essence immediately from God; therefore God is closer to the soul than it is to itself; therefore God is in the ground of the soul with his entire divinity" (*Daz selbe bekantnisse, dâ sich got selben inne bekennet, daz ist eines ieglîchen abgescheidenen geistes bekantnîsse und kein anderz. Diu sêle nimet ir wesen âne mitel von gote; dar umbe ist got der sêle næher, dan si ir selber sî; dar umbe ist got in dem grunde der sêle mit aller sîner gotheit*).[34] This striking statement rests its case on an allusion to Augustine, but takes its final coherence from the complicity of human renunciation, self-annihilation, divine omnipotence, and human deification. The sermons offer many similar evocations of mystical knowledge: "Knowing is higher than life or being, for, insofar as it knows, it has life and being" (*Bekanntnisse ist hoeher dan leben oder wesen, wan in dem, daz ez bekennet, sô hât ez leben und wesen*).[35] "[God's] image is that he knows himself through and through and is nothing but light. When the soul touches him with proper knowledge, then it is like him in this image" (*Sîn bilde ist, daz er sich durchkennet und al ein lieht ist. Swenne in diu sêle rüeret mit rehter bekanntnisse, sô ist si im glîch an dem bilde*).[36] "One must know that to recognize God and to be recognized by God, to see God and to be seen by God, is, in itself, one. In that we recognize and see God, we recognize and see that he makes us recognize and see" (*Ez ist ze wizzene, daz daz ein ist nâch dingen: got bekennen und von got bekant ze sînne und got sehen und von got gesehen ze sînne. In dem bekennen wir got und sehen, daz er uns machet gesehende und bekennende*).[37]

The Dionysian *via negativa*, the regression by which the qualities of the world are denied to the divine, also leads to a denial that God knows particular things:

The masters say that God is a being and a rational being and that He knows all things. But I say: God is neither being nor rational being nor does he recognize this or that. Therefore, God is free of all things, and therefore he *is* all things.

*Die meister sprechent, got der sî ein wesen und ein vernünftic wesen und bekenne alliu dinc. Sô sprechen wir: got enist niht wesen noch vernünftic noch enbekennet niht diz noch daz. Her umbe ist got ledic aller dinge, und her umbe ist er alliu dinc.*[38]

Because all predicates must be lifted from God, he is free to be all in all. God is beyond definition. Hence all things bespeak the unutterable deity. The sermon, an appeal to spiritual poverty, ends by advising that whoever does not understand should not be troubled: until the hearer is like the truth it expresses, its message, which comes immediately (*âne mittel*) from the heart of God, will remain incomprehensible.

Since Eckhart's terms only begin to reveal their full range of implications and their play of association and contradiction in their homiletic context, we need to consider a characteristic sermon from beginning to end.

It is characteristic that Eckhart's sermon on Ecclesiastes 24:30, *Qui audit me,*[39] begins with an elliptical text. What stands out in its scriptural context is the juxtaposition of "hearing" God with "acting" in God. Instead of exploring this pertinent context, Eckhart begins by announcing, rather oddly, that each of the three words, "Who hears me...," might suffice for a sermon unto itself. The notion of a sermon on a single particle seems to border on whimsy. Yet, taken seriously, Eckhart's pronouncement may well have opened the listener to the reflexivity of words which—like the text *Virgo Israel* sung by the nun Hailrat—would have pointed to the one "who hears me." The pattern of an awakening through the word elevates the discrete phrase, the individual experience, to a condition of immediacy before God.

The eternal Wisdom, quotes Eckhart, proclaims that "whoever hears me" is not ashamed. This signifies that whoever is to hear the wisdom of the Father must be "within," "at home," and "One" (192). Three things hinder us in hearing the eternal Word: corporeality, multiplicity, and temporality. Whoever goes beyond these dwells in the spirit, in "unity" and in the "desert." Eckhart, like Mechthild of Magdeburg, sees the desert within as the place of encounter with God. Christ's summons is absorbed into the single word *gelassen*: the hearers should abandon self. This abandonment is the desert in which they are to hear the eternal Word (193).

At this point, Eckhart offers the first of several startling surprises in the course of his sermon, stating: "The very thing that hears is that which is heard in the eternal Word" (*Daz selbe, daz dâ hoeret, daz ist daz selbe, daz dâ gehoeret wirt in dem êwigen worte*—p. 193). The creature who has "gone out"—the noble soul of Eckhart's tract on the man who went out to receive a kingdom in order to return—is God's own Son, for everything God teaches and reveals is actuated nowhere else but in the Son.

After establishing that the destination is the same as the departure, Eckhart expands on the state of *Gelassenheit* in order to clarify the union:

> If you love yourself, you love all others as yourself. As long as you love a single human being less than yourself, you do not truly love yourself—if you do not love all others as yourself, in one human being all human beings: and this human being is God and man.

> *Hâst dû dich selben liep, sô hâst dû alle menschen liep als dich selben. Die wîle dû einen einigen menschen minner liep hâst dan dich selben, dû gewünne dich selben nie liep in der wârheit, dû enhabest denne alle menschen liep als dich selben, in einem menschen alle menschen, und der mensch ist got und mensche.* (195)

Here, unexpectedly, the contours of the Son crystallize out of the interchange of self and others. This thought is then rendered absolute: one should not care more about what happens to one's best friend than about what befalls anyone else. Moreover, Eckhart quotes (and modifies) Paul: "I should be willing to be eternally separated from God for the sake of my friend and for God" ('*ich wolte êwiclîche gescheiden sîn von gote durch mînes vriundes willen und durch got*—195). In the *NIV*, Romans 9:3 states: "For I could wish that I myself were cursed and cut off from Christ for the sake of my brothers, those of my race...." The modification extracts the paradox of abandoning God for the sake of a friend or for the sake of God, as the true perfection that Eckhart now accords to Paul in his willingness. The highest thing that one can abandon is God for the sake of God. Having just urged equanimity in the love of oneself and others, Eckhart now urges a sacrifice which, to his listeners, meant nothing less than accepting eternal loss. We should not underestimate the unedifying severity of this idea for Eckhart's flock. In perfect obedience and willingness, the Apostle Paul went beyond every form of giving and taking in his relationship to God. He took nothing from and gave nothing to God. Instead, states

Eckhart, elliptically: "it was a one and a pure unification. Here, the human being is a true human being..." (*ez ist ein ein und ein lûter einunge. Hie ist der mensche ein wâr mensche...*—197). Most likely, the emphasis fell on the word "true": to live in truth, the human being must renounce all thought of rewards in the service of God. In the monastic society, this meant equal love for all of one's fellows.

The "true" human being is the same as Eckhart's noble human being. Eckhart hints at something uncreated in the soul (197–8). This was one of the teachings that led to a condemnation linking him to the heresy of the Free Spirits. But he goes on to state that everything created is "nothing." The true human being is alien to this createdness. If his human being were to dwell for only a moment in the true being, which is set over against the created nothing, then he, the preacher, would think as little of himself as a worm (198).

Now the sermon moves for the second time from *Gelassenheit*, from the acceptance of hell, to the destination which is already attained in the proper state of abandonment. As all things flow out of God, they are equal (199). Invariably, this trope of the emanation of all things from God appears in connection with the creation by the Word. Here, the contemplative soul that has figuratively gone to hell, like Christ out of obedient love, is returned to a paradise which is already at hand in the equality of all things in God. To bring home the bliss of this divine equality, Eckhart employs two figures. The first is that of the fly which, in God, is equal to the highest angel (199). The second is that of the joy of God's equality; it is compared to a horse playfully running and jumping on a green meadow: the levelness of the meadow of play is the felicity with which God pours out his being. The lowliest of the angels who serve and protect us here below have the same joy and equality as the highest in the celestial hierarchy. If such an angel were commanded to do some seemingly absurd task such as counting caterpillars on a tree, doing so would mean blessedness and God's will (200). As is often the case, the celestial hierarchy is the model for the worldly hierarchy: Eckhart interprets obedience as equality in a manner both medieval and egalitarian. The human creature who is completely in God's will would not even care to be well when ill: "All pain is for him a joy, all multiplicity is a simplicity and a unity..." (*Alliu pîne ist im ein vröude, alliu manicvalticheit ist im ein blôzheit und ein einicheit...*—200). This classical motif is remarkably close to the beautiful lines in Novalis's *Hymns to the Night*: *Und jede Pein/ Wird einst ein Stachel/ Der Wollust sein.*

The true inner asceticism recommended by Eckhart is then translated into knowledge. *Gelassenheit* is like the eye that must be free of all color in order to discern color. As at the beginning of the sermon, this constitutes a paradox of knowledge: "The eye in which I see God is the same eye in which God sees me; my eye and God's eye are *one* eye and *one* sight and *one* knowing and *one* loving" (*Daz ouge, dâ inne ich got sihe, daz ist daz selbe ouge, dâ inne mich got sihet; mîn ouge und gotes ouge daz ist éin ouge und éin gesiht und éin bekennen und éin minnen*—201). This may be altogether Eckhart's clearest formulation of the *unio mystica*. But precisely the same statement is formulated by him in a Scholastic treatise; there he defended himself in making it by referring to Augustine.[40]

Eckhart's mystical state of abandonment is a contemplative asceticism, a renunciation of the world and self that seeks no visionary signs, but instead finds its validation in the world and in a life understood within the divine being. The sermon on the text *"Qui audit me"* concludes that what one should give up is not something one happens to possess, but rather oneself altogether. Whoever gives up all, if only for a moment, but does so completely, is truly *gelassen*.

If the great *summae* of High Scholasticism are appropriately compared to the architecture of the Gothic cathedrals, Eckhart's nonsystematically mystical homiletics can be compared to their interior space. Even in its imagery, his preaching is like the play of light that must have formed the backdrop for his speech. Pellucid and obscure, his sermons embody the eternal light that shines in the darkness without being touched or contained by the darkness. His mysticism, which begins with distance and abandonment in view of the nothingness of all created things, concludes by elevating all words, works, and creatures into the divine light:

> Words also have great power; one could do wonders with words. All words have power from the first Word…. Since like can accomplish so much with like, the soul in its natural light ought to elevate itself into the highest and the purest realm and enter into the angelic light, and with the angelic light make its way into the divine light, and there stand between three lights in their parting of ways, in the heights where the lights strike together. There, the eternal Word utters life into it; there the soul becomes alive and responsive in the Word.

> *Wort hânt ouch grôze kraft; man möhte wunder tuon mit worten. Alliu wort hânt kraft von dem êrsten worte…. Wan glîch in glîchem sô vil würket, dar umbe sol sich diu sêle ûf erheben in irm natiurlîchen lichte in daz hoehste und in daz lûterste und alsô treten in engelischez lieht*

*und mit engelischem liehte komen in göttlich lieht und âlso stân zwis-*
*chen den drin liehten in der wegescheiden, in der hoehe, dâ diu lieht*
*zesamen stôzent. Dâ sprichet ir în daz êwige wort daz leben; dâ wirt*
*diu sêle lebende und widersprechende in dem worte.*[41]

Eckhart's motifs are somewhat like chords resounding in various keys, often surprising and startling us. Yet there are overall oppositions and harmonies: the many and the one, self and others, time and eternity, individual and community. Within the patterns of opposition, the Eckhartian paradox of the inner and the outer is the central enigma. It is in turn keyed to the recurrent references to the eternal Word that takes precedence over the creation in time. The world is seen in aspect, rather than in time, space, or number.

Instead of mobilizing theoretical abstractions to explain away the inconsistencies of his sermons, we would do better to acknowledge the sporadic as integral to the message. If his reasoning habitually jumps from what appears to be an arbitrary pretext (for example, from the meaningfulness of the conjunctive particle *and* to his perennial theme of the birth of God in the soul),[42] the aim is to demonstrate the universal accessibility of the central divine birth by showing that "all words have power from the first Word"—spoken, as Augustine says, by truth itself.

With this in mind, we may be closer to an understanding of such Eckhartian oddities as the metaphor of God as a young horse frolicking on a blooming meadow, or the preacher's declaration that in lieu of any comprehending listeners, he would have been compelled to deliver his sermon before the collection box. Haas views this second example as Eckhart's clear confirmation of the inadequacy of all language (whereby the mystic realizes that his experience is ineffable, but is still compelled to speak of it, so that the powerlessness of language somehow ends up being a deep confirmation of its own power).[43] Perish the thought that the preacher was making a little joke.

Though difficult and profoundly serious, Eckhart's sermons are not grave or ponderous. They have a lightness, which (if the word *humor* offends) is at least closely akin to humor. Haas has observed that the great Franciscan preacher of the thirteenth century, Berthold of Regensburg, preached the end of the world in sermons that contained elements of humor and wordplay. Why should Eckhart have been loathe to mix profound seriousness with lightness? His sermons combine detachment with concentration. A detachment close to humor can be sensed in the casual tone of his anecdotes of the type, "I was once asked what the Father does in heaven. I replied: He gives

birth to his Son, and doing this is such a joy and pleases Him so well
that He does nothing other than give birth to His Son..." (*Ich wart
einest gevrâget, waz der vater tæte in dem himel? Dô sprach ich: er gebirt
sînen sun, und daz werk ist im sô lüstlich und gevellet im sô wol, daz er
niemer anders getuot dan gebern sînen sun...*).[44] The play element here
comes from nonchalantly transferring the notions of passing time by
doing things, from the plane of time to that of eternity. The playful-
ness in Eckhart's metaphor of the divine power as a young horse
prancing about a blossoming meadow is also akin to the stylistic
delight he himself took in antithesis and paradox. There is verbal play
in the superflous repetition of Eckhart's characterizations of God:
"God is in all things. The more he is *in* the things, the more he is outside of the things; the more *within*, the more without, and the more
without the more within" (*Got ist in allen dingen. Ie mê er ist* in *den dingen, ie mê er ist ûz den dingen: ie mê* inne, *ie mê ûze, und ie mê ûze, ie mê*
inne).[45] A single leap on this meadow would have sufficed to make the
point.

A play of the hypothetical imagination is activated when Eckhart
calls upon his congregation to consider two situations in order to
grasp how "the kingdom of God is near at hand":

> First of all, we should know *how* the Kingdom of God is near....
> Therefore, we should know the meaning of this. If I were a king,
> but did not know it myself, I would not be a king. But if I had the
> firm belief that I was a king, and if all people imagined this
> together with me and I knew for certain that all people imagined
> it, then I would be a king, and the entire wealth of the kingdom
> would be mine, and I would lack for none of it.

> *Ze dem êrsten suln wir wizzen, wíe daz rîche gotes uns nâhe ist.... Dar
> umbe suln wir wizzen den sin dâ von. Daz ich ein künic wære und ich
> des nicht enweste, ich enwære niht ein künic. Aber, hæte ich des einen
> ganzen wân, daz ich ein künic wære, und wænden des alle die liute mit
> mir und ich weste daz vür wâr, daz des alle die liute wænden, sô wære
> ich ein künic, und so wære aller der rîchtuom des küniges mîn, und des
> engebræche mir nihtes niht.*[46]

Regarded in its own right as a *jeu d'esprit*, the effect of this imagined
choice of two kings is to dethrone the one who is simply passively
royal and to enthrone the one who receives recognition: even in the
field of political authority, knowing precedes being. This political
implication accords with Eckhart's valuation of humanity over hierar-

chy. But his reference is to the kingdom of God, and his point that the inner certainty acquired through *Gelassenheit* is already within the domain of salvation, and therefore in need of no external verifications. Anticipating certain difficulties of Luther's doctrine of salvation by faith alone, Eckhart's terms of abandonment conceive of a salvation by a kind of *knowing* that surpasses merely believing by virtue of its indestructible inner certainty. If Luther's salvation by faith rather than by works runs the risk of turning faith itself into a work, then, by contrast, Eckhart's salvation by *knowing* seems intent on precluding this very risk: in the state of *Gelassenheit*, the knowing of the serene soul has repudiated the very self that desires rewards. In part for this reason, the early Protestant dissenters against Luther's doctrine of imputed justification were attracted to the term *Gelassenheit*.[47]

In the last decade of his life, Eckhart ran afoul of the increasing repressiveness of his times. The long controversy over poverty had only recently ended with the suppression of the Franciscan Spirituals. In 1328, the judgment of Pope John XXII, the pope who had triumphed over the apostolically impoverished Franciscans, fell upon the Dominican teacher of spiritual poverty.

The question for us is not so much whether Eckhart really violated correct doctrine, as whether the Church had reason to perceive a threat in the event that his kind of Christianity had ever become widespread. It would be misguided to expect Eckhart to have acted out the rebel's openly defiant role (a role which, judging by his writings, he never sought). The affirmation of unity is a strong undercurrent in his thought. Nothing in his writing gives us the impression of an intention to assault institutions in the manner of Luther; but everything in his life and work speaks of an uncompromising pursuit of his own ideal of truth. Eckhart challenged authority with his radical shift of emphasis away from all external knowledge to the inner ground of the soul. If all truth resides in the ground of the soul, then it would appear that nothing can be authentically true for us simply because we are told to believe it.

The radical nature of this challenge is evident when Eckhart preaches that if God could be separated from truth, then one should adhere to truth and not to God: "The truth is so noble, that if it were possible for God to turn away from the truth, I would adhere to the truth and leave God" (*Waz ist diu wârheit? Wârheit ist als edel, wære, daz sich got gekêren möhte von der wârheit, ich wölte mich an die wârheit heften und wölte got lâzen...*).[48] Although Eckhart goes on to confirm that only God and no creature is truth, the confrontation here with the choice *per impossibile* which would adhere to truth rather than to God has the effect of shifting the locus of authority inward. Similarly with respect to justice: "The just human beings take justice so seriously, that, if God were not just, they would not care a bit for God and stand so firmly in justice…that they would not care about the pain of hell or the joy of heaven nor any thing" (*Den gerehten menschen, den ist alsô ernst zu der gerehticheit, wære, daz got nicht gereht wære, sie enahteten eine bône niht ûf got und stânt alsô vaste in der gerehticheit…daz sie niht enahtent pîne der helle noch vröude des himelrîches noch keines dinges*).[49] Eckhart's invocation to conceive of God as distinct from truth or from justice is not an appeal to skepticism. But neither is it an empty phrase: justice is not justice because it comes from God. God is God because he is just. As Augustine had written, justice and truth are known to us by an inner sense, tantamount to an absolute self-certainty.

Two of the articles of indictment against him were concerned with Eckhart's alleged denial of the need for works of faith. The papal bull stopped short of condemning these two indicted pronouncements as heretical, warning instead that without further clarification they would be objectionable. Eckhart's accusers felt that he was undermining the connection between works and the attainment of grace. Since *Gelassenheit* (like the "annihilation" of the noble soul for Marguerite Porete) is total, it annihilates virtue along with good works *as means to an end*. In Eckhart's sermon, *Intravit Jesus in templum*, on driving the merchants and moneychangers out of the temple (Matthew 21:12), the merchants are said to be "good" people. The merchants represent all those who, no matter how well-intentioned in their fasts, vigils, and prayers, expect that God should do something for them in return (*sie wellent daz eine umbe daz ander geben und wellent alsô koufen mit unserem herrn*). This is not so much an evil as it is a hindrance for the pure truth, an encumbrance with self, "with time and with number, with before and with after" (*mit zît und mit zal, mit vor und mit nâch*).[50] Eckhart's rejection of the economy of works and of time and number conveys a critique of a widespread problem of spiritual life, a pattern no doubt familiar to the monks and nuns and layfolk of his time: the increasing subordination of the supreme ends of spiritual life to the private ends of personal justification and the ancillary ends of defending and aggrandizing institutions.

The essential goodness of divine being makes good works an end in themselves: "Whoever were to ask life for a thousand years: 'Why do you live?'—if life could answer, it would speak nothing else but: 'I live in order that I live'" (*Swer daz leben vrâgete tûsent jâr: war umbe lebest dû? solte ez antwürten, ez spræche niht anders wan: ich lebe dar umbe daz ich lebe*).⁵¹ We should react the same way about our performance of works—'I do it in order that I do it!' (*ich würke dar umbe daz ich würke*)—not to receive anything from God. If all things are considered in the manner of the divine utterance that eternally expresses and realizes itself, all creatures and works and all of humanity appreciate in worth precisely because the point of reference is no longer the "self" of the creature: "I tell you: humanity is in the poorest or most despised human being just as perfect as it is in the pope or in the emperor; for humanity in itself is preferable to me than the human being which I carry upon myself" (*Ich spriche: menscheit ist an dem ermsten oder versmæhesten menschen als volkomen als an dem bâbeste oder an dem keiser, wan menscheit in ihr selber ist mir lieber dan der mensche den ich an mir trage*).⁵²

In theory of course, the pope should not have ranked higher before God than the humblest human being. But, as the fate of Marguerite suggests, the message was provocative. Although Eckhart always preached obedience, the suggestion that the life of the spirit should be free from all temporal ambitions and encumbrances was in stark contrast to the conduct of a church engaged in quests of power and intent upon suppressing both the quiet independence of the Beguines and the active stirrings of the Franciscan Spirituals.

Eckhart's inner movement was a turning away from a religion of self-hatred and ambition, rooted in fear, obsessed with human depravity, and therefore bound to an economy of salvation based on works and rewards as external tokens of good will and divine favor. Hildegard taught that the fear of God was the beginning of all wisdom. By contrast, Eckhart preached that, "The human being should not fear God, for whoever fears him flees from him" (*Der mensche ensol got niht vürhten, wan der, der in vürhtet, der vliuhet in*).⁵³ It is against the entire orientation toward human depravity, external authority, and punishments and rewards, that Eckhart's "spark of the soul" is said to incline toward the good and toward God—"even in Hell" (*nochdenne in der helle*).⁵⁴ Eckhart preaches against sin, but without threatening his hearers with damnation or enticing them with rewards.

Before his female hearers Eckhart's theology of the Word also gave rise to egalitarian implications:

They [the just] live eternally "with God," precisely *with* [*bei*] God, neither above nor below. They enact all their works with God, and God with them. St. John speaks: "The Word was with God." It was equal and alongside, not below and not above, but rather equal. When God created man, he created woman from the side of man, so that she would be equal with him. He made her nei-

ther from his head nor from his feet, so that she would be...equal
to him. Thus the just soul should be right alongside of God...

*Sie lebent êwiclîche "bî gote," rehte glîch bî gote, noch unden noch oben.
Sie würkent alliu iriu werk bî gote und got bî in. Sant Johannes sprichet:
"daz wort was bî gote." Ez was alzemâle glîch und was bî neben, noch
undenân noch obenân, sunder glîch. Dô got den menschen machete, do
machete er die vrouwen von des mannes sîten, dar umbe daz si im glîch
wære. Er machete sie niht von dem houbte noch von den vüezen, daz sie
im...glîch wære. Alsô sol diu gerehte sêle glîch bî gote sîn....*[55]

Eckhart's egalitarianism is not conditioned by a correct modern
understanding of gender. It is correlative with his theories of being
and knowing, with the predominance of the eternal One over the
many in time.

Before and during his trial, the offices of inquisition were at
work. It was a period of repression: heretics were being tried and executed, books condemned. Courageously or foolishly, Eckhart seems to
have disregarded this impending threat during much of his life. The
first investigation carried out by his fellow Dominican, Nikolaus of
Strasbourg, in 1325-1326 may have been a preventive maneuver for
anticipating and deflecting the more hostile proceedings planned by
others. It is possible that the subsequent charges brought against him
nevertheless came as a surprise. Though introduced by the Arch-
bishop of Cologne, they were to be pressed by the formidable office of
inquisition. The prosecutors took issue with the content of his objectionable utterances, as well as with their capacity to mislead the laity.
In defending himself, Eckhart either conceded or disavowed minor
points, but upheld the correctness and orthodoxy of his teachings as a
whole. He also pledged in advance to recant, should errors be clearly
demonstrated. In 1326, he journeyed to Avignon in order to appeal in
person to Pope John XXII. Some time prior to the papal condemnation
of April 1329, he died while awaiting the results of the proceedings.
Obviously, we cannot know what he was thinking in Avignon, much
less how he would have reacted to the condemnation.

Another accused theologian was also awaiting a verdict in Avignon: William of Ockham, the founder of the Nominalist school that
led to the *via moderna* and ultimately to the underpinnings of modern
empirical science. Nominalism broke ground for modern empiricism
by distancing itself from a medieval Realism that accepted the real
essence of universals. In Eckhart and Ockham, two opposites in the
spectrum of philosophical alternatives were brought together by

chance and papal indictment. Reporting what he understood of Eckhart's teachings, Ockham registered them only as "absurdities." A watershed of Western thought separated them. We are on the side of Ockham and can therefore only speculate in interpreting the significance of Eckhart's mysticism.

Eckhart, it is clear, knew nothing of our modern outlook in which truth and justice are relational terms, designating no real being or entity in itself. Truth is an all-informing real power. Based on, but going beyond Augustine, Eckhart's concept of truth as indivisible defines his philosophy and mysticism:

> St. Augustine speaks a word which sounds quite unlike him, and is yet quite like him: Nothing is truth that doesn't contain all truth within it. That force [i.e., the "noble force" or the "small spark" of the soul] encompasses all things in the truth. For this force, nothing lies concealed.

> Sant Augustînus sprichet ein wort, daz disem hilet gar unglîche und ist im doch gar glîch: niht enist wârheit, ez enhabe in im beslozzen alle wârheit. Disiu kraft nimet alliu dinc in der wârheit. Dirre kraft enist kein dinc bedecket.[56]

All of Eckhart's mystical terms are aspects of this idea of the structure of truth. All truth is one. Truth, in Scripture or philosophy, is concentrated in an eternal generation that God effects in the innermost citadel of the soul. His sermons are mystical because they include all believers in the reciprocity of the divine knowing. If he had expressed his ideas only in Latin treatises and only for learned readers, his reputation might not now be that of a mystic. It was not his term for himself. Yet before his congregation, theory became revelation as he attempted to disencumber faith of the weight of external authority; as New Testament and Old, philosophy ancient and modern, and the voices of many masters all converged in his assertion of the creative power of recognition. Surrounded by vicious controversy and repression, beset even inside cloistered circles by clamorings for signs of certainty and grace, his tracts and sermons strove to unite all voices in the integral word of divine knowledge.

It was after Eckhart's death that the worst catastrophes of the fourteenth century unfolded. In 1324, Louis the Bavarian, the German king and later Holy Roman Emperor, was excommunicated in another attempt of the papacy to assert its political mastery. The resultant turmoil and uncertainty stimulated another of the shattering controversies over the powers of monarchs and popes. Eminent figures such as William of Ockham and Marsilius of Padua supported the royal position.

There were also conflicts within the spiritual estate. As a result of the excommunication, the clergy in all the territories under Louis's jurisdiction were restricted in performing the Mass and administering the sacraments, a grave state of affairs for any priest concerned with the spiritual well-being of his flock. Among the Dominicans, some complied with the papal order to stop administering the sacraments to their congregation. Others resisted. Popular opinion rallied to the king. In the nun Margaretha Ebner, an impassioned sympathy for the excommunicated king stimulated prayers and mystical transports. After Louis's death, Tauler entreated Margaretha to pray for the dead sovereign and inquired of her how God might judge in such a case. Margaretha prayed to Jesus and learned that despite the excommunication of the king his salvation was assured. Why? Because the king had loved Jesus, and human opinion (that of the pope!) is often deceived.[57] Here the conflict of authority has become topical and political, with a corresponding turn toward a personalistic mysticism.

The pious layfolk and religious of South Germany and the Upper Rhine were drawn into the conflict and forced to choose between allegiance to their sovereign or loyalty to their pope. This and the ensuing confusions came during a period of worsening conditions and unheard of disasters—years of pestilence, floods, famines, and mass hysteria. The Black Plague swept across Europe in 1348. In times like these, the bonds of friendship and shared devotion became fertile.

A characteristic current was that of the "Friends of God." The devout circles of "Friends" were given to a mystical piety that could take various forms. Rulman Merswin was a Strasbourg banker who had been moved by a mystical conversion experience to devote his life to God. He organized a retreat community on a river island (*Grünwörth*). Merswin is also suspected as the secret hand that penned the mystical tracts that he attributed to the mysterious persona of the "Friend of God from the Upper Land" (*Gottesfreund vom Oberland*).[58] From the private languages of medieval nuns to the legendary society of the Rosicrucians, the mystical milieu periodically gave rise to arcane obsessions.

However, the most famous representatives of the mysticism of the Friends of God showed nothing of this inclination. They were Heinrich Seuse (Henry Suso) and Johannes Tauler, both of whom had known the influence of Meister Eckhart.

Seuse had arrived at an important insight through the advice of Eckhart. Born in or near Konstanz around 1295, Seuse eagerly entered the Dominican monastery in Konstanz at the tender age of twelve. Since this was below the minimum age for acceptance, and since donations from his parents may have played a role in Heinrich's premature entry, the young monk suffered for years at the thought that he might have inadvertently committed the mortal sin of simony. His *Anfechtungen*, or agonizing doubts about his justification, stand comparison with those of the young Luther.

It was Eckhart's counsel to Seuse in Cologne that freed him from these tormenting thoughts of mortal sin and damnation. The transition is significant for the study of the evolving forms of German mysticism because it suggests that Seuse passed through the same crisis over admission to or exclusion from grace, which, according to our hypothesis, lies at the root of the visionary mysticism of nuns like Elsbeth of Oye.

The problems of spiritual authority and of deciding between conflicting views did not end for Seuse with Eckhart's consoling advice. When the master was condemned for heresy, the pupil came under suspicion for espousing his teaching. Moreover, during the harsh and uncertain period of the interdiction under King Louis, the public authority of the clergy suffered greatly.

Seuse's tract with the title *Little Book of Truth* (*Büchlein der Wahrheit*) was composed around 1327, before the papal judgment fell against his revered teacher. Defending Eckhart's teachings, Seuse incurred the reprimand of his Dominican superiors. Around 1330, he wrote his *Little Book of Eternal Wisdom* (*Büchlein der ewigen Weisheit*), which he expanded and translated into Latin under the title *Horologium Sapientiae*. A book of letters (*Das Briefbüchlein*) and his *Life* completed the four books of *Das Exemplar*. There is speculation about how much his work may owe to the editorial or authorial assistance of his friend, Elsbeth Stagel, a Dominican nun in Töß who solicited from Seuse accounts of his spiritual experiences. He died in 1366.

Seuse's accounts of his early visionary experiences and his more personal and affective tone place him in the tradition of the older convent mysticism. He records visions, experiences of ecstasy, and self-flagellations. However, this is only one side of Seuse. The visions and self-torments form part of what might be called a developmental novel, *ein Entwicklungsroman*, of his spiritual quests and passages. The decisive turn in his life is his overcoming of his early literal-minded imitations of Christ and Saint Paul. This he accomplishes by replacing his self-inflicted torture with ordeals of a common life which, even without crosses and hair shirts, was arduous enough in his age. After this turning point, Seuse began to devote himself to service to others and to the Divine Wisdom (who is characteristically represented by Seuse as a female figure, identical with Christ). Personal exploits and inner experiences thus acquire an exemplary character. Experience is ennobled by chivalrous self-sacrifice. Humiliations and perils are borne bravely in the service of Lady Wisdom. Since all is for the honor and glory of God, everything terrifying and degrading can be transfigured into the stations of a chivalrous quest: a horrendous encounter with a cutthroat in a dark forest, or the bitter stings of false accusation from a woman who slanders Seuse by announcing that he is the father of her child.

Seuse's *Life* offers a panorama of his times and its customs, its diurnal fears and its spiritual adventures. He had something to offer for everyone. To those in need of images and miracles, he had them in plenty, while to those of a keener mind such as the inquisitive and wise Elsbeth Stagel he could still explicate the subtleties of Eckhart's forbidden mysticism.

In contrast to the colorful roundedness of Seuse, Johannes Tauler (1300–1361) comes down to us mainly as the author of some eighty-four sermons. He was born in Strasbourg and spent the greater part of his life in that city. He was influenced by Eckhart, whom he may have known, and affected by the conflict between the king and the pope. A loyal Dominican, he found refuge in Basel during the period of the interdiction. Like Eckhart, Tauler was entrusted with the pastoral care of Dominican nuns, preaching to them in the vernacular. He also cultivated the lay adherents of the Friends of God.

Tauler's sermons utilize the conceptual symbolism of Eckhart in order to instruct his flock on the itinerary and stations of the inner life. In his usage, the terminology of *Innerlichkeit* acquires transparence and refinement. For Tauler, the stages of spiritual rebirth conform to the classical *purgatio, illuminatio,* and *unio;* and these in turn correspond roughly to a trichotomy of sensory, intellectual, and spiritual faculties. Only the third faculty, the *Seelengrund* or *Seelenfünklein* or *Gemüt*, is created in the image of God. The goal of all spiritual experience is to become *gottförmig,* "deiform." The destiny of worldly existence and spiritual life is to return to God. The divine abyss calls out to the human abyss. The soul longs to lose itself like a drop of water in the deep sea.[59]

In Eckhart's sermons, the terminology of *Innerlichkeit* was employed in order to shatter a contemplative imagery based upon space, time, body, and number. In Tauler, the same terminology tends rather to compose an extensive system of symbolic images that serve as an alternative to a spiritless or superficial religiosity. The purpose is still to bring about a purity of devotion, deeper than any *quid pro quo* of works for salvation. However, Eckhart's radical attempt to lead his listeners to a realm of absolute inner autonomy is less evident in Tauler.

Long considered the work of Tauler, the Christmas sermon on the text of Isaiah 9:6 (the first sermon in Vetter's edition of Tauler), is now attributed by some scholars to Eckhart (though it seems to lack the latter's radical challenge to pictorialism). Since the sermon could conceivably have been composed by either, and since it was known to Luther and still paraphrased by Baader in the nineteenth century, it is perhaps wisest to examine it as a testimony to the continuity and impact of German mysticism.

The basic chord of its well-fashioned composition is sounded in the initial pronouncement that on this day one is celebrating a "three-fold birth." The first of the three births is the one that occurs in the heavenly Father. The second is the birth that occurs out of virginal fertility and purity; and the third the one which should be taking place every day and every moment in the heart of the believer. The Father gives birth by looking into himself, thereby knowing his own being through and through. The eternal birth of the Son within the heavenly Father is perfect because of its eternal repetition. The circular course of the heavenly bodies symbolizes this. For the human creature, this represents the necessity of returning to the origin that is God. Like God, the human creature should go into itself wholly in order to go out from self. The soul replicates the divine pattern in three noble powers: memory, understanding, and will. As in Augustine, because of these three powers, the soul, born between time and eternity, is receptive to God. The sermon continues by evoking the powers of concentration needed for the turn inward. Allegorizing Abraham's journey, the sermon compares it to Christ's call to leave father, mother, and native soil behind in order to find eternal life. Coming back to the middle of the three births, the sermon spiritualizes it as the speaking of the Word in the complete stillness of night from the heart of the Father into the spiritualized virginity of Mary. The sermon closes by calling upon the congregation to be the spiritual mother for this same birth.

Tauler cites Dionysius, Plato, and Aristotle, but no one more often than Augustine. To the latter, he attibutes the idea that God is a unity that "brings about all multiplicity and is all in all things, one in all and all in one" (*ein einformig götlich wesen und wurket doch alle manigfaltikeit und ist al in allen dingen, ein in al und al in ein*). This same thought leads Tauler to praise the labor of a simple plowman as a worship honoring the noble blood of Christ (177, 179), a sentiment anticipating Luther. Tauler memorializes "a dear master" who "spoke from eternity, and you discern it in accordance with time" (*er sprach uss der ewikeit, und ir vernehment es noch der zit*— 69). If it is Eckhart who remains unnamed here, Tauler elsewhere recognizes, as did the dear master, that there is a divine knowledge enacted in the human creature (*dis bekent sich Got in Gotte*—350). Another sermon interprets Hildegard's vision of the fear of God—viewing the image now very differently as an allegory of self-knowledge (379).

In Tauler's sermons, the symbol, trope, allegory, or image is a semiotic coinage that has gained currency to the point that it can be utilized even without the large-scale metaphysical or cosmological frames of reference that molded it. A sermon on John 8:12 projects a cosmic outlook: the elements are all moved to return to their origin; how does it happen that only the human creature does not hasten to return (47)? Tauler concludes with the Johannine light shining in darkness without being received by the darkness. The underlying coordinates of Tauler's semiotic system are what might be termed a directional paradox. The path back leads into the coming state. The path inward is a path outward. Self-recognition is a leaving behind of self. Tauler's sermons became the classic standard of a reflective spirituality. Their popularity survived in Pietistic circles into the nineteenth century.

However, the most consequential offshoot of the reflective school was an anonymous treatise popularized by Luther. It was probably written about 1350, apparently by a monk at the house of the Teutonic Order in Frankfurt am Main. Luther published it on the eve of the Reformation, in 1516. Returning to it in 1518, he declared that, except for the Bible and Saint Augustine, no other book or author had taught him more—averring that it anticipated the new Wittenberg theology. It soon acquired the programmatic title of a *Theologia Deutsch*. For Luther, as well as for the dissenters in the ranks of his Reformation, this work possessed great significance. Scholars have long debated Luther's high praise for the *Theologia* and his debt to the mystics. We will return to this issue in chapter six.

# 4

# The Finite and the Infinite

## The Humanistic Mysticism of Nicholas of Cusa

A century after Seuse and Tauler, Nicholas of Cusa (1401–1464) seems to project the inwardness of the medieval monk's cell outward by envisaging the boundlessness of ·divine being and the universe. Eckhart was an important influence behind the Cusan approach to the problems of time and eternity and of the one and the many.[1] However, the new speculation was of a strikingly distinct cast.

Cusanus turned away from the Eckhartian themes of the inner being, of the spark or birth of the Son in the soul, and instead developed a new form of mystical speculation involving number and measure—criteria the mind uses in researching the external world. The infinitude that is beyond all measure leaves us in a condition of incomprehension between the infinitely great and the infinitely small. There is no proportion of the infinite to the finite. By a standard of perfect exactitude, any human judgment is reduced to imprecision and error, so that, by its own devices, human knowledge is predestined to failure. However, all the irreconcilables are conjoined for Cusanus in the paradoxical "coincidence of opposites." Peering through this central enigma of thought, the finite mind approaches the *deus absconditus*, as the conceptual configuration of Christ. The God who can only be adumbrated by means of speculative thought is revealed in Scripture and known to faith and mystical contemplation.

Cusanus is open to a universe of the most grandiose measure. He entertains the concept of a "privatively" infinite universe—one of which the mind can conceive of no boundary. The Cusan universe is an ensemble of relational constructs conceptually centered in God. During the Renaissance, the world of speculative mysticism would increase in complexity. In the century after Cusanus conceived the outlines of his expansive universe, imaginative images of nature as microcosm and macrocosm were fleshed out in the more influential systems of Agrippa von Nettesheim and Paracelsus.[2]

As a rule, Cusanus is regarded and studied as a philosopher, and rightly so, since he was thoroughly steeped in philosophical and theological erudition. Nevertheless, there are also merits to studying him as a mystic. Many of his key terms are said to be used without clear definition. It is not clear what he means when he writes that the divine things and human things "coincide" in Christ; or when he contends that God is present in all things through the mediation of the universe; or that all things are in all other things.[3] If these ambiguities are reprehensible for a philosopher, they are less so for the mystic whose purpose is to show that all things visible to the eye or the mind are a single mystery, to be addressed not by human reason, but by embracing an even greater mystery. There is no sharp distinction between his philosophical and mystical writings. The seminal speculative work, *De Docta Ignorantia* (*On Learned Ignorance*, 1440), is entirely congruent with the mystical treatise, *De Visione Dei* (1453).

The infinite unity and the coincidence of opposites can be viewed as tokens of Cusanus's life and times. Nikolaus Krebs (or Chryffs) was born, the son of a boatsman, in Kues (*Cusa*) on the Mosel River, from which town his Latin name Cusanus is derived. He was sent to the school of the Brethren of the Common Life in Deventer and briefly attended the University of Heidelberg before continuing his studies at the University of Padua, graduating in jurisprudence. In Padua, he encountered some of the best minds of his age and indulged his passion for all forms of knowledge. A man of universal interests, Nicholas undertook impressive courses of study in the areas of mathematics, astronomy, physics, medicine, classical literature, and the new Humanism. After graduating, he served the Church as a lawyer, assisting the work of the Council of Basel and entering upon a long career as a papal legate and bishop. In addition to the intellectual ferment of his time, its worldly crises and its need for political and ecclesiastic reform occupied him. The hopes of reform were set against new upheavals which were nothing less than earthshaking: the great armed heresy of the Hussites, the conflicts of the popes and the councils, and the impending demise of Constantinople under Turkish onslaught.

Each of the stages of his life confronted him with what was most forward-looking in his age. His schooling in Deventer under the tutelage of the Brethren of the Common Life brought him into the ambiance of a devout lay order that existed without vows. In quiet opposition to the decadence of monasticism, the Brethren practiced outside the religious orders devotion and enlightened service to humanity. The *Devotio Moderna* valued both the inner life and the productive activity of the individual. The Brethren looked back to mystical forbears—Gerard Grote (1340–1384) and the Rhenish mysticism of Jan van Ruysbroeck (1293–1381). The schools of the Brethren would later educate Erasmus and Calvin. During Nicholas's schooling in Deventer, he may have known Thomas à Kempis (1379/80–1471), under whose name *The Imitation of Christ* became one of the most famous devotional works of all time.

The quiet religiosity of the *Devotio Moderna* encouraged Nicholas in a monklike devotion which in its simplicity appears to contrast with the daring of his intellectual enterprises. In Cusanus, liberal-minded intellectuality and simple devotion were surprisingly compatible. In his work, this is reflected in his ideal of the layman who knows that the voice of wisdom is heard not only in the scholarly tomes—in which the learned are often misled by the "authority" of a written word—but also on public "streets and squares."[4] The Cusan ideal of the layman is that of the mind guided by common sense and open to common experience in the quest for truth.

Cusanus, the intellectual, the Humanistic collector of all knowledge, ancient and modern, was spurred on by the scientific progress that had gained momentum during the fourteenth century. To name only one pertinent example, Nicholas Oresme had achieved successes in the field of dynamics and mathematics. Oresme had seriously entertained the hypothesis that the earth revolves around the sun. He had considered many of the counterarguments specious, though in the end he concluded that the argument in favor was insufficient. Copleston writes that Oresme had argued that "God is not only one and unique but also infinite," and that there is no reason why God could not have created a plurality of worlds.[5] Oresme also devised graphs for showing variations in the intensity of motion, thereby depicting a movement in time as a figure in space. Whether or not stimulated by his direct influence, Cusanus was drawn by this same scientific and speculative current. Though not a scientist in a modern sense, his openness to daring theories and proofs by experience led him to speculate about standards of evidence. He wrote that physicians should keep records of the weights of urine or of medicinal herbs, and obtain contrastive measurements of pulse rates for young and old and for the sick and the healthy.

Cusanus took over an expanding and problem-filled picture of the world. Like Oresme, he saw all things as encompassed by the infinite. Space no longer possessed an absolute "up" or "down." Everything moved, including the earth. Measure and direction had always been a feature of the earth, rather like the proportions of a living organism. Direction and distance had pertained to the unique topography of a world *qua* individual. Medieval maps showed this world-individual with an inherent orientation in the radical sense of the word *Orient*: Jerusalem was situated at the top or center of the map. Due to mathematical researches and the increasing interest in geography and exploration, new charts were being devised in the fifteenth century, utilizing degree lines and showing newly discovered regions.

This revolution in measurement contributed to the tenor and symbolism of the Cusan thought. A cartographer in his own right, he once compared the mind to a mapmaker who sits in his chamber in order to receive messages from the senses and compile a map of the city outside. When the map has been completed, the mind as mapmaker dismisses the messengers of sense experience, shuts its doors, and revolves its scrutiny from the city to the activity of mapmaking—in order to obtain a mystical knowledge of God.[6] One can characterize the mysticism of Cusanus as a system of constructs, contrived so as to lead the spectator to the infinite unity of God. This unity was also to imply a greater degree of latitude for the individual in matters of faith.

Balancing unity with diversity is the political agenda behind Cusanus's work. In addition to a lifelong adherence to the pious practical individualism of the *Devotio Moderna* and to Humanistic scholarship, his political involvements shaped his mysticism. If infinity, extension, and number call to mind the mathematical advances of the time, his theme of unity recalls the efforts of his age to shore up the disintegrating late medieval order. Cusanus actively participated in these efforts, devoting the early work *De Concordantia Catholica* to the pursuit of harmony. At the beginning of his career in the Church, the Council of Constance healed the Great Schism of the Church, but at the same council Jan Hus was burned, touching off one of the most violent rifts of medieval Christianity—a vivid reminder of the dissent and oppression that characterized Christendom as much as in the time of Hildegard or Eckhart. An outstanding figure of the late fourteenth century, Jean Gerson, was, like Cusanus, a mystic and a supporter of unity, active both against Hus and in favor of healing the schism and taking the *Devotio Moderna* into the fold. Cusanus became personally involved in the attempts to repair the division of the Eastern and Western churches in order to salvage Constantinople from the impending Ottoman conquest.

During his homeward voyage from Constantinople around the end of 1437 or the beginning of 1438, Cusanus was illuminated with the ideas for *On Learned Ignorance*. These came to him, as:

> things which I have long desired to attain by various doctrinal approaches but could not—until, while I was at sea en route back

from Greece, I was led (by, as I believe, a heavenly gift from the Father of lights, from whom comes every excellent gift) to embrace—in learned ignorance and through a transcending of the incorruptible truths which are humanly knowable—incomprehensible things incomprehensibly.[7]

Compared to Hildegard's visions or Eckhart's divine knowing, this may sound like a mere rhetorical flourish. Yet, there is no reason to assume that this assertion of divine inspiration is any less sincere—or less mystical by our definition—than any other assertion of a knowledge of divine truths from a divine source. This remark made by Cusanus in his dedicatory letter to his old friend Cardinal Julian is just as appropriately proportioned for asserting his authority as were the visionary reports of the nuns for establishing theirs.

Cusanus's seminal experience reflected a pivotal transition in European history. En route home from his historic attempt to reunite a long divided and now acutely threatened Christendom, the scholar and legate received from "the Father of Lights" his understanding of infinite unity and the coincidence of opposites. According to his recollection, the insight into learned ignorance had come to him *as* this wise unknowing itself. The theme of wise ignorance anticipates the Humanistic spirit that is open to all human knowledge, but also aware of the limits of human knowledge. Cusanus can therefore rightly be considered a Humanistic mystic. The challenge to ecclesiastical authority and unity was acute in his period. The Cusan intellectual mysticism seems futile and dilettantish when it gives rise to the practical ecumenicism of *On the Peace of Faith* (*De Pace Fidei*). However, as a theoretical edifice, his work as a whole must be recognized as a spectacular endeavor to address the late medieval challenge to unity.

Many of Cusanus's propositions now appear patently specious. In order to approach him initially from an angle favorable to his thought, we would do well to consider that, from classical times to the present, it has been evident that when one reasons in terms of the infinite, paradoxes arise. Among the classical masters of paradox, Cusanus mentions Parmenides and Zeno.[8] Parmenides, Philo of Alexandria, and Plotinus offered precedents for the conception of God as the One, boundless or infinite. After Cusanus, we might think of Pascal's fearful visions of infinitude in the *Thoughts*, or of Leibniz, who will be discussed in a subsequent chapter, or, in modern times, of Georg Cantor's mathematics of transfinite numbers.

Augustine also offered prototypes for the speculation of

Cusanus. Augustine employed the idiom of an incomprehensible knowing or wise ignorance, *docta ignorantia*. According to the *City of God* (12:18), God, whose wisdom paradoxically transcends the simple and the multiple, incomprehensibly comprehends the infinite.[9] Other Augustinian reflections demonstrated that the human mind is incapable of proceeding by steps from the finite to the infinite or to the infinitesimal. The inconceivability of that which is infinitely great or small had been anticipated by Augustine in *On the Trinity*:

> For we do not conceive the greatness of bodies which we have never seen without the aid of memory.... And our reason in fact goes even further, but the phantasy does not follow; as when our reason proclaims the infinity of number which no vision in the thought of corporeal things has yet grasped. The same reason teaches us that even the tiniest bodies can be divided infinitely; but when we have finally arrived at the slightest and most minute particles which we have seen and still remember, we are no longer capable of gazing upon slighter and more minute phantasies....[10]

The senses see small or large objects. The imagination conceives of even smaller or even larger ones. However, the senses and the imagination reach a point beyond which (in the overall system of Augustine) only the intellectual vision might penetrate. Already for Augustine, then, the incommensurable relation of creature to Creator has its mathematical equivalent in the lack of proportion of the finite to the infinite. By the very nature of things and concepts, an unbridgeable chasm remains between the human and the divine power to conceive.

One of Cusanus's demonstrations of the "coincidence of opposites" proceeds to the conclusion that an infinite straight line contains the triangle, the circle, and all other geometrical figures. If his arguments now appear to be riddled with medieval flukes, his intention was to demonstrate that the finite stands in no proportion to the infinite, even though the finite is measured by the infinite, indeed is, as he puts it, a "contraction" of the infinite. As the circle waxes larger, its curve approaches a straight line. Yet no succession of incrementations can ever flatten its curve. This is exemplary for the relationship of normal knowledge to mystical knowledge: to comprehend the being of God, the mind would have to become one with its object. Since the infinite is incommensurable with the finite, the mind can gain no positive knowledge of God. Since the intellect is not truth it can only approximate its object. The mind will always fall short, since the truth could be comprehended "infinitely more precisely." Cusanus writes that the mind is to truth as a polygon is to a circle in which it is inscribed. The more angles are added to the polygon, the more it resembles the circle: "However, even if the number of its angles is increased *ad infinitum*, the polygon never becomes equal [to the circle] unless it is resolved into an identity with the circle" (DI 1:3, 10).

Human uncertainty is therefore also a correlative of the infinite differences that constitute the plurality of the world. This plurality is embodied concretely in human individuality and in the diversity of things. Uncertainty and multiplicity thus allow for a latitude of opinion; they allow for a tolerance bounded by the one faith or by faith in the One. The uncertainty of all finite knowledge becomes wise, becomes *docta ignorantia*, by recognizing that not human reason but the intellectual vision approaches through grace the higher truth of the world. The gateway to wise ignorance is the "coincidence of opposites."

In order to understand the function of the coincidence of opposites in Cusanus's mysticism, it is necessary to recall the role of medieval analogy. Cusanus retains the medieval notion that the created being of things is full of natural analogies which refer us to the divine being. For Hildegard, the ensembles of visible nature pointed to the eternal truths of God. For Eckhart, the denial of images resulted in an increased reliance on paradoxes—of the inner and outer, of being and nothing. Cusanus equates the visible with the conceivable. Among all things perceptible to our minds, none are more perfect than numbers. All comparison intrinsically presupposes number: "Perhaps for this reason Pythagoras deemed all things to be constituted and understood through the power of numbers" (DI 1:1, 3). Eternity, oneness, Creator, and creature are therefore translated into a code of numerical or symbolic relations. Cusanus thus develops a new mode of analogy in which form or number—things visible to the mind—are developed by seemingly logical steps until an impasse of thought yields an enigmatic symbol: a construct that can be formulated precisely but not conceived by the mind.

Analogy thus acquires a fresh profile in Cusanus, symbolizing what cannot be comprehended by reason.[11] He refers to enigmas— reminding us of the *ainigma* of Paul's word that is translated in the King James Bible as, "through a glass darkly" (1 Corinthians 13:12): "Now we see but a poor reflection; then we shall see face to face. Now I know in part; then I shall know fully, even as I am fully known." The effect of the translation into number and relation is not to obviate or explain away the mysteries of faith, but rather to make them all the more palpable and provocative.

Cusanus's demonstration of the coincidence of opposites recalls
Anselm's ontological proof of God's existence. The Absolute Maximum is that than which there can be no greater: "Hence, since the
absolutely Maximum *is* all that which can be, it is *altogether* actual. And
just as there cannot be a greater, so for that same reason there cannot be
a lesser, since it is all that which can be" (DI 1:4, 11). The doctrine of the
coincidence of opposites is necessary because we can deny no predi-
cate to a God who is the infinite unity. The paradox that in God the
greatest that can be coincides with the smallest that can be, is followed
by elaborate demonstrations that the infinite line contains or enfolds
all figures: the triangle, the curve, the circle, etc. From the infinite line
that enfolds all figures in its infinite unity, book one of *Learned Ignorance* moves to the inconceivable figure of the infinite sphere: "In an
infinite sphere we find that three maximum lines—of length, width,
and depth—meet in a center. But the center of a maximum sphere is
equal to the diameter and the circumference" (DI 1:23, 70). The definition of God as a circle with its center everywhere and its circumference
nowhere has been traced back to ancient roots. The paradox fascinates
the mind by its combination of precision and inconceivability.

In Cusanus, analogy as unlike likeness displays an extreme inner
tension. Nothing in this world is like its divine origin—yet the sensible
is still a "figure" of the supersensible, the temporal still a "figure" of
the eternal.[12] The unlike likeness even projects its parameters back
onto our own world: "Since the Maximum [i.e., God] is like a maximum sphere, we now see clearly that it is the one most simple and
most congruent measure of the whole universe and of all existing
things in the universe, for in it the whole is not greater than the part,
just as an infinite sphere is not greater than an infinite line" (DI 1:23,
72). What can be known and measured is only knowable and measur-
able with reference to what passes beyond knowledge or measure.
Thought is not merely limited by, it may indeed depend on and implicate the unthinkable.

What is still distinctively medieval in his thought is the presentation of a kind of hierarchy of levels of being, each of which corresponds, in a manner that seems remarkable to us, to the transcendent
unity of God. Since the infinite stands in no proportion to the finite,
these levels are not a ladder that we can climb in order to get a glimpse
of God. What the principle of ascent tells us is that all our concepts of
God—and indeed all our notions of the world and its entities—are
inadequate. Conversely, the incommensurability of the infinite and
the finite leaves each level and eventually each human individual to
its own immediate confrontation with the infinite being.

The levels conceptualized in *On Learned Ignorance* are: 1. God, as the "Absolute Maximum" and as the "coincidence of opposites" (whereby these terms are not understood as a positive statement about God, but rather as a circumscriptive term for God, as surpassing our finite understanding); 2. the world, which is called the "maximum contractum" and as such both mirrors and condenses the infinite unity of God; 3. the individual thing or creature, as a "contraction" of the world and hence as a likeness of all other things; 4. Christ as the Absolute Maximum, contracted or concretized in the individual Jesus; and 5. the Church, as the mystical body of Christ. True to the pattern of *omnes in omnibus*, the Church contains a maximum diversity of individuals, each of whom reflects the truth by his or her own lights. *De Docta Ignorantia* concludes in a vision of a Christendom that encompasses diversity while remaining one. This is the voice of the politically minded churchman Cusanus, the figure involved in the disputes of the conciliar and papal parties, who favored first one side and then the other, always in pursuit of unity; the theoretician of compromise in the conflicts between Hussite heterodoxy and Catholic orthodoxy, Eastern and Western Churches, Christians and Muslims. The unity and harmony that could not be attained for parties in the real world of Cusanus is attained by the ideal individuals of his thought: "For 'church' bespeaks a oneness of many [members]—each of whom has his personal truth preserved without confusion of natures or of degrees; but the more *one* the church is, the greater it is; hence, this church—[*viz.,*] the church of the eternally triumphant—is maximal, since no greater union of the church is possible" (DI 3:12, 261).

The Cusan coincidence of opposites conforms not only to a new outlook on society, but also to a changing view of nature. In the Cusan infinite, each part is also infinite. God is "all in all." All finite things are said to be in all other things. Cusanus knew the motif of *quodlibet in quodlibet* from Eckhart's Latin works, where the designation of God as an infinite sphere with its center everywhere, its circumference nowhere, was discussed along with reflections on the mercy of a divine grace, of which the least measure for the Creator is the greatest measure for the creature. Between the inward-looking perspective of medieval reflective mysticism and the vitalistic theories of Renaissance and Baroque nature mysticism, there is a continuity in the use of the scriptural-philosophical motif of *quodlibet in quodlibet* or *omnes in omnibus*.[13] Jasper Hopkins, who has performed a valuable service in distinguishing between errors in the Cusan reasoning and the misunderstandings of its interpreters, characterizes the notion of *quodlibet in quodlibet* as "philosophically bizarre"; its ramifications are "based on an altogether dubious notion of the relation between part and whole."[14] And yet at first glance, the logic of "all in all" is impeccable: if God is in all things, and they are in him, then all things are necessarily in all other things as well.[15] The difficulty—which we should not be surprised to encounter—is simply that we can't make sense of this state of affairs. Therefore, we need to ask if *quodlibet in quodlibet* isn't "bizarre" in much the same way that the coincidence of opposites is bizarre. To rebuke or defend these propositions is not enough. The persistence of the motif of *omnes in omnibus* in German mysticism demands interpretation.

In *On Seeking God* (*De Quaerendo Deum*), Cusanus wrote that if we consider things in nature "with the eye of the intellect," we cannot doubt that in any piece of wood, stone, ore, gold, mustard, or millet seed all possible artful corporeal forms are potentially present (*omnes artificiales corporeas formas in potentia esse*). We know this because each has to contain the circle, triangle, rectangle, cube, and so on, in order to be able to give rise to other forms of animals, fruits, flowers, leaves, trees, as well as the likeness of all forms in this and countless other (possible) worlds. If a human artist can make a likeness of a king from a piece of wood, then so much greater is the skill of the divine Artist who fashions the likeness of all forms from a minute corporeal thing (*de quodlibet minutissimo corpusculo*).[16] In this instance, the *quodlibet in quodlibet* is validated by two considerations: 1. The processes of mutation, growth, flowering, and transformation in nature or salvation (the latter is alluded to in the *granum sinapis*) require that new things are potentially contained in certain other things; 2. the creation of all things from some "minutest corpus" requires that all were initially in one thing. "God therefore does not create out of anything else, but rather out of himself (*ex se*), since he is everything that can be." The fact that God creates from no material except his own being means that all things were in God, and he is still in all, and therefore through him all are in all. In a veritable hymn of paradoxes, God is characterized as "*in omnibus omnia, in nullo nihil et omnia et nihil in ipso ipse, integre, indivise in quolibet quantumcumque parvo et simul in nullo omnium....*"[17] All things in all, in nothing nothing, and indivisible in even the smallest of things! These paradoxes can be taken negatively, as expressions of the limits of rational discourse about God, or they can be taken positively, as a praise for the wonders of a creation in which everything arises from the least seed and the whole is "contracted" into each part.

*Omnes in omnibus* is a mystical precept that subsumes all sources of authority and in turn promises answers to questions in many spheres. The ultimate validation for the Cusan *quodlibet in quodlibet* is the *omnes in omnibus* of the triune God, of whom each trinitarian person can, in its own respective way, be called "all in all": the Father in being, the Son in power, the Spirit in actuation (*Deus pater est omnia in omnibus, Deus filius potest omnia in omnibus, Deus spiritus operatur omnia in omnibus*).[18] To the intellectual vision that sees beyond the finite qualities of matter, the true nature of things mirrors the incomprehensible being of this triune divinity.

In *On Learned Ignorance*, Cusanus approvingly quotes the pre-Socratic Anaxagoras, "*quodlibet esse in quodlibet*,"[19] thereby again confirming his claim that, in some way, all thinkers and all believers are really in agreement. Pythagoras is a source as well. Cusanus has a tendency to equate creation and generation with enumeration or with the construction of form[20]—as if things consisted of points, lines, and figures, intensified into solid objects. Formally and numerically, all things can be said to be in all other things. This doesn't signify that they are in them *actually*. They are enfolded in them in the same way all figures are enfolded into the infinite line. "In a stone all things are stone; in a vegetative soul, vegetative soul; in life, life; in the senses, the senses; in sight, sight; in hearing, hearing; in imagination, imagination; in reason, reason; in intellect, intellect" (DI 2:5, 119).

The idea that everything is in everything clearly owes much to precedent and reasoning. If the one thing is to grow into all things, or any thing turn into any other thing, then there has to be a *tertium quid*, a medium with a universal potential. Indeed, Cusanus recognizes an eternal "creative force" or "virtue" (*virtus creativa*).[21] But on top of these other defining contexts, the term *omnes in omnibus* may also have been an experience, conditioned by his age of conflict and change: a divinely reconfirmed article of faith in times of strife and threatened unity. There is a hint of immediate intuition when Cusanus tells us:

Consider more closely and you will see that each actually existing thing is tranquil because of the fact that in it all things *are* it and that in God it is God. You see that there is a marvelous oneness of things, an admirable equality, and a most wonderful union, so that all things are in all things. You also understand that for this reason there arises a difference and a union of things. For it is not the case that each thing was able to be actually all things.... This, then, caused all things to exist in different degrees.... Therefore, in each thing all things are tranquil, since one degree could not exist without another—just as with the members of a body each contributes [something] to the other, and all are content in all. (DI 2:5, 120)

Anticipating the later panvitalism and universal harmony of the nature mysticism of the Renaissance, Cusanus conceives of unity here as the content of an intuition accessible to all who have eyes to see it. The minutely individualized properties of things can be seen as inherently meaningful. All things are harmonious and beautiful by virtue of their tranquil being in God.

Out of the "enfolding" (*complicans*) Oneness of God, the world and all things in it are incomprehensibly "unfolded" (*explicata*) as manifestations of God. The world is a "contraction" of God. So is everything, in its own way. The universe is a likeness of the Absolute, and all things are images of God, reflected in various mirrors and at various distances. If God were to turn away from the world, the mirror images would vanish. The notion that all things are "contractions" of God is almost as mysterious as the notion of *omnes in omnibus*; however, either term serves the same purpose of conceiving the world, the human being, or the discrete thing, in the manner of an image—shortened or refracted perhaps, but nothing without the divine source which is everything in each individual contracted creation.

Cusanus undertakes a critical assessment of certain notions of nature. He evaluates the merits of the Platonic theory of a world-soul in accounting for the harmony of all motions—which presumably spring from one single guiding motion and entelechy. Although he rejects the doctrine of the world-soul, he finds certain elements attractive in the concept. In discussing it, he makes use of his own terminology of enfolding and contraction. He regards the Aristotelian criticism of Platonism as lacking in "deep discernment." In the final analysis, he rejects the world-soul only to the extent that it is considered as an independent creative agent mediating between the power of God and the motions of nature (DI 2:9 145–150). But since the Platonic concept is useful for his purposes, Cusanus employs "learned ignorance" to resolve the misunderstanding between Platonists and Aristotelians. The true mediating power in nature is the omnipresent Word: "Hence, the connecting necessity is not, as the Platonists maintained, a mind which is inferior to the Begetting Mind; rather, it is the divine Word and Son, equal with the Father. And it is called 'Logos' or 'Essence,' since it is the Essence of all things" (DI 2:9, 149). Cusanus goes on to explain that, "only God is the 'world-soul' and 'world-mind'." The philosophers conceived of the world-soul because they were not adequately instructed about the Divine Word and Absolute Maximum (DI 2:9, 150). Thus Cusanus retains the functions and scope of the world-soul, since it proves useful in discussing order and life in the world; but he integrates nature with the universal informing power of the Word. The debate that he sees between Aristotelians and Platonists is to acquire relevance in the mysticism, philosophy, and theology of the next century. For his part, Cusanus reconfirms a long tradition in combining the Platonic-Neoplatonic understanding of the guiding power of spirit in nature with the Word as the divine utterance of creation:

> Therefore, this spirit, which is called nature, is spread throughout, and contracted by, the entire universe and each of its parts. Hence, nature is the enfolding (so to speak) of all things which occur through motion. But the following example shows how this motion is contracted from the universal into the particular and how order is preserved throughout its gradations. When I say "God exists," this sentence proceeds by means of a certain motion but in such an order that I first articulate the letters, then the syllables, then the words, and then, last of all, the sentence— although the sense of hearing does not discern this order by stages. In like manner, motion descends by stages from the universal [*universum*] unto the particular, where it is contracted by the temporal or natural order. But this motion, or spirit, descends from the Divine Spirit, which moves all things by this motion. Hence, just as in an act of speaking there is a certain spirit [i.e., breath] which proceeds from him who speaks—which is contracted into a sentence, as I mentioned—so God, who is Spirit, is the one from whom all motion descends. For Truth says: "It is not you who speak but the Spirit of your Father who speaks in you." A similar thing holds true for all other motions and operations. (DI 2:10, 153)

As often before, the Word is the term for the unity of the created and uncreated worlds. However, with Cusanus the old mysticism of the cosmic Word is combined with new and remarkably modern theories of the universe. It would be a mistake to see this as a matter of pure scientific deduction. His "corollaries concerning motion" and nature turn the world into a kind of riddle; but, as is to be expected, his solution lies in an article of faith: his conceptualization of the hypostatic union of the two natures in Christ.

*On Learned Ignorance* in any event combines many kinds of speculation, even touching on empirical physics. In the chapter devoted to the "corollaries regarding motion," Cusanus reflects that no motion can be absolutely maximal and none absolutely minimal. The second negation rules out complete rest. No body within the universe, not the fixed stars nor the earth, can be stationary. The earth is not the center of the world; and the sphere of the fixed stars is not its circumference (DI 2:11, 157).

The infinity of divine measure and the inherent inequality and imprecision of all motions and relations not only undermines all certainties; the world here appears to be without bearings. Certainty is to be restored through the paradoxical vision of the inconceivable absolute which is God:

> Precise equidistance to different things cannot be found except in the case of God, because God alone is Infinite Equality. Therefore, He who is the center of the world, viz., the Blessed God, is also the center of the earth, of all spheres, and of all things in the world. Likewise, He is the infinite circumference of all things. (DI 2:11, 157)

If we know now that the imprecision of measurement is not the hindrance to knowledge he saw it to be, Cusanus appears quite forward-looking in his awareness of the relativity of perceptions. He knows that we apprehend motion only through comparison with something fixed. If a passenger on a ship did not know that a body of water was moving or did not see the shore from the ship, he would have no way of recognizing that the ship was in motion. Similarly, every vantage point imagines that it stands at the center of things; the person occupying it thinks that it is immovable and all other things in motion: "assuredly, it would always be the case that if he were on the sun, he would fix a set of poles in relation to himself; if on the earth, another set; on the moon, another; on Mars, another; and so on. Hence, the world-machine will have its center everywhere and its circumference nowhere, so to speak; for God, who is everywhere and nowhere, is its circumference and center" (DI 2:12, 162). Cusanus's world-view, with its relativism and its postulate of God as the Absolute Maximum to whom nothing can be denied, even leads him to regard the likelihood of intelligent life on other planets and stars, and even to recognize that the character of that life would have to reflect its planetary or stellar environment (DI 2:12, 171–172).

The conceptual center of the Cusan world-view is Christ as the "Concept of all Concepts." Book two of *On Learned Ignorance* establishes that the universal differences among all things are organized into species which differ by degree. However, there cannot be an infinite number of degrees, because this would be tantamount to no degrees at all. Nor can one reach the absolute maximum or minimum by an infinite regression. Nor can there be any world-soul, as an independent power between God and material nature. There is a gap in the conceptual structure of the world. The being of the Creator with the infinite fullness of actual and possible being is proximate to the created world, which contracts infinite possibility into finite actuality. This allows Cusanus to formulate the central concepts of his Humanistic system:

> Now, human nature is that [nature] which, though created a little lower than the angels, is elevated above all the [other] works of God; it enfolds intellectual and sensible nature and encloses all things within itself, so that the ancients were right in calling it a microcosm, or a small world. Hence, human nature is that [nature] which, if it were elevated unto a union with Maximality, would be the fullness of all the perfections of each and every thing, so that in humanity all things would attain the supreme gradation. (DI 3:3, 198)

Christ, as the "Absolute Maximum contractum," stands at the new center of the conceptual structure of the world: the "Concept of Concepts." The intricate conceptual framework makes the union of the Absolute Maximum with the contracted maximum appear both necessary and incomprehensible. The real necessity and proof of this union reside for Cusanus in faith and Scripture. The answer to his enigmas is placed at the end of *On Learned Ignorance*. It is his evocation and interpretation of the Word:

> For Jesus—who is blessed forever, who is the goal not only of all understanding (because He is Truth) but also of all sensing (because He is Life), and who, further, is both the goal of all being (because He is Being itself) and the perfection of every creature (because He is God and man)—is, as the goal of every utterance, *there* heard incomprehensibly. For every utterance has come forth from Him and terminates in Him. Whatever truth is in an utterance is from Him. Every utterance has as its goal instruction; therefore, [every utterance] has as its goal Him who is Wisdom itself. "Whatever things were written were written for our instruction." Utterances are befigured in written characters. "By the Word of the Lord the heavens were established." Therefore, all created things are signs of the Word of God. Every corporeal utterance is a sign of a mental word. The cause of every corruptible mental word is an incorruptible word, viz., a concept. Christ is the incarnated Concept of all concepts, for He is

the Word made flesh. Therefore, Jesus is the goal of all things. (DI 3:11, 247)

All created things are divine signs, all words are creatures. The truth or inner meaning of all meanings out of which every created utterance proceeds and to which it returns in its latent intention of revelation is the Concept of all Concepts. The intricate conceptual framework is designed to lead from every direction toward this prearranged outcome. In order to enhance the Word as the final answer to all mysteries, Cusanus heightens and multiplies the mysteries. In the process, he raises new questions, thereby creating a perspective that eventually proves fertile in the natural science of the Renaissance.

Hypothetical philosophical inquiry and unquestioned faith condition one another in Cusanus. This is why there is a thematic concordance of the more speculative works such as *On Learned Ignorance* and *On Conjectures* with the contemplative ones such as *On the Vision of God* (*De Visione Dei*) or *On the Sonship of God* (*De Filiatione Dei*).

In dropping the Eckhartian terms of mystical inwardness,[22] the *function* of Eckhart's terms—the confirmation of an immediate relationship with God—is recovered by means of the paradoxes of reciprocality: In the contemplation of God, seeing and being seen again coincide. Each creature only exists because it is seen by and also sees God.[23] These paradoxes are equivalent to the proposition that all things are contractions of God and of the world as a whole. The finite creature is created in the likeness of the infinite God. Divine infinity corresponds in the world of contraction and finitude to the absolute uniqueness of what is individual.

Cusanus expands on this individuality of being and knowing in his most contemplative work, *The Vision of God*. In it, the relationship of the believer to God is compared to perspective in the portraits that are crafted so that from every angle the eyes of the painted figure look directly into those of the spectator. Thus, writes Cusanus, God faces directly every believer who turns to him. Within God, all natures are embraced. The infinite majesty of God is hence correlative with the unique individuality of every believer. The author of *The Vision of God* inquires in contemplative prayer, "For what is more absurd than to ask that You, who are all in all (*omnia in omnibus*), give Yourself to me?... And while I am quietly reflecting in this manner, You, O Lord, answer me in my heart with the words: 'Be your own and I will be yours' (*'Sis tu tuus et ego ero tuus'*).[24] In this tract, composed for the Benedictine monks at Tegernsee, Cusanus proved that the abstractions

of his speculation concerning the infinite unity of God also had devo-
tional-contemplative equivalents. In chapter ten, the Cusan coincidence of opposites is interpreted so that it functions virtually the same
as Eckhart's unity of seeing and being seen, hearing and being
heard—and so that it is also equated with the Paradise from which the
children of Adam have been barred. Chapter ten utilizes the reflexive
metaphor of Eckhart: the word broadcast by the preacher is like the
speaking-creating of God which touches each individual distinctively.
In chapter eleven, God as the "succession without succession" is compared to the contemplation of a clock: the successive striking of time
can be understood as enfolded simultaneously into the concept of the
clock, unfolding then as successive time.

The mystical faith as it is conceived by Cusanus is mentally alert,
encompassing the contemplation of God, as well as a human self-
awareness and an endless striving for truth—a Faustian motif that can
be traced back to Gregor of Nyssa. The themes of Cusanus's most
characteristically mystical writings form a coherent whole with the
more philosophical works. There is a "seeing of the mind" (*videre mentis*), he writes; this seeing surpasses "the ability to comprehend" (*posse
comprehendere*). After distinguishing that one thing is greater than
another, "the mind's simple power of sight" (*simplex visio mentis*) is
drawn by the desire to view that which is beyond all measure.[25] This is
the supreme object, the *apex theoriae* (as one of his works is called).
Truth is integral, but it has many facets and aspects. According to *On
Learned Ignorance*, the truth, as we discern it, is a temporally contracted
"sign" or "image" of a supratemporal, intellectual, and divine truth
(DI 3:7, 226). This is then amplified to a mystical epistemology in his
*On Conjectures*. Our conjectures are said to arise in our mind, in the
same way that the created external world arises in the infinite divine
ground (*Coniecturas a mente nostra uti realis mundus a divina infinita
ratione prodire oportet*.[26]) Speculative thought is thus itself a contracted
reflection of the infinite divine being.

This daring confirmation of the authority of a conjecturing, seeking, speculating mind is probably the most promising legacy of
Cusanus. He is said to have exerted little influence on later German
philosophy and mysticism (except through Giordano Bruno, who then
transmitted something of his thought to later thinkers, including Leibniz and the German Romantics).[27] The Reformation scarcely knew him
at all; and even within the Catholic Church, his theories lapsed into
discredit or oblivion. As a blow for toleration, his *On the Peace of Faith*
is also rather ambivalent. The cards are always stacked against other
faiths. It has been observed that the goal of his pluralism is unity; and

that his toleration disregarded those who lacked power for rivalling hegemony—the Jews in fifteenth-century Germany.[28]

But neither should one underestimate his universalism or the bold example it set for Humanistic thinking. The mere fact of his knowing and thinking about other religions had a positive effect. It was in Cusanus's spirit of informed Humanism that Johannes Reuchlin (1455–1522) initiated the Hebrew and Kabbalistic studies that provided him the incentive and competence to take a position against the confiscation and burning of Jewish books during the struggle of Humanism against obscurantism at the beginning of the sixteenth century.

Beginning with Cusanus and continuing from the fifteenth through the seventeenth century, the themes of German mysticism are expanded and reinterpreted. There is a great tendency toward syncretism. The inner world of reflective mysticism is replaced by the outer world of nature mysticism. It is portentous—a sign of a tradition at the crossroads—that Cusanus anticipates the Faustian typology, even while warning the readers of *On Learned Ignorance* to be on guard against the evil magician—the wicked counterpart to the mystic's striving for union with God through knowledge and faith. The magicians claim that by faith and with the assistance of magic practices a man can become united with "a nature of influential spirits...akin to himself," and by their power perform miracles involving fire, water, musical knowledge, transformations, or the revelation of things hidden: "For it is evident that with regard to all these [wonders] there is deception as well as a departure from real life and from truth. Accordingly, such [magicians] are bound to alliances, and to pacts of unity, with evil spirits" (DI 3:11, 253). Forming covenants with evil spirits, the magician here emerges as the *wicked* man of faith, striving for forbidden transcendence and illicit knowledge. The magician is the false mystic who perverts theory and practice by usurping higher powers.

The outer limits of transgression have been drawn. The shadowy figure of the magician will soon make his spectacular entrance into German intellectual history: in the historical-legendary theologian Johann Faust, and in the two men of science and magic who will be discussed in the next chapter.

# 5

# Nature and Scripture

## Mysticism Between Renaissance and Reformation

By the second half of the fifteenth century, developments were in progress that would confront the European mind with a world unlike anything hitherto known. In 1453, Constantinople, the capital of a thousand-year-old empire, fell to the Ottomans. The refugees who fled westward included Greek scholars whose presence in Italy increased the familiarity and prestige of the Platonistic tradition. As if to offset the loss of their Eastern half, Europeans were expanding their knowledge to include unheard-of lands and seas.

Humanists were reviving the learning of the past, casting out the dross of tradition, and undermining long-standing beliefs. Cusanus had questioned the Constantine Donation granting temporal powers to the pope. Now, it was exposed as a forgery by Lorenzo Valla, who utilized techniques which became a model for textual criticism. Printing presses were disseminating knowledge in the new mechanically reproduced form. Sixty thousand books had been printed by 1500, two thirds of them in Germany. Even prior to the printing of Luther's German New Testament in September 1522, no less than eighteen printings of the complete Bible had come out in German.[1] As Elizabeth Eisenstein has observed about the rising availability of books, "The sheer increase in the quantity of copies in circulation was actually of immense significance."[2] Old authoritative works were printed no less than new ones. This enriched the mix of opinions without initially favoring one side over the other. It spotlighted questions without answering them.

New divisions appeared within every graduate faculty giving rise to lively pamphlet wars. Like theology, medicine and jurisprudence, pulpit oratory was also caught up in the conflict. Advocacy of the "new learning" and the pursuit of eloquence was taken up by preachers and teachers seeking to implement traditional evangelical goals.[3]

When Eckhart was charged with heresy, he had faced his accusers in isolation. With the print medium, "partisanship" found its requisite weapon and banner. Never before had rival assertions had such a capacity to command immediate attention and partisan engagement. As the Renaissance information revolution followed its soaring curve upward, rival opinions vied for attention and acceptance. A new claim to authority based on the common sense of the people would soon be cited against whole phalanxes of the learned—often enough by the learned themselves.

However, there are indications that the common people were perplexed and frightened. Confusion and anxiety are conveyed by apocalyptic prophecies, like the one that came to light at the Untersberg near Salzburg in the early 1520s (a period in which Paracelsus was no stranger to Salzburg). It was foretold that peasants, henchmen, artisans, and even women would slaughter one another in grim conflict. The survivors would be finished off by a returning Emperor Friedrich of chiliastic legend.[4]

As the events of the Reformation began to unfold in 1517, the individual conscience experienced sharp inner conflicts. In a few compressed years, the ideas of the Reformation were spread far and wide by the new print medium. Flooding Europe, the new doctrines polarized it, fragmented it internally, and set it off from its past. Like our own time, the Reformation was an age in which bridges were burned while they were still being crossed.

German mysticism during the Renaissance and the Reformation responded to the "information revolution" and to the new crises of authority. The great slogans of the age resonated with this background. This applies to the Humanistic return "to the sources," to the Lutheran or Paracelsian appeal to a superior folk knowledge, to Luther's "universal priesthood of the laity" and to his "scriptural principle," as well as to the Spiritualist demand for an "unpartisan" faith, to be effected by a transferral of authority from the outer letter to the inner word and spirit.

The old world was coming to an end. It had to be remade or reborn, to become whatever it had within it to be. Many great figures of the age therefore possessed an epic-heroic quality. Because the ultimate ground of truth was in dispute in every sphere, Agrippa von Nettesheim, Paracelsus, and Luther, each in his own way, had the stature of titans. Endtime and renewal were conjoined in the thinking of this age. Mysticism originated either in the endeavor to synthesize all sources of authority or in the attempt to champion one above all others.

Born in Cologne in 1486, Heinrich Cornelius Agrippa von
Nettesheim vacillated between the tendency to synthesize and the tendency to accord exclusive authority to the Bible. One of the most outstanding scholars of his time, Agrippa is thought to have studied law
and medicine in Cologne before entering the military service of the
emperor. Much of his life was spent wandering through Europe from
station to station: Spain, Paris, Dôle in Burgundy, Avignon, London,
Metz, Northern Italy, Lyon, Antwerp, Bonn. His early preoccupations
included alchemy, Kabbalah, and all forms of magic. Agrippa also pere-
grinated between the diverging intellectual tracks of his age. The poles
of his thought were his early Humanism and Renaissance Neoplatonism and the exclusive biblical authority to which he later gravitated.

During Agrippa's early wanderings, he occupied himself for several years with Johannes Reuchlin's classic work of Christian Kabbalah, *De Verbo Mirifico* (1494). Agrippa studied this work during the
first decade of the sixteenth century. New interest in Jewish mysticism
had been initiated by Marsilio Ficino and Pico della Mirandola. Like
Cusanus's *De Pace Fidei*, Reuchlin's work was composed as a colloquy
of religion. It considered the harmony of the beliefs of Jews, Christians,
and Pythagoreans. While championing the correctness of the Christian
doctrines, Reuchlin brought a new interpretation of the Christian-mys-
tical theme of the Word into play, an interpretation using Kabbalistic
techniques and focusing on numerical values of letters, crowned by the
four-lettered name of God, the Tetragrammaton. After Reuchlin, Kabbalah remained one of the alternative theologies available to dissenters
and mystical theorists. Agrippa's public espousal of Reuchlin's Kabbalism resulted in his being attacked as a heretical "Judaizer" by the
monks who were his bitter life-long opponents.

Like his slightly younger contemporary Paracelsus, or his counterpart of a subsequent era, Bruno (1548–1600), Agrippa was an independent Renaissance man of affairs and letters, a scholar who did not
bow to the mighty. Though dependent on patronage, he was not
enslaved to it. Though credulously immersed in studies of the magic
arts, he retained the critical spirit of the Humanist in his Latin oeuvre.

In Metz, he was successful in defending a girl against whom
charges of witchcraft had been raised on the sole ground that her
mother had been convicted and burned as a witch. Boldly, Agrippa
placed the Dominican inquisitor on the defensive, countercharging
that the denunciation itself heretically denied the efficacy of the sacraments by presuming that the devil could extend his sway congenitally
from mother to daughter.[5] If the defense testifies to Agrippa's good
sense and courage, it should be added that his convictions were those

of a pious Renaissance *Magus* who placed the "ceremonial magic" of religion above its celestial and natural counterparts.

Agrippa's most famous work, *De Occulta Philosophia*,[6] was completed in an initial manuscript form in 1510 and printed in a revised version in 1533. Natural, celestial, and ceremonial magic are the divisions of this work. Its strength lies in its erudition and systematization. Will-Erich Peuckert has characterized it as an attempt to cleanse medieval magic of the old rank demonism and sorcery by reconsidering it in the revisionary light of Ficino's Humanistic Neoplatonism.[7]

What *De Occulta Philosophia* reveals about Agrippa's thought at this stage in his career is a precarious balance of opposing impulses. On the one hand, he accepts much (as undoubtedly any scholarly *Magus* must) on the basis of received authority. On the other hand, however, the mind of the Humanist remains active and critical in evaluating what he encounters or accepts.

Even in its conceptual structure, *De Occulta Philosophia* appears to be a counterpointing of opposites. Agrippa takes over the three-tiered world of Neoplatonism. Nature, the heavens, and the intellectual or angelic world are the three levels. However, true to Hermetic precept, everything present in the lower levels is said to be present on the higher levels. The earthly elements thus exist not only in their debased earthly form, but also in a celestial form, a state untouched by the extremes of heat, cold, or violent change. In the intellectual world, the elements are the ideas. The orderly hierarchy of worlds is held together by God, the sovereign Archetype. This is not the structure of Cusanus; what the two have in common is the effort to conceptualize the universe beneath the dominant concept of God.

Like Cusanus before him, Agrippa sets great store by the notion that all things are in all things. Chapter eight of the first book refers to this as the unanimous opinion of all the Platonists. The motif of *omnes in omnibus* is complemented by the motif of hierarchy. The higher world communicates itself to the lower by means of the "virtues" that operate in things. These are forces, hidden properties, and astral influences in nature. Containing all three worlds within itself, the human microcosm, through knowledge, exerts a magic influence on external nature. Human nature is threefold, as is the constitution of mind. For the Humanist Agrippa, this trichotomous anthropology also gives rise to a doctrine of free will and to an exalted estimation of the human capacity for knowledge and the power that goes with it.

*De Occulta Philosophia* reflects the influence of Johannes Trithemius, abbot of Spanheim, a compiler of magical lore. A study would be called for to determine whether this assiduous perpetuator of medieval theories of magic may have transmitted the influence of Hildegard's writings on nature and medicine to Agrippa and Paracelsus. Trithemius is a referential figure for the early Agrippa.

In the second decade of the sixteenth century, Agrippa came under the influence of John Colet. Colet was distancing himself from Italian Neoplatonism, moving instead toward the Renaissance strain of Paulism that would also attract Lefèvre d'Etaples and Marguerite of Navarre. Colet's lectures on the Apostle Paul delivered at St. Paul's in London were attended by Agrippa.[8] During this period, the *Magus* began to shift from the synthesis of all authorities toward the exaltation of a single authority. Beginning in 1515, Agrippa's writings register the impact of Colet in the theme of the imitation of Christ as well as in an increasing estimation of the Bible as the only reliable source of truth.

Agrippa's development is of particular interest because of its parallels with and disparities from Luther's path during the same period. In his *Liber de Triplici Ratione Cognoscendi Deum*, Agrippa argues that, "ignorance of God is the source of all evils and the origin of all sins."[9] Knowledge of God, according to the *Liber de Triplici Ratione*, is given in three books, the Book of Creatures, the Book of the Law, and the Book of the Gospel: these are God's three successive revelations, granted respectively to heathens, Jews, and Christians. Natural theology, supported by the medieval and mystical notion of the "participation" of things in the divine nature, is here still included as one of the three mainstays of revelation, though the other two are successively higher. The highest possible theology is the knowledge of God effected by the Holy Spirit. The word *faith* is not used in its new sense, but the intention is close enough to Luther's that Kuhlow ventures to assert that of all the Neoplatonically influenced theologians of the period, Agrippa comes closest to the Reformer's doctrines of *sola scriptura* and *sola fide*.[10] Unfortunately, this tells us too little about the reasons for their affinity. Did Agrippa abandon magic for Holy Scripture, or did he expect to find a more efficacious magic in faith?

In the first years of the sixteenth century, alert minds were groping their way toward the step leading beyond opposition to what was seen as outmoded, but the shape of things to come was still unclear. This applies to Agrippa and Paracelsus, as it does to the Luther whose *Letter to the Christian Nobility* of 1520 still stood in the broad front of a universal reform inspired by Humanism. Agrippa's *Declamatio de Incertitudine et Vanitate Scientiarum et Artium atque Excellentia Verbi Dei*, written around the beginning of the year 1526, was a resounding cry of despair over the uncertainty of all knowledge, save that of the "excellent Word of God." The work came out of a period of personal defeat and hopelessness in Agrippa's life, and it coincided with a crisis for the Reformation. In 1525, Luther, after rejecting Erasmus's defense of free will, parted ways with certain erstwhile supporters, rebuffed dissenters, and hardened his own assessment of the infallibity and clarity of the Bible.

In his *Declamatio*, Agrippa cast doubt on all the sciences, including those he had once practiced. Only the scriptural Word of God is reliable. Here was a position close to Luther's own, and with similarities to the biblical focus of Paracelsus during this same period. Yet neither Agrippa nor Paracelsus embraced the Lutheran Reformation. Neither accepted Luther's doctrine of the unfree will, and both eventually came to characterize Luther as a "sectarian" or "heretic."

Regarding our theme of mystical knowledge, it is important to note that the source of continuity in Agrippa's vacillating ideas lies in his reliance on "illumination" as the source of truth—whether for the magician or for the interpreter of Holy Scripture. Nauert's extensive study of *Agrippa and the Crisis of Renaissance Thought* strongly suggests that the theme (though not the experience) of mystical "illumination" was the stabilizing axis of Agrippa's evolution as a thinker:

> As the present study has repeatedly shown, the mystical solution ran through his thought consistently from his earliest to his latest years. If only the mind of man, having been freed from the bonds of the flesh by careful preparation, can attain mystical illumination, then all knowledge and so all power will be its own. Since Agrippa himself did not claim personal experience of his sort, he had to provide a way out for those like himself who were not mystics. This way was to follow the lead of those who had gained such union, that is, simply and humbly to follow the Bible, which is the work of such illuminates. Even for a profound understanding of Scripture, illumination is necessary.... Mysticism and skepticism, far from being opposed, here exist together.[11]

Mystical "illumination" is always the goal: it is sought first in magic, then in the Bible, which is a report of the illumination of others. Agrippa was therefore open to the authority of the Bible during his entire development. As Nauert states, he adhered to "illumination" as a mystical source of truth. This suggests that the same supreme knowledge that Agrippa had initially sought in magic lore was subsequently sought in Scripture. The question for us is whether the magical universe, with its hierarchies of occult powers and influences, vanished for the revisionist author of the *Declamatio*—or did Agrippa merely eschew certain knowledge of it? And if the world of demons did not cease to exist—if, instead, only human control over it and all certain knowledge of it were lost—then wasn't the world perforce a nightmare realm of demons, a slaughterhouse of Satan? This is close to what we in fact find in the thinking of Luther who, as is well known, had no use for Renaissance magic.

Agrippa's magic world did not disappear: he published a revised *De Occulta Philosophia* in 1533, two years before his death. And the satanic world kept its power for a Luther who fervently believed in witches and devils. The demotion of all supernatural authority beyond that of Scripture meant that any supernatural presence (except the divine presence invoked in prayer and the sacraments) lurked in menacing shadows. Over it, humans could exercise no synergistic control of the kind to which the Renaissance magicians had aspired. When Renaissance magic was vanquished by the modern spirit of the Reformation, the hierarchies of demons and spirits were locked into a common world—as a subversive ever-present enemy within.

Agrippa is now all but forgotten, but his imposing figure and the tragic swan song of his *Declamatio* exerted a profound impact on contemporaries and posterity. Montaigne took over thoughts from the *Declamatio* in his own skeptical *Apology for Raymond Sebond*. Rabelais satirized him as "Herr Trippa" in the Third Book of *Pantagruel*. Elsewhere in *Pantagruel*, Rabelais lets Panurge lampoon the idea that a "Great Soul" unites and animates all things in the universe: it is actually the pandemic Debt, the fact that everyone is in hock to everyone else, that convenes and enlivens our world. There is a deeper meaning in this parody. The appeal of *omnes in omnibus* could speak to a deepening sense of malaise fostered by a budding market-driven system. Things were no longer discretely themselves; they were penetrated by invisible forces that insidiously transformed and quickened every activity. All manner of things were giving rise to other things by virtue of the Great Soul of exchange value. With an increased circulation of ideas, teachings, and beliefs came an incumbent desire to reconcile and coordinate them, to separate the certain from the uncertain, the old from the new; and this was the talent of Nettesheim. Like other mystics, he met with difficulties precisely because he attempted to restore and give meaning to his tradition. As an antidemonologist, Jean Bodin denounced him as a wicked sorcerer who, through his pupil Weyer, discredited the laudable campaign to eradicate all witches.

But the most famous memorial to the restlessly doubting and inquiring mind of Agrippa of Nettesheim was created by Goethe in Faust's opening monolog on the futility of all studies:

> I have, alas, studied philosophy,
> Jurisprudence and medicine, too,
> And, worst of all, theology
> With keen endeavor, through and through—
> And here I am, for all my lore,
> The wretched fool I was before.[12]

Goethe's Faust possesses (aside from his obscure namesake) a rival prototype from the German Renaissance. He was a younger contemporary of Luther and Agrippa, a figure difficult to categorize in retrospect: a physician, medical theorist, and philosopher of nature who was also a critic of conditions and institutions, an interpreter of the Bible, and, as we shall see, a mystic in his own right.

Paracelsus was the name he took after 1528 in order to lend his work its unique trademark; but his given name was resounding enough: Theophrastus Bombastus von Hohenheim. Born near the Swiss monastery of Einsiedeln in 1493 or 1494, he grew up in Villach in the South Austrian province of Carinthia. A physician-father was the source of the son's devotion to medicine. Paracelsus learned in various monastery schools, as well as among the miners and peasants of Carinthia. He acquired medical training at the University of Ferrara, and he claimed to have gathered, during wide peregrinations through Europe, what was known and done both by trained practitioners and common people.

Admirers of Paracelsus have contrasted him favorably with Agrippa. Compared with his eclectic, vacillating Humanistic contemporary, Paracelsus has been portrayed as an intrepid seeker and original thinker.[13] However, Paracelsus's most comprehensive theoretical work, the *Astronomia Magna, or the Entire Philosophia Sagax* (1537), was composed not long after the publication of the *Declamatio de Incertitudine et Vanitate de Scientiarum et Artium* and the belated full publication of *De Occulta Philosophia*. And the Paracelsian *Astronomia Magna* was similar to Agrippa's works in cataloguing and comparing the arts and sciences, dividing them into *artes incertae* and *certae*. Agrippa looked to the authority of the Archetype and Word. The physician Paracelsus argued on the grounds of visible nature and palpable experience. Both men accorded supreme authority to the Bible, Christ, and the gospel promise of redemption. If one separates this polestar from the remaining syntheses of their thought, it loses much of its meaning and consequence.

Like Luther and the Humanists, Paracelsus saw the enemy of progress in an entrenched Scholastic establishment. Kristeller has contended that the rift between Platonic and Aristotelian tendencies only began in the time of Paracelsus.

It was only during the sixteenth century that Aristotelianism began to be attacked in its central territory, that is, in natural philosophy. A series of brilliant thinkers, not unaffected by Aristotelianism or other traditions, but original in their basic intention, people like Paracelsus, Telesio, Patrizi, Bruno, and others, began to propose rival systems of cosmology and natural philosophy which made an impression upon their contemporaries and have been of lasting interest to historians of Renaissance thought.[14]

Paracelsus recognized the buttresses of the old and false dogmas in Aristotle, Avicenna, and Galen. The climactic and tragic turning point of his career occurred in Basel, where, in 1527, he burned the established medical textbook in a public action recalling Luther's announcement of the Ninety-Five Theses or his burning of the papal decretals in Wittenberg. Driven out of Basel by his opponents, Paracelsus embarked upon a life as a legendary and impoverished wanderer, practicing medicine and writing his treatises until his death in Salzburg in 1541.

What Paracelsus professes as a *medicus* draws primarily on "the light of nature," which is distinct from, if complementary to, the light of revealed truth. The inclination is therefore strong to exclude him by definition from the mystical tradition. Nevertheless, no comprehensive study of German mysticism can get around him. Few figures are harder to place—or more seminal. He writes about a knowledge *by* divine illumination, and about a knowledge *of* divine forces in nature. Therefore, even though he makes no strong claim to a personal mystical knowledge, he is rightly classified as a mystic. During the early Reformation, the years that also formed Paracelsus, speculation about the nature of God and the meaning of the Bible was so much in the air that it saturated the medical and scientific reformation of this wandering physician. The term *light of nature* changes meaning in the course of his career. Sometimes it is close to spiritual "illumination," sometimes it appears to be independent of revelation, and sometimes it is explicitly subordinated to the superior light of God. At no time is it *antithetical* to Scripture.[15]

As we shall see, Paracelsus is a figure struggling to assert his authority in an epoch of fast-paced developments and changing values. Repeatedly and rather self-consciously, he refers to his critics' invectives. They malign him as a *Lutherus medicorum*, a "grand heretic." Does he reject the association with the reform in theology? Actually, he is offended by their suggestion that he, the great "monarch" of physicians, is a copy of Luther.[16] From the beginning of his career, Paracelsus composed theological tracts with the same confidence he exuded in his medical works. Certain diatribes and defenses are so colorful that we seem to glimpse him arguing about religion with the patrons of some inn. His tone is personal, artless, pugnacious—it is the manner that the Germans admire as earthy in their Alpine brethren. The less polished drafts of his German oeuvre sometimes seem to sustain the allegations of his alcoholism. In Salzburg in 1524, he was swept along by the events of the Peasant Wars. If his role in these events is not certain, his opinions in any event acquired elements of a radical social criticism, mixed with the fervent faith of the period. Far from any opportunism, a sincere gospel of brotherly love informs Paracelsus's self-conception as a physician.

Since from the very beginning of his career Paracelsus simultaneously pursued theological and medical interests, his work reveals the kind of cross-referenced intuitions of nature and Scripture found in Hildegard and other mystics. An early theological treatise on the Trinity makes frequent references to the *Paramirische Schriften,* his medical writings.[17] His thinking is guided by the correspondences of the microcosm and macrocosm, but also by the relationship of the great and small worlds to the divine being.

Already in the *Liber de Sancta Trinitate* of 1524, Paracelsus applies the time-honored instruments of likeness and analogy in writing of Creator and created nature. The result is that both these mirror their counterpart. There is a peculiar naturalism in his argument that there is a "celestial queen" (*himblische künigin*) corresponding to the Virgin Mary, so that the divine Son is able to be "born from two persons, namely from God and from the goddess." However, the Father retains primacy, so that both "persons" are "in one divinity" (*der sun ist geporen von zweier personen, nemblich von gott und der göttin...beiden personen in einer gottheit*).[18]

Kurt Goldammer prepared a new ground for the interpretation of Paracelsus by publishing the theological writings and calling attention to their long-standing relationship to the scientific and medical treatises,[19] and by documenting the eschatological elements in the thought of Paracelsus.[20] The natural world, the human being, and the historical world are all conceived in the light of an eschatological fullness of time. This helps explain the low esteem in which Aristotle, Galen, and Scholasticism are held. Scholasticism had analyzed growth in nature by means of the categories developed by Aristotle for the description of a world which was uncreated and eternal.[21] Both Paracelsus and Luther were convinced that the world was rapidly approaching its end. The red thread of an expanded eschatological principle runs through Paracelsus's medical theory, through his vitalistic naturalism, and through his critique of institutions. Just as there is a succession of ages with a beginning and end, so too, matter, the body, and the cosmos have their natural lifespans.

As a theoretician with polyhistorical interests, Paracelsus confronts us with an envisaged world somewhere between that of the early magician Agrippa and that of the mature Luther: between the eclectic authority of all possible sources and the exclusive authority of Scripture. Gone are the supercelestial tiers. Yet nature is still replete with myriad supersensible "influences." In delineating his understanding of nature, Paracelsus borrows terminologies from the alchemists and mystics, as well as from Luther. In proceeding from the investigation of the great world to the small world, the theoretical physician proceeds, like the mystic, from the visible to the invisible and from the exterior to the interior, *von aussen nach innen*. The human creature is a "mirror" image cast in the elements. Paracelsus also adapts the Lutheran or Spiritualist terminology of "faith" against "works."[22]

The common image of Paracelsus is too much attuned to the fantasizer of nature, who wrote of "elemental spirits," sylphs, undines, salamanders, and gnomes, to accomodate his proximity to the biblical stringency of Luther. The two are distinguished by many doctrinal and philosophical differences. What they share in common is their sense of a real divine presence at work in nature and the human soul. For Luther, it suffices to affirm this power through faith. It is enough that the believer is directed to it in the sacraments. Paracelsus, as it were, diffracts the divine power across a diverse spectrum of colors and forces. Luther's *Letter to the German Nobility* encouraged the medical profession to reform itself without his inexpert counsel. Paracelsus is engaged in healing the mortal body in nature. He sets store by the time-honored precept that God created not only the human being but nature in his own image. Hence, there is a triad of divine "principles" operative in a continuing creation.

In an early treatise, *De Viribus Membrorum* (also entitled *De Spiritu Vitae*), Paracelsus wrote of a "spirit of life": it is present in all members of the body as a single force and is "the highest grain or seed of life" (*ligt in allen glidern des leibs wie...der eine geist die eine kraft in einem wie dem andern, und ist das höchste korn des lebens*).[23] This vital force is ubiquitous in the vital totality of nature: "From all the stars and influences of the entire heavens as far as the firmament extends lies the

force of the *spiritus vitae* and is like an invisible celestial vapor and
unites itself with it as cold and warmth, so that they make a tempera-
ture" (*Aus allem gestirn und influenz des ganzen himels so weit das firmament begreift, ligt die kraft des spiritus vitae und ist gleich einem vopori
coelesti invisibili und unirt sich mit dem als kelte und werme so sie ein tem-
peratur machen*).[24]

The *spiritus vitae* therefore appears to be a mediating power within
nature, like the *spiritus mundi* in Agrippa's *De Occulta Philosophia*. In his
later *De Vera Influentia Rerum*, Paracelsus went beyond the idea of the
omnipresent power of life, taken as if independent of God, by making
the "virtues" or influences into the equivalent of the *rationes seminales* or
*causae primordiales*: "For each virtue is uncreated; that is, God is without
beginning and not created. Thus all virtues and forces were in God
before heaven and earth and before all things were created, when God
was a spirit and hovered over the waters..." (*dan ein ietliche tugent ist
unbeschaffen; das ist, got ist on anfang und nicht beschaffen. so sind alle tugen-
den und kreft in got gewesen, vor himel und erden, und ehe alle ding beschaffen
sind worden, da got ein geist war und schwebet uber die wasser...*).[25] Thus the
immediacy of the eternal powers or virtues in God tells us that God is at
work in every single blade of grass:

> ...so we now know that a plant has the virtue, the question then
> is how does the virtue come into the plant? The answer then is:
> not from the planets, not from the twelve signs [of the zodiac],
> not from the other stars, but rather from God: he has put it in
> there [*der hats dahin geben*]. And how does it happen that food
> and drink become flesh and blood in the human being? Not from
> the heavens, nor from the earth, elements, fruits, nor even from
> the human being, but rather from God, who has effected the
> transmutation so miraculously. So now, [just as] this proceeds
> from God without any intermediation [*on alle mittel*], in the same
> manner [proceed] the virtues....
>
> ...*so wir nun wissen, das das kraut die tugent hat, so ist die frag, wie
> kompt die tugent in das kraut? so ist der bescheit, nicht aus dem plan-
> eten, nicht aus den zwölf zeichen, nit aus den andern sternen, sonder
> aus got, der hats dahin geben. dan wie kompts, das speis und trank im
> menschen blut und fleisch wird? vom himel nicht, auch von der erden,
> element, früchten, noch auch vom menschen nit, sonder von got, der die
> transmutation also wunderbarlich gemacht hat, das sich das in das
> muß verwantlen, und das da muß ein speis sein. so nun das on alle mit-
> tel, durch kein mittel aus got gehet, so sind auch die tugenten....*[26]

Whether they are called forces or influences or virtues, the powers at work within the vital totality of the world are eternal and divine. In affirming this, Paracelsus appears to retract his belief in an astrological dimension of pathology. But his point is actually that the "true influence," acting through the stars, is divine. The wondrousness of this power is comparable to the "transmutation" of the wine and bread in Communion.

The terms in which the Communion is discussed are not Lutheran; however, Paracelsus, like Luther, does affirm the effective presence of God in the sacrament by invoking the real presence of a miraculous divine power throughout the world. Paracelsus at times even approaches a mysticism of emanation reminiscent of Eckhart: there is a kinship of the divine forces and virtues in nature with the soul in the human being: "...and that God has poured the same forces and virtues into nature, just as [he has poured] the soul into the human being, and that [the forces and virtues] are not unlike the soul, except that [the former] were without beginning with God. The soul, however, is a creature" (...*und das got die selbigen kreft und tugent in die natur gossen hat, wie die sêl in menschen, und das die kreft der sêl nicht ungleich sind, alein das sie on anfang bei got gewesen sind. die sêl aber ist ein creatur*).[27]

The soul is created. However, it stems directly from God, just as the divine powers in nature stem directly from God. This is close to reflective mysticism. It seems that the soul would need only look within, need only look to its own origin as soul, to recognize, as Eckhart's mysticism recognizes, its birth and the birth of all creatures in God. If Paracelsus does not take this step, it is not because the premises were alien to him, but because his interests lie in the phenomenal world of nature. The realm of place, time, number, and body imposes its own agenda. Instructed by the light of nature, the physician researches the temporal moments of the eternal powers that affect the health of the patient and the healing potencies of substances and herbs.

But in caring for what is temporal, the *medicus* cannot lose sight of the divine origin of all creation. In *Astronomia Magna*, Paracelsus deduces from the Bible that, since the human being was created last, therefore all creatures are like books and letters in which the human origin and nature can be read. Pursuing this thought, he suggests a regressive reading from the human to the prehuman, to a prime material created from nothing and comparable to the wood used by a carpenter: "the first creatures are made from nothing...but through the Word, corpus [and its spirit] are made, from which corpus thereafter all creatures have been made..." (*die ersten geschöpf seind aus nichten*

*gemacht...aber durch das wort ist das corpus [und sein geist] gemacht wor-
den, aus welchem corpus nachfolgend alle creaturen worden...).*[28]

Though Paracelsus did not accentuate the premises of Logos mysticism, they were hardly alien to his thought. The task of the nature
philosopher is to recognize what is eternal from what is natural and
creatural.[29] This recognition takes place when, so to speak, we read
nature in its "letters and books." This is the rationale for Paracelsus's
famous theory of the "signatures of things." The signatures are the
outer visible qualities from which the medical philosopher intuits the
inner powers or virtues of things: the liver-shaped plant that heals the
liver ailment. As we have seen, the idea behind the signatures has a long
tradition, a tradition shared by Agrippa and other thinkers of this age.

For Paracelsus, the origin and crux from which all codes derive
their meaning and form is divine and eternal. The signatures of things
are the letters and books of a nature that only reveals its full significance in the human being. A kind of Rosetta stone, it would seem, the
human microcosm of our nature is twofold: twofold, immortal and
mortal, and again twofold as the mirror of the macrocosm. There is an
"astral body" and there is an "elemental body." Both have a common
origin in a higher quintessence or *Limus.* In the creation of the human
being, a part of this *Limus* was created to be invisible (the astral body)
and a part to be visible (the elemental body). Educated by the firmament, the astral or sidereal body sees into the inner life of nature.[30]

As a corollary to this theory of knowledge, the *Astronomia Magna*
argues that the philosopher of nature recognizes his own science as
integral to the plan of revelation. As a speculative mystic, Paracelsus
therefore goes far beyond Luther. A difficult but signally important
passage reveals that the knowledge of the philosopher is part of the
theophany:

> Therefore, know that God bears such a love to disclose that
> which is secret in the stars, that, on account [of this disclosure],
> he has created the microcosm, [doing so] not solely in the stars,
> to be secretly revealed in the human work, but rather [in order]
> to reveal all of the natural mysteries of the elements, which could
> not happen without the human being. And God wants that the
> things should become visible which are invisible.

> *Darauf wissent, das got zu eröfnen die heimlikeit im gestirn, ein solche
> lieb darzu tregt, das er von wegen der selbigen dan microcosmum
> beschaffen hat, nicht alein in dem gestirn, das heimlich zu offenbaren
> durch des menschen werk, sonder auch alle natürliche mysteria zu*

*offenbaren, welches one den menschen nit het mögen beschehen. und got wil, das die ding sichtbar werden, was unsichtbar ist.*[31]

It is the "godless" astronomers (in rejecting them, Paracelsus follows a long Christian tradition from Augustine to Pico della Mirandola) who claimed the secrets of the stars could be revealed in some arcane human work. The secrets of nature are revealed in and through human nature.

Studying the microcosm to this end, the physician reads the creation by the light of nature, a reading complementary to the light of the spirit. The uncreated divine power gives the root meaning of the created being: "Everything to which nature gives birth it forms in accordance with the virtue that is thus within the thing, and [the things] are to be understood thus" (*Alles, was die natur gebirt das formirt sie nach dem wesen der tugent so im selbigen ist, und seind also zu verstehen*).[32] This sublime idea that all things have an eternal meaning—anticipated by Hildegard and adapted by Paracelsus to medical ends—inspires interpretations for centuries. Sad to say, its early medical application appears rather mean-spirited, for Paracelsus goes on to state that inner human qualities are reflected in the outer bodily form: thus, as a proverb says, a crooked or crippled body makes for a crooked or crippled mind, and vice versa (*krumer leib gibt krume sinn, krume sinn geben krumen leib*). The later, more sublime variations of the "signature of things" refine the notion that the beautiful forms of created nature are articulations of the eternal Word.

In characterizing the status of Paracelsus in intellectual history, we face a choice between the exaggeratedly negative view coined by a tradition of critics, and the naively positive image cultivated by certain of his admirers. His admirers and critics alike have been confounded by the mixture of naturalistic and spiritual elements in his thinking. It is this very mixture that makes him relevant to the history of German mysticism.

As a mode of philosophy, the thinking of Paracelsus often charts a perilous course between the sublime and the ludicrous. Despite his praise of experience, his "nature" is mediated by numerous received notions, possibly drawn from Neoplatonic, Gnostic, Kabbalistic, and popular sources. Walter Pagel has argued for these sources. The key terms of Paracelsian nature theory are *body* and *spirit*. Bodies are analyzed in terms of forces, qualities, and spirits.[33] At root, all of nature is animate. Its life is a process of combustion. The great variety of forces or spirits that Paracelsus discerns conforms to the vision of a world in which each part is like the whole to the extent that it can become more than its static or inert form.

The reflection of Creator and creation is a two-way mirror. If God is naturalized for Paracelsus, nature is at the same time deified in analogy with the divine nature. Each creature or thing is in turn vitalized in likeness of the total vitality of the world. This vitalization yields one of the most influential of Paracelsus's innovations: the *Tria Prima* of Sulphur, Mercury, and Salt—the three "principles" that are combined to constitute any living organism. When the organism is alive, the principles are indistinguishable; when it is defunct, they can be separated out in the same way that, in an elemental object, they are separated by the alchemist's fire. Sulphur is body for the alchemist: that which burns. Mercury is smoke, for the alchemist: that which is fluid. Salt is compaction, an alkali: that which is fixed.[34] Sulpur, Mercury, Salt can be flesh, blood, bones. Or they can be soul, spirit, body. In all events, the three are united as one in the living being, and only separated in death. Before their union, there is the *prima materia*, after their unity the *ultima materia*. As with the Stoics whose philosophy Paracelsus vaguely mentions as one of his possible antecedents, fire is the symbol of an all-encompassing divine life. The diseases stem from these three "substances" rather than from the four elements with their corresponding humors. Paracelsus calls the elements *matres*, and they are no longer equated with the humors.[35] Instead, by virtue of the *Tria Prima*, all things are said to be in all other things. In point of their vital transformations, all things would appear to be potentially equivalent to all other things.

The dynamic reciprocality and interrelatedness of all things bears out the informing power of the Creator God, who is said to be (in a formulation approximating Cusanus): "all in all, he is the *prima materia* of things, he is the *ultima materia* of things, he is who is all" (*alles in allem, er ist rerum prima materia, er ist rerum ultima materia, er ist der alles ist*).[36] Through creation, things are informed with their own life pattern: "For God created the time that is a harvest in grain, and an autumn in fruit, and thus too he created in the element of water his autumn and harvest" (*Dan hat got die zeit beschaffen, das ein ernde ist im korn, ein herbst im obst, so hat er auch beschaffen dem element wasser sein ernt und herbst auch*).[37] Even the minerals are informed by their own pattern of maturation and destruction.

The intuition of a universal pattern is responsible for the great influence exercised by Paracelsus. For the alchemist or the physician, the recognition that all things are in all other things has pragmatic consequences: metals and chemical substances can be transformed and ennobled; foodstuffs can be metabolized into blood. For the healer of souls, the lesson is rebirth. For the speculative mystic, the teaching of all things means that the highest truths can be discerned by contemplating a simple clump of stone or blade of grass.

Is there any reason to believe that the illuministic coherence of Paracelsus's thought was less responsible for his reputation than any advances he may have achieved in medicine? Paracelsus enjoyed a reputation as a healer. But where is the solid evidence that he was more successful as a physician than his traditionalist competitors? How can we fail to notice that what he presents as "experience," *experientia*, is riddled through and through with the same concept-mongering he decries in his opponents. He may win our assent by ridiculing the Galenists—by inquiring who has ever seen their phlegmatic or choleric humors. But who has ever seen the arcane forces that Paracelsus proposed in their place? If he inspired acclaim and emulation, this can scarcely have been because his followers presciently acknowledged his anticipation of subsequent developments in medicine. It is probably closer to the mark that the mystical and syncretic aspects of his theories were what founded his reputation in his heroic age of learning and research—an age exploding in all sorts of theories, sources, and doctrines.

Paracelsus and Agrippa were men who would know all things; Luther was the man who would know the one necessary thing. Since the writer Luther is not a mystic who reports or teaches mystical knowledge, I have chosen not to devote a full chapter to him, but instead to consider his affinities with the nature mystics in this chapter and with the *Theologia Deutsch* and the Spiritualists in the next. His affinities with mysticism have been the topic of long-standing disputes. Since mysticism has been defined and characterized differently here than in previous studies, it may be possible to cast a new light on the issues. Hartmut Rudolf has summarized the doctrinal similarities and differences of Luther and Paracelsus with respect to the theme of spiritual rebirth.[38] If only their respective doctrines were considered, their distance would be considerable. Yet even their diverging doctrines addressed overriding issues and common concerns. Insights can be gained by considering what Luther and Paracelsus shared by way of the common experience and thinking of their age. And it is also necessary to consider why the mystical writers of coming generations saw fit to combine their respective doctrines.

Our understanding of Luther as well as of Paracelsus suffers from the compartmentalization of the two men into Renaissance and Reformation slots, and perhaps also from a degree of theological aversion to admitting historical relativism in the study of religious doctrine. It is universally acknowledged that, for Luther, faith implicates the whole human being. But the Luther who conceived the doctrine of salvation by faith alone is not necessarily the whole man for scholars, not necessarily the man of his time, the personality who rejoiced in nature and recognized God at work in organic processes, yet also knew that Satan lurked everywhere in the world, who despised witches and devils, loved music and song, went through bouts of rage and depression, but also experienced moods of great joy—the Luther who knew common terrors that are no longer common, but overcame them and captivated his age with his singular acts of courage and defiance. This Luther had things in common with Paracelsus that are not doctrinal. Both understood truth as an "immediate" (*ohne Mittel*) access to a divine power ubiquitous in the world; and both correspondingly upgraded the authority of the scholastically untutored commoner—Luther's lay priest, capable of understanding the Bible, and Paracelsus's nonscholastic plebeian source of knowledge, attuned to the Book of Nature.

There are further parallels in their cultural surroundings. Goldammer has observed that Paracelsus or his imitators associated the notion of the transforming "imagination" with the power of faith and prayer. Indeed, the abuse of this power of faith by sorcerers was even regarded as a kind of evil "anti- or pseudoreligion."[39] Faith and salvation could only mean what they meant to Luther and Paracelsus within their experienced world of fears and superstitions. Their realms of experience—Luther's battle zone of supernatural powers, or Paracelsus's nature rife with invisible forces—are certainly implicated in their respective religious doctrines and medical theories.

No parallel between Luther and Paracelsus is more revealing than that linking their respective notions about the ubiquitous supersensible presence of the divine being and power. Generally speaking, the literature on Luther's doctrine of the *Abendmahl* is not congenial to lateral comparisons—least of all when mysticism is involved. Heinrich Bornkamm stated in 1947 that a problem in discussing this Lutheran doctrine is the fact that the Eucharist has always served as an object of speculation for the "Gnostic, mystical, theosophic, naturalistic, magical-primitive current in Christianity"—from all of which Luther was presumably distinct.[40] Yet insofar as it might be possible to find any good in mystical notions of divine omnipresence, Bornkamm could also conclude that Luther was a better mystic than all the mystics. For Luther was not bound to the literalistic thinking of a Zwingli who supposed that, because Christ sits at the right hand of God, he is not in the bread and wine:

God is for Luther literally in all things, as a force that penetrates and rules everything [als alles durchwaltende Kraft], in fire, in water, in the leaf of a tree, in a stone. Luther has nothing to do with the childish, humanized image of the Creator, who, after he has made the world, now sits enthroned far away in heaven, with the God of naive preachers, who disturbed Jacob Boehme for example so deeply. More conclusively than [Luther], no mysticism has ever enunciated the existence of God in the world.[41]

God is *literally* in all things. This does sound like a mystical idea, but we are told that it was not so for Luther (presumably because he was led to it by a literal reading of the Bible, and the mystics were allegorizers). Luther did employ metaphors in elucidating his doctrine of Communion. One of these is cited by Ernst Sommerlath in his article, *"Abendmahl III. Dogmatisch,"* in *Religion in Geschichte und Gegenwart.* The Communion is a vehicle or bridge, a "pipe" through which the water flows which sates the thirsty. Since the pipe is not meant literally by Luther, the "real presence" sounds like a divine *influentia* of the kind known to Agrippa or Paracelsus. Sommerlath utilizes the word *presence* in characterizing Luther's understanding of the Communion, but states that the doctrine of ubiquity was only an extreme position to which Luther had been driven by Zwingli (as if presence in a limitless number of places were not tantamount to ubiquity). One can dehistoricize the Lutheran doctrine of ubiquity by explaining it as a function of the Christological doctrine of Luther, but was Luther's Christology really so unrelated to his experience of a world full of satanic perils?

Behind these ambiguities lies a long and bitter history of controversies among Protestants. Many of Luther's contemporaries passionately rejected the doctrines of Christ's real presence in the bread and wine and of the ubiquitous presence of God in the world. Calvin and his followers scorned the doctrine of ubiquity as an "absurdity," while some Lutheran theorists enthusiastically overinterpreted their contested teachings. If the opponents of real presence and divine ubiquity scoffed at the superstition of *Allenthalbenheit* and slandered the Lutherans as "cannibals," the defenders of the Lutheran teachings fine-tuned them, inquiring whether the divine body was chewed, swallowed, and digested like food, and speculating as to whether the divine ubiquity was an "illocal omnipresence" or "multipresence," an *omnipraesentia,* a *volipraesentia,* or a *multivolipraesentia.* One prominent Lutheran theologian and extreme ubiquitarian, Johannes Brentz, actually maintained that if a churchmouse were to ingest the sacramental bread, the invisible body of Christ would be present in its rodentine belly.[42]

Yet this controversy of the Reformation and post-Reformation period cannot be written off as orthodox zealotry. As Bornkamm indicates, throughout much of the history of mysticism and folk piety, the Eucharist—a symbol and embodiment of the immediate presence of God—acted as a magnet for contemplation and even as a stimulus to action. In Cusanus's times, the Czech Reformation had demanded that the people receive the Eucharist in both forms, wine as well as bread. Beneath the banner of the Communion chalice, the Hussite armies had routed their imperial and papist opponents. With awe and trembling, the people of Reformationist Wittenberg received back the Eucharist in both forms; and in the wake of the Reformation, the Lutheran lay folk in many parts of Germany would rise up against attempts to modify the doctrine and practices of their *Abendmahl*. To a Christianity dominated by patriarchal and traditional patterns of authority, Christ's invitation to partake of the bread and wine at the Last Supper—his words,

> Take and eat; this is my body…. Drink from it, all of you. This is my blood of the covenant, which is poured out for many for the forgiveness of sins. (Matthew 26:26–28)

appeared as a kind of last will and testament—to which the abandoned children clung in desperation, and over which the haughty heirs quarreled acrimoniously.

Both Luther and Paracelsus were preoccupied throughout their careers with the issues surrounding the sacraments, especially the Communion. Both authored numerous writings on the *Abendmahl*. Their respective doctrines evolved in either case: they differed mutually, and there is no evidence of a common front. However, both Luther and Paracelsus did emphasize body and the divine immanence in their respective theories of the altar sacrament. Moreover, both professed that the taking of the sacramental bread and wine affected the physical being of the believer in an eschatological sense. Even Luther's defenders concede that he maintained this remarkable view in the absense of strict scriptural proofs.[43] Since Luther believed God to be literally present in fire, water, plant, or stone, he might have had no argument with the mere assertion of Agrippa or Paracelsus that the divine *influences* were poured into these things—though he would indeed have questioned by what authority one claimed to make positive statements about the articulations of divine presence and power. Sommerlath and Bornkamm agree that for Luther the sacraments are a *verbum visibile*: they are "signs" *which are what they symbolize*, as

opposed to arbitrary symbols which merely recollect something that
they are not.

Now, if we assume the omnipresence of God, might it not be the
case that—for the Luther who did possess a lyrical sense of nature—
all things (fire, water, leaves, stones) did convey a latent meaning as
real signs, even if the scriptural word has little to say about how to
read them, even if Christ had not bound himself to them in the same
way he bound himself to the bread and wine? Subsequent Lutheran
mystics would then have gone beyond the letter in discerning divine
meanings in all things, but not altogether beyond the spirit of his
teachings.

Luther railed at the "sacramental enthusiasts" who disagreed
with his doctrine; but his own writings in the Eucharistic dispute were
not devoid of mystical traits. In his polemics of 1525 and 1526, he
ridiculed Karlstadt and Zwingli for an inappropriate literalism, presenting their notion of real presence as one in which Christ climbs
down from heaven to enter the bread and wine. According to Luther,
the superior understanding instead teaches that, as far as life or spirit
are concerned, things are more complex *even in nature*. Thus, one seed
of grain gives rise to many ears of corn. One spirit or soul is wholly
present in all parts of the body. One power of vision takes in many
objects of vision, and one voice sent out arouses many listeners.[44]
These metaphors are mystical in the sense that they confirm that the
spiritless (or here we can also say: "literal") characteristics of time,
place, body, and number that hold true for the elemental world do not
hold true for the world under the sway of a life-giving spirit—nor
indeed for the interrelation of the immanent and transcendent orders
of being.

The mysticism of the *Theologia Deutsch*, about which more will be
said in the next chapter, had a profound impact on the early Luther as
well as on his early opponent in the Eucharistic controversy, Karlstadt.
The *Theologia Deutsch* rejected "images." Writing against Karlstadt's
advocacy of the destruction of church art, Luther counselled his opponent to remove the pictures from his heart and leave the ones in the
church alone: the reforming purgation should take place within.

Other formulations of this pivotal phase in Luther's career indi-
cate that he was steeped in mystical and Augustinian paradoxes concerning the divine nature:

...His own [God's] divine nature can be wholly and entirely in
all creatures and in every single individual being in particular,
more deeply, more inwardly, more present than the creature is to

itself, and yet on the other hand may and can be circumscribed nowhere and in no being, so that he actually embraces all things and is in all, but no one being circumscribes him and is in him. (WA 23, 137)

Elsewhere, too, Luther discourses apropos the Eucharist in a way that is reminiscent of Cusanus's *coincidentia oppositorum*:

Nothing is so small but God is still smaller, nothing so large but God is still larger, nothing is so short but God is still shorter, nothing so long but God is still longer, nothing is so broad but God is still broader, nothing so narrow but God is still narrower, and so on. He is an inexpressible being, above and beyond all that can be described or imagined. (WA 26, 339)

It would be quite mistaken to suppose that these paradoxes are quirks or vestiges. The mystical paradoxes of immanence and transcendence are closely linked to Luther's central views on divine omnipotence and faith as against works righteousness. That this is so can be inferred by considering a remarkable passage in Luther's reply to Erasmus, *On the Bound Will* (1525). In an aside of this pivotal work, the Wittenberger rebukes his Humanistic opponent for contending that, if God is (as Luther asserts) omnipresent, then God must be present even in sewers or outhouses. Yes indeed, replies Luther: God has to be present in such places, too. For otherwise, when, as has happened, a martyr is incarcerated in some such disagreeable hole, he would have to refrain from calling out to God until he had been liberated and could repair to a more decorous setting (WA 18, 622–3).

Assuredly, Erasmus would not have denied that Luther's martyr, imprisoned in a sewer, could pray and be heard by God. What separates them here is not just doctrine, but also Luther's refusal to conceive of "action at a distance." In order to hear, see, and respond to the martyr, God, in Luther's understanding of the nature of things, has to be invisibly present alongside the martyr (though not in a form that can be pictured in the literal manner attributed by Luther to Zwingli).

On Luther's Eucharistic doctrine, David Steinmetz recently wrote that, "No theologian before or after Luther has celebrated the universal presence of God more than Luther has. At times, Luther appears in his unguarded statements to veer toward pantheism."[45] Instead of "pantheism," we would do better to think of the interpenetration of immanence and transcendence in German mysticism. Luther's God is not only in all things, but also outside all things; not just passively coextensive with place, but rather wholly present in each place; not thing, but subject. Yet no leaf stirs or grows without God's active power for Luther. The ubiquity of Luther's hidden and revealed deity differs from pantheism, not only in that God extends beyond the visible or finite world. (Even Spinoza was a "panentheist" in the sense that his God has an infinite number of attributes, of which we are aware of only two.) Luther differs fundamentally from what we expect of pantheism in that for him God is wholly present in every place. If we were to transcribe this into a terminology of finite extension, we would be confronted with the paradox that the natural part contains the divine whole, All is in all. Luther's Eucharistic doctrine implies that this is the case for the God who is revealed in Scripture. Paracelsus's medical mysticism conveys the same view for the divine powers revealed in temporal nature.

Paracelsus contracted the eschatological perspective into the life of the individual: "Let everyone consider, when he dies—thus is *his* Final Day" (*gedenk nun ein ieglicher, wann er stirbt: so its séin jungster tag*).[46] Or he compressed it by analogy into the alchemical transformation of the elements from their primal state to their ultimate state. Similarly (though with no concern for medicine or the philosophy of nature), Luther concentrated his eschatological perspective into the life and death of every individual. As the Swiss church historian Walter Nigg has compellingly argued: "Luther refers the hope for the cherished Final Day not, as did the primitive Christians, to the coming of the Kingdom which would arrive with an apocalyptical fanfare. Rather, this longing merges with the death of the individual."[46] This individualization of the endtime perspective is related to an abhorrence for apocalyptic prophesies, harbored by Luther, notwithstanding his sense that he was living in the final age. According to Nigg, the notion of the kingdom is retained as "the Kingdom of God within you" (as Luther and his age read Luke 17:21), that is: as the divine spiritual kingdom, alongside or within the kingdom of our world, which is tantamount to the kingdom of Satan. Luther saw it as one of his greatest accomplishments to have brought about the separation of the two "kingdoms." He thought that a diabolical chaos resulted from allowing them to get mixed up with one another. Similarly, Paracelsus saw it as the task of the alchemical physician, or of the *Vulcanus* within the body, to separate out the poison, the *Ens veneni*, that lurks everywhere in our natural surroundings.

Nigg concluded that Luther's doctrine was of immeasurable importance for German culture:

The inner kingdom had come to him by way of mysticism, but
only Lutheran Protestantism was able to naturalize this notion in
the German nation [*vermochte diese Vorstellung...im deutschen Volk
einzubürgern*]. It is not advisable to deride the often mentioned
German inwardness [*Innerlichkeit*]. For it is not a given of nature,
but a gift given by Christianity. One might fairly say that without this inwardness, Germany would not have become Germany. And this inwardness did not stop at the borders of Germany.... if one thinks of George Fox's wonderful message of the
inner light. The inner kingdom recaptures the Johannine presence of salvation which is the eternal within the human being
that cannot be taken away from him by any misfortune.[47]

In the crisis of his time, Luther reinterpreted the immediacy of an
apocalyptic doom by preparing the individual for death. The mission
of the *Lutherus medicorum* was to accomplish for the temporal life what
Luther had accomplished for the eternal—by confronting and by challenging the power of death.

Although the affinities of Luther and Paracelsus now strike some
scholars as attenuated, during the sixteenth and seventeenth centuries
the parallels were impressive enough for religious minds. A tradition
of nature mystics endeavored to synthesize confessional doctrines
with the pansophic theories of nature inspired by Paracelsus.

One case in point is the influential work called *Azoth* (or: *About
the Tree or Line of Life*).[48] The work was included in the first full edition
of 1589–1591, published by Huser in Silesia. Though probably not by
Paracelsus, the *Liber Azoth* is for this reason all the more interesting as
a compendium, extension, or interpretation of his themes. In *Azoth*,
the natural world can be considered a great correlation of languages,
texts, and words. The word *Azoth* is a concoction of the first and last
letters of the Latin, Greek, and Hebrew alphabets. To the Bible and the
Book of Nature, the Human Book is added (841). The words from
Genesis, "Let there be..." (*Es werde*), are like the Word of which the
Gospel of John speaks in its Prolog (851). As a spirit turned material,
the creative Word is the same as the primal substance which is called
*Yliaster* (from *hyle* and *astrum*, "star stuff").

*Azoth*, the mysterious *materia prima* of the world, is also "the soul
of the great world" (890). The origination of the spirit life of nature
comes about through a kind of generative imagination within this
world-soul (867). This same power is at work in the human microcosm:
it is even encoded into the process of sexual attraction, copulation, and

embryonic formation. The power of imagination also gives birth to what is eternal. The body-engendering potency of the imagination operates when the believer partakes of the bread of Communion. The Eucharist is an angelic bread that gives birth to a new eternal body (892). The *Liber Azoth* not only combines many sources of authority, it also searches for the common essence of cosmogony (as the power that gives birth to the world), sexual desire (the power which informs conception) and the sacramental miracle (the power of rebirth).

The *Liber Azoth* focused on the Eucharist just as it was becoming an object of increasingly bitter controversy, and did so with a clear logic: just as, for Paracelsus, the Bible had held the key to the eschatological coherence of nature, now nature could be consulted for a solution to the doctrinal controversies that arose from the letter of a Scripture taken as the supreme authority. The Scriptures and the macrocosm at every level, the male and the female, the microcosm as body, spirit, and as soul, the wisdom of the ancients, as well as the lore of the common people—all could now be juxtaposed and interpreted conjointly.

# 6

# Letter and Spirit

## Mysticism as Dissent in the German Reformation

During the period in which Paracelsus was struggling to advance his new ideas, a different current of German mysticism was emerging, aimed less at the synthesis of diverse sources of authority than at dissent from doctrinal authoritarianism: the mysticism of the Protestant Spiritualists. Their writings bore an oppositional face, but also a peculiarly individualistic one.

In accordance with the somewhat dated classification system of Ernst Troeltsch, the Spiritualists are the dissenters from the authoritarianism of the Lutheran "scriptural principle," those who (in contrast to the literalism and legalism of sectarian Anabaptism) exalted the "living spirit" above the "dead letter."[1] We know now that the diverse figures referred to as Spiritualists were more complex than this classification can suggest. They shared important views with the early Luther and with the South German Anabaptists.[2] The *Theologia Deutsch* was a common influence on nearly all the Spiritualists of the sixteenth century. In their writings, letter and spirit are correlative with the outer and inner word, and with the visible and invisible church. In seeking a knowledge of God that comes not from the letter, but from the divine Spirit and Word, the Spiritualists turned increasingly to a reflective and speculative mysticism.

After the demise of Müntzer's revolutionary crusade, the Spiritualists emerged as the individualists of Evangelical freedom. Except for Schwenckfeld's conventicles, no group was founded by them. Virtually by definition, their tenets were incapable of giving rise to a new sect, as did the Anabaptist movement. Their immediate influence on religion and society was therefore rather slight. Nevertheless, their impact as critics of orthodoxy can be surmised from the furious reactions of their opponents. As theorists, they were surely ahead of their time. Their writings helped to define the constellations of "mysticism and dissent," a link that has been explored in a book of that title by Steven Ozment.[3]

In the course of two centuries, mystical Spiritualism was represented by figures as diverse as Thomas Müntzer, Hans Denck, Caspar Schwenckfeld, Sebastian Franck, Valentin Weigel, Jacob Boehme, and Anna Ovena Hoyers. In this chapter, I will discuss the appeal of mysticism in the early Reformation and consider the sixteenth-century Spiritualists as mystical writers.

One descriptive way to characterize the early sixteenth century is to recognize the great prevalence of conflicts caused by rival assertions of authority. These ranged from disputes over the prerogatives of popes, emperors, councils, bishops, cities, and all other voices of sanctity or power; through the debates of the Humanists; on down to the quarrels of peasants and lords over rents and common lands. Everywhere, competing claims were being pressed. Often these claims were based on interest, often also on faith, but no doubt most often on a combination of faith and interest. The law student turned monk and theologian who agonized over his own justification before God before he turned the world upside down as a reformer was both of and above this age.

The mysticism of Hildegard had stressed the supremacy of the Church; that of Eckhart the integrity of the individual; and that of Nicholas the unity of opposites with implications for a global reconciliation. Beginning with the Reformation, German mysticism began to flourish increasingly in wildernesses that lay either beyond the *opinio communis* or between opposing orthodoxies. The early Luther who sought answers to agonizing questions concerning justification was attracted to the mystics.[4] Similarly (though with different outcomes), the dissenters who found themselves in an uncertain terrain between rival confessional camps developed mystical rationales. In addition to offering a divine sanction for the seeker or the dissenter, mysticism could address the problems associated with conflict. It could do so either by reconciling the dissenter with the inevitability of persecution, or by projecting a utopian harmony intended to cure the world of its bitter divisions.

This role is intimated already in the *Theologia Deutsch*, the treatise which Luther edited and published (partially in 1516, and completely in 1518, the year after the *Ninety-Five Theses*). Scholars have been puzzled by Luther's statement that this little book in the tradition of Eckhart and Tauler actually anticipated the Reformation. In 1518, Luther wrote that only the Bible and Augustine had taught him more than this small work; he extolled it for anticipating the new Wittenberg theology. As we shall see, the key to Luther's response to the *Theologia Deutsch* has much to do with the conflicts and uncertainties of his time.

We should begin by noting that scholars of the Reformation have cast doubt on the *doctrinal* affinity of Lutheran theology with the *Theologia Deutsch*. The most complete comparisons have been drawn by Ozment. Among other points, Ozment considers that Luther was attracted to the *Theologia* because it featured a devotion freed from fear of punishments and desire for rewards, and because it addressed the whole man, emphasizing an ethic of humility in recognition of the "bitterness" of the Christian life, akin to the Lutheran Theology of the Cross. Both Luther and the anonymous tract recognized the primacy of experience. However, Ozment states that the mystical themes of unification or deification, as well as the notion that the human being has one "eye" in time and another that sees into eternity, should have been uncongenial to Luther. The conclusion is that Luther's theology was a "covenant theology," dependent on Nominalism and fundamentally unmystical.[5]

The differences are real. However, the negative conclusions drawn by Ozment and others presuppose that the comparison itself stands on an even plane. The *Theologia Deutsch*, the sermons of Tauler, and the one or two sermons of Eckhart which Luther may have known (in erroneous attribution to Tauler) were not doctrinal exposés. To compare this mystical treatise (which was presumably aimed at a restricted circle of sympathizers) with articulated doctrinal or polemical statements seems to me to be somewhat like comparing the *Weltanschauung* of a Hobbes or a Rousseau with the legislative innovations of the later legal theoreticians who were impressed by their overall visions. The differences are partly conditioned by the inappropriateness of the comparison itself. It is, if not false, at least misleading to maintain that the mystics believed in something called a ground of the soul in contrast to Luther's sole recognition of the Scriptures. The truth revealed in the ground of the soul was not supposed to be alien to the authority of the Bible. The point was that all truth was one. The human creature had to contain something like this truth within itself in order to have the capacity for true faith. Luther rejected the "spark of the soul," but could the early reformer who was still groping for answers have rejected the underlying idea that the individual has an innate capacity to recognize the truth?

Like Rousseau's utopia in a later century, German mysticism provided the nucleus of an ideal of freedom, truth, and harmony. If the ways in which this "utopia" was interpreted by Luther and by the radical reformers varied considerably, this does not speak against its influence. The *Theologia Deutsch* was not a utopia in the sense of describing a place or a model society, but rather in the sense of resolving conflicts inherent in the real world and presenting the solution in glowing terms. We may not discover his doctrines in the *Theologia Deutsch*, but we can trace certain expressions of Luther's early optimism about the prospects of the reform to the mystical work which he equated with his reforming theology. The *Theologia Deutsch* contrasted with the theological treatises of the *via moderna* or *via antiqua*, not only by its having been written in German instead of Latin, but also by virtue of the simplicity and directness of its whole outlook. Forget doctrines—it seems to beckon—matters are really quite simple. You need only choose clearly between self and God.

The tract conveys no psychological experience. Its author renounces all "images" and begins by quoting Paul: when that which is "perfect" (*das Vollkommene*) has arrived, one casts aside everything "piecemeal." The summons is then amplified by a dual, temporal-eternal perspective. The salient aspect of spiritual life is a human condition poised between eternity and time. Law and grace, freedom and obedience, are the ordinates of decision. Their oppositions are reconciled by a paradox of freedom. As in Eckhart, complete renunciation and obedience leads to absolute spiritual autonomy. The soul poised between eternity and time has to renounce its preoccupation with Mine, Thine, and Self. Obeying and loving God without concern for reward or punishment, the soul finds itself already in an earthly "Paradise."[6] All of creation is declared to be an outer district of a Paradise in which everything is allowed—everything except disobedience to God. Disobedience is tantamount to human selfishness. Like Eckhart, the author of the *Theologia* devalues "works" along with "images."[7] In fact, the two seem to be coupled by an underlying logic. The author warns against those who (like the reputed antinomians of the Free Spirit) imagine that they are above both the law and Christ in their deification. But the author also warns against the knowledge that comes from reading and assenting to the Bible without being moved by it to love God.[8]

Among its implications, the dualistically tempered *Theologia* touches on the contrast of a Bible understood as hearsay truth (a correlative of "time" and "self"), and the contrasting prospect of love, obedience to God, and transcendence of Mine and Thine in an earthly Paradise transfigured by the light of eternity. The little treatise by the anonymous Frankfurter confronts the reader with an enigma. If, in its negative emphasis, it characterizes a false or superficial believer who obeys self instead of God, who knows or believes in "images," and reads the Bible as "history," *what is the positive alternative?*

In no uncertain terms, Luther reported that his theology was confirmed in the *Theologia Deutsch* (WA 1, 378–9). It is too strong a confirmation of affinity to rest solely on the weak psychological category of "experience," or on the tenuous sociological one of a democratization of mysticism. I will suggest instead that the utopian aspect of the *Theologia*—its implicit reconciliation of a radical autonomy in faith with the rightful order of an earthly "Paradise"—held up an ideal that attracted the Luther who was on the verge of empowering the individual with a higher authority, and after Luther the dissenters who adhered to essential points of his Reformation, yet were unable to live with what they saw as its failure in the common domain: Müntzer, who considered Luther inauthentic in his faith and halfhearted or lax in the struggle against error, and Denck, Franck, and Weigel, who saw the new order not only as lax and inauthentic, but also as authoritarian and regressive. As part of their dissent, the Spiritualists rejected the Lutheran doctrine of imputed justification: if the believer has only an imputed justification, without improvement, the door is left open to false certainty and self-satisfaction. This doctrine was rejected by Spiritualists and Pietists. Yet no clear picture emerges for the nontheologian, when Luther and his opponents are seen as motivated exclusively by doctrinal disputes. To concentrate only on doctrines fails to provide a rounded picture of motives and ideas.

Even if we concede that Luther's impulses were fundamentally theological—not social or political—we are left with open questions that point toward the utopian aspect of the *Theologia* and toward the social issues of the time. Is it possible that Luther and his followers could have done otherwise than expect that their theological reforms would bring about a revolutionary transformation of society? Luther had written in 1520 that the papacy had plundered and oppressed Italy worse than the Turk had ravished any conquered country—and was now poised to do the same to Germany. Is it possible that this Luther and those who supported him with body and soul could have maintained the reservation in their hearts that, in replacing an oppressive realm of works righteousness with a new reign of truth and faith, no general improvement was to be expected in common society—because justification is after all only *imputed* by God to the believer who remains *simul justus et peccator*? To assert this might seem like a theologically rigorous interpretation of the Reformation, but it is actually an implicitly cynical one. In its endeavor to safeguard the theological integrity of Luther, it risks turning him into the conscious or unconscious purveyor of a misleading propaganda. Why shouldn't we then consider George Bernard Shaw's diatribe that salvation by faith alone appealed to Lutheran burghers because it offered a cheaper route to heaven than works righteousness? What can really be said against this? Bainton's rejoinder was that since the early Protestants risked their lives and property, they could hardly have been motivated by any mere material interest (i.e., in the ecclesiastical properties that promised an immense transfer of wealth). However, this rejoinder proves nothing of the sort. Even an adventurist in a palace coup risks life and property.

If the reformers had done nothing but proclaim the doctrine of salvation by faith alone and secularize church properties, the cynical view would have prevailed even then. The theological motivations of Luther's actions and the practical reforms of his *Letter to the Nobility* militate against this cynical view. So do the invocations to brotherly love like that of the first *Invocavit* sermon of 1522: Faith without love is not enough; indeed, is no faith at all, but only a counterfeit faith comparable to the reflection of a face in a mirror rather than to the face itself. This mystically tempered metaphor implies that if true faith is in the soul, it has to be reflected outwardly in love for one's fellows. The *Theologia Deutsch* and Luther's *Preface to Romans* became the mainstays of those who sought to reinstitute the early Lutheran ideal of faith united with love, freedom with the common good.

This ideal is symbolized very forcefully at the conclusion of Luther's most influential and seminal work, *On the Freedom of a Christian* (1520). Here, the reformer gives the reader advice that echoes the spirit of the *Theologia Deutsch*: If you want to donate, pray, or fast, then don't do it with the idea of getting something good for yourself in return. Give freely and with the thought that others will have the enjoyment of what you give. If you give thus for their good, then you will be a true Christian. Why should you want a superabundance of goods and good works for yourself, when you have enough in a faith by which God gives you all things? As if to surmount the implication that one form of exchange is being replaced with a more profitable one, Luther—in a manner worthy of Eckhart's warning against the "moneychangers" of faith—combines two characteristic mystical tropes: a fountain overflowing from the superabundance of divine goodness and the paradox whereby the more anything is inside God, the more it also flows out of God. Look, he tells the reader, this is the way the good things of God ought to flow out of one and into another and become common, so that each person will take responsibility for his fellow as if for himself. "Out of Christ, they flow into us.... Out of us, they flow into those who need them" (WA 7, 37). "It follows from this that a Christian does not live in himself, but rather in Christ and his neighbor.... Through faith, the Christian rises above himself and into God, and out of God he descends again beneath himself through

love, even while remaining in God..." This is the true Christian freedom, Luther concludes; it surpasses all other freedoms "as heaven
surpasses earth" (WA 7, 38).

This paradoxical freedom *qua* bondage to God and to one's fellows connects this seminal Lutheran work with the *Theologia*. Freedom
should be reconciled with order through faith and love. Evangelical
freedom from compulsion and self-interest should lead to the utopian
order of an earthly Paradise of freedom, love, justice, and brotherhood. Cast off Roman falsehood and oppression, so goes the message
of Luther. Liberate the world from the corruption of works-in-
exchange-for-grace, and from the papal coercion of believers. Do so,
and—so it appears—the true faith will lead to a bounteous Paradise of
overflowing love and good fellowship.

This is also the Luther who penned his resounding declarations
against every form of coercion in matters of faith. Christ did not want
people to be compelled by fire and sword to believe. We need only
wield "the sword of the spirit, the Word of God," the Bible that has
been discarded under the bench by the pope (WA 7, 139–40). Let people believe, teach, and do, just as they please: the Holy Spirit will win
out in the free-for-all (WA 15, 218–9). And stop hounding the Jews:
they are right to refuse to convert when force is used against them
(WA 11, 314–36). Who, after all, are those who have been persecuted
for their beliefs? The true Christians have always been among the persecuted; the real heretics are the persecutors themselves (WA 7, 317).

The flaw in this utopia of freedom and good fellowship was its
failure to foresee principled disagreement, its inability to brook any
use of Evangelical freedom other than in the manner expected by the
man who framed it. Complicated theories have been advanced to
explain and explain away Luther's subsequent change of heart. The
most cogent explanation for his growing wrath against Catholics,
Protestant "false brethren," and Jews was their unwillingness to see
the light and accept the true faith in conformity with his doctrine.

The doctrine of *sola fide* failed to anticipate the degree to which it
could be abused. It was unable to account for "error," except as diabolical ill will. By the same token, the mystical Spiritualism of the dissenters must be understood with regard to their self-assertion against
Luther's authority. Scholars have clarified the elements of mystical
Spiritualism in the writings of Müntzer, Schwenckfeld, Denck, or
Franck. But if these elements are taken as fixed quantities which originate in the *Theologia Deutsch*, Tauler, or Eckhart, and act as determinants of the paths followed by the dissenters, the interpretation will be
hard pressed to explain why their paths were so different either from

Eckhart's or from one another. A common determinant should have the same effect.

Scholarship can only address the disparities by showing how the elements of mysticism actually served to legitimize the stance of each dissenter within a changing historical situation. What Luther and the dissenters actually discovered in the *Theologia Deutsch* was what was not in it at all: an inspiration to reconcile individual faith with the common good, Evangelical freedom with a just and righteous order, in *a nonmonastic society*. For the dissenting mystics, the key to discovery would lie in the life-giving power waiting within or behind the manifest tyranny of the letter.

In a manner of speaking, the whole excitement and enterprise of the sixteenth century was aimed at resurrecting the "living spirit" mouldering inside the tomb of a dead or false "letter." This applies to the recovery of ancient skills and texts by the Humanists, to the proclamation of the Evangelical spirit by the reformers, and even to Paracelsus's researches into nature. In general, *spirit* functions as a correlative concept. Since what it signifies depends on its assigned opposite, it can imply something different when it is contrasted with letter, law, the flesh, the body, matter, or nature. Each signification lends its own coloring to the contrast, just as the opposites tend to be seen as affiliated.[9] Indeed, reconciling opposites and uniting the many in one are offices of the spirit. Paracelsus, we recall, was engaged in deciphering the "letters" of nature in order to arrive at the recognition of inner spirit-forces. The *Theologia Deutsch* had relatively little to say about the connotations of "spirit"; but it did express a related motif in interpreting the mystical-Pauline unity of "all in One and One in all,"[10] as well as in contrasting the shallowness of a complacent hearsay faith that says, "I know because I read it in Scripture," with a deeper knowledge for which knowing and loving are one.

Luther's older and more radical reforming colleague at Wittenberg, Andreas von Bodenstein (Karlstadt), was the author of a commentary on Augustine's *On the Spirit and the Letter*. He was also a critic of the slow and seemingly halfhearted pace of the reforms. Influenced by the *Theologia Deutsch*, Karlstadt helped propagate the link between dissent, mysticism, and the appeal of spirit over letter. However, Luther himself opened the deepest wellspring in interpreting "letter" and "spirit" as the Pauline-Augustinian correlative of the law and grace.[11] The "spiritual" sense ceased to be the allegory that could be molded conveniently to papal dogma and scholastic philosophy. The living spirit in the letter was unequivocally directed toward personal salvation. The spirit was the one Holy Gospel underlying the Old and the New Testament, the existential essence of all scriptural history.

According to Kühn, the early and more tolerant Luther was a Spiritualist.[12] This was the Luther whose exegesis was far from a later orthodox interpretation of the scriptural principle that came to be based on "verbal inspiration." When Luther's tolerant attitude dissipated after 1525, the shift came in his stance vis-à-vis opponents, lukewarm friends, and wayward supporters. The change brought with it the more dogmatic accents of his reading of the scriptural passages essential to his debate with Erasmus, Karlstadt, or Schwenckfeld. With regard to Luther's doctrines of the Lord's Supper or the bound will, the pertinent scriptural passages were declared to be absolutely clear and unequivocal. Against his insistence on the letter, Luther's opponents cited the spirit.

Each of the Spiritualist dissenters adhered to one of several points in the mystical utopia of freedom and order: Thomas Müntzer seized upon the denial of self and external proofs, magnifying verification into a standard of martyrdom. Schwenckfeld rejected everything external to the living faith, accentuating this rejection with a mystical doctrine of the gradual enhancement of the human being. Hans Denck and Sebastian Franck sought to retain and reinforce the openness and tolerance of the early Luther. The Spiritualism of Valentin Weigel developed into a many-sided response to a new scholasticism and dogmatism.

Although the Spiritualists were more open-minded than their orthodox opponents, the elevation of spirit above letter left the divine provenance of the Bible essentially unchallenged. Moreover, their critique of literalistic authoritarianism was only one hue in the spectrum of their dissent. No small part of what they wrote echoed the early Luther. The point at which Spiritualistic dissent can be said to have crossed the line to become mysticism depended on the intention and perception of the disputing parties themselves. In defending his authority against his challengers, Luther ascribed to them the pejorative mysticism of "Enthusiasts," *Schwärmer*. In shunning the authority of Wittenberg, Müntzer adopted a mystical terminology and insisted on the criterion of an experienced faith (but this faith was in turn supported by biblical prophecy). When the clear letter was wielded by orthodoxy against dissent, its recourse was the living spirit—backed up, to be sure, with a dissenting reading of the Bible. Exiled from every confession, the champions of the spirit identified with the invisible universal church of the persecuted. Isolated in a hostile world, they were thrown back on a knowledge between the individual and

God. The dialectic revolt of spirit against letter developed as a dynamic conflict of ideal and real, doctrine and practice. Indictments either of the dead letter or of the doctrine of forensic justification were intended as assaults on hypocrisy and false authority. Mysticism encouraged dissenters in their revolt or defiance.

Thomas Müntzer (1490–1525) was the most radical champion of spirit over letter. The informing energy of his manifestos and sermons is the popular outrage against the representatives of a discredited sanctity. The same kind of rage was driving common people to taunt priests and strip church interiors, to smash and burn sacred art that had only recently been revered. The people were incensed at having been duped by the emblems of sanctity. "Anguished lay piety" compelled the iconoclasts to destroy the old and search for new warrants of truth.[13] In the rapid movement of a change fired by a spreading hatred of hypocrisy and false authority, it happened more than once that the reformers outstripped and separated off from their founder. For Müntzer, the events were in fulfillment of divine prophesy and in response to the "speaking God" within. Onto those who balked and refused to accept God's will descended the ugly mantle of false sanctity. This soon came to mean Luther himself in the view of Müntzer and his plebeian followers.

This most radical champion of spirit over letter was actually one of the most bookish of reformers.[14] Müntzer's readings included Humanism, Plato, Aristotle, Pico della Mirandola, Augustine and other Fathers, as well as pseudo-Joachite chiliastic writings and the *Theologia Deutsch*. After joining the reform movement, he was recommended by Luther for the ministry of the Saxon town of Zwickau. There, Müntzer came into contact with the stirrings of a plebeian reformation represented by the radical weaver Nikolaus Storch. For Müntzer, the scriptural letter was called to life by a prophetic spirit, an immediate authority, beholden only to the ongoing commands of God. The plebeian prophetic voice blended with Müntzer's theological sources, with his awareness of a revolutionary chiliasm represented by Hussites and Taborites, with his reading of the Lutheran proclamation of Christian freedom, and with the powerful but ambiguous message of the *Theologia Deutsch*, its promised leap from all "piecework" to a new "perfection." The paradox of freedom could be carried to its conclusion by forcibly removing all who clung to the old tyranny, who shirked from the struggle to establish a kingdom of divine justice on earth. The true path was that of the plebeian revolt. Müntzer rallied and led it. Faith was identified with participation in the suffering of Christ through militant struggle against "the godless" who were to be slain to make way for the kingdom of heaven on earth. This was a doctrine tailored for martyrdom, an ending which did not spare Müntzer.

Goertz and Nipperdey have discussed the Spiritualistic and mystical elements in Müntzer's writings.[15] As used by Müntzer, *spirit* is a polemical term. It is the keynote of a theology which stands opposed to that of the *Schriftgelehrten* (Pharisees). Faith does not come from doctrines or, in Luther's manner, from the Scriptures. It comes from "experience." The Lutheran doctrine of salvation by faith and the word is *unerfahren*, "unexperienced," and therefore inauthentic. This is the sentiment of a man caught up in a struggle against the hated power that Luther himself vividly characterized as that of an apocalyptic enemy, the Antichrist.

Notwithstanding his invectives against Luther, Müntzer did not discard biblical authority. To the contrary, he biblicized his own life and struggle. The same voice that had spoken to the prophets was now speaking to and through Müntzer. In a sermon summoning the princes to join the people or be slain for their godlessness, the prophetic world of Daniel overtakes life experience. The "inner word" possesses all authority, as it does for the Spiritualists who come after him; however, for Müntzer, this word is prophetic and revolutionary. It is not an eternal word spoken into the silence of the soul: it is a word spoken in time, about the times.

In 1525, Müntzer's peasants were crushed at the Battle of Frankenhausen. Müntzer was captured, tortured, and executed. Luther's pitiless pamphlets against the rebels came as a shock even to some of his supporters. Luther had formerly sustained the demand that the community should have the right to choose its own pastor. In response to the peasants' revolt, he began to transfer this right to the rulers, one of many shifts toward a retrenchment of political and theological authoritarianism. The death of Müntzer coincided with a turning point in the Reformation.

By 1525, Luther had vanquished Karlstadt, the populistic and puritanical leader of the radical Wittenberg Movement of reform, in a war of words. The tension between the Erasmian Humanists and the Wittenberg theologians resulted in an open rift when Luther published his great treatise of 1525, *On the Bound Will*, his systematic reply to Erasmus's defense of the free will. The debate over the Eucharist was also becoming increasingly hateful, escalated by Luther's condemnation of Zwingli. The debate would eventually divide the Reformation more bitterly than the rift between Lutherans and Papists.

New forms of Protestant dissent surfaced. Adherents of the new
faith began to register their disappointment that the reform they had
embraced was not regenerating Christian society.

In Zurich, the year 1525 saw the first rebaptism performed by a
Swiss Anabaptist sect. The witnessing of the sectarian Anabaptists
was individual and corporate. They practiced adult baptism. They
excluded offenders from their congregations and distanced themselves from Luther on the issue of the Eucharistic sacrament, interpreting the breaking of bread as a "remembrance" of the broken body of
Christ, to be partaken of only by the true congregation of the reborn.

After the demise of Müntzer, the South German and Austrian
Anabaptists expressed various forms of a dissent rooted in part in
medieval theology. Their formulations were almost invariably
touched by the mysticism of the "inner word." Werner Packnull has
characterized the wellspring of this inward authority among the more
orthodox South German Anabaptists:

> For them the appeal to the inner Word was of a more utilitarian
> nature. As representatives of an anticlerical lay movement, it
> provided them with a rallying point of opposition against the
> Reformers' close association of the Word of God with the Scrip-
> tures. An exaggerated view of the importance of the letter sup-
> ported an unwholesome division between laity and clergy. A
> new class of scribes, claiming a monopoly on God's revelation,
> was the consequence. In contrast the inner Word was accessible
> to all men, even the illiterate.[16]

But the "inner word" was also a rallying point for the radicals and
intellectuals.

In January 1525, a young Humanist scholar and teacher named
Hans Denck in the Lutheran city of Nuremberg was expelled by the
magistrates of that city. Denck was accused (along with three assis-
tants of Dürer, the so-called "godless painters") of professing and
spreading heretical teachings. In the interim between his expulsion
and his death in Basel three years later, this solitary figure followed a
restless itinerary along the Upper Rhine through Switzerland and
Southwest Germany. Embracing adult baptism, Denck wrote a number of documents justifying his views. He wandered about, visiting
scattered congregations. After the peasants' defeat, a dissenting
underground abounded in desperate forms of mystical dissent, ranging from the chiliastic visions of the Dreamers' sect to Hans Hut's
"gospel of all creatures," which taught the exemplary patience of

beasts. At what became known as the Synod of Martyrs at Augsburg in August 1527, Hut gathered the remnants of his hard-pressed movement and urged his followers to practice the fraternal love prophesied in the Apocalypse. Denck attended. Hut was imprisoned and died in an escape attempt.[17] Denck found his way to Basel, but succumbed to a plague epidemic in December 1527. The end of his life found him still attempting to rethink his theological positions. Shortly after his death, the imperial mandate at the Diet of Speyer gave the signal for an Anabaptist holocaust.[18] The surviving dissenters who were not reabsorbed into the main confessions were drawn either to the disciplined sects or to a more individualistic dissent. For the independents, the Spiritualistic path had been forged by Denck's individualism and voluntarism. The evolution of his views reveals the characteristic point of departure.

Denck's Augsburg "apologia" of the year 1526 spoke to the controversy that had come to a climax the preceding year with Luther's treatise *On the Bound Will*.[19] In this most pivotal work of the Reformation after *On the Freedom of a Christian*, Luther championed predestination against the Erasmian defense of free will. Luther recognized in the Erasmian defense a recourse for the doctrine of salvation by good works.

This was the decisive turning point for Denck and those who followed his way. Without abandoning their essentially Lutheran emphasis on faith and grace, the Spiritualists beginning with Denck sought to maintain the early Lutheran emphasis on freedom and fraternal love. Denck was indebted to Neoplatonism and the *Theologia Deutsch*. He tended toward a universalistic theology of the Word. The "inner word" is in all. Predestination is rejected on the grounds that it makes God the cause of evil. Denck's reflections betoken the new pluralism of a Spiritualist dissent no longer driven by the militant righteousness of Müntzer. This tendency was to be represented variously by Hans Bünderlin, Sebastian Franck, and Caspar Schwenckfeld.[20]

In December 1525, Luther and his colleagues in Wittenberg received a Silesian visitor, the preeminent reformer of that territory, Caspar Schwenckfeld von Ossig (1489–1561). Schwenckfeld was a reformer of the first hour. He had become concerned about the failure of the church reform to regenerate Evangelical behavior. After much thought and prayer, Schwenckfeld had concluded that Luther's enunciation of the Evangelical doctrine had not removed everything "external" and "fleshly" accruing from the old false doctrine of works, laws, and ceremonies. The Silesian had become convinced that the doctrine of Christ's presence in a Eucharist in which the unregenerate also partook enabled those of shallow faith to secure an external reassurance of salvation in a manner akin to the superficiality of the old practices.

Schwenckfeld met with no success in his attempts to persuade Luther. Although the talks themselves were civil, Luther soon began to connect the Silesian reformer with the other critics of his hardening doctrine of real presence; and, though Schwenckfeld was by no means in full agreement with Zwingli and Karlstadt, he orbited toward the scattered and sundry camp of the dissenters.

In Schwenckfeld, it again becomes evident that the broadest common denominator for the beginnings of Protestant dissent were dissatisfaction with the failed regeneration of Christian life and reluctance to accept an imposed doctrinal hegemony. Beyond this, the tendencies took many directions—Zwingli, the magisterial reformer of Zurich, soon oppressed the Anabaptists, while the Anabaptist sects shunned those with whom they were not of one mind. Schwenckfeld and the other Spiritualists remained opposed both to sectarian dissent and to the authoritarianism of all the established churches, which they called *die Steinkirchen*, "churches of stone." The ambiguity of a nonsectarian articulation of principles was resolved in accordance with the individual personalities of the Spiritualists.

Schwenckfeld was a nobleman who had served several years as a courtier at Silesian courts. His prolific writings reflect the background of his training for the court. The Silesian was known as a calm and forceful speaker. He could also write clearly and with much personal warmth, but his writing retained the self-effacing reserve of the courtier who indulges in no outbursts of passion or flights of style.

As a religious reformer and theorist, Schwenckfeld was repulsed by everything "external" or "of the flesh." This began with the Eucharistic doctrine, which he blamed for many failures of the new faith. The words of institution, "this is my body" in Matthew 26:26, were rather to be interpreted in light of John 6. Christ's glorified resurrected body is a "spiritual food." There is to be a gradual ascent of the fallen human creature toward the glorified Christ. In his *De Cursu Verbi Dei*, the Word is not the preached or printed word of the Bible and not a cosmic Christ, but rather the second person of the Trinity, the incarnate Son.[21] Faith rests in a spiritual encounter with Christ. Schwenckfeld's dissatisfaction with the scriptural principle and the doctrine of real presence was of a piece with his ecclesiology, which looked to the "invisible church," and regarded the institutional church as unworthy. The visible church hangs on sermons and sacraments, yet before the written word can say anything at all to the hearer or reader, the living faith of an "inner word" has to prepare the heart. Schwenckfeld knew this inner voice of the spirit from his own experiences of awakening or conversion in the years 1525 and 1526. Characteristically, his experiences were identical with the agony of his struggle to resolve within himself his stance on the issues that separated him from the Luther whom he revered. Schwenckfeld developed his prioritization of the spirit over the letter within the evolving context of his controversy with Luther over the Eucharist.

Schwenckfeld argues all his points by citing the Bible. He encourages his adherents to look to no other book for guidance.[22] However, the Silesian Spiritualist is also aware that, even if the believer's knowledge of truth coincides with Scripture, it doesn't come out of it, at least not in the sense implicit in the doctrine of "faith from hearing." The Holy Spirit affects the believer, as it were, from the inside outward, not from outside in. Conscience comes into its own in Schwenckfeld's teachings. The religious office of rulers is denied. As rulers, they have no religion.[23]

In 1529, Schwenckfeld was in effect expelled from Silesia at Luther's urging. The exposed situation of the Silesian Protestants who were ruled by a Catholic emperor led Schwenckfeld's princely protector to succumb to pressure from Wittenberg and encourage his coreligionist to enter upon a life of exile in Southwest Germany. In the three decades before his death in 1561, the exile continued to refine and publicize his doctrinal views. The conventicles of his adherents persisted in Southwest Germany, in Silesia, Lusatia, and eventually in Pennsylvania, where they became the Schwenckfelder Church.

Schwenckfeld's independence is characteristic for German Spiritualism after Müntzer. The Spiritualists went their own way. Open to dialog with all groups and tendencies, they were fixed to none. Separately, they developed theories of religious toleration. Although the issues surrounding the Eucharist played an important role for the Spiritualists, they lacked a common trademark such as adult baptism. The manner in which the theme of the spirit was articulated varied considerably.

During the early years of Schwenckfeld's lifelong wandering, many other refugees from the old and new orthodoxies were living in exile or in flight for their lives. The Anabaptists were slain in droves during the years 1528 and 1529. The Lutheran estates, which courageously protested the renewal of the Edict of Worms at the Imperial Diet in Speyer, proffered no challenge to the imperial mandate against the Anabaptists, who were now persecuted by all confessions and magisterial reformers beginning with Zwingli in Zurich.

Only shortly before this period of repression, Luther and his followers had proclaimed to the people that no one should be condemned as a heretic for exercising freedom of faith. As this tolerance
vanished, the preferred charge against heretics became blasphemy. As
Luther explained, the dissenters were still free to believe as they
chose—but merited death for professing their beliefs or practicing
them openly. Luther's initially principled attitude of toleration for the
convictions of others steadily turned into its opposite, culminating in
the fierce anti-Semitic outbursts of his last years. In February 1530,
Luther wrote to his associate Mykonius in Gotha that the rulers were
obliged to execute not only the rebels, but even peaceful Anabaptists
and Zwinglians on account of their blasphemy. Evangelical freedom
yielded to a new orthodoxy prepared to root out error with force. One
encouragement of Luther's hardened position came from the city
scribe of Nuremberg, Lazarus Spengler.

In 1530, Spengler, one of the earliest supporters of the Reformation, undertook an initiative. It was from Nuremberg that Denck and the
"godless painters" had been expelled in 1525, but some elements within
the city were still of the opinion that the city's magistrates should toler-
ate Jews, heathens, Enthusiasts, and Anabaptists, with all their ceremonies and assemblies, come what may. These citizens were wont to
cite Luther's treatise of the year 1523, *On Governmental Authority*, a work
that argued the strongest case that faith is free and should not be sub-
jected to compulsion. Spengler hoped that the leader of the Reformation
could now be persuaded to deliver a public pronouncement more helpful in the pursuit of the new goals of religious conformity. Luther
responded with a reversal of his earlier position. He now placed the consensus above individual belief and accorded to the rulers the right to
appoint the pastors for the people.[24] The most considered philosophical
opposition to this new tendency came from Sebastian Franck.

Since the appearance of studies by Wilhelm Dilthey and Alfred
Hegler toward the end of the nineteenth century, Franck has been
regarded both as the archetypal Spiritualist and as a precursor of
many later intellectual currents. His life (1499–1542) has a special fascination inasmuch as he appears to have experienced personally most
stations of the Reformation: as a Catholic seminarian, an Evangelical
pastor, a Humanistic writer and publicist, a friend of dissenters in
Nuremberg, married to the sister of one of the "godless painters," and
finally as an exile. Franck was driven to remain independent of all
sects and doctrines.

Like Schwenckfeld, Franck's opposition to the moral failings of the Reformation gave his thinking a dualistic cast: flesh and spirit, darkness and light, letter and spirit are pervasive and antagonistic alternatives. But unlike the Silesian noble whose inner life was absorbed in the Bible and whose hopes for a new community were disseminated within his devotional conventicles, Franck is rather the type of the inquisitive intellectual whose republic of the spirit can only be convened from the remnants of all possible sources of learning. Franck composed a "chronicle of heretics," wrote a "History-Bible," published a book on the Turks, compiled a collection of proverbs, dabbled in geography, translated the *Theologia Deutsch* into Latin, and published the writings of Servetus (whose critique of trinitarian doctrine would result in his execution in Calvin's Geneva).

Franck's collecting impulses are evident in his style, in characteristic sentences that delight in the listing of endless synonyms, as if in order to demonstrate that all the outer words over which so much blood was being spilled were interchangeable. More than any dissenter before him, he set about undercutting the basic foundations of the new orthodoxy, doing so not simply by citing the Bible, but by questioning it as a basis for binding doctrines. Instead of reacting to Luther's doctrinal arguments with other doctrines, as did Schwenckfeld, Franck's procedure was to show that Lutheran premises ought to have led to the opposite conclusions.

Franck's career as a publicist had an orthodox beginning in 1528, when he undertook to translate a treatise called *Diallage, hoc est Conciliatio locorum scripturae, qui prima facie inter se pugnare videntur*, written by a pastoral colleague named Andreas Althamer. Althamer's work appears to have been a rebuttal of an unmentioned little tract by Denck. In it, the erstwhile master of St. Sebald's school in Nuremberg had arranged forty seemingly contradictory passages drawn from the Bible opposite one another (*Gegenschriften*). His object had been to bring the reader to the "sole teacher, the Holy Sprit" (*einigen Lehrmeister, dem heiligen Geist*).[25] The Latin reply by Althamer stands in a long tradition of attempts to prove that there are no internal contradictions in the Bible.

In the course of translating Althamer, Franck was to arrive at the principle of a criticism that employed paradoxes in order to curtail the tyranny of the letter and restore the freedom of the spirit. Franck also wrestled with the Lutheran work that set the philosophical agenda for unorthodox Lutherans from Denck to Leibniz: Luther's *On the Bound Will*, a work which saw God outside of Scripture as a *deus absconditus*. For Franck, God was hidden even *in* the Scriptures. Where Luther taught that the human will is bound by divine omnipotence, Franck recognized a will set free by the omnipresent divine power that illuminates the human understanding.[26] This turn of mind was characteristic for the Spiritualists. Luther's predestinarianism and correlative demand for conformity was logically inverted. Arguing from the premises of Luther, first Franck and later Weigel championed a voluntarism and toleration based on the omnipresence of the inner word. Franck's evocation of the inner word present in all things and people shows the logic by which mysticism would surmount the principle of Luther's scriptural authoritarianism.[27] For Franck, the ubiquity of God corresponded to Luther's own justification of the real presence of Christ in the sacrament—but minus Christ's having "bound" himself by his word to the bread and wine.[28] The ubiquitous Word is not "bound": neither is the believer bound to external sacraments or ceremonies. Franck in fact went beyond the later Spiritualists Weigel and Boehme in attaching no importance to the sacraments of baptism or the Eucharist.

Luther's treatise *On the Bound Will* defended the antinomies that result from accepting the "clear word" of the Scriptures in reference to God's predestining power. His earlier work, *On the Freedom of a Christian*, had placed the paradox of human freedom squarely before the reader as: "a Christian is free and a subject to none, a Christian is bound and a servant to all." Denck and Franck accepted the centrality of the paradox in faith, but they did so in a manner that allowed them to avoid Luther's insistence that the human mind should bow before reactionary inferences from "the clear word of Scripture."

Franck's most famous work pursues this seminal undertaking by offering the reader "two hundred-eighty paradoxes" (*Paradoxa Ducenta Octoginta*, 1534). The introduction defines the "paradox" polemically as a *Wiederrede* or contradiction: a paradox is a statement that is incontrovertibly true, and yet rejected by the entire world (*ain Red / die gleichwol gewiß und waar ist / die aber die gantze Welt / und was nach dem Menschen lebt / nichts weniger dann fur waar hält*).[29] Franck's definition is not the work of an elitist Humanism. The *Paradoxes* include folk proverbs. His marshaling of contradictions was a blow struck for dissenters. It challenged the doctrinal fiat from Wittenberg, according to which each territory and city should be ruled by a religious consensus enforced from above. Franck reverted to the early Luther in maintaining that the truth is always guarded by the heroic minority that defies the "world."

Kurt Goldammer has written that Franck's paradoxes are a kind of unresolved dialectic of thesis and antithesis without synthesis.[30] They consist often, but not always, of two or more statements that stand in apparent contradiction. Actually, the paradoxes bring off the balancing act of upholding the dualistic distinction of flesh and spirit, by affirming the freedom of faith, while avoiding the formulation of a new doctrine; for a new doctrine was altogether counter to Franck's intentions. The first of his 280 paradoxes states that "No one knows what God is"; the very last that "The Word, which is a light, spirit and life, suffers no human being's light or gloss." The unknowing of the paradoxes is directed against "self," and for the unity of all beings in God. Paradox 157 teaches that "Love does not sin and can do no injustice." The adjoining text explains that "to sin is nothing but not to love, [nothing] but self will and [self] seeking" (als eigener Wille und Gesuch). The text to paradoxes twenty-nine, thirty, and thirty-one explains that "God is a free, out-poured indwelling good, actuating power, in all things, which dwells in all creatures and brings about all in all" (Gott ist ain frei / außgegoßne inwonende güte / wirkende krafft / inn allen dingen / die in allen Creaturen weset / und alles in allen wirckt). This is the language of the Theologia Deutsch, where "God," "One," and "the Good" are synonyms.

Instead of finding the paradoxes resolved, the reader is urged to attempt a leap beyond the letter of the outer word: the contradictions can only be reconciled by what the author alludes to near the end as the "spirit that no one can write" (Geist, den keiner schreiben kann). It follows from this that the truth for Franck is necessarily individual. Though by no means "subjective" in the modern negative sense, the truth activates itself within, as an undefinable presence. Whatever is turned into a binding doctrine is dead for truth. For Franck, letter and spirit are parallel in function to "flesh" and "spirit" in Luther's Preface to Romans. These are not substances: the whole human creature is in its entirety flesh or spirit, depending on its relationship with the eternal. For Franck, what is thought or articulated is likewise altogether "letter" or altogether "spirit."

"Faith," for Franck, is still the decisive criterion of the Christian religion; but his is a faith that has to be expressed in good works, like the tree that bears good fruit in Luke 6:43. Clearly, these cannot be the works prescribed by the external authority of priests or papal laws, but only the superabundant goodness which—in the earthly Paradise of the Theologia Deutsch or in the conclusion of On Christian Freedom— flows out of God, through the soul that rests in a state of faith and abandonment of self. Fides to Franck is Gelassenheit, the "Sabbath rest" of the soul.[31]

The corollary to Franck's understanding of the spirit is an ethic of tolerance. More than any of the other Spiritualists, he was oriented toward the "invisible church" of all believers. It exists at all times, in all peoples, countries, and confessions. The dogmatists and persecutors are the only real heretics. Those persecuted as heretics have the true faith. It seems, then, that the invisible church can only be defined negatively. Persecution is of significance as a testimony. This concept was handed on to Sebastian Castellio, the dissenter from Savoy who protested the execution of Servetus, and, much later, to Gottfried Arnold (1666–1714), who elaborated Franck's inversion of heresy and faith in a chronicle of the persecutors and persecuted, *The Unpartisan History of Church and Heretics*. Oversimplified as it is, the notion that those who suffer persecution are always the faithful or righteous ones has a modern ring to it. Franck was also a pacifist and a critic of the unjust rulers whom he likened to the predatory eagles of heraldic emblems. He defended the theory that people should learn from world history, from the *History-Bible* (*Geschicht-Bibel*), as he entitled one of his books. While denying that the meaning of the Bible is historical, Franck accorded to an all-encompassing history the significance of a second Bible.

Franck's universalism and modernity invite the supposition that he denied all historicity to revealed truth. But according to Hegler, Franck found "in Christ a complete revelation of the divine being and will."[32] The historical fact of Christ is not challenged by Franck. The life of Christ is said to be so exemplary that all the books and sermons of value could be replenished from it. Yet the historical Christ *per se* is "flesh" and therefore meaningless for faith. Only the inner word, the eternal Word, can generate real faith in the believer. Franck saw the Christ of faith as the eternal Word, present in all places and peoples.

The simultaneous retention of the historical Christ with a rejection of the "historical faith" is a peculiarity that hovers over the paradoxes of Franck and, to some degree, over all the Spiritualists. For Franck, the very act of positing the object of faith as something that can be written and rendered into binding doctrine has an externalizing, falsifying effect. Religion as the "outer word" deadens the living faith, not because the Bible is a nonfactual story, but rather because the "history" and "letter" of Scripture are *per se* false and idolatrous—as objects of faith.

The views of Franck remained elliptical and eclectic. It was only with Valentin Weigel that Spiritualism at last developed the systematic theory required for explaining its opposition to the authoritarianism of *sola scriptura* and *fides historica*.

Weigel, who lived from 1533 until 1588, was the product of a different period. In character at the opposite extreme from the open defiance of the earlier Spiritualists, Weigel represents the type of the underground dissident who writes for the sympathizing few, for posterity, or for his desk drawer. Nevertheless, it was Weigel who dealt the most stinging blow to the new orthodoxy—a blow which earned him the abiding hatred of the zealous Lutheran clergy and theologians. The stations of Weigel's life were those of a typical Lutheran pastor. Educated first in Leipzig and then in Wittenberg, he became pastor of Zschopau in Saxony and remained in this position until his death. Despite his reputation for heresy, much in his writing is concerned with intensifying and deepening the Evangelical faith.

We know from historical accounts that this was truly an age of faith. However, the age of faith had various faces: one free, the other unwilling and coerced, a third driven by faith itself to embrace heterodox positions. Folk piety had always resulted in deviating opinions; there was to be no exception in Protestant times. In the decades of Weigel's youth, study, and pastorate, the suppression of heresies continued in Saxon lands. Accused heretics (or "blasphemers") were tortured, imprisoned, exiled, beheaded, or burned at the stake. The castle of the Wartburg, where Luther had been forced to hide out after the Imperial Diet at Worms, became a prison for a nonviolent Anabaptist, ironically named Fritz Erbe ("heir"). For his crime of disavowing the Evangelical sacraments, Erbe remained imprisoned in the Wartburg until death. Lutheran persecutions—including burnings for reason of heresy—continued in the second half of the sixteenth century. Elector Prince August of Saxony consolidated the faith by enforcing the General Articles of 1557. Schools and churches were inspected to assure that only approved teachings were disseminated. Pastors stood under a binding supervision in matters of doctrine. They could be dismissed with resultant economic ruin. The congregation itself was subject to compulsion. Fines and public detention were mandated for those who failed to attend church.[33]

These strictures threatened punishment in a sphere that had formerly been the domain of a victorious popular freedom. From the beginning of the Reformation, the church sermon had played a central role in the Evangelical movement and a pivotal one in the transition from the old faith. In the early years of the Reformation, the lay folk had demanded Evangelical preachers, sometimes disrupting the sermons of recalcitrant priests. Though still cherished by the common folk, the sermon was becoming integrated into the machinery of control and suppression. The German language possesses several forceful words signifying subordination in a patriarchal society. Not coincidentally, these words allude either to a condition of having no right to speak for oneself or to the basic passivity of hearing: *Unmündigkeit*, *Bevormundung* (the voiceless subordination of the minor), and *Hörigkeit* (the bound subjugation of the slave or servant). It is worth pondering the question how the Lutheran lay folk felt about being returned to their earlier condition of *Unmündigkeit* and *Hörigkeit*, being required to attend the sermon by statutes enforced by the town beadle.

In the only confrontation of Weigel's lifetime, members of his congregation reported on suspicious elements in his sermons. In response to the inquiries of the superintendent, Weigel wrote a defense summarizing the message of his sermons. The defense quotes extensively from Luther, criticizes the historical faith, and even takes its title from the *Theologia Deutsch*. Otherwise, however, Weigel makes his message sound harmonious with orthodox theology. When faced with ruin, he emphasized an Evangelical common ground. However, he interpreted the common ground in a manner that played off Luther against the new Lutheran orthodoxy. As for the complaints brought against him, it seems that Weigel enjoyed sufficient rapport with his flock to avert disaster.

Scholars have divided Weigel's development into three phases: an early period (1570–1571), in which he appropriated the mystical thought of Eckhart, Tauler, and the *Theologia Deutsch*, in search of a solution to the current dispute over justification; a second period, which began the year before the defense with *Know Thyself* (*Gnothi seauton*, 1572) and lasted until 1576, during which time the mystical teachings previously absorbed were interpreted in a more original manner; and a final period (1578–1584) during which Weigel increasingly turned to the nature philosophy of Paracelsus, at the same time developing a more stringent critique of the church.

Since *Know Thyself* was written the year before Weigel's confrontation with the authorities, it presumably indicates the objectionable ideas for which he was denounced to the superintendent. Weigel's introduction counsels the reader to first read the "book of the heart." He admonishes that the "lost child" who is being led only by the "letter," without having seen or known Christ in faith, will reject the call of "know thyself." This lost child—Weigel admonishes severely—will reveal itself as the beast of the Apocalypse. Clearly, self-knowledge is not merely a personal issue for the pastor of Zschopau.

Self-knowledge resonates with the mystical tradition that had come down to Weigel, recalling the *Theologia Deutsch* and Tauler. Self-knowledge is combined by the pastor of Zschopau with the nature mysticism of Paracelsus. The Eckhartian tradition provided Weigel with the assurance that: "There is a great difference between the house and [the] occupant of the house, for the inner is always better and nobler than the visible and external."[34] The polarity of inner and outer offered a position of defense. However, the Paracelsian nature mysticism with its triadic structures provided Weigel a further possibility of synthesis ignored by his Spiritualist precursors. Weigel's mysticism of self-knowledge combines features of epistemology, cosmology, and anthropology, doing so more systematically than the work of any of his mystical predecessors.

To be sure, these features remain within an Augustinian thematic framework. This is evident for Weigel's epistemology and anthropology in chapters nine and ten of *Know Thyself*, and for his cosmology in the opening chapters of his *On the Place of the World* (*Vom Ort der Welt*). Weigel's paralleling of the dual hierarchies—of the world and of the faculties of knowledge—is indebted to Renaissance Neoplatonism. The ascent, upward toward the realm of the intelligences or angels, is also a path inward, into the innermost faculty of the soul, since the latter stems directly from God. This is a familiar itinerary.

What is new is the radical assertion regarding Scripture, that knowledge does not come from without, not from the letter, but rather from within. Weigel makes it clear that he, too, is outraged, both by the moral hypocrisy and by the authoritarian compulsion of the new Protestant world. Like Franck, he is a moralist. However, Franck had scarcely attempted to resolve the problem of how to make positive assertions within the limits of an antidogmatic dissent. Weigel knew of Franck's work, but was a more systematic and patient thinker than his precursor. The clandestine dissenter transformed the precept that knowledge must come from within into what amounts to a doctrine of the mind and its relationship to the world. Self-certainty in the Augustinian tradition offered a foundation stone for Weigel's rejection of all dogmatism.

Even in our natural knowledge—he writes in chapter eleven of *Know Thyself*—there has to be both a knower and an object of knowledge. All vision depends in a decisive manner upon the eye itself: if it is faulty or tinged, the perception will be altered accordingly. Weigel expands this: *all knowledge comes from the knower.* If it came from the object, we would all have the same perception. The very existence of discord is thus construed by Weigel to favor his Spiritualistic epistemology. The anger and dogmatism of the orthodox clergy is a judgment on them: for what they *see* stems from what they *are*. Chapter eighteen goes on to elaborate that the letter is not only the outer word of the Bible. The tyranny of nature is also a form of the "letter."

Like Augustine and Pico della Mirandola before him, Weigel refutes the fatalism of astrology. He does so, not in order to refute superstition. The point is that nature stands in the power of God. This is the sense of the visionary evocation of "the place of the world" in his treatise of that title. Just as all truth comes from within, thus, too, the immanent power of God permeates and sustains this world. Beyond "the place of this world" there is no place, beyond the time of this world no time. The transcendence of the eternal is beyond place and time. The power of God therefore lies in every sense *within*.

In his *Golden Grasp* (*Der güldene Griff*), Weigel takes up a motif already used by Franck, of the book sealed with seven seals in Revelation 5. Weigel explains that this book lies within us. From within us all knowledge proceeds, in the same way that all things have been created by God out of nothing. As Weigel's initial chapter elucidates, all true knowledge comes to him who understands these implications of the creation *ex nihilo*:

> Whoever considers this—I tell you—, that all things have come into being from nothing, have come into being through the Word, from the invisible into the visible, from the spiritual into the physical and corporeal, and [yet] it remains one within the other...thus, all external things flow out from the inner being, and nothing from without inward. Just look: Whence comes the tree? Truly, from out of the astral powers (*aus den astris*) of the stars of the invisible seed. Whence comes the pear? Out of the tree. Whence come snow and hail, rain, fog? Not from the earthly mists, as Aristotle says, but rather from the invisible astral powers of the stars, which make the invisible visible. Now, whence comes the human being? From the *limbus terrae*, that is: from the clump of earth that is indeed the entire world. Invisibly, Adam lay in the world and became corporeal. That out of which one is made one also covets within oneself.... Adam was extracted from all creatures, and all creatures lie within him. From the firmament or stars is his spirit, and therefore Adam has all his art, craft, language, and animal wisdom within him, for what is in the firmament is also in the human being. Beyond this, the human being has an eternal soul from the inspiration of God, together with the Holy Spirit. Therefore the eternal celestial wisdom is also within him; from which can be concluded that all knowledge of divine things is not taken from books, but rather flows from the human being himself into the letters.[35]

All the previous worlds of German mysticism—visible and invisible, outer and inner, nature and Scripture, letter and spirit—are united in a knowledge that unlocks the human, natural, and scriptural "books"—all in the suggestively evoked context of the book with seven seals, in the noetic endtime of an inner, spiritual Revelation.

Ethically, Weigel's Spiritualism is a reaffirmation of the position which, in chapter twelve of the second book of *Know Thyself*, he attributes to Tauler and the *Theologia Deutsch*: good works must be done unconditionally, neither for the sake of any reward, nor out of fear of any punishment. The false human being who is self-centered and self-seeking actually punishes himself. The true Christian who denies himself and seeks only the honor of God will find God in all things. In order to substantiate this point with reference to knowledge, chapter thirteen names Eckhart and inserts an extensive paraphrase of one of his sermons before concluding by citing a Paracelsian treatise.

Weigel's later *Dialog on Christianity* hammers home the point that the Lutheran *imputed* justification—if it lacks for an inner conversion and human improvement—is utterly devoid of any saving grace. Weigel's "preacher" in the *Dialog* represents the orthodox Lutheran position. At the conclusion of the dialog, the preacher discovers to his eternal sorrow that his doctrines of imputed justification and faith from hearing pave the high road to hell.

The trichotomous anthropology that Weigel takes over from Paracelsus facilitates the attempt to find a third path, beyond the antitheses of doctrine which threatened the Protestant world with internecine strife and disintegration toward the end of the sixteenth century. In the following century, faced with intense conflicts between Lutherans and Calvinists and with a general renewal of confessional warfare, Jacob Boehme would undertake to refine the work of synthesis begun by Weigel. The synthesis would offer not only a defense against orthodox repression, but also a visionary basis for affirming pluralism. The subjective pole of the inner spirit is complemented by a large-scale interpretation of spirit in nature and salvational history in Boehme.

Spiritualistic mysticism as it emerged in the century of the Reformation retains a simple core within its increasingly complex conflation of inner and outer worlds. All truth and all goodness comes from within. Any doctrine that reduces the believer to an unfree recipient of the "external word" deprives the Bible of its essential meaning. The living truth that can only reside in the individual draws upon self-knowledge. Hence, it looks to itself instead of imposing its opinions on others. If it is authentic, faith issues in selfless actions.

The complex and rather tortuous evolution of this simple idea of an inner truth is symptomatic of the detours and impasses of the

Reformation. The words from Ferdinand Lasalle's *Franz von Sickingen*, quoted in Arthur Koestler's parable of modern revolution, *Darkness at Noon*, might do to summarize the dialectic of hope and disappointment, the clash of ideal and realization at the root of sixteenth-century Spiritualism:

> Show us not the aim without the way.
> For ends and means on earth are so entangled
> That changing one, you change the other too;
> Each different path brings other ends in view.

German mysticism helped to inspire the "aim" which led to the revolutionary ferment of the Reformation; and when its ends and means had been confounded, mysticism again gathered the hopes and teachings of spiritual renewal and launched them toward more receptive shores.

# 7

# The Part and the Whole

## Jacob Boehme and the Baroque Synthesis

Between the religious wars of the century of Reformation and the unprecedented calamities of the Thirty Years' War, a respite was granted to the conflict-torn Holy Roman Empire. In Middle Europe, this period of calm lasted from the Peace of Augsburg in 1555 to the Defenestration of Prague in 1618—a rare interval of peace for this region. If in the history books the brilliance of Elizabethan England outshines this obscure respite, to some who benefited from it and then watched it draw to a close it may have seemed like a charmed interlude, an enchanted island in time, surrounded by fervent hopes and dire forebodings. Its culture was favored by the intellectual-spiritual climate of the Reformation and the Renaissance—but also chilled by omens of continuing conflict: the St. Bartholomew's Day Massacre in Paris, the Dutch Wars of Independence, and the accelerating momentum of the Counter-Reformation. As the interval came to an end, the mix of longings and forebodings rose to an apocalyptic cacophany, as the dramatic events of the Thirty Years' War began to unfold.

The great doctrinal, scientific, and political problems of the previous century had been left largely unresolved. Nature, Scripture, the body politic, and the individual conscience had all been exposed to a new light of scrutiny. But in each case, there were as many questions as answers. What could have been more compelling than to expect that the great questions were to be answered altogether and upon supreme authority, in a resolution of all the deep mysteries of being?

Mysticism articulated the complicated and tension-ridden composition of this historical culture. Already in the mysticism of Paracelsus, Franck, Weigel, and the pseudo-Paracelsian *Liber Azoth* there was a discernible tendency toward accumulation, theoreticization, and synthesis. At its simplest, this impulse amounted to a gathering and hearing out of disparate voices, as in the writings of Franck where the unifying "spirit" abides in the unutterable paradox. At its most complex, this impulse gave rise to insinuations of immense secrets entailing the coherence of all things. Synthesis and integration extended beyond what can be classed as mysticism. In logic and pedagogy, the system of the French Calvinist Pierre de la Ramée (1515–1572, a victim of the infamous massacre in Paris), provided a new method for organizing all learning and thought. Pope Clement VIII (1592–1605) opened the window to Renaissance syncretism in the theology of Rome. The compendious and eclectic devotional writings of the Lutheran pastor Johann Arndt (1555–1621) laid up the inspirational treasures for the future culture of German Pietism.

But the most spectacular attempts at synthesis in this period did not pursue their aims solely with reasoning or encyclopedic collection. Faced with seemingly unresolvable quandaries, eager minds were attracted to the special vantage of the illuminist or theosophist. The more intractable the conflicts proved, the more appealing the dream of a hidden coherence either favoring one's own side or reconciling all sides in a higher order and harmony. The elusive goals of harmonization were represented variously by the widespread allures of an alchemistic art that drew upon the transforming, dissolving, and combining ("spagyric") powers latent in nature; by the grandiose projects of pansophic theoreticians such as Giordano Bruno, Robert Fludd, or Jan Amos Comenius; and by the telltale furor generated by the Rosicrucian manifestos. These latter enticed by blending the authority of an esoteric antiquity with a Humanistic modernity, nature with religion, East with West. All the powers conferred by knowledge were gathering into the clandestine fraternity of savants, who could be expected to reach out from concealment—rather like the wizard Prospero on his tempest-swept, enchanted island—to heal the ailments of this troubled age.

Of the many remarkable figures of this period, none was more prodigious than the shoemaker-mystic, Jacob Boehme (1575–1624). A man of humble origin and rudimentary education, Boehme was destined to become one of the most renowned and influential writers of his age. His work would still provide stimulation to the great philosophers and poets of the Romantic period two centuries later. In the evolution of German mysticism and its relations with intellectual history, Boehme is a pivotal figure: the one into whom all the earlier currents flowed and out of whom these currents spread after being transformed by the force of his inspiration. Through his influence, the tradition of German mysticism remained in German intellectual life until the nineteenth century.

Boehme is a writer who seems to come out of nowhere and lack the requisite background of education, training, or position. He attributed his gifts to the Holy Spirit, and his admirers further stylized his fame as the "God-taught" theosophist. The legend of his illumination is more famous than his writings. According to his friend Abraham von Franckenberg, the divine inspiration was visited upon the cobbler in 1600, when a sudden gleam of light in a vessel startled him from his labors, causing him to go out of his shop into nature. There, according to this account, Boehme saw into the secret "center" and "heart" of nature, recognizing in the lines and forms of things their revealing "signatures." Though Boehme's references to his illumination are less detailed than this, it is clear from his remarks that this seminal event amounted to a spiritual "rebirth," that it took place in 1600, and that it became the foundation of his writings.

There is truth to the characterization of an inspiration lacking the common prerequisites, but also some exaggeration. Long after his time, his inspiration was interpreted in the light of later concepts of the distinction between rational discursive thought and passive mystical inspiration. Distinctions unknown in his century were superimposed on his work.

Recently, the anachronistic view of Boehme and his work has begun to receive a long-overdue corrective: by Alexandre Koyré, Ernst-Heinz Lemper, Bo Andersson, and my own biographical study focusing on contemporaneous determinants of Boehme's developing thought.[1] In this chapter, I will summarize my own results and place Boehme and his work into the context of the tradition of German mysticism, before turning to the other mystics of his century who are on a par with him in depth and originality.

We know very little about the actual source materials read by Boehme—the works of the "many high masters" which in *Aurora* he professes to having read. However, a surprising number of the themes of German mysticism are reassembled and synthesized in his oeuvre: Hildegard's epic struggle between the forces of good and evil, with nature as the battleground and with the realm of the angels as a model for this world; Eckhart's reflective knowledge which knows God in self-knowledge; Seuse's chivalrous devotion to Lady Wisdom; Tauler's use of parabolic symbols; the Christian Kabbalah and Hermetism of the Renaissance; the paradoxes of all things in all, and of the whole contained in the part; nature as an ensemble of living forces and a meaningful code of signatures coordinated with Scripture; the ubiquity of the divine being and the real presence of the body of Christ in the bread and wine of Communion; the inner word as the spirit that unfolds outward to disclose the hidden sense beneath the letter; the Spiritualists' defense of freedom and toleration, and their individual-istic opposition to orthodox authoritarianism.

The Johannine and Augustinian roots of German mysticism are essential to Boehme's interpretation of creation, his conflation of tem-poral creation and eternal Word, and his evocation of the associations of *lux in tenebris*. These combinations unlock some of his most obscure formulations and symbols. However, around this time-honored the-matic core there are new outgrowths with ancient roots. Gnostic ele-ments come into play to express an extreme alienation at the outset of the Thirty Years' War. He brings a material inherited from Christian Neoplatonism to bear on the relationship of natural or human evil to the goodness and omnipotence of the Creator. Boehme speculates with a theory of qualities and forces and interprets the androgynous Adam in the tradition of Gregor of Nyssa and Erigena. His central concerns are with the creation and its implications for free will, good and evil, and knowledge. Boehme knows a creation *ex Deo* in the tradi-tion of Erigena. Remarkably, evil appears as an aspect of divine being. Evil is not God, but neither is it nothing. The development that is guided toward that light which was "in the beginning" is the ent-elechy of all things, human, divine, and natural. There are strong Lutheran and Paracelsian elements in Boehme's mysticism. All the currents of tradition flow into his complex synthesis—as if he were the relay from which they were to flow back out again to affect writers as diverse as Silesius, Kuhlmann, Zinzendorf, Novalis, Tieck, Baader, and Schopenhauer in Germany, along with others in Holland, Eng-land, France, America, and Russia. The Baroque synthesis is classically exemplified by the mysticism of Boehme.

Boehme must be interpreted in the historical context of his period and region of Upper Lusatia (*die Oberlausitz*). This was a small, predominantly German and Lutheran territory that lay to the east of Electoral Saxony, the heartland of the Reformation, and to the north of the Habsburg-ruled Kingdom of Bohemia, to which Lusatia and Sile-sia were attached as crown lands.

The dilemma of standing between conflicting principles of authority was virtually encoded into the political geography of this region. The unstable condition of being suspended between rival demands for religious and political allegiance was a cross on which the people of this region had been crucified for nearly two centuries. It began with the Hussite Wars of the fifteenth century, continued with the turmoil of the Lutheran Reformation (which left Lusatia torn between its Catholic emperor and its Lutheran faith), and then continued, even more divisively, with the post-Reformation internecine disputes of Lutherans, Anabaptists, Schwenckfeldians, and Crypto-Calvinists. It culminated in 1618, in the new Defenestration of Prague—an action that imitated the Hussite insurrection and inaugurated the bloodiest European war of religion. For two hundred years, the interminable conflicts had flared up all around Upper Lusatia, from Bohemia to Electoral Saxony to Brandenburg and the Silesian duchies (where there were disturbances caused by the introduction of Calvinism), and then back to the Bohemian capital, where the long fuse at last ignited the Thirty Years' War.

To gain a deeper understanding of the historical background of the Baroque duality of celestial and infernal perspectives, it is helpful to take note that even in Boehme's earliest and most optimistic writing, *Aurora* (1612), the threat of religious war and persecution is evoked. It would seem that the real horrors of history were never out of mind. Yet the first three decades of Boehme's life coincided with the extended period of peace and relative harmony between confessions in Middle Europe. This was the heyday of a Prague that still gloried as the capital of the Holy Roman Empire under the Habsburg Emperor and King of Bohemia, Rudolph II. An early, still rather successful period of Rudolph's reign lasted until the turn of the century. This era was adorned by spectacular initiatives in the arts and sciences.

The Rudolphine culture of Prague was also characterized by a relatively high degree of pluralism and tolerance. Protestants of more than one variety, Catholics, and Jews contributed openly to a many-faceted culture that was centrally preoccupied with the elaboration of universal patterns and overarching systems of knowledge. The astronomers Tycho Brahe and Johann Kepler, the artists Giuseppe Arcimboldo and Bartholomäus Spranger, an array of famous alchemists (representatives of a "science" sponsored by many princes during this age), the Kabbalistic mystic Rabbi Löw, and many lesser-known scientists, craftsmen, and thinkers pursued their activities in the vicinity of Rudolph's court. Nearly all aspects of Rudolphine culture—its Humanism, astronomy, alchemy, and mysticism—were shared by the citizens of Boehme's Görlitz, a city familiar even to Kepler and Löw.[2]

The Lusatian satellite of Rudolphine Bohemia also fell within the sphere of influence of an Electoral Saxony that had been the bastion of Protestant culture since Luther's own day. Toward 1600, Dresden and Wittenberg pressured the Lusatians to conform strictly to the orthodox Lutheran Book of Concord. The pressure to conform was exerted by the divines of Wittenberg, sometimes in collusion with the Catholic emperor in Prague.

After 1600, Calvinistic rulers came to power in Brandenburg and Silesia. The political equilibrium was threatened by their more militant opposition to Rome and Habsburg, the religious peace by their rejection of Lutheran practices and doctrines. Notably, the Calvinists denounced the Lutheran doctrines of divine ubiquity and "real presence" in the Eucharist. To the open or clandestine Calvinists and to some of the Humanistically tempered followers of Melanchthon (Philippists), the old Lutheran teachings appeared lax, superstitious, and idolatrous.

The Lutheran Lusatians were again caught in the middle, with challenges to their religious autonomy coming from all sides. They had turned Lutheran in 1526, the same year they came under Habsburg rule. After the Schmalkaldic War, they had narrowly escaped complete subjugation. *De facto*, the Lusatians enjoyed a tenuous state of religious toleration. A variety of religious groups coexisted quietly inside their boundaries, but this meant a constant peril of sliding from the precarious peace and losing their religious autonomy. In a sense, the Lusatians were frozen in time. They were locked into the condition of the early Reformation, when faith rested on the conscience of the individual and not on enforcement by the state. They were outside the Augsburg system of exclusionary territorial confessions, based on political control and creedal conformity. In the Lusatian cities, the religious peace depended on an informal coexistence of the majority Lutherans with several minorities of Catholics, Schwenckfeldians, and Philippists. This pluralistic religious culture was suspended between the orbits of the orthodox Lutheranism of Wittenberg and the cosmopolitanism of Prague.

Boehme's writings bespeak his impassioned allegiance to the freedom of an anachronistic Lutheranism. He expresses opposition to enforced creedal conformity. At the same time, he incorporates numerous influences of the waning Rudolphine era, as it lingered prior to the Counter-Reformation offensive of Emperor Ferdinand II in 1617. The remarkable fact that an uneducated layman could undertake to resolve the religious disputes of his time clearly testifies to the emancipating power of the Lutheran conferral of authority on the individual believer. However, in resuming his writing after being silenced by the ministers and magistrates of his city in 1613, Boehme just as clearly went beyond the limits drawn by Luther and his magisterial successors.

Reflecting the controversies of his region and the piety of his era, Boehme was preoccupied with the defense of the Lutheran doctrine of the "real presence" of the invisible flesh and blood of Christ in the bread and wine of the Eucharistic *Abendmahl*. Johann Georg Gichtel, Boehme's meticulous seventeenth-century editor, devoted over three pages to the heading of *Abendmahl* in the index to the complete works. Boehme's first two books took up the task of defending and interpreting Lutheran Eucharistic doctrine by means of central concepts: that of *siderischer Geist* (sidereal spirit) in *Aurora*, and that of *Wesen* (divine being) in *The Three Principles of Divine Being*. In the context of Boehme's entire oeuvre, the doctrine of the real presence is interpreted in terms of a mystical omnipresence of God. In contrast to Luther, Boehme understood the doctrine of divine ubiquity as an assertion rich in metaphysical consequences. He pursued these consequences in a manner for which Luther might have shown as little acceptance as did the orthodox theologians who condemned Boehme in the seventeenth and eighteenth centuries.

In the turbulent history of Lusatia, the Eucharist had repeatedly been struggled and fought over. The Hussites had marched through the region beneath the banner of the Communion chalice. A century later, their Utraquistic celebration of the Communion in both forms was reinstituted by the Reformation. The Protestants of Boehme's own lifetime knew no more bitter nor more symbolically charged point of contention. The Schwenckfeldians challenged the authority of Lutheran doctrines and institutions by remaining aloof from the *Abendmahl*, calling their abstinence *Stillstand*. When the German Calvinists pressed for political reforms and took a more militant stance vis-à-vis the Catholic powers, they also firmly rejected the Lutheran doctrine of ubiquity. This was no mere appendix to their other reforms: the Lutheran *Abendmahl* was doctrinally similar to the Catholic Communion—an objectionable proximity for militant antipapists.

In the hands of the Lusatian cobbler, the doctrine of divine ubiquity became the foundation of an irenic mysticism which made qualitative variety the complement of the One. This is evident in Boehme's depiction of the utopian Paradise of the angels in *Aurora* (1612). *Aurora* was conceived and written during years when the Lusatians were petitioning their emperor for a Letter of Majesty guaranteeing the toleration of Lutheranism in Lusatia.

Repeatedly pointing to the exemplary aspect of the angelic kingdom, Boehme sketches the ideal configuration of his Paradise. Each individual has a right to his own particular quality and a "natural right" (*ein Natur-Recht*) to dwell in peace in the *locus* of his birth. No angelic prince hinders the free movement of other angels; and no angelic army makes war against any other army—except against the infernal host of the banished Prince Lucifer, who fell attempting to usurp the highest throne, to subjugate the entire Kingdom to his power. In Boehme's view, the divine presence is equally immanent in every locality and angel. The *omnes in omnibus* of free diversity is thus aligned with a harmonious order and reign. The deity who is greater than all things is mirrored in the human creature as a free capacity for redemption, just as the heavenly tincture in the elemental stone or plant intimates a secret capacity to be transformed and perfected.

In his pluralism, the mystic gravitated toward Prague. The order of the cosmos was in serious dispute during the period in which *Aurora* was conceived and composed. Kepler—who was also a man of pansophic interests—was completing his *Astronomia Nova* to resolve scientific questions left open by Copernicus and Brahe. Kepler was no stranger to Boehme's Görlitz, a city in which the new astronomy met with keen interest.

By resolutely affirming heliocentrism, *Aurora* introduced a new factor into German mysticism. Paracelsus, like Hildegard in *Scivias*, still saw the world as an "egg." The geocentrist Weigel still ruminated over "the place of the world." Now, however, in the new astronomy, Boehme confronted what Kepler called the *Mysterium Cosmographicum*. For the shoemaker, this meant that all the given assumptions about the *prima facie* order in nature—all the orders among planets, elements, and elemental humors—were annihilated. A free-floating, potentially chaotic, yet wondrously stable and vital pattern is celebrated in Boehme's *Aurora*, a vision deriving in no small measure from his naive assent to a sun-centered world. Only a divine power present equally in all things and all places can maintain the universal harmony of the planetary, angelic, and political orders.

The world is not stacked and rigged with God on top and the earth on bottom: the very idea depresses Boehme. God is *alles in allem*. Through the divine nature, all things are in all other things. Corresponding to the planets, Boehme knows seven "source-spirits." These *Quellgeister* stem from the tradition of the divine "influences" of Paracelsus and Agrippa, with roots in the *causae primordiales, causae seminales,* and *logoi spermatikoi*. The *Quellgeister* are eternal spirit forces operative in the fallen nature of a world that has been half deadened by the insurrection and fall of Satan and his constituent spirits.

All spirits, good and evil, consist of qualities and force. There are seven qualities, keyed to the traditional influences associated with the planets. Summarized in chapters twenty-five and twenty-six of *Aurora*, the conventional planetary qualities had been tabled in *The Book of Secrets* attributed to Albertus Magnus. Reprinted in Germany

in 1548, *The Liber Secretorum* continued to influence the nature philosophy of the period.[3] Boehme was in conformity with the natural science
and alchemy of his period in extending the qualities to all domains of
nature: to planets, elements, plants, and psychic humors.

As force, the ensemble of the spirit-qualities makes up a divine
substance that *Aurora* calls the *Salitter* or *Sal niter*; it exists in a celestial
and an earthly, half-corrupted form. *Salitter* alludes to the refined and
unrefined forms of saltpeter. This was the essential industrial product
required for the manufacture of gunpowder. *Salitter* was also an object
of alchemistic speculation. One theory propagated in his region saw
"aerial niter" as the substance that sustained all life. The ambiguity of
a common niter and an esoteric *Salitter*—a divine substance and an
earthly substance—was characteristic for alchemistic theory. Alchemy
recognized a philosopher's Mercury or Sulphur with supernatural
powers which corresponded at a higher level to ordinary mercury or
sulphur.[4] Without ignoring the distinction between science and superstition, we have to consider Boehme's ideas in the context of the naturalism of his time. It was a naturalism that could take many forms.
These were embodied not only in the mathematical astronomy of
Kepler, but also in fanciful observations of terrestrial nature, of rocks,
elements, fruits, plants, and animals.

All promptings and prototypes were brought to a white heat and
merged into the synthesis of Boehme's mysticism around 1600. All
spirits, qualities, and beings of the eternal and supernatural order concealed in nature were perceived as being "in one another like a single
thing" in Boehme's vision of the divine omnipresence. Everything is
focused in the "Divine Birth":

> Herewith, I intend to admonish the reader that he should regard
> the Divine Birth properly. You should not think that one spirit
> stands next to another, the way you see the stars in heaven
> standing one next to the other; rather all seven are in one another
> as one spirit...
>
> *Allhier will ich den Leser verwarnet haben, daß er die Göttliche Geburt
> recht betrachte. Du solst nicht dencken, daß ein Geist neben dem
> andern stehe, wie du die Sterne am Himmel siehest neben einander ste-
> hen; sondern sie sind alle 7 in einander wie ein Geist...* (1, *Aurora*, ch.
> 10:40)[5]

This confabulation means that within the pattern of the Divine Birth
there is no hierarchy among the spirits: in the eternal world, as in the

angelic kingdom, none is higher, none lower: "Look, all seven spirits of God are born at once, none is the first and none the last" (*Siehe, es werden alle 7 Geister Gottes zugleich geboren, keiner ist der erste, und keiner ist der letzte...*[1, *Aurora*, ch. 11:6]). God is the power of order in the nonhierarchical world: the God without and the God within. The coincidence of order with freedom, of harmony with equality, is evident for those with eyes to see what is inscribed in nature and in the soul: "for the law of doing what is right is written into nature, and you have the same book in your heart" (*denn das Gesetze, recht zu thun, ist in die Natur geschrieben, und du hast dasselbe Buch in deinem Hertzen* [1, *Aurora*, ch. 11:31]).

    *Aurora* recognizes that there is "no place in heaven nor in this world" where the Divine Birth does not take place. The tiniest "circle" that can be drawn is full of God (1, *Aurora*, ch. 10:60). The Son is born eternally in all creatures, in stones, leaves, and grass: "for the birth of the Holy Trinity is everywhere" (*denn die Geburt der Heil. Dreyfaltigkeit ist überall* [1, *Aurora*, ch. 8:82, 84]). "So near to you is God that the birth of the Holy Trinity also takes place in your heart; all three persons are born in your heart, God Father, Son, Holy Spirit" (*Also nahe ist dir Gott, daß die Geburt der H. Dreyfaltigkeit auch in deinem Hertzen geschiht; es werden alle 3 Personen in deinem Hertzen geboren, Gott Vater, Sohn, H. Geist* [1, *Aurora*, ch. 10:58]).

    God is everywhere: the recognition of this is both ecstatic and problematic, for it will elicit a compendious and ever more complex system of thought and intuition in reply to the follow-up question:

> Now you ask: Since God is everywhere, and is himself everything, how does it happen then that in this world there is such cold and heat; and also that all creatures bite and strike each other, and there is nothing but pure grimness in this world?

> *Nun fragst du: weil denn Gott überall ist, und selber alles ist, wie kommts dann, daß in dieser Welt solche Kälte und Hitze ist; dazu beissen und schlagen sich alle Creaturen, und ist nichts denn eitel Grimmigkeit in dieser Welt?* (1, *Aurora*, ch. 9:42)

The problem of evil in a world filled with suffering—a world in which humans behave like wild beasts—is taken up on the brink of war, when Boehme attempts to look into the depths of subjective being.

    As the Thirty Years' War began, Boehme broke the silence imposed on him by his pastoral and civic censors. His second book supplemented the theme of the ongoing creation effected by the source-spirits with themes having to do with the creation of an angelic Adam who became human, by falling from his erstwhile state of grace into his present condition of a hunted animal. With *The Three Principles of Divine Being* (*Von den Drey Principien Göttliches Wesens*), the mystic inaugurated a further endeavor that lasted until his death in 1624: to interpret divine ubiquity, to explain the rise and fall of the world and of human life in time. Since time is the refracted image of eternity, the eternal and temporal worlds, Creator and creature, One and many, have to be understood altogether through one another. Like the Spiritualists before him, Boehme wanted to overcome the "historical faith." The historical faith had failed because it had attempted to grasp the objects of faith as historical happenings, bound to the external scriptural letter. For the mystic, *Historia* and *Buchstabe* are extraneous to the human existence that is the subject of faith.

The pattern of the seven qualities is construed in a manner that reveals the configuration of the eternal birth at the core of all becoming: a single divine process is at work in the cosmic genesis of the world, in nature, procreation, the birth of an infant, or the regeneration of the soul. The key is the reinterpretation of the *creatio ex nihilo*: the tenet enunciated by Luther in his *On the Bound Will*. Even Weigel still adhered to it. But Boehme interprets the *ex nihilo* as a creation in which God draws upon no other material than his own hypostatized will. *Ex nihilo* is in reality *ex Deo*: therefore not "historical," but rather an ongoing and eternal process. God is omnipresent in the world because the world is made by God out of God: through the divine *Fiat* of creation, which is the same as the divine Word and light of redemption. Boehme's *creatio ex Deo* reverses the Lutheran-Calvinist doctrine of predestination, at the same time opening the door to a new correlation of biblical and philosophical knowledge. It is the central and formative idea in his thinking. Against the creation *ex nihilo*, Boehme's reflexive process of creation sanctions his doctrines of free will and rebirth. The creation *ex Deo* grounds the divine ubiquity and suggests the homology of all processes.

Further implications include Boehme's cosmic vitalism and theory of signatures. The world is seen as a mirror or outer expression of the inner divine will. Creation and faith become united in the creative imagination. We recall that for Eckhart knowing was said to precede being, and that God continually created all things in the soul. For Boehme, the creation *ex Deo* likewise creates eternally from within, as if every particle of the world were continually exploding out of an obscure longing into being in order to witness the light of eternity. In eternity, the divine will can be said to imagine itself into being, as does

the regenerated soul in a Now that takes leave of all the obscure com-
pulsions and delusions that are the correlatives of time and history. In
Boehme's pivotal second work,

> The consequences of the eternal self-generation of the divinity
> extend down the chain of being, thus: (1) We know already from
> *Aurora* that the angels were created out of God; they are finite
> but perfect miniatures of the Divine Being. (2) Man was not cre-
> ated out of a mere clump of earth, but rather out of a finer mater-
> ial, a *Limbus* or *Quinta Essentia*, which came into existence during
> an apotheosized cosmogony. (3) God did not create the first
> woman out of a mere rib extracted from Adam, but rather out of
> all the vital "essences" of Adam. (4) Even the animals are not
> simply formed out of clay; for they have a spirit in them that is
> not reducible to mere earth and water. (5) Plants have a life in
> them that cannot be resynthesized from the materials into which
> they decompose. (6) Finally, even the lifeless elements are pene-
> trated by the force of the Word which revitalizes vegetation.
> Hence, when the elements separated off from one another at the
> beginning of the world, each element was left teeming with
> invisible "elemental spirits" of its own kind. This shows that the
> "circle of life" is everywhere, complete in each creature and
> latent in each element.[6]

The circle of life is the pattern of dynamic force-qualities at work
everywhere. Understood in its aspect of simultaneity, this pattern
interprets the eternal being of God. Understood in the pattern of its
succession, it interprets the processes of nature and history: the emergence of life in the elements, the origination of the world in the matrix
of a darkness engendered by Lucifer's insurrection and fall, and the
succession of the stages of human history, prefigured in Genesis and
climaxing in the fire-world preceding the great apocalyptic awakening
of humankind, the Age of the Lily that blossoms toward midnight.
Boehme expected the last age to succeed the chaos and bloodshed that
engulfed his region.

In the final age, the human creature is to be restored to the state of
wholeness and awareness which stood at the beginning of the human
odyssey, to the condition of the angelic, androgynous first Adam. This
Adam's total seeing (without sleep in his mind or night in his eyes) is
to be restored in the mystical recognition of the coherence of all things,
in the intuition of the "signatures" of the world. These are the symbolic
qualities that awaken the awareness of a common origin of all crea-

tures in the transcendent divine "Unground" (*der Ungrund*)—a term for the limitlessness and indeterminacy of the hidden God whose creation is also a process of self-recognition.

The reflective aspect of the divine process is embodied in the Noble Virgin of Divine Wisdom, a figure adapted by Boehme from the intertestamental Wisdom literature of the Bible and enriched by Platonic affinities. The Noble Virgin Sophia allowed Boehme to incorporate the values of knowledge into his Lutheran fundamentals. Through the power of self-knowledge, the Virgin of Divine Wisdom performs the work of a transforming imagination—in a *creatio ex se* that reinterprets the Lutheran *sola fide*: the hidden God in nature eternally gives birth to its triune self out of the nothingness of the eternal will. The same wonder occurs in the rebirth of the believer.

For Boehme, the double perspective of a truth that is confirmed both by biblical revelation and by a "philosophy" ancient and modern reconfirms the many-faceted nearness of God. Just as his mysticism rejects predestination, so too does it disassociate itself from a prophecy based on the apocalyptic certainties drawn from the Book of Revelation. Faith concerns itself with the present and with eternity, not with history. There is an inner prophecy, preoccupied with a present existence seen as a reflection of the eternal being. The recognition of the power of eternity at work in time is the light of a knowledge that comes with the annihilation of the selfish will. The true self-knowledge is also a knowledge of the timeless divine omnipresence in nature.

Boehme's treatise in reply to the historical and literal chiliasm of Stiefel and Meth (who were preparing their followers for the imminent Second Coming) provides the biblical key to his spiritualistic prophecy, when he writes that the whole human being must be restored:

> ...and the whole man, as God created him in Adam, shall again stand in the quality and force of Christ, and again live in Jehova's light and force. For when Christ has completed everything, He is to give back the realm in rebirth to His Father, and God shall be all in all, as it was before the times of the world.

> ...*und soll der gantze Mensch, wie ihn Gott in Adam schuf, in Christi Eigenschaft und Kraft wieder darstehen, und wieder in Jehovae Licht und Kraft leben; Denn wenn Christus alles vollendet hat, so soll Er das Reich in der Wiedergeburt seinem Vater wieder überantworten, und soll seyn Gott alles in allem, wie es war vor den Zeiten der Welt.* (5, Anti-Stiefelius, book 2, sec. 168)

The biblical reference is to 1 Corinthians 15:24–28, one of the *loci classici* for the Pauline *omnes in omnibus*. It is the key to Boehme's singular use of prophesy. The second book proclaimed at the start of the war (a war during which the combatant parties drew for their propaganda scenarios upon the endtime battles of the Apocalypse), that the eternal world of a restored Paradise was latent in this world:

> Thus then, it is now recognizable to us, that God is All in all, and [that He] fulfills all, as it stands written: Am I not He who fulfills all things [*der alles erfüllet*]? (Ephesians 1:23) Thus, we know that the pure holy element in Paradise is his dwelling place: this is the second principle, [and] the same stands in all things: and [yet] the thing, as a dead, dark thing born out of it [*als eine todte finstere Ausgeburt*], does not recognize it, just as the pot does not know the potter, and thus does not grasp or take hold of it.

> *So uns dann nun erkentlich ist, daß Gott Alles in allem ist, und alles erfüllet, wie geschrieben stehet: Bin nicht ich der alles erfüllet? (Eph. 1:23) so wissen wir, daß das reine heilige Element im Paradeis seine Wohnung ist, das ist das andere Principium, dasselbe stehet in allen Dingen: und das Ding, als eine todte Ausgeburt, kennet es nicht, als der Topf seinen Töpfer, auch so ergreiffet oder fasset ers nicht.* (2, Principien, 22:39)

The failure to grasp the maker is the inability of the darkness to grasp the light. To conceive of the light is to be translated and reborn: from the "dark-world" of a fallen nature, caught up in strife and time, into the "light-world," which is the eternal origin of this world of transience and suffering. The divine world is called the second principle, and it is latently omnipresent in this world.

For Boehme, writing near the end of a long tradition, the union of worlds has become exceedingly complex, but all the more vividly felt. The latent presence of the eternal world in this world, of all things in all, sets the pattern of his mysticism. The signatures of things are clues that link what is present to the eternal. There are eternal grounds for the "historical" facts of Adam and Eve, for the curse of the earth, for the scourge of war. Recognizing the presence of eternity in time translates the believer from this world into an eternal one latent within it—a natural world of tranquil beauty. To believe and confess this doctrine of mystical rebirth is to reject the authority of false clerics and unregenerate rulers. Boehme's serenity is paired with antiauthoritarianism.

Divine ubiquity guaranteed order and freedom to Boehme's religious identity and to the confessional integrity of Lusatia. What connects the Lutheran doctrine with its extraordinary political-confessional extension is the mediating vision of his nature mysticism and philosophy. This was the catalyst for his inspiration and the substance of many of his reflections. All nature is Boehme's "living witness." In itself, the knowledge of scholars and scientists is inadequate (1, *Aurora*, ch. 22:11). Nature is full of secrets hidden beneath the letter (1, *Aurora*, ch. 21:1). Scripture and nature have to be understood with reference to one another. Intuitively, anyone can recognize from the existence of the natural and human creation, "that in these things a still more powerful force has to be present which has created all of this" (*daß in diesen Dingen noch eine mächtigere Kraft vorhanden sey, die dieses alles also geschaffen habe* [1, *Aurora*, ch. 22:11]).

The world calls for interpretation. If Boehme's mysticism can be ascribed to an experience, it is that of his intuition of a mystery of the world, constituted by the presence of good and evil in all things and by the concealment of God in nature. If all things in nature mean something, their key lies concealed in us and beneath the outer letter of Scripture. The clue of all clues is the power of the eternal Word in nature. The Word appears in many embodiments: as the rationale for the "nature language," as the intuitive codes of the "signatures of things," as process and product, the "speaking word" and the "spoken word" of creation. At root, the world is God's struggle for self-understanding and self-expression. Creation as sense and utterance guides the divine process of the world. Boehme interprets the eternal Word of creation and redemption as the pattern of all reality. The power that informs all things is the divine will to emerge from the darkness of anger, fear, and violence into the divine light of knowledge and harmony. The answer to the riddle of the world lies in recognizing that the life of the world is itself a quest for divine knowledge. Good is what realizes this light; evil is the darkness that fails the path of self-knowledge.

Earlier mystics also recognized this mystery. Cusanus marvelled at the coherence of the world. Agrippa knew of a higher concealed power in nature, present also within the human creature. He evoked it as the occult power of the *Magus* in an utterance which so impressed Schopenhauer that the philosopher used it as the motto of the second book of *The World as Will and Representation: Nos habitat, non tartara, sed nec sidera coeli: Spiritus in nobis qui viget, illa facit* ("It dwells within us, not in the nether world, nor in the stars of the heavens: the Spirit living within us effects all this").[7] But whereas Agrippa saw the *mirandorum operator* as the power of the magician, Boehme rejected the magician as a Faustian seducer ("...the sorcerer sits by the way and will deceive many a one": *der Zauberer sitzet im Wege, und wird manchen verblenden—* 1, *Aurora*, ch. 22:21). Either of these nature mystics presented the hidden power as perceptible in both an external and an internal nature. The inner force of all forces and the outer signatures that express what is hidden are the constants of the German mystical tradition, with consequences extending far beyond it.

In the eighteenth century, Herder would take the organic integrity of cultures as the expression of natural or organic forces. Lavater would use similar terms to characterize the expression of inner character in human physiognomy. In the nineteenth century, Schopenhauer would again utilize Boehme's terminology in his secular philosophy of the metaphysical will. What he retained was an approach to the world that looked not merely for cause, but for the meaning of things, an approach pursued even by Wittgenstein.

Boehme died in 1624. During and after the Thirty Years' War, his memory was cultivated as part of a mystical and pansophic heritage by his friend Abraham von Franckenberg (1593–1652) and other devotees. Among those who were to encounter his mysticism after the war, Friedrich Breckling (1629–1711) and Johann Georg Gichtel (1638–1710) are of prominence. They were Germans who found a freer environment for their dissenting spiritual development in Amsterdam. Through these and similar channels, a German mystical synthesis became known to ever-wider circles in Germany, Holland, England, and France. In the judgment of Erich Beyreuther, Boehme was to become the father of the "enthusiastic" or "radical" wing of Pietism. Beyond radical Pietists such as Gottfried Arnold (1666–1714), Boehme and Paracelsus also nourished the esoteric inclinations of Nikolaus Ludwig von Zinzendorf (1700–1760),[8] Friedrich Christoph Oetinger (1702–1782), and others. Philipp Jakob Spener (1635–1705) remained cooler in his assessment, and his reserve eventually prevailed in Pietistic circles. On the whole, the more accessible and orthodox Johann Arndt (1555–1621) probably exercised a greater and more lasting influence on the culture of German Pietism.[9] If the reputation of the shoemaker-mystic tended to affect the thoroughgoing nonconformists, this was in keeping with the individualistic tendency of Spiritualism.

Baroque mysticism proved particularly attractive for devout intellectuals and artists. It should be born in mind that Jacob Boehme was not the only purveyor of the mystical tradition. Two contemporaneous collectors and disseminators of mystical themes were the

Schwenckfeldian Daniel Sudermann (1550–1631) and the Cologne
Jesuit Maximilian Sandaeus (1578–1656). The great Lutheran hymnist
Paul Gerhardt (1607–1676) is credited by Gerhard Rödding with the
creation of a "unique synthesis of mystical piety and Lutheran faith,"
achieved by incorporating mystical materials from Bernard of Clairvaux, Arndt, and Martin Moller.[10] Moller, who died in 1606, was the
mystically inclined Lutheran pastor of Boehme's Görlitz, the compiler
of a collection of devotional materials called the *Meditationes Sanctorum Patrum.*

Because of the imaginative and suggestive nature of Boehme's
writings, his earliest postwar impact was spectacular in the poets who
were the experimenters and avant-gardists of the Baroque Age, the Silesian poets who knew his work: Daniel Czepko (1605–1660), Angelus
Silesius (Johannes Scheffler, 1624–1677), and Quirinus Kuhlmann
(1651–1689). Czepko wrote during the war, Scheffler and Kuhlmann
soon after the Peace of Westphalia (1648) permanently divided Germany. Despite their shared sources and common origin, these two postwar poets went in diametrically opposite directions in devoting themselves to the conversion of the world: Scheffler as a Catholic convert and
priest, and Kuhlmann as an idiosyncratic Protestant millenarian.

The structure of mysticism in Baroque poetry is determined by
the mystical totality. God is everywhere and all-powerful, *omnes in
omnibus.* Hence, the mind and poetic imagination are confronted with
an almost endless array of paradoxes and puzzles. In solving them,
the reader passes through a kind of transforming mirror, exchanging
worldly wisdom for divine wisdom and thereby assimilating time to
eternity. The pansophic theme of totality with its characteristic triad of
principles known from Paracelsus and Boehme is joined in this poetry
by a dualistically tempered mysticism of the kind associated with Eckhart or the *Theologia Deutsch.*

Nature mysticism and reflective mysticism differ in their appearance, but not in essence. We recall that in Eckhart, and again in Weigel
and Boehme, the mysticism of omnipresence was combined with a
speculation, aimed at confronting the human mind with a kind of
inverted mirror image of itself. Peering at its enigmatic image,
"through a glass darkly" at what Boehme called the "hidden man" of
the soul, the soul recognizes the inverted figure of God.

Associated with Franckenberg's circle toward the end of the
Thirty Years' War, Daniel Czepko was a master of the rhymed epi-
grammatic couplet—the formal vehicle for the polished and mirror-
like paradoxes that were refined to an unsurpassable degree by these
poets. In addition to Boehme's influence, there is a clear reception of

the motifs of Eckhart and the *Theologia Deutsch* in Czepko's work:[11]
"When God created the world...," the poet writes, "I flowed out with
everything, and yet remained in him" (*Da Gott die Welt erschuff..., Ich
floß mit allem aus, und war doch in ihm blieben*).[12] The soul is "a spark,
fallen into this body"—"Therefore, it strives heavenward, and finds
itself in all things" (*Die Seel ist als ein Funck in diesen Leib gefallen,/
Drumb wil sie in Himmel auf, und findet sich in allen*).[13] The couplets of
Czepko's *Sexcenta Monodisticha Sapientum* are a play of opposites,
divine and human, eternal and temporal, beginning and ending with
the signs of alpha and omega:

*alpha und omega*

*Anfang*                    *Ende*

*im*

*Ende*                    *Anfang*

*Das Ende, das du suchst, das schleuß in Anfang ein,*
*Wilt du auf Erden weis', im Himmel seelig seyn.*[14]

Here, Czepko offers a visible-verbal emblematic mirror for his chief
mystical theme. *Anfang* means beginning, *Ende* is end. The two lines
can thus be rendered:

The end which you seek: enclose it in beginning,
If you want to be wise on earth and blessed in heaven.

In interpreting this exhortation to invert, the mind is to be
prompted to flesh out the other facets of antithesis, thereby mentally
rounding out the part into a crystalline whole. In this case, the recou-
pling of "the end," as the object of human desire, back into God, as the
absolute point of departure, is intended to refigure the fleeting linearity of time into the circularity and permanence of eternity, thereby
conjoining wisdom with bliss and marrying heaven with earth.

In Czepko's epigrams, the premises of nature mysticism are conjoined with the dual perspective of reflective mysticism. As to the former, we are assured that all things are a book. Thus:

Everything full of God.
The blade of grass is a book, if you but seek to open it,
You can learn about creation and all wisdom from it.
*Alles voll Gott.*
*Das Gräslein ist ein Buch, suchst du es aufzuschliessen,*
*Du kanst die Schöpfung draus und alle Weisheit wissen.*[15]

This Boehmian reading of the blade of grass discloses the oneness of all things. Another epigram (*Alles in Eines*, "All into One") conveys that just as meaning (*Sinn*) has a bark or rind (*Rind*), and life a plant (*Kraut*), everything is one, if viewed in its essential being.[16] The life of the world grows meaning like the outer bark enclosing the inner source from which all things sprout.

In Czepko's epigrams, the divine omnipresence is aspectual, an angle on things:

> Not to yourself.
> See all things in God, and God in all things,
> You'll see that everything in him can be compared.
> *Nicht zu dir.*
> *Schau alle Ding in Gott, und Gott in allen an,*
> *Du siehst, daß alles sich in ihm vergleichen kan.*[17]

The axis on which all the epigrams turn is that of One-All-None-Word-World-Creator-Creature. Refracted through the conversions of *omnes in omnibus*, all things are likenesses of all other things: the world becomes an endless mirroring of God. Unjustly eclipsed by Silesius, Czepko's epigrams display in their love of inversion and irony an affinity with concrete poetry. There is subtle wit in the evocation of God as an ocean entirely within and entirely surrounding the subject. Against the dizziness which this ought to evoke, the poet prescribes: *Halt sein Geboth* ("Keep—i.e., hang onto—his commandment"). In an age of scientific inquiry, Czepko's God-centered view of nature counsels that whoever would ascertain the truth about all things will succeed, if he can find the right door to but one thing.[18]

The manifest irony of inversion and equation of one in all and all in one gives rise to endless subtleties for the master of the mystical epigram who called himself Angelus Silesius.[19]

Johannes Scheffler, christened a Lutheran in 1624, the year of Boehme's death, hailed from Breslau and studied at Strasbourg, Leiden in Holland (a vital center for the Protestant dissenters during the seventeenth century), and Catholic Padua. Finishing his medical studies, Scheffler returned to Germany shortly after the Thirty Years' War came to a close. Accepting a position as a court physician in Lutheran-orthodox Oels, he became friends with the aging and erudite Franckenberg. As a poet, Scheffler came up against the narrow-minded censorship of the Lutheran clergy. He converted to Roman Catholicism, demonstrating his conviction by becoming a priest and an activist in the Counter-

Reformationist campaign to reinstitute Catholicism in Silesia. Most of the poetic writings of Scheffler-Silesius, including his most famous *Cherubinic Wanderer* (*Der Cherubinische Wandersmann*), were published during the interval between his conversion and his ordination.

There is some evidence of a Catholic partisanship in the epigrams in the *Cherubinic Wanderer*, as, for example, in this apparent critique of the Lutheran *sola fidei*:

> Love is the soul of faith.
> Faith alone is dead, it cannot live
> Until it's been given its soul, love.
> *Die Lieb' ists Glaubens Seele.*
> *Der Glaub allein ist Todt / Er kan nicht eher Leben /*
> *Biß daß jhm seine Seel die Liebe wird gegeben.*[20]

An Evangelical Pietist might also have accepted this couplet with the proviso that faith without love is not faith at all. The orthodox Lutheran Formula of Concord conceded, "That good works must certainly and without doubt follow a true faith (provided only it be not a dead but a living faith), as fruits of a good tree."[21] Yet a subtle provocation does make itself felt, as it does again when the poet writes that, "Scripture without spirit is nothing" (2, no. 137):

> Scripture without spirit is nothing.
> Scripture is scripture, nothing else. My consolation is essentiality,
> And that God speaks in me the word of eternity.
> *Schrifft ohne Geist ist nichts.*
> *Die Schrifft ist Schrifft sonst nichts. Mein Trost ist Wesenheit /*
> *Und daß Gott in mir spricht das Wort der Ewigkeit.*

The epigrams are full of statements that appear heterodox by a literal standard, but are intended to challenge the mind in the manner of the Spiritualists, that is, without spelling out new doctrines *per se*. The technique of challenging orthodoxy and complacency by means of daring statements had precedents in Eckhart, Franck, and Boehme.

As in Czepko's poetry, the paradoxes are premised both on divine omnipresence and on the union of opposites, as in the poem, "God does not live without me" (1, no. 8):

> God does not live without me.
> I know that without me God cannot live an instant,
> If I come to naught, he must for want give up the ghost.

*Gott lebt nicht ohne mich.*
*Jch weiß daß ohne mich Gott nicht ein Nun kan leben /*
*Werd' ich zu nicht Er muß von Noth den Geist aufgeben.*

The God who is *Omnes in omnibus* necessarily—Silesius makes this
clear—exists by virtue of the same essence for me as I for him. As with
Eckhart, the denial of every external certainty of logic and letter
should result in an unconditional inner certainty. At the same time,
this refocusing of faith conjoins the human *I* with the divine *Thou*
within a mysterious abyss. The "pure divinity" is an "uncreated sea"
(1, no. 3), while the self-reflective *I* becomes a question mark, only
answered in God. Thus the poem, "One does not know what one is"
(1, no. 5):

> One does not know what one is.
> I don't know what I am, I am not what I know:
> A thing and not a thing: A dot and a circle.
> > *Man weiß nicht was man ist.*
> *Jch weiß nicht was ich bin / Jch bin nicht was ich weiß:*
> *Ein ding und nit ein ding: Ein stüpffchin und ein kreiß.*

The uncertainty of the mystic's unknowing of self as the path to the
unknown God coincides here with the absolute precision and certainty of the symbol of God as center and circumference: the dot dwin-
dles to nothing but thereby radiates outward to become the symbol of
eternity. The point and circle are revisited in this evocation of the
divine center and circumference (3, no. 148):

> God is my point and circle.
> God is my center when I enclose him in me:
> My circumference, when from love I dissolve in him.
> > *Gott ist mein Punct und Kreiß.*
> *Gott ist mein mittelpunct wenn ich Jhn in mich schlisse:*
> *Mein Umbkreiß dann / wenn ich aus Lieb' in Jhn zerflisse.*

One can discern here, as if between the lines, a kind of kinetic afterimage of the classical fountain symbolism of confluence, as well as the
associated paradox of *totus intus, totus extra*. The more it concentrates
the God within, the more the soul dissolves in the ocean of divinity.

Silesius also uses *Ort* and *Zeit*, "place" and "time" (as did Eckhart or Weigel), to circumscribe "world" (1, no,.185):

> Place itself is in you.
> Not you are in the place; the place, it is in you!
> Should you cast it out, eternity stands already here.
> *Der Orth ist selbst in dir.*
> *Nicht du bist in dem Orth / der Orth der ist in dir!*
> *Wirfstu jhn auß / so steht die Ewigkeit schon hier.*

This is the kind of couplet that encourages comparison with Kant's transcendental philosophy; but actually the paradox follows from the underlying tenet of divine omnipresence.

For the sake of coming closer to the rhyme of the original, we can replace *Ort* with "world" in the related couplet (1, no. 205):

> The world is the word.
> The world and the *word* are One, and if not for the world,
> (By Eternal Eternity!), there would not be the *word*.
> *Der Ort ist das* Wort.
> *Der ort und's* Wort *ist Eins / und wäre nicht der ort /*
> *(Bey Ewger Ewigkeit!) es wäre nicht das* Wort.

The *locus* of the world, to recall Weigel's title, is the cradle of the Word. Word and world exist for one another in the divine plan. The unity of all in all, Creator in creature, light and Word within world, achieves a perfect unity of absolute mystery and transparent clarity, of content with form, in these gemlike epigrams of Angelus Silesius.

Baroque mysticism took an extravagant turn in the life and work of the younger poet Quirinus Kuhlmann (1651–1689). Kuhlmann was also a native of Breslau, also a student at Leiden. Early in life, Kuhlmann displayed prodigious talents as a budding poet and scholar. He was driven by a desire for fame and by the ambition to accumulate and artfully combine the humanistic learning of the centuries. In Leiden, he came in contact with radical dissenting circles. He also read Boehme's *Mysterium Magnum*, the massive Genesis commentary which synthesized all the mystical themes of the legendary cobbler. Influenced by Boehme's work, the quest for totality acquired an explosive focus in Kuhlmann. From now on, all life experiences and all current events were transfigured to portentous symbols of the dawning final age of the *Kühlreich*, his "Cool Kingdom." For reasons not altogether clear, messianic enthusiasms were having a heyday in the late seventeenth century. A similar case has been made famous by Scholem: that of the Lurian Kabbalist and false Messiah, Sabbatai Sevi, whose reputation stirred Jews to ecstasy during the same era.[22]

The inexorable logic of conspiracy theory seized control of Kuhlmann's imagination. Anything that struck him as congruent with the pattern of darkness and light in his thinking was *ipso facto* true. His conspiratorial mentality was also nourished by a rich material of biblical and mystical allusion. Kuhlmann interpreted his own name in accordance with a Boehmian symbolism, justifying it by Acts 3:19 which spoke in the Latin Bible of coming "times of refreshment," *tempus refrigerii* (the champion of the coming age was thereby signalled as the *Refrigerator*). His apocalyptic opponent was one Edward Coleman, the secretary to King James II and a reconverted Catholic who was suspected of an intention of recatholicizing England. Coleman became *Kohlemann*: the nemesis who heaped up the satanic coals that were to be "cooled" by the saving Kuhlmann and *Refrigerator*.

The poetic product of this scheme of allusions was the cycle of his ecstatic "Cool-Psalms," the *Kühlpsalter*. A unique work of religious and poetic art, the *Cool-Psaltery* should be interpreted against its own prosaic background which, though unintentionally, is very much like Don Quixote's true circumstances—in glimmering between the lines. When the poet completes the fourteenth "Cool-Psalm" by surmounting one of his attacks of despair, he concludes tellingly: "I have no enemy but Myself in this world."

With his dedicated circle of supporters, Kuhlmann undertook expeditions to Istanbul in order to convert the Grand Turk to Christianity and the Cool-Monarchy. An expedition to Jerusalem to convert the Jews got as far as Geneva. The final expedition to convert the Czar of all Russia ended tragically: in Moscow, Kuhlmann was denounced by a Lutheran pastor. He was condemned to death and burned at the stake in a tar-filled bathhouse. Though he was dismayed by this sentence, there is evidence to suggest that he arranged certain events of his life to fit the prophetic pattern.[23] Many things about Kuhlmann are dubious. That he was a poet and a man of deep sincerity is not among them.

As a poet, Kuhlmann is a unique and heroic figure. He pits his word of divine inspiration against the prosaic banalities of the late-Baroque world—the period in which the fervor of the Age of Faith was beginning to fade before enlightened sobriety, or take refuge in private religiosity. The era of epic struggles, of signs and wonders, was receding. The cynical war-weary world of the novelist Grimmelshausen had arrived. Jacob Boehme and Jan Amos Comenius were the towering legends of a tragic-heroic age of glory and revelation. Inspired by their visions, and unwilling to accept the failures of their prophesies, Kuhlmann sought to make good in his own person on what he only imperfectly understood.

Although far more would need to be said about the art of the late-Baroque poets, nearly all of them show tendecies of evolving from synthesis to experimentation and eclecticism. Other mystical poets sought to create a studied poetic expression of the relationship of creature to Creator. Christian Knorr von Rosenroth (1636–1689) drew extensively on Kabbalism in his poetical and theoretical works. A Lower Austrian Protestant who lived in Nuremberg, Catharina Regina von Greiffenberg (1633–1694), was influenced by the linguistic experimentation of the intellectuals of that city. The Catholic Jesuit and lyricist, Friedrich Spee (1591–1635), studied the works of Spanish poets and mystics and composed a different kind of mystical poetry in which nature sings the praises of the Creator. Spee was also an early critic of witchcraft persecutions, the courageous author of *Cautio Criminalis*, against the practices of witch trials.

Reacting in part to the confessional fragmentation of life in a strife-torn Germany, the faithful of the seventeenth century were drawn to emblematic syntheses. One of the most remarkable products of this impulse is the unique tableau created at Bad Teinach near Calw in Southwest Germany: the *Bad Teinacher Lehrtafel*.[24] This church painting, designed in the format of a winged altar, was an instructional-devotional work of symbolic complexity employing esoteric and Kabbalistic motifs. At times, eclecticism resembled a supraconfessional ecumenical culture. This can be seen in the writings of the Catholic scholar Athanasius Kircher (1602–1680), with whom Kuhlmann eagerly corresponded.

In the radical Pietism and tolerance of Gottfried Arnold, eclecticism and historicism went hand in hand. Arnold not only defended the persecuted heretics of the past but also—as Peter Erb has shown—made use of mystical and spiritual texts from the Middle Ages to his own time.[25] More will be said about Arnold with respect to the theme of German pluralism.

As we have seen throughout this study, the themes of the mystic are never exclusive to mysticism. Nevertheless, its most striking forms perennially blossomed in environments in which authority was in crisis. Repeatedly reinterpreted, the half-doctrinal, half-visionary notion of the omnipresent divine power in nature and the soul continued to nourish popular religious enthusiasms and philosophical speculation before being redirected to the Romantic understanding of nature and imagination.

# 8

# Diversity and Unity

## Mysticism Between Pietism and Enlightenment

Except for Novalis, the Baroque mystics are the last who are both original and influential in German literary and intellectual history. Gerhard Tersteegen, Friedrich Christoph Oetinger, or Michael Hahn cannot fairly be stigmatized as minor mystics. However, compared to Boehme or Silesius, they are minor figures in the history of letters and ideas.

The impact of mysticism in the seventeenth and eighteenth centuries can be pursued in the dispersal of its themes and in the lingering influence of Boehme or Weigel. One of the most significant outgrowths of German mysticism is what I will refer to here as "German pluralism." This term is intended to signify a common impulse discernible within a wide variety of tendencies. At its root, German pluralism represents a reaction against the attempt to impose doctrinal hegemony of any kind; at its most developed, it is a sanctioning and affirmation of whatever is particular, organic, unique, or subject to defamation and persecution.

It should be noted that the image of orthodox German Protestantism that emerges when one focuses on its dissenters is slanted. The boundaries between orthodoxy and Pietism were not altogether rigid. Nor was mainstream Lutheranism as petrified, as closed-minded, or even as hostile to mysticism as it appears from the invectives of the dissenters. The Lutheran pastorate nurtured much of the intellectual culture of Germany. It should be added that the early eighteenth century found the Pietists—those erstwhile outsiders and challengers of orthodoxy—assuming the role of rigid authoritarians against an occasional alliance of professional clergy and enlightened intellectuals. Still, both the fervor of Pietism and the cooler light of the *Aufklärung* at some point defined themselves through their oppositon to a rigid tradition based on the outer or literal word of the Bible. Viewed retrospectively, there was a powerful rationale for the multiform rebellion against the shallowness and narrowness of religious life, and against a clerical establishment that rested its case on the authority of the Bible. Scriptural authority had served to fan the flames of Germany's destruction and was now quite powerless to surmount her continued division.[1] The offshoots of mysticism took various forms, from religious introspection and Enthusiasm, to ecumenicism and radical protest, and eventually to the residual elements of Spiritualism retained even by some major representatives of the German Enlightenment.

Much has been written tracing the influence of mysticism in the religious sensibility of the late seventeenth and eighteenth centuries.[2] The roots of Pietism lie in a confessionally divided Germany and in a widespread desire for a more personal, devout, active, and transforming religious way of life than the official clergy and its religious practices could provide. Speculative mysticism is by no means absent in Pietism, but it is secondary. Here, I will discuss the concepts and experiences of the major Pietists, Philipp Jakob Spener (1635–1705), August Hermann Francke (1663–1727), Nikolaus Ludwig von Zinzendorf (1700–1760), and Friedrich Christoph Oetinger (1702–1782) in order to suggest how their respective concepts or experiences of rebirth, conversion, or awakening echo mystical themes.

In the early Pietism of Spener's *Pia Desideria* (1675), the mystic's inner voice reasserted itself in the theme of "rebirth": in the inner, God-induced conversion which gives rise to the "new man" who is a creature not of nature, but of grace, in whom faith and good works are united.[3] In contradistinction to the orthodox doctrine of an imputed forensic justification (but harkening back to the early Lutheran prefaces to Romans or the *Theologia Deutsch*), Spener's forward-looking belief in "rebirth" recaptured one of the central themes of Boehme's Baroque synthesis. The new teaching of rebirth found a fertile soil in a Brandenburg torn by dissension between Lutherans and Reformed (Calvinists), where the state, in attempting to reconcile the two confesssions, violated the conscience of believers. In his plea for interconfessional toleration, Spener argued that grace should not be adjudged by men on confessional or doctrinal grounds. Spener distinguished fundamentally between the "world" and the "Kingdom of God." He contended that the eternal kingdom could become manifest before the end of time.[4] Spener's plea for tolerance of the individual conscience was a voice of moderation and conciliation.

In the conversion experience of August Hermann Francke, the mysticism of Augustine, Tauler, Arndt, and Molinos played a role. Francke reinforced the pattern of subsequent Pietism by minutely observing and analyzing his experience. His account indicates that the challenged authority of faith and Scripture was pivotal.

As a young student of biblical exegesis, Francke had been asked to prepare a sermon contrasting the living faith in John 20:31 with the shallow faith of complacency and unthinking habit. In considering his task, Francke fell into a state of uncertainty about his own inner conviction and about the trustworthiness of the Bible. After hours of despair, all his doubts were at last dispelled through fervent prayer. Francke experienced rebirth. His subsequent leadership with its dual emphasis on inner fervor and on active, organized charity made the city and university of Halle a bastion of Pietism.

Francke's conversion and the innumerable kindred experiences observed and recorded by the Pietists deepened the introspective aspect of German culture even beyond religious circles. August Langen's study of the vocabulary of German Pietism argues that the Pietistic language of introspection that developed in the confessional memoirs had a more profound effect on the German psychological novel of the late eighteenth century than did the foreign models of Rousseau or Richardson.[5]

A third figure who exercised an influence comparable to that of Spener and Francke is Count Zinzendorf. A pupil of Francke's Halle-based Pietism, Zinzendorf's contributions to the tradition of German mysticism were to take several forms. Zinzendorf was powerfully moved by his contemplation of the Passion of Christ. Once—while gazing at a manneristic painting of the Crucifixion which bore the inscription, "I suffered this for you, what have you done for me?"—Zinzendorf felt touched to the quick.[6] Out of this kind of contemplation, he developed a Christocentric "theology of blood and wounds" (*Blut- und Wundentheologie*), expressed in a language that now appears quite alien because of its preoccupation with anatomical details and its Baroque mixture of German and foreign words. The most lasting contribution of Count Zinzendorf lay in organizing the Brethren of Herrnhut in Upper Lusatia. This was an ecumenical community uniting Protestant refugees from Bohemia who were divided along sectarian lines. The model communities of the Herrnhuter endured and later provided formative impulses to Schleiermacher and Novalis.

However, there was another side to the success of the pastoral efforts of men like Zinzendorf. Pietistic introspection was standardizing the life of the soul. Langen points out that Pietistic reports of rebirth and awakening follow a stereotyped pattern.[7] The program of Pietism had highlighted the need for "an authentic and vitally significant experience of God on the part of individual Christians."[8] Yet Pietistic pastoral efforts in the end encouraged an achievement-oriented organization of religious experience. It was the founder of Herrnhut who was to discover in himself that the theories of spiritual awakening and conversion could become meaningless. The conversionary stages of "penitential struggle" (*Bußkampf*) and "breakthrough" (*Durchbruch*) that he had been encouraging in others did not apply to him.[9] Zinzendorf gradually underwent a rapprochement with the doctrine of forensic justification.

The systematization of the inner life was depriving it of its aura of wonder. In an eighteenth-century Pietism that had taken a firm stand against reason and science, inner experience and knowledge of nature were to become quaint curiosities. In the eighteenth-century Pietism of Zinzendorf and Oetinger, nature mysticism reemerged as a rebellion against reason. As a child, Zinzendorf had struggled with doubts about a faith challenged by science and reason. As an adult, he came to cherish mystical Spiritualism and nature mysticism. This inclination is even more pronounced in his contemporary Oetinger.

Though Spener's cooler attitude prevailed toward Boehme's pansophic mysticism, individual Pietists, including Zinzendorf, Oetinger, and the alchemistic physician who treated the young Goethe in Frankfurt, continued to be fascinated with Baroque nature mysticism.[10] Around 1600, pansophic mysticism had still interacted amicably with science in bolstering the authority of the scriptural word; however, after 1700 pansophy came to stand in an alliance with biblicism against reason. Like Zinzendorf, Oetinger belongs to this second phase. Though a trained theologian and a Lutheran churchman, Oetinger was also touched by popular religiosity and nature mysticism.

Long before his speculative interests, Oetinger had known the experiential mysticism of the devotional word. A childhood event remembered from his bedtime devotions indicates his keen ability to react to the spiritual import of words:

> I came to the song "Swing up to your God, you troubled soul!" [*Schwing dich auf zu deinem Gott, du betrübte Seele!*] With no idea of being troubled, I was eagerly driven to understand what it is to swing oneself up to God. I therefore exerted myself inwardly before God, and behold! I felt myself swung up into God. I prayed through my song. There was no word which didn't leave a clear light in my soul. In my life, I have felt nothing more joyous.[11]

Here, it is clearly not the crisis of authority, but rather the desire to know, learn, and understand that triggers the mystical experience. What is uniquely mystical in Oetinger often responds to conflicts stemming from his desire to learn. Something of the Faustian rage for all knowledge always smoldered in the breast of this respectable churchman.

Oetinger also underwent the kind of inner awakening that responds to a personal crisis of authority—to what Magdalene Maier-Petersen has analyzed as the characteristic identity crisis at the root of the Pietistic awakening.[12] Attracted in childhood as much to secular as to religious learning, Oetinger read not only the Bible but also books about nature and natural history and travel literature. Under the influence of a mother who was more worldly than his father, he aspired to study law in order to become a government official. As a pupil, he rebelled against the Evangelical seminary at Blaubeuern. Trapped between parental encouragements and conflicting loyalties, Oetinger found himself in what Maier-Petersen calls a classical "double-bind conflict."

In his eighteenth year, Oetinger underwent a crisis brought about by the necessity of deciding once and for all between the secular or the religious course of studies. Through prayer, he experienced his awakening. It amounted to his firm decision for the pastorate. Nevertheless, Oetinger's pastoral career would always be accompanied by mystical and pansophic researches and studies.

A miller in the university town of Tübingen first persuaded the young theology student that Boehme's writings were "the best theology." In his youth, Oetinger had read Leibniz, but from this encounter on he instead turned to nature mysticism as an alternative to rationalism. He was destined to spend a lifetime engaged in avocational studies of Boehme and Swedenborg. His prolific mind was forever in quest of the secret knowledge promised by practical alchemy, emblematics, or Swedenborg's mysticism.[13] The most assiduous German student of Swedenborg and a prodigious theosophist in his own right, Oetinger expended his energies in pursuit of theology, alchemy, Kabbalah, and the study of biblical and mystical symbolism. In this, he maintained the tradition of Renaissance panvitalism, including the theory of the signature. Oetinger still stood in the old tradition, for which nature, Scripture, and the human creature are the parallel texts in which God is revealed. His contemporary, the Pietist and theologian, Johann Albrecht Bengel (1687–1752), was engaged in the construction of a biblical exegesis which took scriptural figures literally. For Oetinger as well, figures of expression were to acquire a kind of "spirit-corporeality" (Geistleiblichkeit). Following the German mystical tradition, Oetinger in his own way took the sacred word as a reality. In elaborating his scriptural and mystical "concept of life," he paralleled the developments in philosophy that led from Leibniz, through Herder, eventually to the modern vitalistic philosophy (*Lebensphilosophie*).[14] However, in his own day, the new rationalism occupied the critical ground. Except for the emblematic studies, Oetinger's theorizing produced little that survived his century. Faced with an increasingly unbridgeable gap between scientific and biblical knowledge, he reinvented his own nature out of Scripture, with the guidance of an increasingly antiquarian pansophic mysticism taken over from Paracelsus and Boehme.

Spener, Francke, Zinzendorf, and Oetinger, each in his own way, were men whose energies and interests were directed toward an organized following or congregation. Missionary activities, as well as irenic or ecumenical sentiments, are responsible for the much-cited Pietistic attitude of tolerance. Before turning to its philosophical counterpart in the pluralistic philosophies of Leibniz and Herder, it is worthwhile to consider the radicalism and individualism of several of the inheritors of the mystical tradition. Gottfried Arnold is the most influential and also the most fertile for the rise of a modern theory and ideology of tolerance. However, some obscure and forgotten figures also merit attention. Not only do their idiosyncracies extend our understanding of the diversity of types engendered by the German mystical tradition, they also show how the influence of Weigel and Boehme was transmitted in popular circles.

The most curious of these is a Dutch peasant, a figure for whom the designation *Enthusiast* (*Schwärmer*) might have been invented. In considering him, we step outside German territory, but we remain squarely within a mystical tradition that proceeded from Boehme. Bornkamm has shown how his legacy was maintained by the common people.[15] For more than two centuries, the exemplary career of the shoemaker of Görlitz encouraged both plebeian mysticism and nonconformity. In the view of Beyreuther, Boehme fathered the "enthusiastic" and "radical" wing of German Pietism. Friedrich Breckling (1629–1711) and Johann Georg Gichtel (1638-1710) were the German dissenters who sought refuge in Holland, broadcasting the influence of Boehme. Gichtel did so by bringing out the first printed edition of his complete works (Amsterdam, 1689). A later Southwest German plebeian theosophist Michael Hahn (1758–1819) was a peasant's son who organized devotional communities that lasted into this century.[16] If the more accessible and orthodox books of Arndt exercised the greater overall influence on the culture of Pietism, the exemplary shoemaker reinforced the eccentricities of the radical individualists.

The power of this influence is evident in the memoir of the remarkable illumination of Hemme Hayen in Johann Heinrich Reitz's *Historie der Wiedergeborenen* (*History of the Reborn*).[17] Hayen was a man of humble origin, born in the Dutch coastal country in 1633. His childhood and youth were marked by grave hardships. His stepfather, an Anabaptist, warned him to be virtuous and go his own way in search of salvation. With the encouragement of his mother, young Hayen earnestly read the Bible and other pious literature such as Thomas à Kempis's *Imitation of Christ*. As a young husband and father, Hayen experienced still more hardships with his wife and twelve children, many of whom died in infancy. He embittered his own existence with self-accusations, and could look forward only to a future of never-ending severity. At one point, he recalls reading that a person ought not to love God for the sake of heaven. The notion seemed strange to him.

Within this constricted horizon, Hayen had the good fortune to know an unorthodox Lutheran village pastor who was open to conversation and who had read some of Boehme's writings. There were also Mennonites in the vicinity; more sectarian in spirit, they were bound to a rule of formal membership. The melancholy young man faced a choice between becoming a member of their sect or going his own way in accordance with the advice of his stepfather (*Historie* 5, 173–174).

On a Sunday in February 1666, Hemme Hayen experienced his awakening. He had summoned one of the Mennonites to examine the broken leg of his son and to talk about the Mennonite religion, but even before the visitor arrived, the father had been awakened by the spirit. He immediately began to think of certain sayings from the Bible. More than before, he understood these sayings "spiritually": "and in them, I had a very deep vision, such as had never happened to me before." In his aroused condition, he not only understood the sense of the biblical words that came to mind: whatever his senses alighted upon, he now "grasped in a spiritual manner"; and he discerned a "supernatural, quite inexpressible, and probably altogether inhuman and heavenly sweetness in my soul and a communion with the common being" (of all things)—so that he cried out for joy (175–176).

In this condition, he woke up his wife and explained to her the reason for his joy. Through him, his wife partook of his experience. Unable to contain himself, he continued to shout. The Mennonite arrived, dressed the son's injured leg, and ate with the family. Hayen accompanied him part of the way home. They talked about Jacob Boehme, who was now constantly on his mind. The Mennonite inquired whether Boehme had been "one of our people," and Hayen was saddened and irritated by the realization that the sectarian wanted to bind God's blessing to his own congregation (177).

At home again, the spiritual awakening continued to labor within him for several days on end. His account of the process of this awakening is the record of one spiritual adventure after another. The entire process is placed in doctrinal context by a conversation with his sympathetic village pastor: The attainment of grace is not bound to any sect, nor is the millenium bound to a particular juncture in time. The path to God is an individual one. By the same token, the final age *accompanies* normal time, and is made known to those individuals whose number may already be very great. Agreeing about these things, Hayen and the pastor were moved to tears (179).

A very different, and considerably more famous case is that of the German ribbon weaver and mystic, Gerhard Tersteegen (1697–1769). Tersteegen was a product of the Reformed (Calvinistic) Protestant region on the Lower Rhine. At the time of his birth, his home city of Moers was a Dutch possession. Like Hayen, he was imaginatively gifted. Finding the mercantile profession of his youth to be unsatisfactory for his temperament, he took up the craft of a weaver, devoting his life to prayer and meditation. Tersteegen wrote devotional tracts, poems, and song texts which became standards of German hymnals. Although he participated in conventicles and even acted as a spiritual counsellor, he always remained reserved and humble, eschewing celebrity and importance within his circles.

Unlike Boehme or Hayen, Tersteegen was trained in school in classical languages; he might have studied theology if the means of his family had been sufficient. Instead, he was sent as an apprentice at age fifteen to Mühlheim on the Ruhr. There, he came into contact with the mystical conventicles of separatists who stood aloof from the official church. For dissenters of the previous century, men such as Gichtel or Breckling, separatism had led to prison or exile. Tersteegen appears to have been a rather timid individual. It is therefore quite possible that his association with nonconformist circles was a source of anxiety.

According to some accounts, Tersteegen's signal conversion experience took place while he was still an apprentice. He was passing through a forest on his way to Duisburg. Beset by severe colic pains and fearing for his life, he prayed to be spared long enough to prepare himself for eternity. The pains disappeared, and from that time on he devoted himself to a virtually monastic life of work, prayer, and study, never marrying. An additional influence on his mysticism came from the Quietism of Madame Guyon who taught a will-less renunciation akin to Eckhart's teaching of *Gelassenheit*. Tersteegen's ideal of a self-less love of God went beyond common devotion by striving to accept the divine will in a condition of indifference even to heaven or hell.[18]

As an imaginative poet, Tersteegen wrote songs such as "God is present" (*Gott ist gegenwärtig*), "I worship the power of love" (*Ich bete an die Macht der Liebe*), or "Great God in whom I hover" (*Großer Gott, in dem ich schwebe*), which long remained in use in German lands. These hymns circle around the divine presence in which the soul seeks a calm surpassing the world of the senses, as in the hymn, "Weary spirit, go now to rest" (*Müder Geist, nun kehr zur Ruh*):

> Weary spirit, go now to rest
> And forget all pictures,
> Close your eyes softly;
> What is not God, let be forgotten,
> Be quiet for the Lord and hold still for him,
> That he may enact [in you] what he wants.
> *Müder Geist, nun kehr zur Ruh*
> *und vergiß der Bilder alle,*
> *schleuß die Augen sachte zu;*
> *was nicht Gott ist, dir entfalle!*
> *Schweig dem Herrn und halt ihm still,*
> *daß er wirke, was er will!*[19]

The silent prayer once recommended by Augustine, the rejection of all images by Eckhart, the renunciation in which the human will submits completely to the divine—these are traditions dear to the heart of Tersteegen. Among the individualistic mystics, the quietistic Tersteegen is at the opposite end of the spectrum from the rebels of radical Pietism.

During and after the three decades of a war fought with confessional slogans, the atmosphere of conflict and bigotry led to a defensive reaction in the tradition of Spiritualist dissent. An impressive and largely neglected voice of protest was that of the North German protest poetess, Anna Ovena Hoyers (1584–1655). Classically educated, Hoyers was the daughter of an astronomer and of a wealthy family. Married young and widowed early, she became the friend and outspoken defender of dissenters. A protester against war and bigotry, she emigrated to Sweden after quarreling bitterly with the orthodox pastorate of her native Schleswig.

A nineteenth-century scholar called her the fiercest woman ever to polemicize in German (*Nie wol hat eine Frau so ungestüm polemisiert, wie diese herbe Kämpferin*[20]). In fact, her small body of poetic writings and one published collection range from sensitive poems written for her children, to moving church hymns, to exceedingly blunt and effective attacks on those who preached war and kowtowed to princes:

> The old proverb states quite correctly:
> Satan feeds on clerics and shits out soldiers.
> I think that things are in a very bad way,
> When a clergyman carries the insignia of war...
> *Das alte Sprichwort sagt gar recht:*
> *Satan frisst Pfaffen / scheist Lantz-Knecht.*
> *Mich dunckt die Sachen stehen sehr schlecht /*
> *Wann ein Geistlicher führt Kriegszeichen...*[21]

To Hoyers, the clergy are mere hindrances on the path to truth. They block out the light for the common folk (*Dem g'meinen Mann nehmt ihr das liecht*).[22] The orthodox clergymen only display humility when preaching before a congregation of "potentates" (*Da sind die Pfaffen ander Leut...*). They cater to the powerful by preaching the cause of war.[23]

Hoyers's protest is grounded in an oppositional Spiritualism that appropriates authority to the individual by asserting that, "Spirit is the master, and the letter the slave / If I'm to enjoy the power of the Word / The Lord himself must unlock my heart." (*Der Geist ist Herr / der Buchstab Knecht / So ich des Worts Krafft soll geniessen / Muß der Herr selbst mein Hertz auffschliessen*). Spiritualism is for Hoyers the banner under which all dissenters and doctrinal individualists are gathered. "Whoever comes along and talks of the spirit," she writes, is "accused as a heretic, imprisoned or driven into exile, slandered as a Schwenckfeldian and a visionary (*Phantast*), a Rosicrucian, Enthusiast, Chiliast, Weigelian, Davidian, Neutralist..." (*Kommt einer her und sagt vom Geist/ Der wird sehr übel abgeweis't / Und alß ein Ketzer hart verklaget / Incarcerirt oder verjaget / Genant Schwenckfelder und Phantast / Rosenkreutzer, Enthusiast / Chiliast, Weigelianist / Davidianer, Neutralist...*).[24] All the "sects," whether loyal to Luther, Calvin, Flacius, or the pope, are greedy exploiters who proclaim the letter in ignorance of the spirit. When these false shepherds have been swept aside, the people will rejoice and thank God for deliverance.[25] There were other agitators of her kind who were associated with the name of Valentin Weigel and proclaimed the living "spirit" against the dead "letter" of the orthodox clergy during the Thirty Years' War in Germany.[26]

As a protester, Hoyers wields a rhetoric of Spiritualistic mysticism in order to defend all the defamed believers of her own period.

Gottfried Arnold (1666–1714), whose writing was mentioned in the preceding chapter, was born eleven years after the death of Hoyers, during more peaceful times. Influenced by Spener and familiar with the writings of Sebastian Franck, Arnold extended the Spiritualist defense of heresy to the past. As a scholarly historian of the Church, he defended all heresies and championed nonconformism. To Arnold, all who had suffered persecution were the true church. To the institutional churches—the churches of walls and stone, reviled by all the Spiritualists from Boehme on—Arnold sounded the death knell in his virulent "Grave Song for Babylon" (*Babels Grab-Lied*). According to Benz, a line can be traced from the radical individualism of Arnold, via Johann Christian Edelmann, to Friedrich Nietzsche.[27]

According to Erich Seeberg, the influence of Boehme's nature theories were coupled with the mystique of the *Theologia Deutsch* in encouraging Arnold to conceive of mystical theology as a true "supraconfessional consensus of all times."[28] The Luther who deserved veneration was the interpreter of the Bible and the *Theologia Deutsch*—the Luther who distinguished sharply between law and gospel, between *deus absconditus* and *deus revelatus*.[29] Arnold mobilized his arsenal of concepts, including the trichotomous anthropology, Boehmian metaphysical-theological voluntarism, and the concept of the human microcosm,[30] thereby underscoring the singularity of each individual within the divine plan, a motif shared with the less radical Tersteegen.[31]

Seeberg also sets forth a strong case that Arnold encouraged the ahistorical, nonintellectual understanding of mysticism.[32] This may be true. However, it is surely inappropriate to assess the great *cri de coeur* of Arnold's history of the church and its heretics solely by parochial scholarly standards. As a champion of individual dignity, Arnold is sovereign. Among the radical Pietists, he alone occupies a commanding position in intellectual history as a whole. In his period and thought, he is a watershed figure in what Hazard called *la crise de conscience européene*.

When we turn from Pietism to the German Enlightenment, we again recognize echoes of mysticism. This is true for Gottfried Wilhelm Leibniz (1646–1716). At times, it appears almost as if Leibniz had understood his philosophical and mathematical thinking as a luminary's search for concealed patterns. It is as if his objective in logic had been a better Lullian art of combination; his goal in mathematics an improved numerology; as if his task in the philosophy of his *Theodicy* and *Monadology* had been a better theosophic-pansophic speculation.[33] Certain historians of philosophy have come close to classifying Leibniz as a mystic, and there are grounds for this.[34] But it is also an exaggeration, inasmuch as his thought is clearly grounded in human reason, and since he neither claims nor teaches a divine knowledge like that of Eckhart, Paracelsus, Agrippa, Boehme, or the Spiritualists.

Pluralism, this specialty of the German Enlightenment, is close to the heart of the unsystematic system elaborated by the philosopher, scientist, and mathematician. In Leibniz, pluralism is accorded the highest sort of rational justification. Beyond reacting against the conflicts engendered by religious disputes, he confirms that diversity is essential to the divine scheme of nature. In this he continues the tradition of Cusanus, Boehme, and Arnold.

With avid interest, Leibniz sought and read the writings of Weigel, Silesius, Boehme, Kuhlmann, and sundry other dissenters, mystics, and Spiritualists. He shared with Weigel and Boehme a tradition rooted in Plato and Augustine, a tradition nourished by Neoplatonic Renaissance theories of the universal coherence of things, as well as by Luther's *De Servo Arbitrio*. He also recorded his stylistic evaluations of the mystics, criticizing the storminess of Arnold and preferring the gentler style of Thomas à Kempis, Boehme, or Spener.[35]

In Leibniz, the motifs of mystical illuminism are blended almost indistinguishably into the philosophical vocabulary of his rationalism. If reason is compelling and universal for Leibniz, he could nonetheless write that, "the true and the good in our knowledge is an emanation of the divine light."[36] This trajectory of thought can be read as a response to the new Cartesian outlook in philosophy (an outlook that had no place for the anthropological trichotomy in which spirit in its many forms had played the central role). The Cartesian dualism pressed home a dichotomy of matter and mind. It was in response to this dualism that Leibniz formulated his quintessentially pluralistic and, some would say, mystical theory of the monads. The monad was the vitalistic microcosm that made it possible to surmount the difficulties Leibniz perceived in the philosophy of his rivals.

In his *Theodicy*, Leibniz acknowledged the Spiritualists and mystics as forerunners in addressing the universal questions of the creation, coherence, and vitality of the world.[37] In taking up the problem of causality raised by Newton, Leibniz at the same time wrote of the controversy between Lutherans and Calvinists over the nature of Christ's presence in the Eucharist. He analyzed the doctrine of real presence in terms of the concept of *action at a distance*.[38] His *Theodicy* substituted the rational concept of a preestablished harmony for the Platonic, mystical, or Spiritualist theories of the World Soul or omnipresent divine Spirit. We can see from this how the themes of the mystics were becoming absorbed into the new philosophy.

The pattern of Leibniz's monadic metaphysics is clearly that of *omnes in omnibus*. Everything contains everything else. God is in all things, and all things are in God. The unity of infinite and finite worlds foreshadowed by Cusanus or Boehme is conceptualized by Leibniz with the aid of reason and mathematics. The same laws and logic apply everywhere. The God of Liebniz is characterized by this *harmonia universalis*.

For Leibniz, the tradition of *Logosmystik* evolves into the universal system of an *All-Logik*. God is the Word, and his revealed signs are the symbols of mathematics and logic. Mathematics can overcome the gulf between the infinite and the finite by means of an infinitesimal measure that recognizes the endless progression of degrees (still denied by Cusanus). The monadology of Leibniz is a metaphysics of plurality and uniqueness rather than of quantity—a world system that constructs the universe out of an infinite number of absolutely unique individuals, preharmonized with one another and with the whole by God. This is a rational view of the world, but clearly it is also a visionary one: "The universe is a sort of fluid, entirely of a piece and like an ocean without bounds; all movements are sustained and continued on to infinity, though imperceptibly, like the circles which arise from a stone tossed into water..." (Letter to Princess Sophie, February 6, 1706). All things act upon all other things and are influenced by all other things.

This universe is conceived by Leibniz as a visionary totality. Nature is characterized by an infinite depth and by a ubiquitous latent vitalism. Leibniz observes that every piece of matter may be imagined as a garden full of plants or as a pond full of fish, whereby every branch of every plant, every part of every animal, and every drop of liquid is in turn the same kind of garden or pond (*Monadology* 35:67). Each monad is a unit composed of desire and perception, an organism that reflects (or, as Leibniz puts it, "expresses") in its unextended interior the whole of things.

Each monad is absolutely distinct, an individuality linked to the other monads only through the preestablished harmony of the whole. All monads are also alike, as mirrors of the world. But since each mirrors the world from the perspective of its own position, each expresses the world from its unique vantage point. Hans Heinz Holz has noted that this coexistence of an identity of the object with an infinite plurality of vantage points laid the ground for Leibniz's pluralism by allowing for differences of opinion without sacrificing the absolute integrity of the truth. According to Holz, the Leibnizian paradigm of one truth observed from many vantage points was to furnish the pattern for Lessing's parables of religious tolerance.[39]

The early reception of Leibniz's monadology was dependent upon the broader crosscurrent of Deism in the Enlightenment, a current that began with his contemporary Shaftesbury (1671–1713), dominating Leibniz's successor, Christian Wolff. This once extraordinarily influential, but now largely forgotten, thinker adapted the preestablished harmony, while freely admitting that he could do nothing with the monadology.

Wolff took from the *Theodicy* the concept of God as a supreme understanding that selects the best of all possible worlds. The best is the one in which all things can be explained mechanically and causally. This was a philosophy which largely, though not entirely, banished from the world its mystery. (The relations of matter and spirit remained incomprehensible; and it has been said, too, that Wolff's concept of God retained a devotional inwardness that stands comparison with the profound religious sentiment of the compositions of Johann Sebastian Bach.) However, the tenor and content of his system, coupled with his praise for the moral philosophy of Confucius, were sufficient to provoke the wrath of the Halle Pietists, including that of Francke, in 1721. Their scurrilous public and private campaign against Wolff did much to create a recognized boundary line between the cultures of reason and faith.[40] With the dismissal of Wolff, the battle lines were drawn between the patriarchal culture of the forefathers and the free movement of progress.

Initially, this conflict had been a three-sided standoff of Pietism, orthodoxy, and Enlightenment. Prior to the dismissal of Wolff, Pietists and *Aufklärer* had been allied for a time. Now, a new alliance of Enlightenment with orthodoxy came into play. It was only feasible because an orthodoxy still preoccupied with correct doctrine as yet saw no necessary rift between biblical exegesis and scientific rationalism. In the late seventeenth century, the orthodox precept of the "verbal inspiration" of the entire Bible was still marching in stride with the scientific spirit. It was only in the eighteenth century that it became jarringly apparent that the Bible in its literal sense was incompatible with the new scientific understanding of the world.[41] By Lessing's time, the shift of positions had come full circle, so that this champion of reason employed the old terminology of spirit and letter against an opposing front that stood on verbal inspiration and biblical inerrancy. Eventually, it would be left to Hamann and Herder to take the hegemonic authority of reason to task in the name of an irreducibly particular divine meaning and human expressiveness; and it would be left to Hegel to seek the living "spirit" behind the "letter" of both Scripture and reason—in the historical and intellectual life of the world.

What we have inherited is the distorted retrospective view that forgets all the shifting alliances and recognizes only a chasm between the pious Bible-thumpers on the one hand and the vanguard of modern enlightenment on the other. The former are the bigoted know-nothings of Luise Gottsched's *Pietistry in a Reinforced Skirt* (*Die Pietisterey im Fischbein-Rocke*, 1736)—a parody of self-righteous sectarianism, which one enjoys without noticing that it supports the view that the professional clergy, not women or menials, ought to have the say in religious matters.

When the conflict revolved to the two-sided struggle between the voices of Enlightenment who questioned verbal inspiration and the absolute defenders of scriptural authority, the opposition followed the traditional pattern of German dissent. This was the case with Gotthold Ephraim Lessing (1729–1781). Before Lessing edited the *Fragments* of the Deist Hermann Samuel Reimarus (1694–1768), the Deists in Germany had known persecution and enforced silence. Lessing's *Axiomata* (*Anti-Goeze*, 1778) took a position against the authoritarianism of an orthodox biblicism, the new "scriptural principle." Lessing not only distinguished between the "letter" and the "spirit" of the Bible, he denied that the truth of Christianity lay in its given "historical" facticity (as had, in a different context, the mystical, Spiritualistic, and early Lutheran critique of the *fides historica*). Instead, Lessing sought inner characteristics of validity. His controversy with the Lutheran orthodoxy gave rise to the great drama of pluralistic tolerance, *Nathan the Wise* (1779).

Lessing knew the writings of Sebastian Franck and Valentin Weigel.[42] In his essay, *The Education of the Human Race* (1777), he argued for an understanding of revelation as a progressive education of humankind, a progression involving several stages, in which divergent forms of communication and instruction are appropriate. This was conceptually more advanced but otherwise similar to Sebastian Franck's ideas on history and revelation. Lessing's understanding of God as a being whose thinking is his creating refashioned the reflective mysticism of the Middle Ages. Lessing also focused on John, cited the Augustinian *locus classicus* of the Gospel as the fulfillment of the Platonist books, and emphasized love as the message of the Gospel.

The eighteenth-century influence of Pietism proved fruitful when it interacted critically with rationalism. Oetinger's fame as the "Magus of the South" had its traditional counterpart in a "Magus of the North": Johann Georg Hamann (1730–1788). Hamann stood in a more discriminating relationship both to the mystical culture of the past and to the new philosophy of Kant, with whom he engaged in a close but adversarial interaction.

Hamann's object of interest was the word of language, the word of God in the Bible. His references and motifs drawn from the traditions of mysticism and Pietism were subordinated to this linguistic interest. Hamann believed that language was of divine origin and therefore central to understanding the relationship of Creator and creature. By renouncing the experimental projects of speculative nature mysticism (which still occupied Oetinger), Hamann was able to direct the quest for an inspired communication with God toward the salient area in which innovative and lasting results could be achieved. Not the signatures of an external creation, but rather the linguistic signs themselves revealed the privileged avenue to God. Leibniz had been led to formulate something akin to mysticism by the Cartesian problem of mind and matter. Hamann was now led by his opposition to Kantian rationalism to formulate a critical theory in which meaning and expression eclipsed universal reason and blind material causation.

In his *Aesthetica in Nuce* and in his letters to Kant, Hamann reinterpreted the old similitude of nature and Scripture. As the Word, God is a "writer," his text nature. The Kantian philosophy appears to Hamann as a new philosophical literalism and a potential orthodoxy of its own. Indeed, even "mysticism" in a pejorative sense is embodied by the Kantian critique of religion.[43] According to Hamann, Kant's "physics for children" could do no more than aspire to explain an elementary "ABC" of the world. However: "Every impression of nature in the human being is not only a reminder, but a guarantee of the basic truth: Who the LORD is" (*Aesthetica in Nuce*). Here again, the parallels of nature, meaning, and perception reproduce the old mystical triads in a new context—now, however, in opposition to the new "literalism" of reason. Despite his similarities with Boehme, Hamann took offense at being likened by Kant to the creator of the Baroque nature language.[44] The connotation of the mystic as one who pretends to a knowledge of God from some other source than the Bible was something that Hamann—as a Lutheran and as an interlocutor of Rationalists—wished to avoid.[45]

Johann Gottfried Herder (1744–1803) is the figure in whom the pluralistic and expressionistic impulses of the mystical tradition came to fruition. There is some confusion about the mystical roots of these impulses in Herder. Characteristically, Isaiah Berlin's otherwise revealing discussion of what he calls an "expressionistic" philosophy contradicts itself concerning Herder's relationship to the mystical tradition. In a comparison with Hamann, Herder's affinity with mysticism is categorically denied: "Unlike his teacher Hamann, Herder was decisively influenced by the findings of natural science; he gave them a vitalistic but not the mystical or theosophical interpretation favoured by Hemsterhuis, Lavater, and other 'intuitivists.'" And again: "Herder remained free of mysticism." But at another point in the same essay—again regarding Herder's view of nature—Berlin recognizes "mysticism" as the key to the vitalism and individualism in Herder's vision of nature:

> However much lip service Herder may have paid to 'natural kinds,' in general he conceived of nature as a unity in which the *Kräfte*—the mysterious, dynamic, purpose-seeking forces, the interplay of which constitutes all movement and growth—flow into each other, clash, combine, coalesce. These forces are not causal and mechanical as in Descartes; nor insulated from each other as in the *Monadology* of Leibniz; his notion of them owes more to neo-Platonic and Renaissance mysticism, and, perhaps, to Erigena's *Natura naturans* than to the sciences of his time. For Herder reality is a kind of symbiosis of these *Kräfte* (whose character remains obscure) with an environment that is conceived in somewhat static terms; if the environment is altered too abruptly, the result is some kind of collapse. Herder found more and more evidence for this. Transplanted flowers decay in unsympathetic climates; so do human beings.[46]

A view of nature closer to Herder's than that of Erigena—and indeed one in which it would be more accurate to say that forces combine, clash, and coalesce in an environment that fashions the expressive particularities of organisms—is that of Boehme's *Aurora* or *Signatura Rerum*. Boehme knew the qualitative uniqueness and rootedness of things in an environment. In *Signatura Rerum*, this rootedness is said to mold the character of things so that they express or mirror the ubiquitous creative power of God.

Like Boehme, Herder recognized this power as a divine process, homologous within and without, in things invisible and visible, in God, nature, and the soul:

> There develops from these given principles a philosophy of the soul, of the universe, of the divinity, beyond which I can imagine nothing more uplifting. In every minutest part of the infinite, rules the truth, wisdom, goodness of the whole: in every percep-

tion (*Erkenntnis*) as in every sensation, the image of God is reflected: in the former, with rays or with a shimmer of the pure light, in the latter with colors into which the ray of the sun has divided. Perception (*Erkennen*) is an enjoying of the radiance of the sun, which is mirrored in each ray; feeling (*Empfindung*) is the play of the colors of the rainbow, beautiful, true, but only as an oblique reflection of the sun.[47]

Causation within the natural world and perception of the external world possess a nimbus in this passage that could not have shone any brighter in a pansophic treatise: the light of reason reveals the truth of the whole in every particle.

Herder's understanding of God and nature is very much in the tradition of the nature mysticism that had discerned in every organism and every part of the world the operation of the full divine force and wisdom: hence, the unique individuality of each organism. There is something fundamentally Lutheran in the preoccupation with the invisible power and wisdom of God at work shaping the unique being of each individual thing in nature. As Luther had proclaimed in his defense of his doctrines of ubiquity and real presence: (God) "fashions each little grain particularly in all parts, within and everywhere..." (*Denn er macht ja ein iglich Körnlin besonders ynn allen stucken, innwendig und allenthalben...*").[48] Far from Luther's sense of things (and yet also in conformity with it) is Leibniz's argument that the particles of nature are like machine parts that are so infinitely articulated that no aspect of any component can be nonfunctional and senseless. Luther and Leibniz (as well as Spinoza) are in the background of Herder's philosophy of organic individualism. A full study would be needed to trace the motifs associated with the pluralism that attains its classical form in the thought of Leibniz and Herder—in a philosophy that reflects and sublimates the confessional and political fragmentation of German lands in the waning days of a defunct empire.

In Herder's "Spinoza Conversations" (*Gott. Einige Gespräche*, first version, 1787), Spinoza's pantheism is reconsidered in a manner emphasizing vitalism and particularity. Herder surmounts the duality of the Spinozist attributes of thought and extension: what we call "matter" is actually an array of vitalistic forces. These are lawful forces. Yet nature has an inner core that remains hidden to us. We can only discover laws and discernible forms; their inner being remains inaccessible. If Herder took his stand on the side of philosophical rationalism (to the exclusion of introvertive mysticism with its brooding upon the inner being and will in nature), he retained the awareness that a metaphysical center would always remain concealed to the investigative initiative of reason and science. Later, Schopenhauer would approach Herder's *vis occulta* by an inner path, reasoning that, if what we see from without is force, we know this force from within—as the ubiquitous latent will.

In eighteenth-century poetic depictions of nature, the old correspondences of nature, Scripture, and creature, of microcosm and macrocosm, could still shimmer through the veil of facticity. This is evident, for example, in Barthold Hinrich Brockes's poem *The Little Flower, Forget-me-not* (*Das Blümlein Vergißmeinnicht*), where every single "blade of grass"—*Blatt* can mean "page" as well as "leaf"!—is "inscribed" with lines; and every vein is illuminated with light, so that it stands as a "letter" in the "ABC of the World." The same visionary outlook on nature is evident in Albrecht von Haller's *On the Origin of Evil* (*Über den Ursprung des Übels*), when "our world" is carried like a grain of sand "in the sea of the heavens." This quality is evident in Friedrich Gottlieb Klopstock's *The Rite of Spring* (*Die Frühlingsfeier*): the cosmic immensity of "the ocean of worlds" appears overwhelming. Or again in Friedrich Karl Kasimir von Creuz's *Essay on the Soul* (*Versuch über die Seele*). The gradual depersonalization of the universe during the Enlightenment didn't diminish its awesome solemnity. Moreover, even after nature had been definitively removed from the context of faith—notably in the philosophy of Schopenhauer and Nietzsche—the cosmos would still be brought into focus by questions of meaning rather than of causation.

Certainly, we should distinguish the thinker in Herder from Hamann or Leibniz, from the older mysticism, the new Pietism, and the sentiments of Klopstock or Lavater. In all, however, there are echoes of the themes of individuality and harmony, inner and outer, visible and invisible, carried over from the mystical and Pietistic tradition. In all, the understanding of the world, of nature and the human being, is preoccupied as much with meaning and interpretation as with causal explanation. Causality and meaning are inextricably mixed together in this tradition.

Robert Clark wrote on the impact of Herder's Pietistic family background:

In the Pietistic movement there was a powerful latent individualism, most notably exemplified by Hamann, but also in Herder, who from boyhood had been encouraged to read Arndt's *True Christianity* and to depend upon its prayerful interpretation of the Bible. The habit of individual, independent interpretation could easily be transferred to other subjects. Herder's early success as a critic stemmed from his youthful Pietism, as strengthened and clarified by his thoughtful and critical reading of secular philosophy.[49]

When expression in the human realm rises from language to writing and written literature (*Schrift*), something of the living spirit is lost to the encroachments of the dead letter:

> [It is] not only that with the letters the living accents and gestures gradually disappear—the ones that had previously created such a powerful access to the heart; not only that dialects, and with them even the characteristic idioms of individual tribes and peoples thereby became fewer; the memory of human beings was also weakened, as was their lively power of mind (*Geisteskraft*), in the presence of this artificial aid of the transcribed forms of thought (*vorgezeichneter Gedankenformen*).[50]

Herder adds that, due to the vitiating power of scholarly learning and books, the human soul might long ago have been stifled had not providence provided it fresh "air" by means of "various destructive revolutions" (*durch mancherlei zerstörende Revolutionen*). Herder uses the term *revolution* in analogy to the disasters and transformations which, in his view, assisted in the formation of the natural world. Nevertheless, the fact that the human "revolution" has the purpose of freeing humanity from the reign of an accumulated, stifling learning (the stiff poetics of Gottsched) allows us to see a continuum between the dissent of the Spiritualist and the rebellion of the Romantic revolutionary of the *Sturm und Drang* period.

The German pluralism of spirit over letter had strengths and weaknesses. Opposition to the oppressiveness of the letter has the inherent flaw that, virtually by definition, it resists being written into law to safeguard against repression. Spiritualistic tolerance can only act prior to or outside the law. At best, German pluralism, as it evolved from Cusanus and Boehme to Herder, was imaginative in its capacity for affirming, not merely suffering, diversity.[51] Herder saw nations and their cultures as natural organisms. Their literary and linguistic manifestations express a character unique to them alone. The notion of the singularity of nations may be an incipient nationalistic ideology; in Herder, it is a foundation for tolerance and the appreciation of diversity.

Gerhard Kaiser's *Pietismus und Patriotismus im literarischen Deutschland* traces the metaphor of the garden, rich in diverse plants and herbs—the symbol of a human variety that expresses the divine goodness and will—from Boehme to Herder and beyond to the Romantics Schleiermacher and Steffens.[52] Kaiser takes stock of the extensive genealogy of Boehme's metaphor, comparing it to that of God as the boundless circle with an omnipresent center.[53]

As we have seen, the biblical-philosophical source material for the terminology of pluralism prioritizes the trope of *omnes in omnibus* conveying the Pauline *pleroma*, the end of the world as the "fullness" of time, when God reveals himself as "all in all."[54] *Omnes in omnibus* merged with the Neoplatonic theme of the necessary reciprocality of One and many in German pluralism. By contrast, the Apocalypse offered a prototype for a national identity in which a life-and-death struggle of good against evil is paramount. The Apocalypse offered the archetypal format for religious war propaganda, as well as for the mythology of National Socialism.[55] Moreover, the Lutheran or Pietistic mysticism of the Passion, with its idolization of salvation through blood and death beneath "the banner of the holy wound," proved to be readily adaptable for nationalistic war propaganda at the beginning of the nineteenth century.[56] By contrast, the motifs associated here with the Pauline *pleroma* offer support for the themes of a redeeming knowledge and universal brotherhood of nations. Though motifs and symbols are not the real actors in history, their symbolic languages can nonetheless clarify for us how the roles of nationalism have been conceived as myth and executed in reality.

# 9

# Nature and Imagination

## Romantic Mysticism from Novalis to Schopenhauer

In the two decades before and the two after 1800, Germany may have witnessed more changes in every sphere, may have borne more high drama and known more creative personalities and ideas than in any comparable interval: Kant's critical revolution, the audacious philosophies of the Idealists, the rainbow of writers and literary schools, *Sturm und Drang, Klassik,* Romanticism, the French Revolution, Goethe, Napoleon, the War of Liberation.

One strain in this many-sided transition was a resurgence of mysticism—a mysticism stimulated in no small part by opposition to Kantian and Voltairean rationalism. In 1791, a man named Karl von Eckartshausen, a jurist and Munich government bureaucrat with avid literary interests, published a book with the title *Mystical Nights* (*Mistische Nächte*). It signaled the author's recent change of interest from science and enlightenment toward the esoteric and mystical. The book attempted to marshal the diverse arguments of Platonism, Herder, the love mysticism of Saint Francis, and the "soul-electricity" of Mesmer, to seize back the light from the Enlightenment by championing the precept that: "It is only faith, my brother, that leads to knowledge!" (*Der Glaube, mein Bruder! führt erst zum Wissen*).[1] Although mysticism and occultism had persisted during the Enlightenment, Eckartshausen's book was a harbinger of a new Romantic mysticism.

The new mysticism came at the end of the Enlightenment, just as a new German nationalism was about to be lifted out of the cradle. Hindsight therefore readily, perhaps too readily, discerns the seed of a later irrationalism. According to one reading of history, the German national character, having failed to progress along the normative track of political development, began to accumulate the cultural and psychological substance for National Socialism. In order to assess the role of mysticism before and during the Romantic period, we should again consider historical context, literary tradition, and the principle of an authority that could either strengthen demands for conformity or validate the prerogatives of the individual.

In the decades around 1800, the situation was remarkably analo-
gous, *mutatis mutandis*, to what had prevailed two centuries earlier at
the beginning of the Thirty Years' War—also a period of cultural and
scientific awakening in Germany. During that distant age, Germans
had been confronted by vexing controversies over predestination,
ubiquity, the *Abendmahl*, and the proper understanding of the Scriptures: these issues had been debated as having implications for war
and peace, for Germany and humankind as a whole. Two centuries
later, Germans were again confronted with universal questions. The
new questions were directed to the socio-political order by the French
Revolution (with which many Germans initially sympathized), and to
the natural, metaphysical, or anthropological orders by the Kantian
revolution of critical thought. Despite the distance of these theoretical
issues from the earlier doctrinal ones, the Kantian philosophy imposed
an agenda of problems of a scope comparable to the Baroque crisis.
These questions again touched on the relationships of faith and knowledge, freedom and necessity. Where the earlier theological controversies revolved around the relationship of the soul to the deity and
inquired about the hidden God, the new philosophical debates instead
revolved around the relationship of subject and object, and asked
about the unknowable reality of the Kantian noumenon or "Thing in
Itself." In the earlier age, the Lutheran *deus absconditus* was a God both
hidden and omnipresent in nature. This nature had been held together
by ubiquitous occult forces. The earlier nature mysticism of the Age of
Faith had endeavored to understand the *deus absconditus* with reference to the concealed power of a *vis occulta* in nature; and it had
approached both the natural forces and the hidden God by way of the
inner life of the soul, so that questions of theology, nature, and psychology all appeared to be suggestively linked. Now, toward 1800, a
similar constellation was asserting itself. It would soon release comparable energies and popularize kindred themes. Considerations of
national character aside, the situations were homologous.

The inner and the outer, the visible and the invisible, the finite
and the infinite realms were again themes for debate, as was the entire
order of life in Germany and Europe. Novalis, Goethe, and Schopenhauer all knew both the old culture of Pietism and the new revolutions
in science and philosophy. Since the terms of the older mysticism were
still, however marginally, in currency, they only needed to be brought
back into the center of intellectual life and reinterpreted. Novalis was
to accomplish this in the sphere of poetics by reinterpreting the relationships of outer and inner in the sense of an imagination that creates
and recreates nature. Ultimately, Schopenhauer would secularize the

new and old mysticism with his theory of the relationship of the Will to a grim nature from which there was no escape.

The thematic material of German mysticism was slated for rediscovery, with or without its religious authenticity, as an essential component of what we might call *la matière allemande*. It is hardly surprising that, as the Germans began to search for their national identity in their past, the scintillating worlds of cosmic expansiveness and mystical introspection were caught in the mirror of their self-identification. If the following brief discussion is necessarily sketchy, its purpose is to demonstrate the relevance of mystical themes to the concerns of an age. The boundary line between religious mysticism and its resonances in a secular poetry and philosophy will be crossed freely in order to consider the rather extensive contribution of mystical themes to German literature and ideas as a whole.

This is nowhere more evident than with Goethe, for whom the stuff of German mysticism indeed became an artistic-intellectual subject matter—and one which met his deepest needs as a poet and speculative thinker. The young Goethe's most important encounter with this material took place during the physical crisis of his illness in Frankfurt in 1769. This was the period of his warm acquaintance with the Pietistic friend of his family, Fräulein von Klettenberg (1723–1774); of his successful treatment by a Pietistic physician given to alchemistic theories and remedies; of his amused and captivated immersion in pansophic speculation, experiment, literature, and lore. The existential turning point of his illness and recovery helped solidify a thematic material which, in its broadest outlines, included not only alchemy and Pietism, but also Neoplatonism, Johannine speculation about the divine Word, Swedenborg, the legendary personalities of Paracelsus or Agrippa von Nettesheim, and the Arnoldian defense of heresy that would justify the role of the nonconformist and outsider for the young Goethe. Many, if not all, facets of the German mystical tradition penetrated, via an imaginative prism, into Goethe's work: as the Renaissance magic and mysticism of *Faust*, the "Confessions of a Beautiful Soul" in *Wilhelm Meister's Apprenticeship*, and as a contributing factor to Goethe's native sense of the inherent meaningfulness of nature as symbol.

Goethe's chief guide during his youthful infatuation with alchemistic experimentation was Georg von Welling's *Opus Mago-Cabbalisticum et Theosophicum*. This was an early eighteenth-century compendium extracted from Paracelsus and Boehme. It offered Goethe a compendium of pansophic commonplaces, strong in point of systematization, but rather weak in language, imagery, and expression.[2] It would be inaccurate to claim Welling as a pivotal figure whose influence would qualify Goethe as a clandestine mystic in his own right. Welling is too thin a conduit; and what Goethe received from or shared with German mysticism came to him from many sources.

Goethe's development as a writer paralleled the concurrent evolution from the culture of the Enlightenment to Romanticism. During Goethe's early manhood, Kant's development was progressing toward the so-called "Copernican Revolution" of his turn toward pure subjectivity. No one can deny Kant's radical innovations vis-à-vis his forerunners, yet neither can it be said that his thinking was without precedent. Augustine and Descartes before Kant had in some sense anticipated the view that the truth could be "obtained without going outside of subjective experience."[3] In his *Metakritik* (1784), Hamann had relished the satisfaction of calling attention to a forerunner of the new critical philosophy, whom he characterized as the "eleatic, mystical, and enthusiastic Bishop of Cloyne, George Berkeley." In point of philosophical *doctrine*, Kant had nothing of the mystic about him. But in point of *theme*, his turn toward pure subjectivity bears an undisputed similarity and kinship with Berkeley's *esse est percipi*—or for that matter with the prioritization of knowing before being by the forgotten Eckhart. Just as Luther's paradox of faith in a hidden yet omnipresent God had once encouraged the two related impulses of introspective mysticism and nature philosophy, and just as the real Copernican revolution of the sixteenth century had left open the great Faustian question of what held the world together in its inmost being, Kant's epistemological revolution now left many questions unanswered, even while placing them in a fresh perspective. There was a curious irony in either instance: the mystical enthusiasm that Luther had wanted to eliminate, like the mystical metaphysics which Kant had intended to exclude, was in the end stimulated by the watershed achievements of either of these reformers.

The revival of mysticism responded to developments in the sphere of thought. As Copleston says of Kant's successors, "the Kantian theory of knowledge [was] inflated into a metaphysics of reality." And this ultimately meant that, "Absolute thought or reason [was] regarded as an activity, as productive reason which posits or expresses itself in the world.... Inasmuch as reality is looked on as the self-expression or self-unfolding of an absolute thought or reason, there is a marked tendency in German idealism to assimilate the causal relation to the logical relation of implication."[4] In Fichte and Schelling, the logical relation becomes a process of implicating, *qua* creating. This would then lead to the view of the Absolute as a divine subject that expresses itself by unfolding the structures of reality: as the Absolute Spirit in history of Hegel and Schelling. Fichte had conceived a theory of mind, as equivalent to imagination: the absolute ego posits the external world of nature. Fichte is the pivotal figure in discussions of the affinities of mysticism with Idealism and Romanticism.[5]

In the evolution from Idealism to Romanticism, it was not only the true but also the beautiful that inspired novel enterprises. Here again, Kant's esthetics had broken ground by enhancing the status of subjectivity and attributing to mind a more autonomous role than in earlier esthetic theories. Eventually, this meant that beauty, taste, and genius were to be supplanted by the terms *poetry* and *imagination* in an emerging Romantic theory of "the absolute autonomy of art."[6]

In this environment, the whole tradition of German mysticism blossomed anew, not only as a subject matter, but as a source of inspiration, ideas, and symbols. The memory of the mystics had been cultivated in the Pietistic circles that nurtured early Romantics such as Schleiermacher and Novalis. Romanticism now discovered its forebears, particularly Boehme, as if digging up some buried treasure. The erstwhile doctrinal concerns of German mysticism were forgotten. As if to outbid the issues raised by Kant and Fichte, mysticism offered concepts rich in mythic overtones and redolent of poetry. Where the new philosophy could only proffer the dry assertion "that the world in its entirety had to be considered as the product of creative thought or reason,"[7] the mystics offered elaborations which could summon forth the latent excitement of colorless philosophical abstractions. The world is virtually imagined into being by the divine Spirit.

Creative thought was interpreted as the "creative imagination." Faivre has characterized this ancient notion as *la faculté qu'aurait l'imagination d'agir sur le monde extérieur, directement ou par l'intermédiaire d'un 'médiateur plastique'*. The "creative imagination" magically touches and transforms the exterior world. The notion has been traced from its Neoplatonic and mystical sources through the Renaissance to the Romantic age, when it again unfolds in the metaphysical implications of Schelling's philosophy of art as "the power of imagination, or of synthesis, on which all creation rests" (*die Kraft der Ineinsbildung, auf welcher alle Schöpfung beruht*)—above all in Novalis's "magical idealism."[8] Certain traditional motifs of German mysticism were echoed in this theme of the creative imagination as a transcendent power that expresses itself in the visible external world. It was akin to Eckhart's elevation of knowing above being. In Paracelsus and Boehme, the creative imagination coincided with the theory of the signatures which demonstrated that nature can be read as an array of letters to decipher the virtues of things—a "code of the world."[9]

With the Romantic theologian Friedrich Schleiermacher (1768–1834), a further motif was restored which augmented the theme of nature and imagination: that of the infinite as the object of all authentic religion. After the controversy of Friedrich Heinrich Jacobi and Moses Mendelsohn over Spinoza during the years 1785 and 1786, pantheism had become an influential doctrine in Germany. Schleiermacher's characterization of God as the infinite was not inspired by Cusanus. His thinking was influenced by the Pietism of his schooling, by an intense study of Fichte and Kant, by his encounter with a Spinozist pantheism which seemed to bridge the gap between religion and philosophy, and by his interaction with Novalis (who shared Schleiermacher's Pietistic background and philosophical interests). Pietism, Idealism, and Spinozism gave rise to the theory by which Schleiermacher merged the infinitude of nature and the inner depth of feeling in a Romantic attempt to surmount the dead letter of orthodox or enlightenment theology.

In an environment in which the older religious culture of Germany was still very much alive, and in a period in which the political and intellectual order in Europe was being shaken to its foundations, many facets of the German mystical theme were thus coming together to form a pattern that could be interpreted in poetic literature. In order to see what this meant in the living history of the Romantics, we should briefly consider how German Romantic culture was experienced by a commentator who was neither a German by birth nor a mystic by temperament. The Scandinavian-born naturalist Henrik Steffens (1773–1845) lived, studied, and launched his university career in Romantic Germany. His memoirs *Was ich erlebte* (*What I Experienced*) recount a pilgrimage through the stations of the Romantic cultural world.

Steffens's Romantic world includes his Danish childhood and early curiosity about distant lands. It includes the impact of news of the French Revolution on his family members, as well as what he recollects as "the deepest mystery of Christianity," the Lutheran Communion of his childhood.[10] The Romantic world comes to life in the adventure of Steffens's nighttime ride through the Grillenburg Forest to Dresden (where he visited a gallery and was suddenly overcome with emotion, even bursting into tears at the sight of the Sistine Madonna, an icon for the Catholic-nostalgic sentiments of the Protestant Romantics). Among his portraits of famous acquaintances of the Jena period such as Novalis, Tieck, Fichte, and Schelling, one of the most memorable is that of the eccentric autodidactic physicist, Johann Wilhelm Ritter (1776–1810), the discoverer of the effects of ultraviolet rays. Ritter was a figure half out of the esoteric tradition, a *Grübler* deeply immersed in Boehme and Paracelsus, yet also at the threshold of the modern understanding of electricity. Steffens recollects that the Galvanic column was for tellurian physics what Kepler's laws had been for the physics of heavenly bodies; and he recalls Ritter's obsessive experiments with Galvanic effects, utilizing frog legs as an electroscope.[11] The mass excitement over Mesmer's medical-physical-psychological pseudoscience was only a few years hence (on the verge of being revived by Gotthilf Heinrich von Schubert, 1780–1860). Between the lines of Steffens's memoir, one can readily imagine how the new vision of a nature animated by mythic polarities and sympathetic powers was insinuating itself into the thought and poetic enthusiasm of the Romantic mind. Hovering above the whole age is the authority of Goethe, scientist and poet, whose *Faust* was a moving tableau of German Renaissance mysticism in all its facets.

Steffens distinguishes between the obsessiveness of Ritter and the murky mysticism of the philosopher Baader on the one hand, and the nonmystical philosophy of Schelling and Fichte on the other. Though the former enjoy his critical respect, it is only the latter who are accessible to the rational mind: "Baader had stepped out of the dark regions of mysticism; Schelling on the other hand out of the bright region of the scientific speculation of the time."[12] More recently, Ernst Benz reclaimed Schelling and Fichte (the latter to a lesser degree because of religious objections) for an Idealistic philosophical mysticism first formulated by Eckhart and Boehme.[13] The distinction drawn by Steffens is tantamount to that between *Mystizismus* and *Mystik*. *Mystizismus* is a pejorative in German, while during Steffens's period *Mystik* acquired an increasingly historicistic connotation.

In Jena, Steffens also knew Friedrich von Hardenberg, the great early-Romantic poet Novalis. Though Steffens denied that Novalis was a mystic, he did so on grounds that are irrelevant to our definition: The mind of Novalis did not attempt to flee behind the world of the senses; rather, writes Steffens, Novalis was a mind "at home within the secret place," which contemporary philosophers had been undertaking to penetrate by means of their speculative methods. This enticing character portrait accounts, according to Steffens, for the fact that Novalis was equally adept in poetry, philosophy, and science.[14]

At the time of their acquaintance, the mystical-religious transformation of the *Sophien-Erlebnis*—the visionary awakening of the poet at the graveside of his beloved—was already behind Novalis. Engaged to his second fiancé, it was only a few weeks before his early death at the age of twenty-nine.[15] Critics have contended that the devotion to Sophia and the ecstasy experienced at her graveside are literary stylizations. This is undoubtedly true. But before excluding Novalis from the mystical canon, one would have to offer the example of any other mystical poet whose experiences were not imaginatively stylized.

As a mystical poet, Novalis brings to culmination the tradition of German mysticism, the tradition of Boehme whose work became known to him through Tieck. Of a Pietistic family, the many-sided Novalis was a brilliant and imaginative thinker who studied the works of Kant and Fichte and followed the latest developments in the sciences. He was also engaged in practical affairs as a student of mining.

The encyclopedic materials of Novalis's poetic thought are gathered in the journal of his years as a student of mining in Freiberg, *Das allgemeine Brouillon* (1798/1799). Here, amidst reflections on poetry and the physical sciences, Novalis asserts that, "The higher philosophy treats the *marriage of nature and spirit*" (*Die höhere Phil[osophie] behandelt* die Ehe von Natur und Geist).[16] The method of the reflective fragments is to reapply the traditional terms of transcendence and immanence to the world of nature in order to highlight the dimensions of the spirit within it. Under the heading of a "spiritual physics" (*Geistige Phys[ik]*), he concludes that, "Our thinking is purely but a galvanisation—a touching of the terrestrial spirit—of the *spiritual atmosphere*—by a heavenly, extraterrestrial spirit. All thinking etc. is thus in itself already a *sympraxis* in a higher sense" (*Unser Denken ist schlechterdings nur eine Galvanisation—eine Berührung des irdischen Geistes—der* geistigen Atmosphäre—*durch einen himmlischen außerirdischen Geist. Alles Denken etc. ist also an sich schon eine* Sympraxis *im höhern Sinn*).[17] It seems that for Novalis all thinking and all things thought could be broken up—like rays passing through a spectral glass—into the color bands of the transcendent spirit. Writing on "Cosmology," he notes that the immanent "atmosphere of the universe" must be a "synthesis of heaven and earth."[18] Again on "Cosmology," he writes: "What is outer is what is inner, raised to the condition of a secret— / (Perhaps also vice versa)" (*Das Äußre ist ein in Geheimnißzustand erhobenes Innre— / [Vielleicht auch umgekehrt]*).[19] "Time is *inner* space—space is *external time*" (*Zeit ist* innerer *Raum—Raum ist* äußere Zeit).[20] Even what might seem most abstract to us crystallizes into imagined worlds for Novalis:

> Everything *real* [which has been] created out of *nothing*, as for example, numbers and abstract expressions—has a wonderful relationship with things of another world—with endless series of

strange combinations and relationships—as though with a mathematical and abstract world in itself—with a *poetic mathematical
and abstract world.*

*Alles aus* Nichts *erschaffene* Reale, *wie z.B. die Zahlen und die
abstracten Ausdrücke—hat eine wunderbare Verwandtschaft mit Dingen
einer andern Welt—mit unendlichen sonderbaren Combinationen und
Verhältnissen—gleichsam mit einer mathem[atischen] und abstracten
Welt an sich—mit einer* poëtischen mathem[atischen] *und abstracten
Welt.*[21]

Because all things bring to light this complexity of immanence and transcendence, all things possess the order and meaning of utterance:
"Everywhere there is a grammatical mysticism...Grammar. It is not only
the human being that speaks—the universe also *speaks*—everything
speaks—unending languages. / Doctrine of the signatures" (*Überall
liegt eine grammatische Mystik....Gram[matik]. Der Mensch spricht nicht
allein—auch das Universum spricht—alles spricht—unendliche Sprachen. /
Lehre von den Signaturen*).[22] The much traded and handed down signature should have been virtually threadbare by 1800, yet under the touch
of the Romantic poet, it refurbished itself with the notion of a cosmic cre-
ativity. God, the world-soul, the human soul, and each human life are
part of a process—like a living text that is transforming and revising
itself and hence maturing by means of a self-education, encompassing
physics no less than the human psyche:

The soul should become spirit—the body world. The world is not
yet finished—as little as [is] the world-spirit—Out of One God an
All-God [*Allgott*] should come to be. Out of One World—an All-
world [*Weltall* = "universe"]. Common physics—higher physics.
The human being is common prose—he should become higher
prose—all-encompassing prose. Education of the spirit is coedu-
cation (*Mitbildung*) of the world-spirit—and therefore *religion.*

*Die Seele soll Geist—der Körper Welt werden. Die Welt ist noch nicht
fertig—so wenig wie der Weltgeist—Aus Einem Gott soll ein Allgott
werden. Aus Einer Welt—ein Weltall. Gemeine Physik—höhere
Physik. Der Mensch ist gemeine Prosa—er soll höhere Prosa—allum-
fassende Prosa werden. Bildung des Geistes ist Mitbildung des Welt-
geistes—und also* Religion.[23]

Novalis's speculative mysticism had the breadth of past German mysticism, but was also deepened by Idealistic philosophy and empirical
science and dramatized by world history in the making.

In the narrative prose of *Heinrich von Ofterdingen*, a poeticized world is said to have arisen through the power of a "sympathy" animating nature. *The Apprentices of Sais* (*Die Lehrlinge zu Sais*) begins by evoking a great "writing in ciphers" (*jener großen Chiffernschrift*) that is observable everywhere: "on wings, eggshells, in clouds, in the snow, in crystals and in stone formations, on frozen waters, in the interior and exterior of mountains, of plants, of animals, of humans," etc. (*auf Flügeln, Eierschalen, in Wolken, im Schnee, in Kristallen und in Steinbildungen, auf gefrierenden Wassern, im Innern und Äußern der Gebirge, der Pflanzen, der Tiere, der Menschen...*). Everywhere there is this miraculous writing. In *Hymns to Night* (*Hymnen an die Nacht*) or the *Spiritual Songs* (*Geistliche Lieder*), the dimensions of the mystical worlds are folded up into the characteristics of everyday experience, lending it a magical richness. Day and night are two distinct worlds in the *Hymns*. Night, as a world of dream and imagination, occupies the higher place in the mystical dichotomy. The *Songs* echo with a mysticism recalling motifs ranging from the convent piety of medieval nuns to the high mystery of the Lutheran *Abendmahl*. It is remarkable that the poetry of Novalis could find its way into the Protestant hymn books of his own time—as well as into avant-garde theories of the later French Symbolists.

Nowhere is the reinterpretation of the mysticism of worlds more poetically fertile than in the *Hymns to Night*. These begin with a prose charged with the contrasts of the mystical spheres, which grow ever deeper and more laden with resonances, until the prosaic tensions are as if discharged in ecstatic verses—just as the world itself was to be poetically transformed by the Romantic imagination. The world of daylight is the world of a magically transfigured phenomenal reality. While the visible world sinks, as if into a "deep grave" (a variant on the motif of the divine eclipse in negative theology), the inner world of night begins to glow with a boundless depth of feeling. As the resonances of day and night are pitched to the point of incandescence, evoking loss and then resurrection as the return of God, the lyrical persona is transformed in the incomparable lines:

> Over I float,
> And every pain
> Will someday be
> A pang of ecstasy.
> *Hinüber wall ich,*
> *Und jede Pein*
> *Wird einst ein Stachel*
> *Der Wollust sein.*

Profoundly religious and influenced both by philosophical Idealism and by the mysticism of Boehme, Novalis stands at the beginning of a Romantic spectrum. At the opposite extreme is the philosophy of a Schopenhauer. Again influenced by Kant, Pietism, and Boehme, Schopenhauer reinterpreted the Romantic vision that had become bereft of its erstwhile optimistic faith, transforming it into the opposite of Novalis's childlike trust in the goodness of the cosmos.

The magical atmosphere of the fairy tale in the work of Novalis has a parallel in the allegorically Oriental ambiance of *The Tale of the Naked Saint* (*Ein wunderbares morgenländisches Märchen von einem nackten Heiligen*), the work of the youthful Wilhelm Heinrich Wackenroder (1773–1798). As in Novalis, the mystical tradition is transformed into a fairy tale, extolling the cosmic power of love.

There are two world realities: that of a "naked saint," who is convinced that if he desists from cranking "the wheel of time," the entire universe will grind to a halt; and that of the pair of lovers whose melody touches off the transfiguration of the naked saint into a celestial creature. In general, mysticism and myth are taken to be opposites. Yet Wackenroder's juxtaposition of the worlds of temporal drudgery and erotic imagination engenders the motifs of his parable of the meaning of nature. The world is not pushed by slavish exertion: it is drawn by love. Again, this is a theme of enchantment recapitulated, in horror, by Schopenhauer: drudgery and desire are two sides of the one metaphysical Will.

Romantic nature is rendered ambiguous by twilight or moonlight. Romantic imagination is contiguous with the world of dreams, with the "nocturnal side of science" explored by the psychologist Schubert. Dusk appears as a threshold to another world in the landscapes and seascapes of Caspar David Friedrich (1774–1840). Friedrich's abrupt juxtapositions of heavens and earth, shore and sea, foreground and unattainable depths, lends these opposites the aura of distinct, facing worlds. Instead of being integrated by traditional pictorial hierarchies, the worlds that confront one another across the abrupt chasm are only united by an all-encompassing infinitude—the divinity present according to the artist in "every particle of sand." This saturation in the infinite isolates objects and heightens their expressiveness. Trees, rocks, summits, or spires seem like mystical signatures, pointing the displaced spectator across metaphysical boundaries. Tiny human figures or sailing ships appear as if in search of a passage. Friedrich's relation to nature was religious, his view of painting contemplative. His precept as an artist was to close the outer eye and begin by viewing things with the eye of the mind, subjecting nature to imagination. Contemporary observers recognized "mysticism" in his work.

The *Apocalyptic Fragment* (1804) of Karoline von Günderode yields a disturbing view of an imagined nature on the scale of Friedrich's seascapes. The visionary "I" of the fragment stands on a high cliff above the sea, facing east, as morning, noon, evening, and night race across the arc of the sky. The entranced subject wants to plunge into the dawn or the night, in order to be sucked into their rapid tempo and not live so slowly. The visionary subject wearies and falls asleep, and recognizes instead an infinite sea that is perfectly calm, yet moved in its depths. Fog and clouds rise from it and give birth to more and more varied forms: the subject is overcome by dizziness and fear, until consciousness and memory disintegrate "like a torch in a storm." Waking up with a lost sense of time, the subject now becomes aware of having rested in the womb of the calm sea, like a drop of dew, having rejoiced in the air and the sun, and having associated with the "twilight and the rainbow's seven-colored drops," circling the hidden moon with her playmates. The past disappears. The subject belongs only to the present, but, driven by a longing, wanders about in the boundless element (*sehnend trieb ich mich umher im Unendlichen*). In the fragment, the tenses and referential time frames are obscured, until the subject feels the limits of her self dissolve, with an ensuing realization that all things are but one; and that there are no boundaries between "body" and "spirit," "time" and "eternity," "visible and invisible." All things persist in change, as "an infinite life." In 1806, at the age of twenty-six, Günderode committed suicide in despair after her lover, a noted professor, had become reconciled with his wife.

Wackenroder's phantasmagorical orientalism anticipates the Romantic discovery of Indian mysticism: a development that was to become a recurrent preoccupation of the Germans—and one that encouraged the general understanding of mysticism as a universal religion or mode of consciousness. Hermann Hesse wrote *The Journey to the East*, but this journey had begun much earlier, in Herder's interest in Hindu culture, and in the philosophical quest launched by Friedrich Schlegel's essay of 1808, *On the Language and Wisdom of the Indians* (*Über die Sprache und Weisheit der Indier*). Although Schlegel's essay was based on philological researches, he misconstrued Hindu religion as a form of pantheism. His point was directed against a pantheism that he attributed to Schelling. If the erroneous image of Eastern religions has since been corrected, the Romantic identification of mysticism with pantheism would prove more persistent. During Schlegel's career, his Orientalist phase was soon overshadowed by his much-publicized conversion to Catholicism.[24]

In Friedrich Schlegel, the pantheistic-Idealistic impulses of early Romanticism are transformed—aided by a transitional influence of Boehme—into a full-blown Christian philosophy that takes leave of Fichte in order to reassert the soul. The soul is interpreted within a characteristic constellation of references: to the mysterious force of electricity (which Schlegel compares with the scientific discoveries of the Renaissance), to the engulfment of the finite in an infinite being for which the soul longs, to the meaning of historical epochs, to history heightened by eschatology, and to a Romantic view of mysticism as essential to the interpretation of both biblical and philosophical objects, moreover to the Romantic "philosophy of life."[25]

Johann Joseph von Görres (1776–1848), who heard Schlegel's Orientalist lectures with eagerness, was destined to become one of the most influential interpreters of mythology and mysticism. He would also embody certain new antirational impulses most fully. Having gone through the stages of an early enthusiasm for the French Revolution followed by German nationalism (for which he was persecuted by the Prussian government), from a Romantic-universalistic interest in myths and mysticism to a narrowly Catholic mystagogy allied with his rejection of rationalism and materialism, Görres encourages the equation of the mystical with the irrational and the reactionary.[26] His compendious *Die christliche Mystik* (1836) offers a sweeping overview of Christian mysticism—but trimmed to exclude Protestantism and heresy. With Görres, the "politics" of mysticism were amended. Schleiermacher had cemented the liberal associations of mysticism with a cosmopolitan pantheism; Görres now reinforced the association with Catholic supernaturalism and Romantic medievalist nostalgia.

By contrast, the many-sided philosopher, lay theologian, political theorist, inventor, and scholar Franz Xaver von Baader (1765–1841) defies the characterization of the liberal pantheist or reactionary irrationalist. A devout Catholic, Baader was also much influenced by Boehme. He was open-minded enough to be capable of sympathizing with English trade unionist and feminist ideas. Baader was anticlerical, antipapal, and a committed Russophile. His career spans a lifetime, from his early "Storm and Stress" efforts to come to terms with Kant to a post-Romantic era, when his ideas were eclipsed by the success of empirical realism.

Beginning with his early aversion to the emphasis on human autonomy in the philosophy of German Idealism, Baader strove to penetrate to the inner life of matter. His philosophy of life accorded a central role to Eros, even while recognizing the real existence of evil, of a fallen Adamic state, and of the ensuing necessity of redemption.

These were themes that would be taken up in a darker key by Schopenhauer. While adhering to doctrine and revelation, Baader in fact anticipated certain aspects of the philosophical system of the great pessimist—whose originality and significance the mercurial man of faith was among the first to recognize.[27]

Baader's greatest scholarly achievement was a reevaluation, thorough enough to amount to a rediscovery, of Meister Eckhart. Beginning in 1786, German scholars had begun to take notice of the master who preceded the more familiar Tauler and Seuse. After the turn of the century, Baader completed this process by studying the available materials more carefully and introducing Eckhart as the "greatest" of German mystics.[28] Baader also pursued his goal of a "religious philosophy" by interpreting Boehme's mysticism with the aid of an Idealist philosophical vocabulary.[29]

In Friedrich Schlegel, Schelling, and Hegel, Idealism turned not only to nature and spirit, but also increasingly to history. Schelling (1775–1854) undertook to elaborate the theoretical implications of myths and mysticism in a system of philosophy less esoteric than that of his senior by ten years, Baader. Throughout most of his career, Schelling partook of the Romantic fascination with Boehme. However, according to Robert Brown, it was in the mature system beginning in 1809 that this source of inspiration began to bear fruit.[30] In approaching the problem of the free will in his essay *On Human Freedom* (1809), Schelling labored at the task of overcoming the determinism of Spinozistic pantheism. The high point of Boehme's influence came in the treatise on *The Ages of the World* (*Die Weltalter*, 1811–1815). Boehme's characterization of the eternal structure of God is interpreted by Schelling as the ground of an unfolding "history of religious consciousness," a history that reaches its apogee in "the age of the Spirit, when the actualization of God's life in history will be completed. This will be the end of history, the definitive restoration of fallen consciousness, and of all being, to communion with God."[31]

Schelling's concept of the culmination of spirit in history brings us to the more famous philosophy of history of Georg Wilhelm Friedrich Hegel (1770–1831). Hegel's early philosophy was in part a reaction against that of the younger Schelling.

Hegel's *Phenomenology of Spirit* was published in 1807. An early interest in religion had nourished the beginnings of his thought, and it developed in an environment in which mysticism ranked as the illustrious ancestral image of the new philosophy: a model with which contemporary thought could identify, with or without shared articles of faith. Hegel was prodigious in his praise of the rediscovered Eckhart or the widely cherished Boehme. Introduced to Eckhart's sermons by Baader, Hegel soon extolled them in a lecture: the *Meister* had anticipated his own concepts.[32] Lecturing on the history of philosophy, he praised Boehme as the "first German philosopher."[33] This confronts us with the difficult question of Hegel's debt to mysticism.

If nothing else, the coloration of German mysticism could be expected to rub off on Hegel's philosophical writing. After all, he shared philosophical origins with the mystics—Neoplatonism, especially that of Proklos. A drive toward a totality of vision and a kinship with the terminologies of Spiritualism are evinced by the solemn dicta of Hegel's *Phenomenology*: "The true is the whole. The whole, however, is nothing less than the being which completes itself through its development" (*Das Wahre ist das Ganze. Das Ganze aber ist nur das durch seine Entwicklung sich vollendende Wesen*). The totality parallels the development of the individual. Individual fulfillment may come nearest to mysticism in Hegel's interpretation of the *mors mystica*: the transformation effected by a spiritual "death" of the human subject.[34] Hegel's doctrine of death and freedom has been compared to Eckhart's *Gelassenheit* and "birth of the Son in the soul." (The mystical motif of the *mors mystica* is taken up again by Heidegger.) Comparing Proklos and Hegel, Beierwaltes considered either thinker less a mystic than the culminating figure in an overdeveloped metaphysical tradition.[35] In view of the richness of Hegel's sources, it is unlikely that his central propositions were decisively dependent on mysticism. However, Hegelian philosophy is clearly more than a set of cold propositions. It is also a style and atmosphere of thought. If the philosopher himself acknowledged an affinity with Eckhart and Boehme, then the attempt to cleanse him of every association with the mystics is surely tendentious and anachronistic.

On the whole, the discussions of mysticism that occurred in Germany in the wake of Hegel's philosophy did much to generate our own modern contradictions in the use of this term. Mysticism was pantheism, heresy, atheism, acosmism, monism, dualism, superstition; it was a universal religion and it was also the true matrix of German culture and thought. The philosophical problems of the nineteenth century were projected back into the mysticism of Eckhart or Boehme, while the real channels of their influence on modern philosophy were overlooked or forgotten.[36]

More than Schelling or Hegel, the philosopher who terminates the Romantic period by drastically secularizing its religious and mystical themes, channeling them toward the literature, art, and thought of modernism, is the much-neglected Arthur Schopenhauer (1788–1860). In America, the popular esteem in which Nietzsche is now held as a prophet of modernism disregards the magnitude of his debt to Schopenhauer. Yet even the few non-German admirers of the earlier of these two kindred thinkers have ignored Schopenhauer's debt to older German mysticism, to Pietism, and, above all, to Boehme. Reinterpreting German mysticism, Schopenhauer replaced its religious center with the idea of a conscious life sustained by the transcendent irrational power of a metaphysical "will." The Will interprets Kant's Thing in Itself.

During the decisive juncture in the evolution of his thinking, Schopenhauer studied the mysticism of Boehme.[37] In 1814, he transcribed a passage from *Signatura Rerum* in which Boehme identified the metaphysical Will with "desire," "hunger," "longing," and "seeking."[38] In addition to the world-generating "will," the surrounding section of *Signatura Rerum* refers to the desirous will that engenders the qualities of all existing things. The covetous contraction of the primal desire (which, because it is primal, can have no external object) gives rise to the hardness and coldness of stones and earth. An ensuing, opposing impulse elicits movement and life. Within the "Being of all beings," arises an "animosity" (*Wiederwertigkeit*) and "struggle" (*Streit*), as each entity attempts to "subdue or kill" the other, in order to carry over the essence or spirit of the other into an extraneous form (*in eine andere Gestaltnis einführet*).[39] For Boehme, the boundless longing of the "First Will" or "Eternal Will" went into itself thereby creating being out of its own "nothingness." Boehme's will "finds itself" in the "second principle" and is redeemed by the power of a love that overcomes the divine anger. In many points, Boehme's thought anticipates Schopenhauer, for whom the absolute Will beyond time and space gives rise to the phenomenal qualities of individuals, and to an incessant striving, struggle, and suffering in nature and society.

As in the confessional literature of Lutheran Pietism, which Schopenhauer makes a point of citing in support of his concepts, knowledge leads to repentance: "*Repentance* never results from the fact that the will has changed—this is impossible—but from a change of knowledge."[40] Self-knowledge is a recognition of the utter vanity of existence: a fleeting *now* between a past and a future which are in themselves not existent. Like a bookkeeper who has recognized the capital insolvency of his firm, the enlightened mind persuades itself to forego all striving. With a mixture of compassion for suffering and selfless delight in the ideal beauty of things, Schopenhauer's ascetic steers toward the nirvana of a pure nothing, characterized by the Pauline word of a calm that surpasses all reason or understanding.

With Schopenhauer, we are already in the aftermath of German religious mysticism. With some justice, he can be considered the counterpart to the Novalis who interpreted mysticism poetically at the beginning of the Romantic period. The nature that was for Novalis a source of delight is for Schopenhauer a vale of sorrow. But even in Schopenhauer, the outlook of German speculative mysticism is still in evidence. The salient question is still the meaning of the world, even though the cosmos has become a panorama of stunning meaninglessness:

> In endless space countless luminous spheres, round each of which some dozen smaller illuminated ones revolve, hot at the core and covered over with a hard cold crust; on this crust a mouldy film has produced living and knowing beings: this is empirical truth, the real, the world. Yet for a being who thinks, it is a precarious position to stand on one of those numberless spheres freely floating in boundless space, without knowing whence and whither, and to be only one of innumerable similar beings that throng, press, and toil, restlessly and rapidly arising and passing away in the beginningless and endless time.[41]

This is not merely "the real." It is a reality behind which a central sun has set, casting fearful and fantastic hues. The Will is an omnipresent demonic force in a world bereft of the faith of a young Schopenhauer who still treasured the wistful, melancholy, devotional poetry of Matthias Claudius's *Wandsbeck Messenger*. What remains from the mystical heritage is Schopenhauer's appropriation of the *signatura rerum* for an interpretive and intuitive philosophy that searches for the meaning of the world. The world as an object of interpretation, as a conundrum of signs which enfolds its erstwhile transcendent dimensions within human experience—this focus in Schopenhauer points beyond him toward Nietzsche, Freud, and modernism.

Nietzsche seems to have recognized that Schopenhauer's negation of theology was an ironic echo of the negative theology of mysticism. The mystical or religious cast of Nietzsche's language has drawn the attention and comment of scholars, Kämpfert on the work as a whole and Grundlehner for the poems.[42] In *Beyond Good and Evil*, Nietzsche wrote of "a great ladder of religious cruelty." Its first stage is human sacrifice. The second stage sacrifices the strongest natural instincts in a spirit of Christian asceticism.

And finally—what remains that could be sacrificed? Don't we in the end have to sacrifice everything consolatory, holy, and heal-

ing; all hope, all belief in invisible harmony, in future blessedness and justice? Don't we have to sacrifice God himself and
idolize a rock, the forces of stupidity, of gravity, fate, nothingness—all in order to be sufficiently cruel to ourselves. To sacrifice God for nothingness—this is the paradoxical mystery of ultimate cruelty that remained in store for the generation now
growing up. All of us know something about it already.[43]

This is the voice of the seer whose eyes behold the coming age.

# Conclusion:
# Wittgenstein and the Aftermath
# of German Mysticism

In confirming the affinity of modernism with mysticism, we should avoid the sensationalism of Monsieur Jourdain's cunning tutor in rhetoric who amazes his pupil by informing him that he has been speaking prose his entire life. But as with Molière's *Bourgeois Gentilhomme*, the sensationalism cannot be deflated by denying the "prose," but only by demystifying the understanding of what it is. The affinity of modernism with mysticism has been confirmed by the modern writers and philosophers themselves too often to allow for denials. Whether the affinity suffices to characterize modernism itself as a form of mysticism depends upon one's definition and on the modernist. The definition employed in this study has confined it to German Christian mysticism, without denying that the matter can be seen differently and more broadly.

A broader characteristic of mysticism is its challenge to the common understanding of "the world," with its accepted values and sense of life and reality. In this, mysticism approximates a modernist literature that likewise challenges reality, with all its categories of experience, thought, identity, time, language, and culture. Since what is articulated by the mystic surpasses common knowledge and experience, mysticism often manifests itself *in extremis*. Nietzsche, the defiant individualist who questions and "transvalues all values," is demonstrably close to the mystics in his language and style.

The fictional qualities of Kafka's writing recognize in the *petits faits vrais* of reality the banal yet mysterious tokens of transcendence. Authority at its apex is inaccessible. However, the castle hierarchy can be circumvented (so we are told in a key episode) through a sort of inward flight, a turn that surmounts the endless divisions and gradations of the great bureaucracy. The "secret"—we learn from the minor castle functionary named Bürgel—is that the hierarchy is structured so that even the smallest sphere of authority (*Zuständigkeit*) encompasses the whole: this makes a penetration of all barriers conceivable. The thought of this breakthrough is described in ecstatic terms—as if it were a mystical union effected by love.[1]

Rilke's *Stundenbuch* (*The Book of Hours*, first part: 1899) casts the artist in the role of a monk and mystic, on intimate terms with God. Robert Musil and Hugo von Hofmannsthal can be added to the list of major modern writers who associated their most ambitious works with themes of mysticism.[2] The poetry and art of the Expressionists in their moods of ecstasy and despair projected an interior atmosphere in visions of the crisis and agony of the world. The famous collection of Expressionistic poetry, *Menschheitsdämmerung* ("The Dawn—or Dusk— of Humanity," 1920), encompasses many poems that explicitly incorporate the themes of the mystical quest for God.

Not only varied facets of mysticism, but also the mysticism of various religions attracts the attention of artists, writers, and scholars. The latter include Gershom Scholem, the preeminent scholar of Jewish mysticism, Walter Benjamin, and Hans Jonas who interprets Gnosticism in the light of Existentialism. Also drawn to the mystics are political minds of every persuasion: from the Anarchist Gustav Landauer, to the radical or Marxist philosopher of hope Ernst Bloch, to the Nietzschean reactionary and sometime monarchist Rudolf Pannwitz. Attempts are made to appropriate the mystical tradition into the culture and ideology of organized groups. These range from the Nazi Party—whose ideologue, Alfred Rosenberg, attempted to claim the German mystics as Nordic-Aryan aristocrats in his scholarly travesty (*The Myth of the Twentieth Century*)[3]—to the rather humane and cultivated "anthroposophical" followers of Rudolf Steiner, a charismatic theorist whose studies of mysticism are valid works of scholarship (though colored with the peculiar atmosphere of turn-of-the-century Austrian culture). At the beginning of this century, a resurgent conservative German nationalism discovered congenial elements in mysticism[4]—but then so did radicals, rebels, and moderates.

Mysticism as a covert bond for a society of outsiders can be traced back to medieval and ancient sects. The followings of Freud or Jung have displayed the absorption in the inner life or in the symbol, and, at times, the sectarianism of religious movements. More characteristic for the present role of mysticism is its attractiveness as a refuge of the individual disaffected with organized confessions or with conformist society as a whole. Often trivialized, the themes of mysticism have been widely current in the everyday culture of twentieth-century life.

The nineteenth-century discussions of mysticism bequeathed to this century all the prototypes for its eclectic mysticism—everything from the unabashed superstition, to the nondiscursive equivalent of Idealist philosophy, to the notion of a pantheistic materialism. Marx considered the leap from the use value of the commodity to its exchange value to be a source of "the mystical." In an ironical aside, *Das Kapital* augured (apropos the cessation of all challenges to the established order of things after 1848—a standstill alleviated only by the Taipeng Revolt in China and by seances in the West) that, "when all the world stood still, China and the tables moved—*pour encourager les autres.*"[5] Some reflex of this displaced movement may well be operative in the current academic rage for "theory." Initially the opposite of "practice," theory became practice by resurrecting the mystic's love of baroque symbolic systems, concealed motives and intricate interpretations—of the world as literature and of literature as the world. Already in ancient times, the word *theoria* designated mystical contemplation.

Before the turn of the century, the physicist-philosopher Ernst Mach arrived at a kind of secular unification mysticism in analyzing the parameters of experience. In developing the foundations of modern mathematics, Georg Cantor—who believed that his set theory had been revealed to him by God—formulated paradoxes distantly akin to those of Cusanus. Albert Einstein challenged the common and scientific image of the universe more radically than the boldest nature mystic. Goltschnigg has shown that the vitalism of *Lebensphilosophie*, the personalism of Martin Buber, and the language analysis of *Sprachkritik* discovered a kindred spirit in mysticism. German philosophy, in seeking to encompass the whole of reality, set it over against nothingness. Discourse is contrasted with mystical silence. The most original modern philosophers, Martin Heidegger and Ludwig Wittgenstein, introduced mystical allusions and themes into their philosophical reflections.[6]

In conclusion, we can do no better than to consider the famous ending of Wittgenstein's *Tractatus logico-philosophicus*—a *summa* of the aftermath of German mysticism. The following decimally ordered statements are included among the closing propositions: "The meaning of the world (*der Sinn der Welt*) has to lie outside of it" (6.41). "Not *how* the world is, is the mystical (*das Mystische*), but *that* it is" (6.44). "There is indeed that which is unutterable. It *shows* itself, it is the mystical (*das Mystische*)" (6.522). "About that which one cannot speak one must remain silent" (7).

Wittgenstein did not write these statements out of a religious conviction of the kind that has been under discussion here. Aside from the themes of mysticism current in the intellectual culture of Wittgenstein's environment, Schopenhauer's philosophical secularization of the tradition of German mysticism was known to him.[7] What the closing propositions of the *Tractatus* offer is a vestige of the German tradition of speculative mysticism—a kind of afterimage of structures

shared by Hildegard, Eckhart, and Boehme, reduced now of their theological content. When Wittgenstein refers to *das Mystische*, what is
implied is not a personal union with God, not the union of subject and
object. Wittgenstein's "mysticism" is, in the German speculative tradition, a mysticism of the world: "The world of the happy individual is a
different one from that of the unhappy individual" (6.43). "The intuition of the world *sub specie aeterni* is its intuition as-a-limited-whole.
The feeling of the world as a limited whole is the mystical" (6.45).

"World" means the intuited or felt world of the individual. To
speak of the world is for the philosopher to be restricted to logical sentences. Yet to intuit or feel about the world is to view it in accordance
with the question of its meaning—the view of the speculative mystic.
The intuited world as a whole can be accorded no meaning on the
basis of any of the statements that the philosopher could logically
utter, for all such statements could only represent states of affairs
*within* the totality of states of affairs that constitute the world. This is
why the meaning of the world can only lie outside the world, and why
the meaning of the world is *ipso facto* unutterable.

Nevertheless, the philosopher confirms that the unutterable
*shows* itself: "it is the mystical" (6.522). The meaning of the world—the
mystical—"shows itself" in the feeling that the world is a limited
whole—not in any state of affairs that might be expressed by means of
logical sentences. "*How* the world is, is for that which is higher (*für das
Höhere*), a matter of complete indifference. God doesn't reveal himself
*in* the world" (6.432). "The facts all belong to the problem, not to the
solution" (6.4321). "Not *how* the world is, is the mystical, but *that* it is"
(6.44). We are reminded of the mystic's sense of contemplative wonder, which does not aspire to explain things logically or causally. For
Wittgenstein, the world as a "whole" has become the sole—indeci-
pherable—signature.

The *Tractatus* thus ends with afterimages of the German mystical
tradition. The statement, "it *shows* itself," evokes a theophany. Given
the choice of terms, there can be little doubt that Wittgenstein intended
such associations, though his use radically takes leave of the tradition
of all prior theophany. In the same context, he indicates that the answer
to the problem of the meaning of life comes in that the question, the
riddle, disappears (6.521). Eckhart, we recall, put the matter in similar
terms: *Whoever were to ask life for a thousand years: 'Why do you live?'—if
life could answer, it would say nothing but: 'I live in order that I live.'*

For Wittgenstein, as for Eckhart, the true standard of a good
action can have as little to do with punishment and reward as "the
meaning of life" or of "the world" can be specified with reference to

states of affairs that lie within the world: "it is clear that ethics has nothing to do with punishment and reward in the usual sense" (6.422). Just as Eckhart—in denying rewards and punishments to good works and thoughts—thereby also cast out "time" in favor of eternity, so Wittgenstein seeks to equate his notion of "to live eternally" with "to live in the present": "If one does not understand by eternity the endless duration of time but rather timelessness, then he lives eternally who lives in the present" (6.4311). For Wittgenstein, there is another kind of reward: it does not consist of anything accorded to the ethical action within the world. The *Tractatus* states that, through the good action, the world becomes a different world in its entirety: "It must, so to speak, decrease or increase as a whole.... The world of the happy individual is a different one from that of the unhappy individual" (6.43). The eternal—this backdrop against which the world is to be intuited or felt as "a limited whole"—proves to be identical with the world of the experienced present: the present is limitless in the same way that our field of vision is limitless (6.4311).

These statements at the end of the *Tractatus* do not convey a mystical system. Wittgenstein states that whoever understands them, in so doing recognizes them to be nonsensical. The person who understands them does so by transcending them: "He has to throw away the ladder, so to speak, after he has climbed up it.... He has to overcome these sentences, then he will see the world correctly" (6.54). To extract philosophical or mystical tenets from the conclusion of the *Tractatus* would be to miss the point.

What we can say is that Wittgenstein's formulations present us with an ultimate, truncated form of our theme of the union of worlds, of time and eternity, immanence and transcendence; of the good as a rebirth or translation of the reborn into another mode of being; of the question of the meaning of things, the world, or life; of the intuition of the world as a manifestation or expression of the hidden God; and, finally, of the unutterable *es*, which *shows* itself but cannot be expressed: "About what one cannot speak one must remain silent" (7).

If all logical and meaningful propositions about the world are semantically and logically linked, deriving their meaning and system from their ensemble, then the world as a limited whole is either meaningless, or it is an expression of what lies beyond it. The interpretive relationship of immanence and transcendence therefore constitutes the *mystical*, as it has throughout the German tradition.

Were the writings of the mystics only illicit violations of Wittgenstein's rule of silence? At the very least, their speech expanded the universe of discourse.

# Notes

## Introduction

1. Madame de Staël, *De L'Allemagne* (Paris: Dido Frère, 1847), 546.

2. See Gottfried Fischer, *Geschichte der Entdeckung der deutschen Mystiker Eckhart, Tauler und Seuse im XIX. Jahrhundert* (Freiburg i. Ue.: Hess, 1931), 1 (*Als der Begriff 'deutsche Mystik' geprägt wurde, hat man den Hauptton auf das Wort 'deutsch' gelegt. Er stammt bezeichnenderweise von einem Hegelschüler, Karl Rosenkranz, der ihn zuerst in einem Aufsatz als Rezension zu Diepenbrocks Seuse-Ausgabe (1829) in den 'Berliner Jahrbüchern für wissenschaftliche Kritik' verwendete.*)

3. See Ernst Benz, *Swedenborg in Deutschland. F. C. Oetingers und Immanuel Kants Auseinandersetzung mit der Person und Lehre Emanuel Swedenborgs* (Frankfurt am Main: Klostermann, 1947), vii, 271–72.

4. See Steven T. Katz, "The 'Conservative' Character of Mystical Experience," in Steven T. Katz, ed., *Mysticism and Religious Traditions* (Oxford: Oxford University Press, 1983); Wayne Proudfoot, "Mysticism," in Proudfoot, *Religious Experience* (Berkeley: University of California Press, 1985); Gershom Scholem, *Major Trends in Jewish Mysticism* (New York: Schocken, 1946), 6.

5. See Kurt Flasch, "Meister Eckhart—Versuch, ihn aus dem mystischen Strom zu retten," in Peter Koslowski, ed., *Gnosis und Mystik in der Geschichte der Philosophie* (Zurich: Artemis, 1988), 94–110.

6. Heribert Fischer, *Meister Eckhart. Einführung in sein philosophisches Denken* (Freiburg, Munich: Verlag Karl Alber, 1974), p. 139.

7. Alois M. Haas, *Sermo Mysticus: Studien zu Theologie und Sprache der deutschen Mystik* (Freiburg/Switzerland: Universitäts-Verlag, 1989), pp. 22–23, 24–25.

8. Emil Brunner, *Die Mystik und das Wort. Der Gegensatz zwischen moderner Religionsauffassung und christlichem Glauben dargestellt an der Theologie Schleiermachers*, second, much revised edition (Tübingen: Mohr, 1928); Gerhard Wehr, *Die deutsche Mystik. Mystische Erfahrung und theosophische Weltsicht—eine Einführung in Leben und Werk der großen deutschen Sucher nach Gott* (Bern: Barth Verlag, 1988).

9. Friedrich-Wilhelm Wentzlaff-Eggebert, *Deutsche Mystik zwischen Mittelalter und Neuzeit. Einheit und Wandlung ihrer Erscheinungsformen* (Berlin: de Gruyter, 1969).

10. See Josef Quint, "Mystik und Sprache," in Kurt Ruh, ed., *Altdeutsche und altniederländische Mystik* (Darmstadt: Wissenschaftliche Buchgesellschaft, 1964), 122 (*Denn mystisches Erkennen ist auf das denkende Erfassen des All-Einen, in dem alle Unterschiede, alle Seinsbesonderungen, alle getrennten Denkinhalte aufgehoben sind, gerichtet*).

11. See Jürgen Hübner, "Johannes Kepler," in Martin Greschat, ed., *Orthodoxie und Pietismus* (Stuttgart: Kohlhammer, 1982), 65–78.

12. See Frank E. Manuel, *The Religion of Isaac Newton* (Freemantle Lectures, 1973; includes two Appendices: A. Fragments from a Treatise on Revelation, and B. "Of the...Day of Judgment and World to Come") (Oxford: Clarendon Press, 1974).

13. In his later scholarship, W. R. Inge recognized the essential role of authority in mysticism. See his "Authority and the Inner Light," in W. R. Inge, *Mysticism in Religion* (Chicago: University of Chicago Press, 1948), 13 ("What is the province of authority in religion, and what, for a Christian, is the seat of authority? These are the first questions which anyone who discusses the place of mysticism in religion must try to answer. For this kind of religion stands or falls by what we believe about the trustworthiness of what is called the inner light or the testimony of the Holy Spirit, which sometimes comes into conflict with other voices claiming to speak with final authority").

14. Jacob Böhme, *Mysterium Magnum* in *Sämmtliche Schriften* 7 (Stuttgart: Frommanns Verlag, 1958), 8 [2.6] (*Wann ich einen Stein oder Erden-Klumpen aufhebe und ansehe, so sehe ich das Obere und das Untere, ja die gantze Welt darinnen...*).

15. See Evelyn Underhill, *Mysticism: A Study in the Nature and Development of Man's Spiritual Consciousness* (New York: Noonday Press, 1955).

16. Cf. Ernst Benz, "Vision und Liturgie," *Die Vision. Erfahrungsformen und Bilderwelt* (Stuttgart: Klett Verlag, 1969), pp. 467–8 (*Bezeichnenderweise haben bei den großen theologischen Abendmahlsstreitigkeiten des frühen Mittelalters, die sich in der nachkarolingischen Zeit unter Führung des Paschasius Radbertus und des Ratramus in der karolingischen Reichskirche erhoben, beide Parteien, sowohl die Realisten wie auch die Symbolisten, sich auf Abendmahlsvisionen von Zeitgenossen berufen, die sich als Beweis für die Richtigkeit ihrer theologischen Auslegung verwenden ließen*).

17. Katz, "The 'Conservative' Character of Mystical Experience," in *Mysticism and Religious Traditions*, 3ff.

18. Meister Eckhart, *Deutsche Werke* 1, ed. Josef Quint (Stuttgart: Kohlhammer, 1971), 156 (*Quasi stella matutina*).

19. Paracelsus, *Astronomia Magna, oder die ganze Philosophia Sagax der großen und kleinen Welt* (1537/38), in *Sämtliche Werke* 12, ed. Karl Sudhoff (Munich: Oldenbourg, 1930), 32.

## Chapter 1. The Union of Worlds

1. Jasper Hopkins notes in the Introduction to his *Nicholas of Cusa's Debate with John Wenck* (Minneapolis: Banning Press, 1984), 3, that Wenck, was "interested in Pseudo-Dionysius and wrote a commentary on *The Celestial Hierarchy*." Cf. Klaus D. Kuhnekath, *Die Philosophie des Johannes Wenck von Herrenbreg im Vergleich zu den Lehren des Nikolaus von Kues* (Inaugural Dissertation, University of Cologne, 1975), xv, lists the writings of Wenck, including the commentary on Dionysius (1455).

2. Recalling the intertestamental Wisdom literature, Paul uses the term in 1 Corinthians 12:6, 1 Corinthians 15:28, Ephesians 1:23, and Colossians 3:10–11; but unlike other mystical motifs, "all in all" is not identified with a particular passage.

3. See *Ave, gratia plena*, in Meister Eckhart, *Deutsche Werke* 1, ed. Josef Quint (Stuttgart: Kohlhammer, 1958), 389.

4. *Ave, gratia plena*, 385.

5. Jacob Böhme, *Von den Drey Principien Göttliches Wesens*, in *Sämmtliche Schriften* 2, (Stuttgart: Frommanns Verlag, 1955), 64–69.

6. Böhme, *Principien*, 78–79.

7. Böhme, *Principien*, 66.

8. Citations are from *The City of God*, in *The Great Books* 18, trans. Marcus Dods (Chicago: Encyclopedia Britannica Inc., 1952).

9. See Marie-Dominique Chenu, O.P., "Die Platonismen des XII. Jahrhunderts," in *Platonismus in der Philosophie des Mittelalters*, ed. Werner Beierwaltes (Darmstadt: Wissenschaftliche Buchgesellschaft, 1969), 268–316, esp. 279; cf. Friedrich Ohly, "Vom geistigen Sinn des Wortes im Mittelalter," in Ohly, *Schriften zur mittelalterlichen Bedeutungsforschung* (Darmstadt: Wissenschaftliche Buchgesellschaft, 1977, 1–31.

10. In an article that must have gone against the atmosphere of the times, Josef Koch—in the *Jahres-Bericht der Schlesischen Gesellschaft für vaterländische Cultur* 101 (1928): 134–148—characterized Eckhart's debt to Moses Maimonides in no uncertain terms: *Soweit ich bisher urteilen kann, scheint mir Eckhart weit stärker als ein Scholastiker vor ihm von Maimonides beeinflußt zu sein. Alexander von Hales, Albertus Magnus, Thomas von Aquin haben sicher vieles von dem Rabbi gelernt und übernommen. Aber wie oft bekämpfen sie ihn auch! Bei Eckhart habe ich bisher keine Kritik an ihm gefunden. Der Rabbi ist für ihn eine Autorität, der höchstens Augustinus überlegen ist"* In Koch, *Kleine Schriften* 1 (Roma: Edizioni di Storia e Letteratura, 1973), 349–65 (citation on p. 365).

11. See Eckhart, *Lateinische Werke* 2 (In his exposition on the Book of Wis-

dom, Eckhart cites the Augustinian locus classicus from *De Vera Religione: Noli foras ire, in te ipsum redi, in interiori homine habitat veritas;* in *Deutsche Werke* 2, p. 100, Eckhart cites Augustine, *Confessiones* 4, ch. 12, n. 18: *got hât alliu dinc geschaffen, niht daz er sie lieze gewerden und gienge er sînen wec, mêr: er ist in in bliben.—non enim fecit atque abiit, sed ex illo in illo sunt.* The motif of the birth of the Son in the heart was traced from its scriptural antecedents (Paul in Gal. 4:19: "My dear children, for whom I am again in the pains of childbirth until Christ is formed in you...") through its evolution in Patristic literature by Hugo Rahner S.J., "Die Gottesgeburt. Die Lehre der Kirchenväter von der Geburt Christi im Herzen des Gläubigen," *Zeitschrift für katholische Theologie* 59 (1935): 333–418.

12. Boehme's *Aurora* may well have echoed Augustine's *City of God* with respect to the impossiblity of Moses having witnessed the creation (*Schriften* 1, 277; CD 11.24, 4). What is even more certain is his faithful paraphrasing of a bizarre report of the *medici* who are said to dissect living bodies in search of life (1, 391; cf. CD 22.24). Since Boehme did not read Latin, we must assume that he relied on the work or assistance of a third party.

13. Martin Moller, *Meditationes Sanctorum Patrum. Schöne/ Andechtige Gebet/ Tröstliche Sprüche/ Gottselige Gedanken/ Trewe Bußvermanungen/ Hertzliche Dancksagungen...aus den heyligen Altvätern* (Görlitz: 1592). First printed in 1584, this volume had gone through numerous printings by the turn of the century.

14. See Gershom Scholem, "Schöpfung aus Nichts und Selbstverschränkung Gottes," in *Über einige Grundbegriffe des Judentums* (Frankfurt/M.: Suhrkamp, 1970), 67ff.

15. Hildegard of Bingen, *Der Mensch in der Verantwortung. Das Buch der Lebensverdienste (Liber Vitae Meritorum)*, trans. Heinrich Schipperges, (Salzburg: Otto Müller Verlag, 1972), 51 (*Das soll heißen: Sein Herz sollte durch die einströmende Fülle vieler und großer Wunder gestärkt werden, damit er so auch den anderen den Aufbau der Tugendkräfte vermittele. Deshalb empfing er geheime, die Zukunft enthüllende Worte, die sonst den Menschen verborgen sind. Sie wissen ja nicht, durch wen und woher sie gesprochen und wie und welcher Art sie gewesen sind.... Denn sie liegen ganz und gar in den geheimsten Tiefen des Geistigen, dem der im Fleisch gefangene Mensch so fremd ist*).

16. Cf. Josef Koch, "Über die Lichtsymbolik im Bereich der Philosophie und der Mystik des Mittelalters," in *Studium Generale* 11:13 (1960): 653–70 (esp. p. 653).

17. Thomas Aquinas, *Summa Theologica*, pt. 1, quest. 1, art. 10, in *Great Books* 19 (Chicago: Encyclopedia Britannica, 1952), 9–10.

18. Armand Maurer, "Analogy in Patristic and Medieval Thought," in *Dictionary of the History of Ideas* 1, ed. Philip P. Wiener (New York: Scribner's, 1973), 64.

19. Cf. Maurer, "Analogy," 67.

20. See Josef Koch, "Zur Analogielehre Meister Eckharts," in *Kleine Schriften* 1 (Rome: Edizioni di Storia e Letteratura, 1973), 396 (*Man müsse m.E. vor allem auf Augustinus hinweisen, und zwar auf drei Gruppen von Texten: 1. solche Stellen, wo Augustinus das Sein der Geschöpfe als Sein und Nichtsein kennzeichnet; 2. solche, wo er von der* justitia, veritas usw. *spricht, von der her alles wahr ist, und alle gerecht sind, die gerecht sind; 3. endlich den Text, der den Vergeich mit der Sonne [cf.* De Gen. ad litt. *VIII c. 12] enthält, auf den sich sowohl Thomas wie Eckhart berufen, letzterer aber, wie mir scheint, mit grösserem Recht*). Even when other (Dionysian or experiential) sources are elevated by scholars, the influence of Augustine remains beyond dispute. Cf. Emilie Zum Brunn and Alain de Libera, *Maître Eckhart. Métaphysique du Verbe et théologie negative* (Paris: Beauchesne, 1984), 41 (*C'est certainement dans l'oeuvre d'Augustine—l'auteur le plus fréquemment cité par Maître Eckhart et dont on constate à tout moment l'influence dans ses écrits, même lorsque le théologien n'est pas cité nommément—que se trouve l'une des sources principales de l'ontologie eckhartienne de la conversion*). Erwin Waldschütz in *Denken und Erfahren des Grunds. Zur philosophischen Deutung Meister Eckharts* (Vienna: Herder, 1989), 28–32, notes the prominence of Augustine in Eckhart's heresy defense.

21. Dionysius the Areopagite, *The Mystical Theology,* trans. C.E. Rolt, (London: SPCK, 1940), 194.

22. Dionysius, *The Divine Names* (ch. 1.7), 62–63.

23. Dionysius, *The Divine Names* (ch. 4.8), 98.

24. Ernst Robert Curtius, *European Literature and the Middle Ages,* trans. Willard R. Trask, (Princeton: Princeton University Press, 1973), 319–26.

25. Erigena, *Patrologia Latina* 122, p. 1195C (*Praefatio, Versio Ambiguorum S. Maximi:...usque ad simplicissimam omnium unitatem, quae in Deo est et Deus est; ita ut et Deus omnia sit, et omnia Deus sint*). Cf. Augustine, *De Trinitate* 9.5, *Corpus Christianorum Series Latina* (Turnholt: Brepols, 1968), 50, p. 300 (*At in illis tribus cum se nouit mens et amat se, manet trinitas, mens, amor, notitia; et nulla commixtione confunditur quamuis et singula sint in se ipsis et inuicem tota in totis, siue singula in binis siue bina in singulis, ataque* omnia in omnibus—italics in the original).

26. See Alois Winklhofer, "Die Logosmystik des Heinrich Seuse," in *Heinrich Seuse. Studien zum 600. Todestag (1366–1966),* ed. Ephrem M. Filthaut, (Cologne: Albertus Magnus Verlag, 1966), 213–32.

27. See Joseph Leon Blau, *The Christian Interpretation of the Cabala in the Renaissance* (New York: Columbia University Press, 1944).

## Chapter 2. The Visible and the Invisible

1. See Gerhard Wehr, "Franziskanische Mystik—*Die sieben Wege zu Gott*," in Wehr, *Die deutsche Mystik,* 109–19; Kurt Ruh, *Bonaventura Deutsch: Ein*

*Beitrag zur deutschen Franziskaner-Mystik und Scholastik* (Bern: Franke Verlag, 1956).

2. Benz, *Die Vision*, 253ff., 452ff.

3. Peter Dinzelbacher, "Körperliche und seelische Vorbedingungen religiöser Träume und Visionen," in *I Sogni nel Medioevo (Seminario Internazionale, Roma, a cura di Tullio Gregory. Lessico Intellettuale Europeo)* (Rome: Edizione dell'Ateneo, 1985), 57–86. See also Dinzelbacher, *Vision und Visionsliteratur im Mittelalter* (Stuttgart: Hiersemann, 1981); and Johanna Lanczkowski, "Einführung," *Erhebe dich, meine seele,* ed. and intro. by Lanczkowski (Stuttgart: Reclam, 1988), 9.

4. See Benz, *Die Vision* ("Vision und Krankheit"), 15–34; cf. Dinzelbacher, "Körperliche und seelische Vorbedingungen"; and *ibid.*, "Rollenverweigerung, religiöser Aufbruch und mystisches Erleben mittelalterlicher Frauen," in *Religiöse Frauenbewegung und mystische Frömmigkeit im Mittelalter,* ed. Peter Dinzelbacher and Dieter R. Bauer (Vienna: Böhlau Verlag, 1988), 1–58.

5. Hildegard, *Scivias, Praefatio,* in *Patrologia Latina* 197, 354B.

6. In fact, the main themes of *Scivias* were also taken up in the musical play written and composed by Hildegard during the decade in which she produced her first book of visions. From a fine recent recording of this proto-opera, the modern listener can get a sense both of the magisterial beauty of Hildegard's Latin and of the supple vividness of a conception that lent itself as much to musical interpretation as it did to illustration in the exquisite miniatures of the Rupertsberg codex of *Scivias*. Ensemble für Musik des Mittelalters, *Hildegard von Bingen, Ordo virtutum. Sequentia* (Harmonia Mundi).

7. Expanding on a theory of Charles Singer, Flanagan cites the writings of Oliver Sacks on migraine disorders and demonstrates that the light stars and castellated structures described in the visions of *Scivias* or depicted in the manuscript illuminations correspond to the symptoms of "scintillating scotomata." The sequence of attack, resolution, and rebound, the latter involving an increased mental or physical activity, matches the phases of Hildegard's extended visionary experiences. Sabina Flanagan, *Hildegard of Bingen* (London: Routledge, 1989), 199ff.

8. See Adelgundis Führkötter and Josef Sudbrack, "Hildegard von Bingen," in Gerhard Ruhbach and Josef Sudbrack, eds., *Große Mystiker. Leben und Wirken* (Munich: Beck Verlag, 1984), 122–41.

9. Dinzelbacher, *Vision und Visionsliteratur*, 228.

10. Herbert Grundmann, *Neue Beiträge zur Geschichte der religiösen Bewegungen im Mittelalter*, in *Ausgewählte Aufsätze*, 1 (Stuttgart: Hiersemann, 1976), 47–50, 57–61.

11. Grundmann, *Beiträge*, 76–77.

12. Grundmann, *Beiträge*, 56.

13. Grundmann, *Beiträge*, 72–73.

14. Berta Widmer, *Heilsordnung und Zeitgeschehen in der Mystik Hildegards von Bingen* (Basel: Helbing & Lichtenhahn, 1955), 225ff. Widmer's study is one of the best and most neglected.

15. Cited in Latin from *Patrologia Latina* (*Scivias*) 197, p. 389D; in English from, *Scivias*, trans. Bruce Hozeski, with forewords by Matthew Fox, O.P., and Adelgundis Führkötter, O.S.B. (Santa Fe: Bear & Co., 1986), 14, 16.

16. *Patrologia Latina* 197, 410B.

17. *Patrologia Latina* 197, 446C.

18. *Patrologia Latina* 197, 455A.

19. *Scivias*, ed. Fox, 21.

20. *Patrologia Latina* 197, 400D.

21. *Scivias*, ed., Fox, 28.

22. *Patrologia Latina* 197, 404D–405A.

23. Heinrich Schipperges, *Die Welt der Engel bei Hildegard von Bingen* (Salzburg: Müller, 1979), 126ff. ("Die Welt der Engel als Archetyp der Gesellschaft").

24. Cf. Eckhart, *Deutsche Werke* 2, p. 676 (*Vir meus servus tuus mortuus est*); 659–60 (*Ecco ego mitto angelum meum*).

25. See Elisabeth Newman, *Sister of Wisdom: St. Hildegard's Theology of the Feminine* (Berkeley: University of California Press, 1987); and Elisabeth Gössmann, "*Ipsa enim quasi domus sapientiae*—Die Frau ist gleichsam das Haus der Weisheit. Zur frauenbezogenen Spiritualität Hildegards von Bingen," in "*Eine Höhe, über die nichts geht*": *spezielle Glaubenserfahrung in der Frauenmystik?* ed. Margot Schmidt and Dieter R. Bauer (Stuttgart: Frommann-Holzboog, 1986), 1–18.

26. Hildegard's letters to kings and high churchmen are reproduced in *Hildegard of Bingen's Book of Divine Works, with Letters and Songs*, trans. Robert Cunningham, ed. and intro. by Matthew Fox (Santa Fe: Bear & Co., 1987).

27. Hildegard of Bingen, *Der Mensch in der Verantwortung. Das Buch der Lebensverdienste (Liber Vitae Meritorum)*, trans. and commentary by Heinrich Schipperges (Salzburg: Müller Verlag, 1972), 44–6.

28. Hildegard, *Der Mensch*, 42: *Gleichwohl hat Er wie auf Seinen Schultern dem Menschen eine Art Kriegsdienst auferlegt, indem Er ihn auf die Geset-*

*zesvorschriften des Alten Bundes verpflichtete. Diese waren sozusagen der Schall des Wortes, wenn auch nicht das Wort selber. Zunächst nämlich wird der Schall des Wortes vernommen, dann erst wird das Wort verstanden. So war auch das alte Gesetz der Schall und Schatten des Wortes, auf welche hin das Wort selber, Christus, erschien.*

29. Monika Klaes, "Zu Schau und Deutung des Kosmos bei Hildegard von Bingen," in *Kosmos und Mensch aus der Sicht Hildegards von Bingen*, ed. Adelgundis Führkötter (Mainz: Verlag der Gesellschaft für Mittelrheinische Kirchengeschichte, 1987), 48.

30. *Liber Divinorum Operum*, in *Patrologia Latina* 197, 743C–D.

31. *Patrologia Latina* 197, 822B–ff.

32. *Patrologia Latina* 197, 890D–891A.

33. Sabina Flanagan, *Hildegard of Bingen (1098–1179)* (London: Routledge, 1989), 190, 191.

34. Flanagan, *Hildegard*, 180–83.

35. Hildegard, *Der Mensch*, 174.

36. M.-D. Chenu, O.P., *Nature, Man, and Society in the Twelfth Century: Essays on New Theological Perspectives in the Latin West*, preface by Etienne Gilson; selected, ed. and trans. by Jerome Taylor and Lester K. Little (Chicago: University of Chicago Press, 1968), 20.

37. See Johannes Zahlten, *Creatio Mundi. Darstellungen der sechs Schöpfungstage und das naturwissenschaftliche Weltbild im Mittelalter* (Stuttgart: Klett-Cotta, 1979).

38. See Heinrich Schipperges, "Kosmologische Aspekte der Lebensordnung und Lebensführung bei Hildegard von Bingen," in *Kosmos und Mensch aus der Sicht Hildegards von Bingen*, ed. Adelgundis Führkötter (Mainz: Verlag der Gesellschaft für Mittelrheinische Kirchengeschichte, 1987), 1–26.

39. See Robert L. Benson and Gildes Constable with Carol D. Lanham, eds., *Renaissance and Renewal in the Twelfth Century* (Cambridge: Harvard University Press, 1982); Chenu, *Nature, Man, and Society in the Twelfth Century*, esp. 18–37.

40. Heinrich Schipperges, an expert on both Hildegard and Paracelsus, takes note that he at least knew of her. See Schipperges, *Die Entienlehre des Paracelsus. Aufbau und Umriß seiner theoretischen Pathologie* (Berlin: Springer-Verlag, 1988), 49, 52.

41. *Die Visionen der heiligen Elisabeth, und Schriften der Äbte Ekbert und Emecho von Schönau.* (Nach den Originalhandschriften), ed. Friedrich W. E.

Roth (Brünn: Verlag der "Studien aus dem Benedictiner- und Cistercienser-Orden," 1884), visions 20, 40.

42. Mechthild of Magdeburg, *"Das fließende Licht der Gottheit"* (*Nach der Einsiedler Handschrift in kritischem Vergleich mit der gesamten Überlieferung*), ed. Hans Neumann and Gisela Vollmann-Profe (Munich: Artemis, 1990). (Page references in parentheses refer to this edition.)

43. Fritz Martini wrote that Wolfram's language rendered the supernatural in terms of the physical, while lending reality a new depth and mystery: *Das Überwirkliche wird körperhaft—die Wirklichkeit wird hintergründig und geheimnisvoll; auch in seiner Sprache vermählen sich das Göttlich-Geistige und das Irdisch-Sinnliche.* In Martini, *Deutsche Literaturgeschichte von den Anfängen bis zur Gegenwart* (Stuttgart: Kröner, 1965), 48.

44. Cf. *Das Buch vom strömenden Lob* (*The Book of Flowing Praise*), selected, translated and introduced by Hans Urs von Balthasar (Einsiedeln: Johannes Verlag, 1955).

45. Hackeborn, *Das Buch vom strömenden Lob*, 41.

46. Parenthetical page references will refer to the German translation, *Gesandter der göttlichen Liebe*, trans. Johanna Lanczkowski (Darmstadt: Wissenschaftliche Buchgesellschaft, 1989).

47. See Michael Figura, "Herz Jesu," in Peter Dinzelbacher, ed., *Wörterbuch der Mystik* (Stuttgart: Kröner Verlag, 1989).

48. Caroline Walker Bynum, *Jesus as Mother: Studies in the Spirituality of the High Middle Ages* (Berkeley: University of California Press, 1982), 146–53, 247–62.

49. See Siegfried Ringler, *Viten- und Offenbarungsliteratur in Frauenklöstern des Mittelalters. Quellen und Studien* (Zurich and Munich: Artemis, 1980), 8–11.

50. See Caroline Walker Bynum, *Holy Feast and Holy Fast: The Religious Significance of Food to Medieval Women* (Berkeley: University of California Press, 1987. A recent book on female asceticism, *Holy Anorexia*, cites studies by Ida Magli and expresses caution against the notion that medieval religious women were bored and oppressed by their cloistered routines. See Rudolph M. Bell, *Holy Anorexia* (Chicago: University of Chicago Press, 1985), 54. Bell cites Ida Magli, "Il problema antropologico-culturale del monachesimo femminile," in *Enciclopedia delle religioni* (Florence, 1972), 3:627–41.

51. Walter Blank, *Die Nonnenviten des 14. Jahrhunderts* (Inaugural Dissertation, Freiburg/Breisgau, 1962), 120–3; Philip Strauch, *Margaretha Ebner und Heinrich von Nördlingen. Ein Beitrag zur Geschichte der deutschen Mystik* (Tübingen: Mohr, 1882; Reprint: Amsterdam: Schippers, 1966), xxxvi.

52. See Blank, *Nonnenviten*, 117–8 (music and sounds), 120–1 (levitations); Reinhold Hammerstein, *Die Musik der Engel* (Bern: Franke, 1962); Hildegard of Bingen, *Wörterbuch der Unbekannten Sprache (Lingua Ignota)* (Basel: Verlag der Basler Hildegard-Gesellschaft, 1986).

53. Walter Muschg, *Die Mystik in der Schweiz* (Frauenfeld and Leipzig: Huber Verlag, 1935), 196–204. Muschg extensively offers his own translation from Elsbeth's *Büchlein des Lebens und der Offenbarung*. On the likelihood of editorial interventions in the original manuscript, see: Peter Ochsenbein, "Leidensmystik in dominikanischen Frauenklöstern des 14. Jahrhunderts am Beispiel der Elsbeth von Oye," in *Religiöse Frauenbewegung*, 353–72.

54. Muschg, *Mystik*, 200–201 (Elsbeth's dialog), 203–204 (Muschg's critique).

55. Otto Langer, *Mystische Erfahrung und spirituelle Theologie. Zu Meister Eckharts Auseinandersetzung mit der Frauenfrömmigkeit seiner Zeit* (Munich: Artemis, 1987), 113–14.

## Chapter 3. The Outer and the Inner

1. *Qui sequitur iustitiam*, in Eckhart, *Deutsche Werke* 2, ed. Josef Quint (Stuttgart: Kohlhammer, 1971), 293.

2. See Friedrich-Wilhelm Wentzlaff-Eggebert, *Studien zur Lebenslehre Taulers* (Berlin: Gruyter, 1940), on the union of the active and comtemplative life in Dominican mysticism; and Dietmar Mieth, *Die Einheit von Vita activa und Vita contemplativa* (Inaugural Dissertation, Regensburg, 1969).

3. For an overview, see Richard Kieckhefer, *Repression of Heresy in Medieval Germany* (Philadelphia: University of Pennsylvania Press, 1979), 19ff. ("The War Against Beghards and Beguines").

4. Fischer, *Meister Eckhart*; Waldschütz, *Denken und Erfahren des Grundes*; Kurt Flasch, "Die Intention Meister Eckharts," in *Sprache und Begriff*. Festschrift B. Liebrucks (Meisenheim am Glan: 1974): 292–318; Burkhard Mojsisch, *Meister Eckhart. Analogie, Univozität und Einheit* (Hamburg: Felix Meiner Verlag, 1983), 6 (a summary of further literature on this issue).

5. See Haas, *Sermo Mysticus*, esp. 136ff.

6. Langer, *Mystische Erfahrung*; Kurt Ruh, *Meister Eckhart. Theologe, Prediger, Mystiker* (Munich: Beck Verlag, 1985).

7. Eckhart the philosopher was already familiar to Baader and Hegel who saw him as a forerunner. Eckhart's interactions with Scholastic philosophy and with female piety were first elucidated by Heinrich Seuse Denifle and Wilhelm Preger. See Ernst Soudek, *Meister Eckhart* (Stuttgart: Metzler, 1973), esp. 53ff.

8. *Utrum in Deo sit idem esse et intelligere,* see: *Quaestiones Parisienses...*, in Eckhart, *Lateinische Werke* 5, ed. Bernhard Geyer (Stuttgart: Kohlhammer, 1936), 37ff.

9. Lossky and others have discussed these ambibuities with respect to Eckhart's negative theology. See Vladimir Lossky, *Théologie négative et connaissance de Dieu chez Maître Eckhart* (Paris: Vrin, 1960), 207–220. It appears doubtful that all propositions by Eckhart can be brought into a contradiction-free system.

10. Eckhart, *Prologi in Opus Tripartitum,* in *Lateinische Werke* 1.2, ed. Loris Sturlese (Stuttgart: Kohlhammer, 1987), 28.

11. Eckhart, *Expositio Libri Genesis (Exhordium hoc scripturae Genesis tractat Augustinus diffuse, specialiter Super Genesim ad litteram et Super Genesim contra Manichaeos et in tribus ultimis libris Confessionum),* in *Lateinische Werke* 1, ed. Konrad Weiss (Stuttgart: Kohlhammer, 1964), 186. Cf. also Jürgen Eberle, *Die Schöpfung in ihren Ursachen. Untersuchung zum Begriff der Idee in den lateinischen Werken Meister Eckharts* (Inaugural Dissertation, Cologne, 1972), esp. 47–51.

12. Cf. Kurt Flasch, ed., *Von Meister Dietrich zu Meister Eckhart* (Hamburg: Felix Meiner, 1984).

13. See Maurer, "Analogy in Patristic and Medieval Thought," in *Dictionary of the History of Ideas* 1, 64–67; Kurt Ruh, *Meister Eckhart,* 82–86; Mojsisch, *Meister Eckhart;* Josef Koch, "Zur Analogielehre Meister Eckharts," in *Altdeutsche und altniederländische Mystik,* ed. Kurt Ruh (Darmstadt: Wissenschaftliche Buchgesellschaft, 1964), 275–308.

14. Mojsisch, *Meister Eckhart,* 6–10.

15. Mojsisch, *Meister Eckhart,* 69 (*Die Formel "totus intus, totus foris" taucht nicht nur bei Eckhart häufig auf, sondern besitzt auch—mit terminologischen Abwandlungen—eine reiche Tradition: Plotin, Proklus, Hilarius, Augustin, Gregor der Große, Johannes Eriugena, Abelard, Bernhard von Clairvaux, Petrus Lombardus, Alanus ab Insulis, Bonaventura, (nach Eckhart) Heinrich Seuse, Nikolaus von Kues, Angelus Silesius und Francesco Patrizzi.*)

16. See Ruh, *Eckhart,* 95ff.

17. See Ruh, *Eckhart,* 96ff. Cf. "Marguerite Porete," in Zum Brunn and Epiney-Burgard, eds., *Women Mystics,* 143–175.

18. Norman Cohn concluded that the heresy of the Free Spirit constituted "an elite of amoral supermen," precursors of Nietzsche. See *The Pursuit of the Millenium: Revolutionary Millenarians and Mystical Anarchists in the Middle Ages* (New York: Oxford University Press, 1970), 163ff. Cf. Franz-Josef Schweitzer, *Der Freiheitsbegriff der deutschen Mystik. Seine Beziehung zur Ketzerei der "Brüder und Schwester vom Freien Geist," mit besonderer Rücksicht auf den pseudoeckartischen Traktat "Schwester Katrei"* (Frankfurt/Main: Peter Lang, 1981).

19. Cf. Ruh, *Eckhart*, 113.

20. See Langer, *Mystische Erfahrung*, 115–124.

21. Ruh, *Eckhart*, 115ff.

22. *Daz buoch der götlîchen troestungen (Liber Benedictus)*, in Eckhart, *Deutsche Werke* 5, ed. Josef Quint (Stuttgart: Kohlhammer, 1963), 9.

23. *Consideravit semitas*, in Eckhart, *Deutsche Werke* 2, 136.

24. *Praedica verbum*, in Eckhart, *Deutsche Werke* 2, 96.

25. Muschg, *Mystik*, 189ff., 192–93.

26. *Die rede der underscheidunge* 2, in Eckhart, *Deutsche Werke* 5, 191.

27. *Die rede*, 221.

28. *Quasi stella matutina*, in Eckhart, *Deutsche Werke* 1, 143.

29. *Ave, gratia plena*, in Eckhart *Deutsche Werke* 1, 376–7.

30. *Quasi stella matutina*, in Eckhart, *Deutsche Werke* 1, 156.

31. Hugo Rahner, S.J., "Die Gottesgeburt," *Zeitschrift für katholische Theologie* 59 (1935): 333–418.

32. *Adolescens, tibi dico*, in Eckhart, *Deutsche Werke* 2, 306.

33. See Benno Schmoldt, *Die deutsche Begriffsprache Meister Eckharts* (Heidelberg: Quelle & Meyer, 1954), 15–27 ("*bekantnisse—verstantnisse*").

34. *In diebus suis placuit*, in Eckhart, *Deutsche Werke* 1, 162.

35. *In occisione gladii*, in Eckhart, *Deutsche Werke* 1, 129.

36. *Consideravit semitas*, in Eckhart, *Deutsche Werke* 2, 135.

37. *Videte qualem caritatem*, in Eckhart, *Deutsche Werke* 3, 310–311.

38. *Beati pauperes spiritu*, in Eckhart, *Deutsche Werke* 2, 497.

39. In Eckhart, *Deutsche Werke* 1, 192–203 (subsequent page references to this sermon appear in parentheses).

40. Eckhart, *Deutsche Werke* 1, 201, note 4.

41. *Adolescens, tibi dico*, in Eckhart, *Deutsche Werke* 1, 306–7.

42. *Postquam completi*, in Eckhart, *Deutsche Werke* 2, 337.

43. Haas, *Sermo mysticus*, 29.

44. *Omne datum optimum*, in Eckhart, *Deutsche Werke* 1, 72.

45. *Praedica verbum*, in Eckhart, *Deutsche Werke* 2, 94.

46. *Scitote, quia prope*, in Eckhart, *Deutsche Werke* 3, 140–141.

47. See Ludwig Völker, "Gelassenheit," in *Getempert und Gemischet* (*Festschrift* for Wolfgang Mohr), ed. Franz Hundschnurcher und Ulrich Müller (Göttingen: Kümmerle, 1972), 281–312.

48. *Mulier, venit hora*, in Eckhart, *Deutsche Werke* 2, 24–25.

49. *Iusti vivent*, in Eckhart, *Deutsche Werke* 1, 103.

50. *Intravit Jesus*, in Eckhart, *Deutsche Werke* 1, 7, 11.

51. *In hoc apparuit*, in Eckhart, *Deutsche Werke* 1, 91–92.

52. *Moyses orabat*, in Eckhart, *Deutsche Werke* 2, 18.

53. *Ave, gratia plena*, in Eckhart, *Deutsche Werke* 1, 385.

54. *Homo quidam fecit*, in Eckhart, *Deutsche Werke* 1, 333.

55. *Iusti vivent*, in Eckhart, *Deutsche Werke* 1, 106–7.

56. *Implementum est*, in Eckhart, *Deutsche Werke* 1, 184.

57. There is a readable account of the mysticism of this period by Wilhelm Preger, *Geschichte der deutschen Mystik im Mittelalter* 2 (Reprint of the edition of 1874–1893; Aalen: Zeller, 1962), 289–292. Cf. Philipp Strauch, *Margaretha Ebner und Heinrich von Nördlingen*, xxxii–ff.

58. A summary of the literature on Merswin and a translation of his writings has been provided by Thomas S. Kepler, *Mystical Writings of Rulman Merswin* (Philadelphia: Westminster Press, 1960).

59. Johannes Tauler, *Die Predigten Taulers, aus der Engelsberger und der Freiburger Handschrift sowie aus Schmidts Abschriften der ehemaligen Straßburger Handschriften*, ed. Ferdinand Vetter (Berlin: Weidmann, 1910), 378 (subsequent page references in parentheses refer to this edition).

## Chapter 4. The Finite and the Infinite

1. See Herbert Wackerzapp, *Der Einfluß Meister Eckharts auf die ersten philosophischen Schriften des Nikolaus von Kues (1440–1450)* (Münster: Aschendorffsche Verlagsbuchhandlung, 1962), esp. 105ff., 111ff., 116ff. (Eckhart's relevant points were based on our usual texts of Genesis and the Johannine Prolog. Even the geometrical symbolism of Nicholas is encountered in these Latin treatises of Eckhart.)

2. It is certain that Nettesheim and probable that Paracelsus knew of Nicholas. See Kurt Goldammer, "Das Menschenbild des Paracelsus zwischen theologischer Tradition, Mythologie und Naturwissenschaft," in *Paracelsus in neuen Horizonten: Gesammelte Aufsätze* (Vienna: Verband der Wissenschaftlichen Gesellschaften Österreichs, 1986), 219. But their kinship is an indirect one: the similarity of their conceptual apparatus may also derive from third sources.

3. On philosophical difficulties, see Jasper Hopkins, *Nicholas of Cusa on Learned Ignorance* (Minneapolis: Banning Press, 2nd edition 1985, 2nd printing 1990), 14, 24ff.; *Nicholas of Cusa's Debate with John Wenck* (Minneapolis: Banning Press, 1984), 7.

4. See Nikolaus von Kues, *Idiota de sapientia*, in *Philosophisch-Theologische Schriften* 3, ed. Leo Gabriel, trans. Dietlind und Wilhelm Dupré (Wien: Herder, 1964–1967), 422. (*Idiota*: "*Hoc est quod aiebam, scilicet te duci auctoritate et decipi. Scripsit aliquis verbum illud, cui credis. Ego autem tibi dico, quod sapientia foris clamat in plateis; et est clamor eius, quoniam ipsa habitat altissimis.*") Cf. in the same volume, *Idiota de mente* and *Idiota de staticis experimentis*.

5. See Frederick Copleston, S. J., *The History of Philosophy* 3, part 1 (New York: Image Books, 1953), 172–6.

6. Kues, *Philosophisch-Theologische Schriften 3, Compendium* ch. 8, 707–11.

7. Jasper Hopkins, *Nicholas of Cusa on Learned Ignorance* (Minneapolis: Banning Press, 2nd edition 1985, 2nd printing 1990), 158. (Subsequent citations to *Docta Ignorantia* (DI) are referenced to the Hopkins translation by book, chapter, and section.)

8. See *De Principio (Der Ursprung)*, in *Philosophisch-Theologische Schriften* 2:245–7.

9. See Augustine, *De Civitate Dei*, 12:19, in *Corpus Christianorum Series Latina* (Turnholt: Brepols, 1955), 375–6. In idiom, Cusanus's letter to Julian seems to mimic the use of oxymoron and paradox in the work by Augustine ("*[Deus]...cuius sapientia simpliciter multiplex et uniformiter multiformis tam incomprehensibili comprehensione omnia inconprehensiblia conprehendit, ut, quaecumque nova et dissimilia consequentia praecedentibus si semper facere vellet, inordinata et inprovisa habere non posset, nec ea provideret ex proximo tempore, sed aeterna preaescientia contineret*"). That Augustine made use of the term *docta ignorantia* is mentioned in Karl Jaspers, *Nikolaus Cusanus* (Munich: Piper Verlag, 1987), 23.

10. Augustine, *The Trinity*, bk. 11 (St. Paul: Daughters of St. Paul, 1965), 213; *De Trinitate* 11:10, in *Corpus Christianorum Series Latina* 50 (Turnholt: Brepols, 1968), 354–5. (*Nam neque ipsas magnitudines corporum quas numquam uidimus sine ope memoriae cogitamus. [Quantum enim spatii solet occupare per magnitudinem mundi noster obtutus, in tantum extendimus quaslibet corporum moles*

*cum eas maximas cogitamus.] Et ratio quidem pergit in ampliora, sed phantasia non sequitur. Sequitur quippe cum infinitatem quoque numeri ratio renuntiet, quam nulla uisio corporalia cogitantis apprehendit. Eadem ratio docet minutissima etiam corpuscula infinite diuidi; cum tamen ad eas tenuitates uel minutias peruentum fuerit quas uisas meminimus, exiliores minutioresque phantasias iam non possumus intueri, quamuis ratio non desinat persequi ac diuidere. [Ita nulla corporalia nisi aut ea quae meminimus aut ex his quae meminimus cogitamus.])*

11. As Hopkins puts it, "Because analogies do not correspond to any reality to be found in Infinite Being or its relations, they are better called illustrations. Nicholas himself calls them *aenigmata*, i.e., symbolisms; and he uses them to direct the mind's reflection so that the mind's ignorance may be learned." *Nicholas of Cusa on Learned Ignorance*, 16.

12. For example, *De Principio* states: *Nihil igitur in hoc mundo est eius similitudinem habens, cum non sit designabile nec imaginabile.... Mundus sensibilis est insensibilis mundi figura et temporalis mundus aeterni et intemporalis figura, Philosophisch-Theologische Schriften* 2 (Vienna: Herder, 1966), 254.

13. In Cusanus's marginal notations on Eckhart, *quodlibet in quodlibet* is a coincidence of opposites in the propositions about grace as the greatest and the smallest, and for the allusion to God's omnipresent center. See Dietrich Mahnke, *Unendliche Sphäre und Allmittelpunkt* (Haale/Saale: Niemeyer Verlag, 1937), 77–78. (*Aus eigenhändigen Randbemerkungen in seinem...Handexemplar von Meister Eckharts "Opus tripartitum" geht zunächst hervor, daß er bei der religiösen Verwertung der geometrischen Symbolik mit vollem Wissen und Willen mittelalterliche Traditionen fortsetzt. In einer der nur hier erhaltenen lateinischen Predigten, in der Eckhart sagt: "Nach den Lehrern genügt die kleinste Gnade, um den Sünden zu widerstehen. Denn das Kleinste von Gott [minimum dei] ist das Größte hinsichtlich aller Kreatur," und zur Bekräftigung den Satz einer "Autorität" anführt, "daß 'Gott eine geistige Kugel ist, deren Mittelpunkt überall, [deren] Umfang nirgends [ist]'," hat der Kusaner das letztere Zitat am Rande durch eine Wellenlinie und Wiederholung der Anfangsworte "quod deus" als besonders interessant hervorgehoben. Ferner hat er in Eckharts Erklärung von Jesus Sirach, Kap. 24, V. 23/24, wo es heißt: "in göttlichen Dingen ist jedes in jedem und das Größte im Kleinsten," sei, "wie ein Weiser sagt, 'Gott eine unendliche geistige Kugel ist deren Mittelpunkt samt dem Umfang überall ist' und 'die ebensoviele Umfänge wie Punkte hat,' wie im gleichen Buche geschrieben wird," die den beiden Zitaten vorangehenden Eckhartschen Worte und den Anfang des ersten Zitats durch eine Wellenlinie hervorgehoben und die Worte "in divinis quodlibet in quodlibet maximum in minimo" wiederholt.*)

14. Hopkins, *Nicholas of Cusa on Learned Ignorance*, 24–25.

15. Cusanus's exact words are: *Nam cum manifestum sit ex primo libro Deum ita esse in omnibus, quod omnia sunt in ipso, et nunc constet Deum quasi mediante universo esse in omnibus, hinc omnia in omnibus esse constat et quodlibet in quodlibet. De Docta Ignorantia* 2:5, cited from: *Philosophisch-Theologische Schriften* 1:344.

16. Kues, *De Filiatione Dei (Die Gotteskindschaft)*, in *Philosophisch-Theologische Schriften* 2:600–3.

17. *Trialogus de Possest (Das Können-Ist)* in *Philosophisch-Theologische Schriften* 2:356–7.

18. *De dato patris luminum,* in Kues, *Philosophisch-Theologische Schriften* 2:672.

19. Cited from Kues, *De docta Ignorantia* 2, 5, *Philosophisch-Theologische Schriften* 1:334.

20. Elsewhere, Cusanus says that the creating of the Creator is like the reasoning or counting of the reason. See *De dato patris luminum,* in *Philosophisch-Theologische Schriften* 2:662 (*Et hoc ipsum est creatoris creare, quod est rationis ratiocinari seu numerari*).

21. *Trialogus de possest,* 272.

22. Cusanus drops or deemphasizes Eckhart's cluster of notions having to do with the spark of the soul and generation of the only-begotten Son in the soul of the believer. See Jasper Hopkins, *Nicholas of Cusa's Dialectical Mysticism: Text, Translation, and Interpretive Study of "De Visione Dei"* (Minneapolis: Arthur J. Banning Press, 1985), 29–30.

23. See *The Vision of God,* trans. Hopkins in *Nicholas of Cusa's Dialectical Mysticism,* 131 ("To see You is not other than that You see the one who sees You"), 173 ("You appeared to me as invisible by every creature since you are an infinite and hidden God. Infinity, however, is incomprehensible by every mode of comprehending. Later, you appeared to me as visible by all [creatures] because a thing exists insofar as You see it, and *it would not exist actually unless it saw you"—italics added*).

24. Cusanus, *The Vision of God,* cited from Hopkins, *Nicholas of Cusa's Dialectical Mysticism,* 145–7.

25. See *De apice theoriae,* in Nikolaus von Kues, *Philosophisch-Theologische Schriften* 2:373 (*Posse igitur videre mentis excellit posse comprehendere. Unde simplex visio mentis non est visio comprehensiva, sed de comprehensiva se elevat ad videndum incomprehensibile, uti dum videt unum maius alio comprehensive, se elevat ut videat illud, quo non potest maius. Et hoc quidem est infinitum maius omni mensurabili seu comprehensibili*).

26. *De coniecturis,* in Kues, *Philosophisch-Theologische Schriften* 2:6–7.

27. Cf. Karl Jaspers, *Nikolaus Cusanus* (Munich: Piper, 1987), 226ff.

28. See Charles G. Nauert, Jr., *Toleration in the Thought of Nicholaus of Cusa* (M.A. Thesis, University of Illinois). According to Nauert, Cusanus even acted to increase restrictions placed on German Jews.

## Chapter 5. Nature and Scripture

1. See Heimo Reinitzer, *Biblia deutsch. Luthers Bibelübersetzung und ihre Tradition* (Wolfenbüttel: Herzog August Bibliothek, 1983), 85.

2. Elizabeth Eisenstein, *The Printing Press as an Agent of Change: Communications and Cultural Transformations in Early-Modern Europe* 1 (Cambridge: Cambridge University Press, 1979), 169.

3. Eisenstein, *The Printing Press*, 174.

4. Will-Erich Peuckert, *Die große Wende. Das apokalyptische Saeculum und Luther* (Hamburg: Claasen & Goverts, 1948), 160.

5. See Heiko A. Oberman, "The Power of Witchcraft: devil and devotion," in *Masters of the Reformation: The Emergence of a New Intellectual Climate in Europe*, trans. Dennis Martin (Cambridge: Cambridge University Press, 1981), 158–86.

6. There is a somewhat antiquated English translation, originally published in 1651: Henry Cornelius Agrippa von Nettesheim, *Three Books of Occult Philosophy or Magic*, ed. Willis F. Whitehead (Chicago: Hahn and Whitehead, 1898).

7. See Will-Erich Peuckert, *Pansophie. Ein Versuch zur Geschichte der weißen und schwarzen Magie* (Berlin: Schmidt Verlag, 1976).

8. Hermann F. W. Kuhlow, *Die Imitatio Christi und ihre kosmologische Überfremdung. Die theologischen Grundgedanken des Agrippa von Nettesheim* (Berlin and Hamburg: Lutherisches Verlagshaus, 1967), 40ff.

9. Cited according to Kuhlow, *Agrippa*, 46 (*Ignorantia Dei omnium malorum fons est et origo peccatorum…*).

10. Kuhlow, *Agrippa*, 49.

11. Charles G. Nauert, Jr., *Agrippa and the Crisis of Renaissance Thought* (Urbana: University of Illinois Press, 1965), 315.

12. Goethe, *Faust* 1, trans. Walter Kaufmann (New York: Doubleday, 1963), 93.

13. Cf. Erwin Jaeckle, "Paracelsus und Agrippa von Nettesheim," in *Nova Acta Paracelsica* 2 (1945): 83–109.

14. See Paul Oskar Kristeller, *Renaissance Thought: The Classic, Scholastic, and Humanist Strains* (New York: Harper, 1955), 44.

15. See Kurt Goldammer, "Lichtsymbolik in philosophischer Weltanschauung, Mystik und Theosophie vom 15. bis zum 17. Jahrhundert," in *Studium Generale* 11:13 (1960): 670–81.

16. Paracelsus, *Paragranum* (1530), in *Sämtliche Schriften*, div. 1, vol. 8, ed. Karl Sudhoff (Munich: Barth, 1924), 38, 43.

17. Paracelsus, *Liber de Sancta Trinitate* (1524), in *Sämtliche Werke*, div. 2, vol. 3, ed. Kurt Goldammer (Wiesbaden: Steiner Verlag, 1986), 235ff., esp. 241, 242, 255, 262, 246.

18. Paracelsus, *Liber de Sancta Trinitate*, in *Werke*, 2, 3:246.

19. See Kurt Goldammer, "Das theologische Werk des Paracelsus—eine Ehrenschuld der Wissenschaft," in *Nova Acta Paracelsica* 8 (1954): 78–102.

20. See Kurt Goldammer, "Paracelsische Eschatologie," in *Nova Acta Paracelsica* 5 (1948): 45–85; "Paracelsische Eschatologie zum Verständnis der Anthropologie und Kosmologie Hohenheims," in *Nova Acta Paracelsica* 6 (1952): 68–102.

21. On the difficulties in the application of these categories to the creation, see Nicholas H. Steneck, *Science and Creation in the Middle Ages: Henry of Langenstein (d. 1397) on Genesis* (Notre Dame: University of Notre Dame Press, 1976), 35ff.

22. See *Paragranum*, 42 (*die grossen arcana, so uns got mitteilt*), 53, 55 (*erfarenheit*), 59, 63 (*ein kunst aus got, nicht aus dem himmel*), 69 (*die neue geburt*), 71 (*dan was verborgen begriffen wird, gibt allein den glauben; den ausgang und das volkomen geben die werk. die werk seind sichtlich…*), etc.

23. Paracelsus, "De Viribus Membrorum" auch "De Spiritus vitae" benant, in *Schriften*, 1, 3:15.

24. Paracelsus, *De Viribus Membrorum*, 17.

25. Paracelsus, *De Vera Influentia*, in *Schriften* 1, 14:215.

26. Paracelsus, *De Vera Influentia*, 218–19.

27. Paracelsus, *De Vera Influentia*, 221.

28. Paracelsus, *Astronomia Magna, oder die ganze Philosophia Sagax der großen und kleinen Welt* (1537/38), in *Schriften* 1, 12:32, 33.

29. Paracelsus, *Astronomia Magna*, 29.

30. Cf. Paracelsus, *Paragranum*, 41–42; *Opus Paramirum, Schriften* 1, 9:94; *Astronomia Magna, Schriften* 1, 12:20–21, 58–59.

31. Paracelsus, *Astronomia Magna*, 58–59.

32. Paracelsus, *Astronomia Magna*, 172.

33. See Walter Pagel, *Das medizinische Weltbild des Paracelsus. Seine Zusammenhänge mit Neuplatonismus und Gnosis* (Wiesbaden: Steiner Verlag, 1962), 47ff.

34. Paracelsus, *Opus Paramirum*, 83.

35. Paracelsus, *Opus Paramirum*, 48.

36. Paracelsus, *De Viribus Membrorum*, in *Schriften*, 1, 3:34.

37. Paracelsus, *De Viribus Membrorum*, 35.

38. Hartmut Rudolf, "Einige Geschichtspunkte zum Thema 'Paracelsus und Luther'," in *Archiv für Reformationsgeschichte* 72 (1981): 34–54.

39. Kurt Goldammer, "Magie bei Paracelsus," in Kurt Müller, Heinrich Schepers, and Wilhelm Totok, ed., *Magia Naturalis und die Entstehung der modernen Naturwissenschaften* (Wiesbaden: Steiner Verlag, 1978), 33.

40. Heinrich Bornkamm, *Luthers geistige Welt* (Lüneburg: Heliand-Verlag, 1947), 104. Cf. Erich Roth, *Sacrament nach Luther* (Berlin: Verlag Alfred Tölpelmann, 1952).

41. Bornkamm, *Luthers geistige Welt*, 110 (*Gott ist für Luther buchstäblich in allen Dingen, als alles durchwaltende Kraft, im Feuer, im Wasser, im Baumblatt, im Stein. Luther hat mit dem kindlichen, vermenschlichten Bilde von dem Schöpfer, der, nachdem er die Welt gemacht, nun fern von ihr im Himmel thront, mit dem Gott naiver Prediger, der z.B. Jakob Boehme so tief gequält hat, nichts zu tun. Eindringender als er hat auch die Mystik das Dasein Gottes in der Welt nicht ausgesprochen*).

42. Philip Schaff, *Creeds of Christendom* 1 (New York: Harper and Brothers, 1919), 284–90.

43. See Johannes Hemleben, *Paracelsus. Revolutionär, Arzt und Christ* (Stuttgart: Verlag Huber, 1973), 171 (*Deutlich ist, daß es dem Theophrast vor aller Abendmahlstheologie um ein Verständnis der Auferstehung, des Auferstehungsleibes geht...*); cf. Paracelsus, *Das Nachtmahl des Herrn*, ed. Gerhard Degeller (Basel: Hybernia Verlag, 1950); Ernst Sommerlath, *Der Sinn des Abendmahls nach Luthers Gedanken über das Abendmahl, 1527–29* (Leipzig: Dörffling & Franke, 1930), 81–90, esp. 83 (Sommerlath summarizes Luther's unscriptural view of the physical-eschatological effect: *Es geht im Abendmahl, wie es beim Sterben Christi zuging.... So wird der Leib hineingezogen in die Unsterblichkeit.... Auf ausdrückliche Schriftstellen konnte sich Luther bei dieser Meinung nicht berufen*); cf. 57 (*eschatologische Spannung im Abendmahl*); 117–20 (Luther saw *Abendmahl* as the Word in John 1).

44. See Luther, *Sermon von dem Sacrament des leibs und bluts Christi, widder die Schwarmgeister*, in *Werke* 19 (Weimar: Böhlau, 1908), 478–9, 492–3. Subsequent references to Luther will refer to this edition (WA), by volume and page.

45. David C. Steinmetz, *Luther in Context* (Bloomington: Indiana University Press, 1986), 83. I am obliged to Steinmetz for the previous two passages from Luther.

46. Paracelcus, *De Genealogia Christi*, in *Werke*, 2, 3: 90.

47. Walter Nigg, *Das ewige Reich. Geschichte einer Sehnsucht und einer Enttäuschung* (Zurich: Rentsch Verlag, 1944), 211.

48. Nigg, *Das ewige Reich*, 219.

49. Paracelsus, *Sämtliche Werke nach der 10-bändigen Huserschen Gesamtausgabe (1589–1591)* 4, ed. and annotated, Bernhard Aschner (Jena: Fischer Verlag, 1932), 841–96.

## Chapter 6. Letter and Spirit

1. The article on "Spiritualisten, religiöse" in *Religion in Geschichte und Gegenwart* (Tübingen: Mohr, 1962) summarizes the history of this term which echoes Luther's invective against *Geisterei und Schwärmerei*, but came into use in the mid-nineteenth century as a scholarly designation for the Quakers with their doctrine of the "inner light," and for similar tendencies in the early Reformation. From Harnack to Hegler and Troeltsch, the Spiritualist gradually acquired distinguishable contours as an "ideal type" imperfectly covering various figures, groups, and doctrines.

2. See Werner O. Packull, *Mysticism and the Early South German-Austrian Anabaptist Movement (1525–1531)* (Scottsdale, Pa.: Herald Press, 1977). I am grateful to Peter Erb for calling my attention to this book.

3. Steven E. Ozment, *Mysticism and Dissent: Religious Ideology and Social Protest in the Sixteenth Century* (New Haven: Yale University Press, 1973).

4. Cf. Bernd Moeller, "Tauler und Luther," in *La Mystique Rhénane (Colloque de Strasbourg)* (Paris: Presse Universitaires de France, 1961). Almost as an aside, Moeller makes the point which I believe is essential for the attraction of mysticism to the young Luther. He was searching for answers in divine matters: *Luther steht der eigentlichen Mystik zu dieser Zeit, um 1516, noch mit einer gewissen Unschlüssigkeit, suchend zögernd gegenüber; er hat in den Jahren des Umbrechens seiner theologischen Gedanken...in der Mystik mit einem gewissen Recht Bundesgenossenschaft, Bestätigung gespürt auch wohl nach Anlehnung gesucht* (p. 164).

5. See Ozment, *Mysticism and Dissent*, 17–25; ibid., "Eckhart and Luther: German Mysticism and Protestantism," in *The Thomist* v. 2, no. 2 (1978): 259–80; Heinrich Bornkamm, *Eckhart and Luther* (Stuttgart: 1936); and Moeller, "Tauler und Luther," op. cit., 164 (*Dennoch gilt, genau genommen, auch für diese Jahre vor 1517 schon die kategorische Feststellung: 'Luther war kein Mystiker'*).

6. *Der Frankfurter*, Eine deutsche Theologie, trans. and intro. Joseph Bernhardt (Leipzig: Insel-Verlag, 1920), 180; *The Theologia Germanica of Martin Luther*, trans., intro. and comment, Bengt Hoffmann, pref. Bengt Hägglund (New York: Paulist Press, 1980), 136. (These editions are based on two versions of the work.)

7. Der Frankfurter, *Eine deutsche Theologie*, 96, 103; cf. *The Theologia Germanica of Martin Luther*, 62, 68, 136.

8. Der Frankfurter, *Eine deutsche Theologie*, 157ff., 167–8; *The Theologia Germanica of Martin Luther*, 114ff.; 125.

9. See G. Ebeling, "Geist und Buchstabe" W. Wieland, "Geist, philosophisch" in *Die Religion in Geschichte und Gegenwart*, third edition (1956).

10. Der Frankfurter, *Eine deutsche Theologie*, 169, 177; *The Theologia Germanica of Martin Luther*, 126, 134.

11. Cf. Ebeling, "Geist und Buchstabe."

12. Johannes Kühn, *Toleranz und Offenbarung* (Leipzig: Meiner, 1923), 124ff.

13. See Steven Ozment, *The Reformation in the Cities: The Appeal of Protestantism to Sixteenth-Century Germany and Switzerland* (New Haven: Yale University Press, 1975), 42–46.

14. On the contrast in his education and background with the plebeian radicals of his movement, and on the range of his readings, see Ulrich Bubenheimer, *Thomas Müntzer. Herkunft und Bildung* (Leiden: Brill, 1989), 230–6.

15. See Thomas Nipperdey, *Reformation—Revolution—Utopie* (Göttingen: Vandenhoeck & Ruprecht, 1975), 38ff.; H.-J. Goertz, *Innere und Äußere Ordnung in der Theologie Thomas Müntzers* (Leiden: Brill, 1967).

16. Packull, *Mysticism*, 180.

17. See Gottfried Seebaß, "Hans Hut. Der leidende Rächer," in *Radikale Reformatoren*, ed. Hans-Jürgen Goertz (Munich: C. H. Beck Verlag, 1978), 44–50, esp. 48.

18. See Hans-Jürgen Goertz, *Die Täufer. Geschichte und Deutung* (Munich: C. H. Beck Verlag, 1980), 138. (Of all executions of Anabaptists between 1525 and 1618, forty-one percent followed the Diet of Speyer in the years 1528 and 1529.)

19. See John Denck, "Whether God Is the Cause of Evil, in *Spiritual and Anabaptist Writers*, ed. George H. Williams and Angel M. Mergal (Philadelphia: Westminster Press, 1957).

20. See Werner O. Packull, "Hans Denck: Auf der Flucht vor dem Dogmatismus," in *Radikale Reformatoren*.

21. See R. Emmet McGlaughlin, *Caspar Schwenckfeld: Reluctant Radical, His Life to 1540* (New Haven: Yale University Press, 1986), 96ff.

22. See Karl Ecke, *Schwenckfeld, Luther und der Gedanke einer apostolischen Reformation* (Berlin: Warneck, 1911), 38ff., 44–45.

23. See Kühn, "Schwenckfeld," *Toleranz und Offenbarung*, 140ff., esp. 142–7.

24. See Nikolaus Paulus, *Protestantismus und Toleranz im 16. Jahrhundert* (Freiburg/Breisgau: Herder, 1911), 32–61. Of the numerous publications on tolerance and the Reformation, this contribution by a distinguished scholar was perhaps the best documented. It should have definitively laid to rest the legend that Luther only advocated the persecution of dissenters because of the threat of rebellion. See also Joseph Lecler, *Toleration and Reformation*, vol. 1 (New York: Association Press, 1960).

25. Hegler, *Geist und Schrift*, 30.

26. Hegler, *Geist und Schrift*, 35, 43 (Hegler shows the initial subtlety of Francks "shift" from Luther to Althamer).

27. The ubiquity of the inner word is summarized by Horst Weigelt, *Sebastian Franck und die Lutherische Reformation* (Gütersloh: Mohn, 1972), 24 (*Das innere Wort ist in allen Kreaturen vorhanden, also auch in der unbedeutendsten Wiesenpflanze, in der Stechmücke und in der Baumblüte; besonders findet es sich aber im Menschen wegen der Imago Dei. Es ist also sowohl in den alttestamentlichen Frommen, wie Adam, Abel, Henoch, Noah, Abraham, Lot, Hiob als auch in den Heiden*).

28. See Franck, *Chronica, Zeytbuch und geschychtbibel von anbegyn biß inn diß gegenwertig M.D.xxxj. jar* (1531), 421 [on Luther's doctrine of the Eucharist]: *Das der leib und blut Christi nit allein in der creatur des Weins und brots leiplich und wesenlich / sunder auch in allen creaturen / und in einer yeden besunder / auch in den geringsten baumblätlin sey / aber hie bindet sich Christus mitt seinem wort an.* (This must be read with reference to Luther's *Wider die Schwermgeister*.)

29. Sebastian Franck, *Paradoxa Ducenta Octoginta* (Ulm: Varnier, 1534), 1.

30. Kurt Goldammer, "Der Toleranzgedanke bei Franck und Weigel," im *Archiv für Reformationsgeschichte* 47:2 (1956):180–211.

31. See Weigelt, *Sebastian Franck*, 23, 33–34.

32. Hegler, *Geist und Schrift*, 185 ff., 192, 198 (meaninglessness of the historical Christ *per se* ), 200 (universality of the Word); cf. Weigelt, *Sebastian Frank*, 24–25.

33. Paulus, *Toleranz*, 312–24 (Lutheran executions in Saxony, 308–26; on Fritz Erbe, 313ff.; the General Articles, 317ff.; compulsory church attendance, 318ff.).

34. Valentin Weigel, *Gnothi seauton*, in *Ausgewählte Werke*, ed. Siegfried Wollgast (Stuttgart: Kohlhammer, 1977), 183.

35. Translated from Weigel, *Ausgewählte Werke*, 369–70.

## Chapter 7. The Part and the Whole

1. See Bo Andersson, *"Du solst wissen es ist aus keinem stein gesogen"; Studien zu Jacob Böhmes "Aurora" oder "Morgen Röte im auffgang"* (Stockholm: Almqvist & Wiksell, 1986); Alexandre Koyré, *La philosophie de Jacob Boehme* (Paris: Vrin, 1979); Ernst-Heinz Lemper, *Jakob Böhme: Leben und Werk* (Berlin: Union Verlag, 1976); Andrew Weeks, *Boehme: An Intellectual Biography of the Seventeenth-Century Philosopher and Mystic* (Albany: State University of New York Press, 1991).

2. A most impressive overview of Rudolphine Prague is found in the two-volume exhibition catalog which contains excellent scholarly essays on various scientific, theoretical, and artistic aspects of *Prag um 1600. Kunst und Kultur am Hofe Rudolfs II.* (Vienna: Luca Verlag, 1988).

3. See *The Book of Secrets of Albertus Magnus of the Virtues of Herbs, Stones and Certain Beasts, Also a Book of the Marvels of the World*, ed. and intro. Michael Best and Frank H. Brightman (Oxford: Oxford University Press, 1973).

4. See Lawrence M. Principe and Andrew Weeks, "Jacob Boehme's Divine Substance *Salitter*: Its Nature, Origin, and Relationship to Seventeenth-Century Scientific Theories," in *British Journal of the History of Science* 22 (1989): 52–61.

5. Jacob Böhme, *Sämliche Schriften*, ed. Will-Erich Peuckert and August Faust (Stuttgart: Frommanns Verlag, 1955–61) 1, 121. All German citations of Boehme are drawn from this facsimile of the 1730 Amsterdam edition originally edited by Johann Georg Gichtel. References are by volume, brief title, chapter, and section.

6. Weeks, *Boehme*, 98.

7. For a discussion of the context of Agrippa's pronouncement, see Wolf-Dieter Müller-Jahncke, "Von Ficino zu Agrippa. Der Magia-Begriff des Renaissance-Humanismus im Überblick," in Antoine Faivre and Rolf Christian Zimmermann, *Epochen der Naturmystik* (Berlin: Schmidt Verlag, 1979), 50 (Agrippa is cited to *Opera* 2 (*Epistolae*), 874).

8. See Leiv Aalen, "Die 'esoterische' Theologie des Grafen von Zinzendorf. Zur Auseinandersetzung mit der Abhandlung von Pierre Deghaye: La doctrine ésotérique de Zinzendorf," in *Pietismus—Herrnhutertum—Erweckungsbewegung* (Festschrift für Erich Beyreuther), ed. Dietrich Meyer (Cologne: Rheinland-Verlag, 1982), 207–63.

9. See Erich Beyreuther, *Geschichte des Pietismus* (Stuttgart: Steinkopf, 1978), 20–35.

10. Gerhard Rödding, "Paul Gerhardt," in *Deutsche Dichter* 2 (Stuttgart: Reclam, 1988), 191.

11. See Daniel von Czepko, *Geistliche Schriften*, ed. Werner Milch (Darmstadt: Wissenschaftliche Buchgesellschaft, 1963; reprinted from *Einzelschriften der Schlesischen Geschichte* vol. 4: Breslau, 1930).

12. Czepko, *Sexcenta Monodisticha Sapientum (SMS)*, in *Schriften*, 241.

13. Czepko, *SMS*, 228.

14. Czepko, *SMS*, 220.

15. Czepko, *SMS*, 240.

16. Czepko, *SMS*, 237.

17. Czepko, *SMS*, 220.

18. Czepko, *SMS*, 228 (*Überall*), 242 (*Eines offenbahret alles*).

19. See Th. C. van Stockum, *Zwischen Jakob Böhme und Johann Scheffler: Abraham von Franckenberg (1593–1652) und Daniel Czepko von Reigersfeld (1605–1660)* (Amsterdam: N. V. Noord-Hollandsche Uitgevers Maatschappij, 1967), esp. 16–17.

20. Cited by book and number from Angelus Silesius, *Cherubinischer Wandersmann (Kritische Ausgabe)* (Stuttgart: Reclam, 1984), 23, no. 164.

21. See *The Creeds of Christendom*, ed. Philip Schaff (New York: Harper, 1899), 122.

22. For the image of Sevi in German literature, see Hans Jacob Christoffel von Grimmelshausen, *Courage, the Adventuress* and *The False Messiah* (Princeton: Princeton University Press, 1964). The tale of the False Messiah has been excerpted, translated, and introduced by Hans Speier, with valuable notes on the baroque fame of Sabbatai Sevi.

23. See Walter Dietze, *Quirinus Kuhlmann. Ketzer und Poet* (Berlin: Rütten und Loening, 1963).

24. Ernst Harnischfeger, *Mystik im Barock. Das Weltbild der Teinacher Lehrtafel* (Stuttgart: Verlag Urachhaus, 1980).

25. Peter C. Erb, *Pietists, Protestants, and Mysticism: The Use of Late Medieval Spiritual Texts in the Work of Gottfried Arnold (1666–1714)* (Metuchen, N.J. & London: Scarecrow Press, 1989).

## Chapter 8. Diversity and Unity

1. The alliances of early Enlightenment and early Pietism are traced very concretely in Eduard Winter, *Frühaufklärung. Der Kampf gegen den Konfes-*

*sionalismus in Mittel- und Osteuropa und die deutsch-slawische Begegnung* (Berlin: Akademie-Verlag, 1966).

2. See Martin Schmidt, "Speners Wiedergeburtslehre" (1951) and "Die Bedeutung der Mystik für die Bekehrung August Hermann Franckes" (1966), in Martin Greschat, ed., *Zur neueren Pietismusforschung* (Darmstadt: Wissenschaftliche Buchgesellschaft, 1977); and Horst Weigelt, "Der reformierte Pietismus in Deutschland," *Pietismus-Studien*, part 1 (Stuttgart: Calwer Verlag, 1965), 21–22. Joseph B. Dallett gives a good account of the continuation of mystical impulses in the Baroque Age in "The Mystical Quest for God," in Gerhart Hoffmeister, ed., *German Baroque Literature* (New York: Ungar, 1983), 270–92.

3. See Martin Schmidt, "Speners Wiedergeburtslehre," in *Zur neueren Pietismusforschung*, 9–33; and Martin Schmidt, "Pietismus und das moderne Denken," in *Pietismus und moderne Welt*, ed. Kurt Aland (Witten: Luther-Verlag, 1974), 9–74; Philip Jacob Spener, *Pia Desideria*, ed. Kurt Aland (Berlin: de Gruyter, 1955).

4. See Klaus Deppermann, "Pietismus und moderner Staat," in *Pietismus und moderne Welt*, ed. Kurt Aland 82–83.

5. August Langen, *Der Wortschatz des deutschen Pietismus* (Tübingen: Niemeyer Verlag, 1968), 433.

6. Cf. Martin Schmidt, *Pietismus* (Stuttgart: Kohlhammer, 1983), 95.

7. See Langen, *Der Wortschatz des deutschen Pietismus*, 13, 15.

8. F. Ernst Stoeffler, *German Pietism During the 18th Century* (Leiden: Brill, 1973), ix.

9. Erich Beyreuther, *Geschichte des Pietismus* (Stuttgart: Steinkopf, 1978), 193.

10. See Beyreuther, *Geschichte des Pietismus*, 20–35.

11. Translated from citation in Gerhard Wehr, *Die deutsche Mystik* (Bern: Barth Verlag, 1988), 288.

12. Magdalene Maier-Peterson, "Oetinger," *Der "Fingerzeig Gottes" und die "Zeichen der Zeit"* (Stuttgart: Verlag Heinz, 1984).

13. Maier-Petersen, "Oetinger," in *"Fingerzeig Gottes,"* esp. 315–16, 379ff.

14. Piepmeier writes of Oetinger that, "The developed structure of reality as the Word of God, as the speech of God, implicitly and explicitly indicates the structure of his concept of God and makes clear what revelation means for him." Rainer Piepmeier, "Friedrich Christoph Oetinger," in Peter Koslowski, ed., *Gnosis und Mystik in der Geschichte der Philosophie*, 219.

15. See Heinrich Bornkamm, "Pietistische Mittler zwischen Jakob Böhme und dem deutschen Idealismus," in *Der Pietismus in Gestalten und Wirkungen* (Martin Schmidt zum 65. Geburtstag), ed. Heinrich Bornkamm, Freidrich Heyer, Alfred Schindler (Bielefeld: Luther-Verlag, 1975), 139–54.

16. See Wehr, "Michael Hahn—'Christus ist der Weg,'" in *Die deutsche Mystik*, 304–9.

17. The report from Johann Heinrich Reitz's *Historie der Wiedergeborenen* (published in seven parts, 1698–1745), reprinted, vol. 2, ed. Hans-Jürgen Schrader (Tübingen: Niemeyer, 1982), 169–98; also reproduced in Werner Mahrholz, ed., *Der deutsche Pietismus. Eine Auswahl von Zeugnissen, Urkunden und Bekenntnissen aus dem 17., 18. und 19. Jahrhundert* (Berlin: Furche-Verlag, 1921), 37–57.

18. Arno Pagel, *Gerhard Tersteegen: Ein Leben in der Gegenwart Gottes* (Giessen and Basel: Brunnen-Verlag, 1960), 4–7, 18ff., 21. Cf. Friedrich Winter, *Die Frömmigkeit Gerhard Tersteegens in ihrem Verhältnis zur französisch-quietistischen Mystik* (Neuwied: Heusersche Buchdruckerei, 1927).

19. Cited from Pagel, *Tersteegen*, 51.

20. See Erich Schmidt, "Hoyer," *Allgemeine Deutsche Biographie*, 13 (Leipzig: Duncker und Humblot, 1881), 217. More favorable and more informative about the unpublished work is the article by Johanna Goedeking-Fries in *Neue Deutsche Biographie* (1971).

21. Anna Ovena Hoyers, *Geistliche und weltliche Poemata* (Amsterdam: Elzevier, 1650), 238.

22. Hoyers, *Poemata*, 67.

23. Hoyers, *Poemata*, 63.

24. Hoyers, *Poemata*, 164–5.

25. Hoyers, *Poemata*, 29–30, 63, 64.

26. Cf. Julius Otto Opel, *Valentin Weigel. Ein Beitrag zur Literatur- und Culturgeschichte Deutschlands im 17. Jahrhundert* (Leipzig: T. O. Weigel, 1864), see esp. ch. 13 (*Der Weigelianismus während des dreißigjährigen Krieges*), 298–339.

27. See Ernst Benz, *Nietzsches Ideen zur Geschichte des Christentums und der Kirchen* (Leiden: Brill, 1956), 122–34 (*Nietzsche und der deutsche Spiritualism*).

28. Erich Seeberg, *Gottfried Arnold; die Wissenschaft und Mystik seiner Zeit. Studien zur Historiographie und zur Mystik* (Meerane i.S.: Herzog, 1923), 97–98, 105–6.

29. Seeberg, *Arnold*, 107, 112, 170.

30. Seeberg, *Arnold*, 157–8.

31. Seeberg, *Arnold*, 167, 173, 179.

32. Seeberg, *Arnold*, 213.

33. See Leroy E. Loemker, *Struggle for Synthesis: The Seventeenth Century Background for Leibniz's Synthesis of Order and Freedom* (Cambridge: Harvard University Press, 1972); Allison Coudert, "Some Theories of A Natural Language From the Renaissance to the Seventeenth Century," and George Macdonald Ross, "Leibniz and Alchemy," in *Magia Naturalis*, 56–118, 166–80; Friedrich Heer, "Einführung," *Gottfried Wilhelm Leibniz*, ed. and selected by Friedrich Heer (Frankfurt/M: Fischer, 1958).

34. Cf.: George Boas, *Dominant Themes of Modern Philosophy* (New York: Ronald Press Co., 1957), 272ff.

35. See Werner Schuffenhauer and Klaus Steiner, ed., *Martin Luther und die deutsche bürgerliche Philosophie, 1517–1845* (Berlin: Akademie Verlag, 1983), 81, 82–83, 85, 86.

36. Leibniz, *Philosophische Schriften* 3 (Berlin: Weidmannsche Buchhandlung, 1887), 660.

37. Leibniz, *Theodicy* (La Salle, Illinois: Open Court, 1988), ed. and intro. Austin Farrer, trans. E. M. Huggard, 79–80.

38. Leibniz, *Theodicy*, 84–85.

39. Hans Heinz Holz, "Lessing und Leibniz. Pluralismus, Perspektivität und Wahrheit," in Peter Freimark, Franklin Kopitzsch, and Helga Slessarew, eds., *Lessing und die Toleranz* (Detroit: Wayne State University Press, 1986), 17–18.

40. See F. Brüggemann, "Einführung," *Das Weltbild der deutschen Aufklärung. Philosophische Grundlagen und literarische Auswirkung: Leibniz, Wolff, Gottsched, Brockes, Haller,* ed. F. Brüggemann (Leipzig: Reclam, 1930).

41. See Martin Greschat, "Orthodoxie und Pietismus. Einleitung," *Orthodoxie und Pietismus,* ed. Martin Greschat (Stuttgart: Kohlhammer, 1982).

42. See Wolfgang Gericke, "Lessings theologische Gesamtauffassung" (Introduction), *Sechs theologische Schriften Gotthold Ephraim Lessings* (Berlin: Evangelische Verlagsanstalt, 1985), 9–62; and Harald Schultze, "Lessings Verhältnis zum Spiritualismus," in Schultze, *Lessings Toleranzbegriff. Eine theologische Studie* (Göttingen: Vandenhoeck & Ruprecht, 1969).

43. See W. M. Alexander, *Johann Georg Hamann, Philosophy and Faith* (The Hague: Martinus Nijhoff, 1966), 106ff.

44. Rudolf Unger, *Hamann und die Aufklärung. Studien zur Vorgeschichte des romantischen Geists im 18. Jahrhundert* (Tübingen: Niemeyer, 1968), 1:160.

45. Isaiah Berlin, *Herder and the Enlightenment* in *Vico and Herder. Two Studies in the History of Ideas* (New York: Random House, 1977), 166. Writing of the "expressionism" of Hamann and Herder, Isaiah Berlin said this about the Northern "Magus": "Hamann was a Christian touched by mysticism: he looked upon the world, upon nature and history, as the speech of God to man; God's words were hieroglyphs, often tormentingly dark, or they were allegories, or they were symbols which opened doors to the vision of the truth which, if only men saw and heard aright, answered the questions of their heads and hearts."

46. Berlin, *Vico and Herder*, 166–7, 176–7.

47. Herder, *Vom Erkennen und Empfinden* (1774), in *Werke* 2 (Munich: Hanser, 1987), 558.

48. Martin Luther, *Daß diese Worte Christi "Das ist mein Leib" noch fest stehen, wider die Schwärmgeister* (1527), in *Werke* 23 (Weimar: Böhlau, 1901), 137.

49. Robert T. Clark, Jr., *Herder: His Life and Thought* (Berkeley: University of California Press, 1955), 181.

50. J. G. Herder, *Ideen zur Philosophie der Geschichte der Menschheit* (Wiesbaden: Fourier, 1985), 235–6 [see last paragraph of book 9, section 2].

51. For the (not undisputed) theory that mysticism, as opposed to propheticism, is fundamentally conducive to religious tolerance, see Gustav Mensching, *Tolerance and Truth in Religion*, trans. H.-J. Kimkeit (University, Al.: University of Alabama Press, 1971).

52. Gerhard Kaiser, "Völkerfamilie oder Sendungsidee," *Pietismus und Patriotismus im literarischen Deutschland. Ein Beitrag zum Problem der Säkularisation* (Wiesbaden: Steiner Verlag, 1961).

53. Kaiser, *Pietismus und Patriotismus*, 206, 212.

54. See *"Pleroma,"* in Gerhard Kittel and Gerhard Friedrich, *Theological Dictionary of the New Testament* (Grand Rapids: Eerdmans, 1968)."

55. See Weeks, *Boehme*, 130–5.

56. See Beyreuther, *Geschichte des Pietismus*, 225; cf. Koppel Shub Pinson, *Pietism as a Factor in the Rise of German Nationalism* (New York: Octagon Books, 1968); Carl Hinrichs, *Preussentum und Pietismus. Der Pietismus in Brandenburg als religiös-soziale Reformbewegung* (Göttingen: Vandenhoeck und Ruprecht, 1971).

## Chapter 9. Nature and Imagination

1. Karl von Eckartshausen, *Mistische Nächte, oder der Schlüssel zu den Geheimnissen des Wunderbaren. Ein Nachtrag zu den Auffschlüssen über Magie* (Munich: Lentner, 1791), 13, 19, 23, 54, 139, 250. Cf. Oppenheim, "Eckartshausen," in *Neue Deutsche Biographie* 5 (Berlin: Duncker & Humblot, 1968).

2. See Joachim Telle, "Zum *Opus mago-cabbalisticum et theosophicum* von Georg von Welling," *Euphorion* 77, no. 4 (1983): 359–79. (Telle's notes also provide an overview of the literature relevant to the topic of Goethe and nature mysticism.) See also Julius Richter, "Jakob Böhme und Goethe. Eine strukturpsychologische Untersuchung," *Jahrbuch des Freien Deutschen Hochstifts* (1934/35): 3–55. (Though Goethe only mentioned Boehme in a sole citation— citing the legend of Boehme's sudden illumination—Richter is able to point to a number of general similarities in their outlook.)

3. The case for the Cartesian-Kantian originality is made by M. F. Burnyeat, in "Idealism and Greek Philosophy: What Descartes Saw and Berkeley Misses," *The Philosophical Review* XCI, no. 1 (January 1982): 3–40.

4. Frederick Copleston, S.J., *A History of Philosophy* 7 (New York: Garden City, 1963), 23, 19, 22.

5. See Ernst von Bracken, *Meister Eckhart und Fichte* (Würzburg: Triltsch Verlag, 1943). (This is a comparison rather than an influence study.) Géza von Molnár, *Novalis' "Fichte Studies"* (The Hague: Mouton, 1970).

6. See Armand Nivelle, *Frühromantische Dichtungstheorie* (Berlin: Gruyter Verlag, 1970), 12–14.

7. Copleston, *Philosophy* 7:19.

8. Antoine Faivre, "L'imagination creatrice (fonction magique et fondement mythique de l'image)," in *Revue d'Allemagne* 13:2 (April–June 1981): 355–90.

9. See Christoph Wegener, *Der Code der Welt. Das Prinzip der Ähnlichkeit in seiner Bedeutung und Funktion für die Paracelsische Naturphilosophie und Erkenntnislehre* (Frankfurt/M.: Peter Lang, 1988), 170ff.

10. Henrich Steffens, *Was ich erlebte* 1 (Breslau: Verlag Josef Max, 1840), 152–3.

11. Steffens, *Was ich erlebte* 4:87–93. See also Erich Worbs, "Johann Wilhelm Ritter, der romantische Physiker, und Jakob Böhme," in *Aurora* 33 (1973): 63–76.

12. Steffens, *Was ich erlebte* 4:78.

13. Ernst Benz, *Schelling. Werden und Wirken seines Denkens* (Zürich: Rhein-Verlag, 1955).

14. Steffens, *Was ich erlebte* 4:321–2.

15. Steffens, *Was ich erlebte* 4:320–5.

16. Novalis, *Das allgemeine Brouillon,* in Novalis, *Schriften, Das philosophische Werk* 2, ed. Richard Samuel, Hans-Joachim Mähl, and Gerhard Schulz (Stuttgart: Kohlhammer, 1960), 247.

17. Novalis, *Brouillon,* 263.

18. Novalis, *Brouillon,* 263.

19. Novalis, *Brouillon,* 293.

20. Novalis, *Brouillon,* 455.

21. Novalis, *Brouillon,* 440–1.

22. Novalis, *Brouillon,* 267–8.

23. Novalis, *Brouillon,* 316–7.

24. See Ursula Struc-Oppenberg, Introduction to *Über die Sprache und Weisheit der Indier,* in Friedrich Schlegel, *Studien zur Philosophie und Theologie, Kritische Friedrich-Schlegel-Ausgabe* 8, ed. and intro. Ernst Behler and Ursula Struc-Oppenberg (Munich: Schönigh, 1975), clxxxvii ff., esp. ccvii.

25. See Constantin Behler, "Friedrich Schlegel (1772–1829)," in Emerich Coreth S.J., Walter M. Neidl, and Georg Pfligersdorffer, ed., *Christliche Philosophie im katholischen Denken des 19. und 20. Jahrhunderts* 1 (Graz: Verlag Styria, 1987), 174–201, esp. 185–6, 189–91, 194–5.

26. For more positive assessments of Görres, see Reinhard Habel, *Josef Görres. Studien über den Zusammenhang von Natur, Geschichte und Mythos in seinen Schriften* (Wiesbaden: Steiner Verlag, 1960); Sister Mary Gonzaga, *The Mysticism of Görres as a Reaction Against Rationalism* (Dissertation, Catholic University of America, Washington, 1920); Robert Saitschick, *Joseph Görres und die abendländische Kultur* (Freiburg/Br.: Olten Verlag, 1953).

27. See David Baumgardt, "Das Reifen der neuen, an der Mystik genährten Weltauffassung bis zur völligen Abbiegung von der Philosophie des klassischen deutschen Idealismus," section 3, *Franz von Baader und die philosophische Romantik* (Haale/Saale: Niemeyer Verlag, 1927). For a positive perspective on Baader, see Gerd-Klaus Kaltenbrunner, "Ältervater und Novalis. Leben und Werk Franz von Baaders," in Franz von Baader, *Sätze aus der erotischen Philosophie und andere Schriften,* ed. Gerd-Klaus Kaltenbrunner (Frankfurt/M.: Insel Verlag, 1966); see also Herbert Raab, "Franz von Baader," in *Christliche Philosophie im katholischen Denken des 19. und 20. Jahrhunderts* 1, ed. Emerich Coreth, Walter M. Neidel, and Georg Pfligersdorffer (Graz: Verlag Styria, 1987). For a view of the anti-Kantian irrationalist, see E. Klamroth,

*Die Weltanschauung Franz von Baaders in ihrem Gegensatz zu Kant* (Dissertation, Freie Universität Berlin, 1965).

28. See Degenhardt, *Studien zum Wandel des Eckhartbildes*, 111–4.

29. See Franz Xaver von Baader, *Vorlesungen und Erläuterungen zu Jacob Böhmes Lehre*, in *Sämtliche Werke* 13, ed. Julius Hamberger (Leipzig, 1855; reprint, Aalen: Scientia Verlag, 1963).

30. Robert F. Brown, *The Later Philosophy of Schelling: The Influence of Boehme on the Works of 1809–1815* (Lewisburg: Bucknell University Press, 1977), 116.

31. Brown, *Schelling*, 261.

32. Degenhardt, *Studien zum Wandel des Eckhartbildes*, 114–5.

33. Hegel, "Jakob Böhme," in *Vorlesungen über die Geschichte der Philosophie 3*, *Werke* 20 (Frankfurt/M: Suhrkamp, 1971), 91ff.

34. See Werner Beierwaltes, "Hegel und Proklos," *Platonismus und Idealismus* (Frankfurt/M.: Klostermann, 1972), 144ff., 154–187; David Walsh, "The Historical Dialectic of Spirit: Jacob Boehme's Influence on Hegel," and Eric von der Luft, "Comment," in Robert L. Perkins (ed.), *History and System* (Albany: State University of New York Press, 1984); Theo Kobusch, "Freiheit und Tod. Die Tradition der 'mors mystica' und ihre Vollendung in Hegels Philosophie," *Theologische Quartalschriften*, 164:3 (1984): 185–203; Emil L. Fackenheim, *The Religious Dimension in Hegel's Thought* (Bloomington: Indiana University Press, 1967); and Katharina Comoth, "Hegel's *Logik* und die spekulative Mystik, " in *Hegel-Studien* 19 (1984): 65–93.

35. See Beierwaltes, "Hegel und Proklos," in *Platonismus und Idealismus*, 182 (*Beide—Proklos und Hegel—markieren in je verschiedener Weise und Intensität eine konsequenzenreiche Erfüllung und Wende im geschichtlichen Gang des philosophischen Denkens. Uns erscheinen sie freilich weniger als 'Mysten'...sondern als die Vollender einer sich selbst schon überfordernden metaphysischen Tradition und zugleich als die in gewissem Sinne tragischen Initiatoren der Formalisierbarkeit ihres eigenen Gedankens*).

36. See Degenhart, *Studien zum Wandel des Eckhartbildes*, 115ff.

37. See Andrew Weeks, "Schopenhauer and Böhme," in *Schopenhauer-Jahrbuch* 73 (1992): 7–17. While still a student of philosophy in 1811 (long before his reception of Sanskrit literature), Schopenhauer demonstrated his familiarity with German mysticism by observing Schelling's unreferenced borrowings from Boehme. Schopenhauer's earliest critics recognized their kinship; and Thomas Mann could still refer to Schopenhauer as a "mixture of Voltaire and Jacob Boehme." However, the connection has been largely forgotten in this century.

38. See Arthur Schopenhauer, *Der handschriftliche Nachlaß* 2, ed. Arthur Hübscher (Frankfurt/M.: Kramer, 1966), 226, 352, 379; and vol. 1 (Schopenhauer's notes while working out the ideas of his main work), 50, 52, 144–5, 160–1; for the full citation of Boehme written in the margin of Kant's *Critique of Pure Reason*, see Schopenhauer, *Sämtliche Werke* 13, ed. Paul Deussen (Munich: Piper, 1926), 225. On the importance of the year 1814 for the author of *The World as Will and Representation*, see Arthur Hübscher, *Denker gegen den Strom* (Bonn: Bouvier, 1973), 44–46, 136–8.

39. See Boehme, *Schriften* 6:13ff.

40. Schopenhauer, *The World as Will and Representation* 1, trans. E. F. J. Payne (New York: Dover, 1966), 296.

41. Schopenhauer, *The World as Will and Representation* 2:3.

42. See Manfred Kaempfert, *Säkularisation und neue Heiligkeit. Religiöse und religionsbezogene Sprache bei Friedrich Nietzsche* (Berlin: Erich Schmidt Verlag, 1971); Philip Grundlehner, *The Poetry of Friedrich Nietzsche* (Oxford: Oxford University Press, 1986). With reference to Nietzsche's poems, Grundlehner observed that, "The inner sphere of private experience, no matter how tenuous, nevertheless represents to the poet a possibility of obliterating the boundaries between himself and the outer world to achieve a mystical vision. In fact, the vocabulary Nietzsche employs is close to that of the mystics and pietists" (p. 302).

43. Nietzsche, *Beyond Good and Evil*, trans. Marianne Cowan (Chicago: Regnery, 1955), 61–62.

## Conclusion

1. For a discussion of the Bürgel episode in chapter eighteen of Kafka's *Castle*, see Andrew Weeks, *The Paradox of the Employee: Variants of a Social Theme in Modern Literature* (Bern: Peter Lang, 1980), 105–11; cf. Franz Kafka, *Das Schloß* (Frankfurt/M.: Fischer Verlag, 1973), 222 (*Das Geheimnis steckt in den Vorschriften über die Zuständigkeit...*).

2. See Dietmar Goltschnigg, *Mystische Tradition im Roman Robert Musils. Martin Bubers "Ekstatische Konfessionen" im "Mann ohne Eigenschaften"* (Heidelberg: Lothar Stiehm Verlag, 1974); Andrew Weeks, "Hofmannsthal, Pannwitz und der Turm" in *Jahrbuch des Freien Deutschen Hochstifts* (1987): 336–59.

3. An excellent account of the Nazi appropriation of Meister Eckhart is found in Ingeborg Degenhardt, *Studien zum Wandel des Eckhartbildes* (Leiden: Brill, 1967), 261ff.

4. See Klaus Jeziorkowski, "Empor ins Licht. Gnostizismus und Licht-

Symbolik in Deutschland um 1900," in *The Turn of the Century: German Literature and Art, 1890–1915* (Bonn: Bouvier-Grundmann, 1981), 171–96.

5. Karl Marx, *Das Kapital* 1 (Berlin: Dietz Verlag, 1972), 85, n. 25.

6. See John D. Caputo, *The Mystical Element in Heidegger's Thought* (New York: Fordham University Press, 1986); Dietmar Goltschnigg, *Mystische Tradition*, 19–23; Gustav Landauer, *Skepsis und Mystik. Versuch im Anschluß an Mauthners Sprachkritik* (Berlin: Fontane, 1903); Martin Buber, *Ekstatische Konfessionen* (Jena: Diederichs, 1909). See Warren Dauben, *Georg Cantor: His Mathematics and Philosophy of the Infinite* (Cambridge: Harvard University Press, 1979), 147 ("It is also significant that Cantor believed in the absolute truth of his set theory because it was *revealed* to him by God"); Goltschnigg, *Mystische Tradition*, 19–25.

7. On the influence of Schopenhauer and William James, see Ray Monk, *Ludwig Wittgenstein: The Duty of Genius* (London: Cape, 1990); cf. W. Donald Hudson, *Wittgenstein and Religious Belief* (New York: St. Martin's Press, 1975).

# Select Bibliography

## Aspects of Mysticism

Albert, Karl, *Mystik und Philosophie*. Sankt Augustin: Verlag Hans Richarz, 1986.

Dinzelbacher, Peter, ed. *Wörterbuch der Mystik*. Stuttgart: Kröner Verlag, 1989.

Katz, Steven T., ed. *Mysticism and Philosophical Analysis*. New York: Oxford University Press, 1978.

———, ed. *Mysticism and Religious Traditions*. Oxford: Oxford University Press, 1983.

Koslowski, Peter, ed. *Gnosis und Mystik in der Geschichte der Philosophie*. Zurich and Munich: Artemis Verlag, 1988.

Otto, Rudolf. *Mysticism East and West: A Comparative Analysis of the Nature of Mysticism*. New York: Macmillan, 1932.

Ruh, Kurt. *Geschichte der abendländischen Mystik* (Vol. 1: *Die Grundlegung durch die Kirchenväter und die Mönchstheologie des 12. Jahrhunderts*). Munich: C. H. Beck Verlag, 1990.

———., ed. *Abendländische Mystik im Mittelalter* (Symposion Kloster Engelberg, 1984). Stuttgart: Metzler, 1986.

Ruhbach, Gerhard, and Josef Sudbrack, ed. *Große Mystiker. Leben und Wirken*. Munich: Verlag C. H. Beck, 1984.

Scholem, Gershom. *Major Trends in Jewish Mysticism*. New York: Schocken Books, 1969.

———. *Über einige Grundbegriffe des Judentums*. Frankfurt/M.: Suhrkamp, 1970.

Suzuki, Daisetz Teitaro. *Mysticism: Christian and Bhuddist*. Westport: Greenwood Press, 1975.

Szarmach, Paul, ed. *An Introduction to the Medieval Mystics of Europe: Fourteen Original Essays*. Albany: State University of New York Press, 1984.

Underhill, Evelyn. *Mysticism. A Study in the Nature and Development of Man's Spiritual Consciousness* (1910). Reprint: New York: Noonday Press, 1955.

Woods, Richard, O. P., ed. *Understanding Mysticism*. Garden City: Image Books, 1980.


## Ancient, Biblical, and Philosophical Sources

Barnstone, Willis, ed. *The Other Bible*. San Francisco: Harper & Row, 1984.

———. *The Poetics of Ecstasy: Varieties of Ekstasis from Sappho to Borges*. New York: Holmes & Meier, 1983.

Beierwaltes, Werner, ed. *Platonismus in der Philosophie des Mittelalters*. Darmstadt: Wissenschaftliche Buchgesellschaft, 1969.

———, ed. *Eriugena redivivus. Zur Wirkungsgeschichte seines Denkens im Mittelalter und im Übergang zur Neuzeit (Vorträge des Internationalen Eriugena-Colloquiums)*. Heidelberg: Universitätsverlag, 1987.

Bernhardt, Joseph. *Die Philosophische Mystik des Mittelalters von ihren antiken Ursprüngen bis zur Renaissance*. Munich: Verlag Ernst Reinhardt, 1922.

Ehrhardt, Arnold. *The Beginning: A Study in the Greek Philosophical Approach to the Concept of Creation from Anaximander to St. John*. New York: Barnes and Noble, 1968.

von Ivánka, Endre. *Plato Christianus. Übernahme und Umgestaltung des Platonismus durch die Väter*. Einsiedeln: Johannes Verlag, 1964.

Jonas, Hans. *The Gnostic Religion. The Message of the Alien God and the Beginnings of Christianity*. Boston: Beacon Press, 1958.

Sandmel, Samuel. *Philo of Alexandria: An Introduction*. Oxford: Oxford University Press, 1979.

Sorabji, Richard. *Time, Creation, and the Continuum: Theories in Antiquity and the Early Middle Ages*. Ithaca: Cornell University Press, 1983.


## Traditions of German Mysticism

Degenhardt, Ingeborg. *Studien zum Wandel des Eckhartbildes*. Leiden: Brill, 1967.

Greith, E. *Die deutsche Mystik im Prediger-Orden (von 1250- 1350), nach ihren Grundlehren, Liedern und Lebensbildern aus handschriftlichen Quellen*. Freiburg/Breisgau, 1861. Reprint: Amsterdam: Rodopi, 1965.

Haas, Alois Maria. *Geistliches Mittelalter*. Freiburg/Sw.: Universitätsverlag, 1984.

———. *Sermo Mysticus: Studien zu Theologie und Sprache der deutschen Mystik*. Freiburg, Switzerland: Universitätsverlag, 1989.

Koch, Josef. *Kleine Schriften*, vol. 1. Rome: Edizioni di Storia et Letteratura, 1973.

Kunisch, Hermann. *Zur deutschen Mystik des Mittelalters und ihrer Nachwirkung*. In Kunisch, *Kleine Scriften*. Berlin: Duncker & Humblot, 1968.

Muschg, Walter. *Die Mystik in der Schweiz, 1200-1500*. Frauenfeld and Leipzig: Verlag Huber, 1935.

Preger, Wilhelm. *Geschichte der deutschen Mystik*. Reprint of the edition of 1874 and 1893 (Aalen: Otto Zeller, 1962).

Ruh, Kurt. *Bonaventura Deutsch: Ein Beitrag zur deutschen Franziskaner-Mystik und Scholastik*. Bern: Franke Verlag, 1956.

Wehr, Gerhard. *Die deutsche Mystik. Mystische Erfahrung und theosophische Welt-sicht—eine Einführung in Leben und Werk der großen deutschen Sucher nach Gott*. Bern, Munich, Vienna: Barth Verlag, 1988.

Wentzlaff-Eggebert, Friedrich-Wilhelm. *Deutsche Mystik zwischen Mittelalter und Neuzeit. Einheit und Wandlung ihrer Erscheinungsformen*. Berlin: Gruyter, 1969.

## Medieval Mysticism

Bynum, Caroline Walker. *Holy Feast and Holy Fast: The Religious Significance of Food to Medieval Women*. Berkeley: University of California Press, 1987.

———. *Jesus as Mother: Studies in the Spirituality of the High Middle Ages*. Berkeley: University of California Press, 1982.

Colloque de Strasbourg. *La Mystique Rhénane*. Paris: Presses Universitaires de France, 1963.

Davies, Oliver. *God Within: The Mystical Tradition of Northern Europe*. Foreword by Rowan Williams. New York: Paulist Press, 1988.

Dinzelbacher, Peter and Dieter R. Bauer, eds. *Frauenmystik im Mittelalter*. Stuttgart: Schwabenverlag, 1985.

———. *Religiöse Frauenbewegung und mystische Frömmigkeit im Mittelalter*. Vienna: Böhlau, 1988.

Lewis, Gertrud Jaron. *Bibliographie zur deutschen Frauenmystik des Mittelalters*. Berlin: Schmidt Verlag, 1989.

Ringler, Siegfried. *Viten- und Offenbarungsliteratur in Frauenklöstern des Mittelalters*. Zurich and Munich: Artemis Verlag, 1980.

Schmidt, Margot, and Dieter R. Bauer, eds. *"Eine Höhe, über die nichts geht."* *Spezielle Glaubenserfahrung in der Frauenmystik?* Stuttgart-Bad Canstatt: Frommann-Holzboog, 1986.

Ruh, Kurt, ed. *Altdeutsche und altniederländische Mystik.* Darmstadt: Wissenschaftliche Buchgesellschaft, 1964.

Langer, Otto. *Mystische Erfahrung und spirituelle Theologie. Zu Meister Eckharts Auseinandersetzung mit der Frauenfrömmigkeit seiner Zeit.* Munich: Artemis, 1987.

## Renaissance, Reformation, Baroque

Emrich, Wilhelm. *Deutsche Literatur der Barockzeit.* Königstein/Taunus: Suhrkamp, 1988.

Faivre, Antoine, and Christian Zimmermann, eds. *Epochen der Naturmystik. Hermetische Tradition im wissenschaftlichen Fortschritt.* Berlin: Schmidt Verlag, 1979.

Goldammer, Kurt, ed. and intro. *Paracelsus: Vom Licht der Natur und des Geistes. Eine Auswahl.* Stuttgart: Reclam, 1979.

——. *Paracelsus in neuen Horizonten: gesammelte Aufsätze.* Vienna: Verband der Wissenschaftlichen Gesellschaften Österreichs, 1986. (Salzburger Beiträge zur Paracelsusforschung, Folge 24).

Hopkins, Jasper. *Nicholas of Cusa's Dialectical Mysticism: Text Translation, and Interpretive Study of "De Visione Dei.".* Minneapolis: Arthur J. Banning Press, 1985.

——. *Nicholas of Cusa on Learned Ignorance: A Translation and Appraisal of "De Docta Ignorantia"* (Second edition, 1985; second printing, 1990). Minneapolis: Arthur J. Banning Press, 1985.

Jaspers, Karl. *Anselm and Nicholas of Cusa,* ed. Hannah Arendt, trans. Ralph Manheim. New York: Harcourt Brace & Jovanovich, 1974.

Koyré, Alexandre. *Mystiques, spirituels, alchimistes du XVIe siècle allemande.* Paris: Gallimard, 1971.

Mahnke, Dietrich. *Unendliche Sphäre und Allmittelpunkt.* Haale/Saale: Niemeyer Verlag, 1937.

Nauert, Charles G., Jr. *Agrippa and the Crisis of Renaissance Thought.* Urbana: University of Illinois Press, 1965.

Pagel, Walter. *Paracelsus. An Introduction to Philosophical Medicine in the Era of the Renaissance.* Basel: Karger, 1958.

Peuckert, Will-Erich. *Pansophie. Ein Versuch zur Geschichte der weissen und schwarzen Magie.* Berlin: Schmidt Verlag, 1976.

Hoffmann, Bengt R. *Luther and the Mystics: A Re-Examination of Luther's Spiritual Experience and his Relationship to the Mystics.* Minneapolis: Augsburg Publishing House, 1976.

Oberman, Heiko A. *"Simul Gemitus et Raptus*: Luther and Mysticism." In *The Reformation in Medieval Perspective,* ed. Steven E. Ozment. Chicago: Quadrangle Books, 1971.

Ozment, Steven E. *Mysticism and Dissent: Religious Ideology and Social Protest in the Sixteenth Century.* New Haven: Yale University Press, 1973.

Packull, Werner O. *Mysticism and the Early South German-Austrian Anabaptist Movement, 1525-1531.* Scottsdale, Pa.: Herald Press, 1977.

Weeks, Andrew. *Boehme: An Intellectual Biography of the Seventeenth Century Philosopher and Mystic.* Albany: SUNY Press, 1991.

Williams, George H., and Angel M. Mergal, eds. *Spiritualist and Anabaptist Writers.* Philadelphia: Westminster, 1957.

## Pietism to Enlightenment

Beyer-Frölich, Marianne. *Pietismus und Rationalismus.* (The memoirs excerpted in this anthology range from August Hermann Francke to Albrecht Haller.) Leibzig: Reclam, 1933.

Erb, Peter C. *Pietists, Protestants, and Mysticism: The Use of Late Medeival Spiritual Texts in the Work of Gottfried Arnold (1666-1714). Pietist and Wesleyan Studies,* 2. Metuchen, N.J. and London: Scarecrow Press, 1989.

Greschat, Martin, ed. *Orthodoxie und Pietismus.* Stuttgart: Kohlhammer, 1982.

Mahrholz, Werner, ed. *Der deutsche Pietismus. Eine Auswahl von Zeugnissen, Urkunden und Bekenntnissen aus dem 17., 18. und 19. Jahrhundert.* Berlin: Furche-Verlag, 1921.

Maier-Petersen, Magdalene. *Der "Fingerzeig Gottes" und die "Zeichen der Zeit."* Stuttgart: Verlag Heinz, 1984.

Müller, Kurt, Heinrich Schepper, and Wilhelm Totok, eds. *Magia Naturalis und die Entstehung der modernen Naturwissenschaften.* Wiesbaden: Steiner Verlag, 1978.

Schmidt-Biggemann, Wilhelm. *Theodizee und Tatsachen. Das philosophische Profil der deutschen Aufklärung.* Frankfurt/M.: Suhrkamp, 1988.

## Romantic and Modern Relations

Benz, Ernst. *Theologie der Elektrizität. Zur Begegnung und Auseinandersetzung von Theologie und Naturwissenschaft im 17. und 18. Jahrhundert.* Steiner: Wiesbaden, 1971.

———. *Schelling. Werden und Wirken seines Denkens.* Zurich: Rhein-Verlag, 1955 (translated by Blair Reynolds and Eunice M. Paul, *The Mystical Sources of German Romantic Philosophy.* Allison Park: Pickwick, 1983).

Brown, Robert F. *The Later Philosophy of Schelling: The Influence of Boehme on the Works of 1809-1815.* Lewisburg: Bucknell University Press, 1977.

Caputo, John D. *The Mystical Elements in Heidegger's Thought.* New York: Fordham University Press, 1986.

Comoth, Katharina. "Hegels 'Logik' und die spekulative Mystik. Über Typen des trinitarischen Symbolons." In *Hegel-Studien* 19 (1984): 65-93.

Friedrichsmeyer, Sara. *The Androgyne in Early German Romanticism: Friedrich Schlegel, Novalis and the Metaphysics of Love.* Bern: Peter Lang, 1983.

Goldammer, Kurt. *Paracelsus in der deutschen Romantik. Eine Untersuchung zur Geschichte der Paracelsus-Rezeption und zu geistesgeschichtlichen Hintergründen der Romantik.* Vienna: Verband der wissenschaftlichen Gesellschaften Österreiches, 1980.

Goltschnigg, Dietmar. "Einleitung," *Mystische Tradition im Roman Robert Musils. Martin Bubers "Ekstatische Konfessionen" im "Mann ohne Eigenschaften.* Heidelberg: Stiehm Verlag, 1974.

Hudson, W. Donald. *Wittgenstein and Religious Belief.* New York: St. Martins Press, 1975.

Maaß, Fritz-Dieter. *Mystik im Gespräch. Materialien zur Mystik- Diskussion in der katholischen und evangelischen Theologie Deutschlands nach dem Ersten Weltkrieg.* Würzburg: Echter Verlag, 1972.

Tatar, Maria M. *Spellbound: Studies on Mesmerism and Literature* (Princeton: Princeton University Press, 1978).

Zimmermann, Hans Dieter. *Rationalität und Mystik.* Frankfurt/M.: Insel Verlag, 1981.

# Index

Mechthild of Hackeborn, 40, 58, 62
Mechthild of Magdeburg, 12, 35, 39,
    40, 58–62, 76–77, 83
Melanchthon, Philipp, 174
Mendelsohn, Moses, 220
Merswin, Rulman, 94
Mesmer, Franz Anton, 215, 221
Meth, Ezechiel, 181
Molinos, Miguel de, 194
Moller, Martin, 28, 185
Montaigne, Michel de, 123
Moses 16, 19, 20, 74
Müntzer, Thomas, 143–144, 147, 149,
    151–155, 157
Muschg, Walter, 65–66
Musil, Robert, 234

Nettesheim. *See* Agrippa
Newton, Isaac, 8, 204
Nicholas of Cusa (Cusanus), 7, 11,
    27, 35–36, 99–119, 132–136, 183,
    204–205, 212, 220, 235
Nietzsche, Friedrich, 1, 11, 61, 203,
    211, 230–231, 233
Nigg, Walter, 139–140
Nikolaus of Strassburg, 92
Novalis, 1, 6, 9, 11–12, 31, 37, 85, 172,
    193, 195, 216, 219, 221– 225, 231

Oetinger, Friedrich Christoph, 184,
    193–194, 196–197, 207, 208
Oresme, Nicholas, 101
Origen, 10, 16, 70–71
Ozment, Steven, 143, 145

Pagel, Walter, 131
Pannwitz, Rudolf, 234
Paracelsus, x, 1–2, 7, 9, 12, 28, 30–31,
    34, 57, 99, 118–119, 121–122,
    124–125, 127–134, 136, 139–140,
    143, 150, 167, 169, 176, 184–105,
    204, 217, 219, 221
Parmenides, 103

Pascal, Blaise, 103
Paul the Apostle, 20, 26, 31–32, 34,
    79, 84, 121, 146
Peuckert, Will–Erich, 120
Philo Judaeus of Alexandria, 10, 16,
    33, 103
Pico della Mirandola, Giovanni, 119,
    131, 152, 165
Pietists/Pietism, 1, 2, 6, 11, 15, 28, 59,
    170, 184, 188, 192–198, 201, 203,
    206–208, 211–213, 216–219, 220,
    222, 225, 230
Plato, 97, 152, 204
Plotinus, 10, 29, 103
Porete, Marguerite, 75–76, 90–91
Preger, Wilhelm, 72
Pseudo–Dionysius. *See* Dionysius
Pythagoras, 105, 109

Quint, Josef, 5, 82

Reformation, German, 1, 2, 6, 80, 118,
    122–123, 136, 144–147, 153–155,
    158–159, 163, 167–169, 172, 174,
    175
Renaissance, 1, 2, 5, 6, 9, 10, 12, 27,
    29, 34, 36, 55, 107, 110, 118–123,
    133, 169–171, 197, 204, 209, 217
Reuchlin, Johannes, 116, 119
Ricardis the nun, 56
Richardson, Samuel, 195
Rilke, Rainer Maria, 234
Ritter, Johann Wilhelm, 220–221
Romantics/Romanticism, 1, 2, 9, 10,
    12, 29–32, 170, 215, 219, 225–227,
    231
Rosenberg, Alfred, 234
Rosenroth, Christian Knorr von, 192
Rousseau, Jean Jacques, 145, 195
Rudolph of Biberach, 39
Ruh, Kurt, 5, 72, 75–76
Ruysbroeck, Jan van, 101